Holistic Nursing

A Handbook for Practice

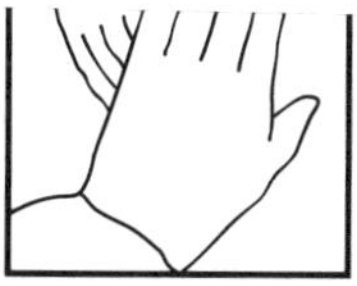

Holistic Nursing

A Handbook for Practice

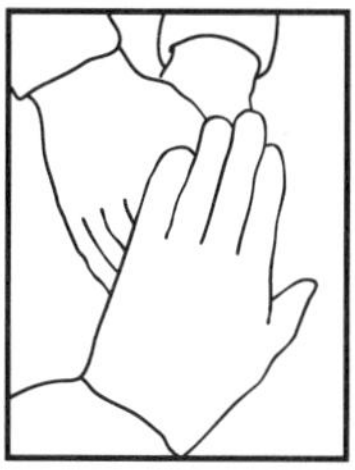

Barbara Montgomery Dossey, RN, MS, FAAN
Director, Holistic Nursing Consultants
Santa Fe, New Mexico
Co-Director, Bodymind Systems
Temple, Texas

Lynn Keegan, RN, PhD
Associate Professor, University of Texas
Health Science Center at San Antonio, Texas
Co-DIrector, Bodymind Systems
Temple, Texas

Cathie E. Guzzetta, RN, PhD, FAAN
Director, Holistic Nursing Consultants,
Dallas, Texas
Editor-In-Chief,
Capsules & Comments in Critical Care Nursing

Leslie Gooding Kolkmeier, RN, MEd
Private Practice
Applied Psychophysiology and Counseling
Plano, Texas

Endorsed by the American Holistic Nurses' Association

An Aspen Publication®
Aspen Publishers, Inc.
Gaithersburg, Maryland
1988

Library of Congress Cataloging-in-Publication Data

Holistic nursing: a handbook for practice /
Barbara Montgomery Dossey . . . [et al.].
p. cm.
"An Aspen publication."
Includes bibliographies and index.
ISBN: 0-87189-776-8
1. Holistic nursing. I. Dossey, Barbara Montgomery.
[DNLM: 1. Holistic Health. 2. Nursing. 3. Philosophy, Nursing.
WY 86 H7325]
RT42.H65 1988
613-dc19
DNLM/DLC 88-14534
for Library of Congress
CIP

Editorial Resources: Ruth Bloom

Library of Congress Catalog Card Number: 88-14534
ISBN: 0-87189-776-8 (Hardback)
ISBN: 0-8342-0399-5 (Paperback)

Printed in the United States of America

5 6 7 8

This book is dedicated to
all Nurse Healers—
for nursing, if it is ***truly*** nursing
is healing.

Cover Design

Nursing is an art; and if it is to be made
an art,
it requires as exclusive a devotion, as hard
a preparation, as any painter's or sculptor's
work;
for what is the having to do with dead
canvas or cold marble,
compared with having to do with the living
spirit—the temple of God's spirit?
It is one of the Fine Arts;
I had almost said,
the finest of Fine Arts.

FLORENCE NIGHTINGALE

The cover photograph, titled "Transition," is the work of John Haynsworth of John Haynsworth Photography, 86 Highland Park Village, Dallas, TX 75205. We also wish to thank Flora Clark and Brooke Wilson.

The cover photograph originally appeared on the cover of the inaugural edition of *Capsules & Comments in Critical Care Nursing*, © 1993, edited by Cathie E. Guzzetta, RN, PhD, and published by Mosby, Inc., 11830 Westline Industrial Drive, St. Louis, MO 63146. Reprinted with permission.

Table of Contents

Foreword .... **xi**

Preface .... **xv**

Acknowledgments .... **xix**

Reviewers .... **xxi**

UNIT I—THE INWARD JOURNEY **1**

Chapter 1—Holism and the Circle of Human Potential **3**
Barbara Montgomery Dossey and Lynn Keegan

Nurse Healer Objectives 3
Definitions 4
In Search of the Whole Person 5
Self-Assessments 5
Circle of Human Potential 13
Summary 20
Directions for Future Research 20
Nurse Healer Reflections 21

Chapter 2—The Transpersonal Self and States of Consciousness **23**
Barbara Montgomery Dossey

Nurse Healer Objectives: The Transpersonal Self and States of Consciousness 23
Definitions 24
Foundations for Healing 25
The Transpersonal Self 29
States of Consciousness 33

Summary 35
Directions for Future Research 35
Nurse Healer Reflections 36

Chapter 3—Nurse as Healer: Toward the Inward Journey 39
Barbara Montgomery Dossey

Nurse Healer Objectives: Nurse As Healer 39
Definitions 40
Toward the Inward Journey 41
Summary 51
Directions for Future Research 52
Nurse Healer Reflections 52

UNIT II—CONSCIOUS JOURNEY TOWARD WHOLENESS 55

Chapter 4—The History and Future of Healing 57
Lynn Keegan

Nurse Healer Objectives: The History and Future of Healing ... 57
Definitions 58
Healing in Antiquity 58
Scientific Revolution 63
The Future of Healing 69
Summary 73
Directions for Future Research 74
Nurse Healer Reflections 74

Chapter 5—The Psychophysiology of Bodymind Healing 77
Barbara Montgomery Dossey

Nurse Healer Objectives: The Psychophysiology of Bodymind Healing 77
Definitions 78
Natural Systems Theory, Information Theory, and Transduction 79
Placebo Effect 81
State-Dependent Learning 82
Where are the Brain Centers? 83
Mind Modulation of the Autonomic Nervous System 84
Mind Modulation of the Endocrine System 86
The Mind-Gene Connection 89
Mind Modulation of the Immune System 89
Mind Modulation of the Neuropeptide System 91
What Next? 94
Summary 95

Directions for Future Research 95
Nurse Healer Reflections 95

UNIT III—THEORY AND PRACTICE OF HOLISTIC NURSING 99

Chapter 6—Nursing Process and Standards of Care 101
Cathie E. Guzzetta

Nurse Healer Objectives 101
Definitions 102
Nursing Process 102
Holistic Assessment 103
Nursing Diagnoses 107
Client Outcomes 115
Plan 115
Implementation 116
Evaluation 116
Standards of Care 117
Summary 124
Directions for Future Research 124
Nurse Healer Reflections 124

Chapter 7—Wellness, Values, Clarification, and Motivation 127
Barbara Montgomery Dossey and Cathie E. Guzzetta

Nurse Healer Objectives 127
Definitions 128
Contemporary Nursing 128
Toward Wellness 129
Values Clarification 134
Human Motivational Model 137
Worksite Wellness 141
Summary 142
Directions for Future Research 143
Nurse Healer Reflections 143

Chapter 8—Research and Holistic Implications 147
Cathie E. Guzzetta

Nurse Healer Objectives 147
Definitions 148
Wellness Model 148
Holistic Research Methods 149
Identifying Holistic Variables 151
Evaluating Holistic Interventions 151
Objectivity and Scientific Investigation 153

Summary 153
Directions for Future Research 153
Nurse Healer Reflections 154

UNIT IV—STRATEGIES TO STRENGTHEN THE WHOLE PERSON 157

Chapter 9—Nutrition, Exercise, and Movement: Nourishing the Bodymind 159
Lynn Keegan

Nurse Healer Objectives 159
Definitions 160
Theory and Research 161
General Explanations: Nutrition, Exercise, Movement 164
Nursing Process 170
Summary 177
Directions for Future Research 178
Nurse Healer Reflections 178

Chapter 10—Environment: Protecting Our Personal and Planetary Home 181
Lynn Keegan

Nurse Healer Objectives 181
Definitions 182
Theory and Research 182
General Explanations: Environment 186
Nursing Process 187
Summary 193
Directions for Future Research 193
Nurse Healer Reflections 193

Chapter 11—Relaxation: Opening the Door to Change 195
Leslie Gooding Kolkmeier

Nurse Healer Objectives 196
Definitions 196
Theory and Research 197
General Explanations 201
Nursing Process 205
Summary 219
Directions for Future Research 220
Nurse Healer Reflections 220

Chapter 12—Imagery: Awakening the Inner Healer 223
Barbara Montgomery Dossey

Nurse Healer Objectives 223
Definitions 224
Theory and Research 225
General Explanations 228
Nursing Process 233
Summary 259
Directions for Future Research 259
Nurse Healer Reflections 259

Chapter 13—Music Therapy: Hearing the Melody of the Soul 263
Cathie E. Guzzetta

Nurse Healer Objectives 264
Definitions 264
Theory and Research 265
General Explanations 269
Nursing Process 275
Summary 285
Directions for Future Research 285
Nurse Healer Reflections 285

Chapter 14—Play and Laughter: Moving Toward Harmony 289
Leslie Gooding Kolkmeier

Nurse Healer Objectives 290
Definitions 290
Theory and Research 291
General Explanations 293
Nursing Process 296
Summary 302
Directions for Future Research 302
Nurse Healer Reflections 302

Chapter 15—Relationships: Learning the Patterns and Processes 305
Barbara Montgomery Dossey

Nurse Healer Objectives 305
Definitions 306
Theory and Research 306
General Explanations: Relationships 309
Nursing Process 312
Summary 328

Directions for Future Research 328
Nurse Healer Reflections 328

Chapter 16—Touch: Connecting with the Healing Power 331
Lynn Keegan

Nurse Healer Objectives 331
Definitions 332
Theory and Research 333
General Explanations 337
Nursing Process 341
Summary 352
Directions for Future Research 353
Nurse Healer Reflections 353

Chapter 17—Self-Reflection: Consulting the Truth Within 357
Leslie Gooding Kolkmeier

Nurse Healer Objectives 358
Definitions 358
Theory and Research 359
General Explanations 360
Nursing Process 364
Summary 386
Directions for Future Research 387
Nurse Healer Reflections 387

Appendix A—NANDA Diagnosis Qualifiers 389
Cathie E. Guzzetta

Appendix B—Unitary Person Assessment Tool Prototype 391
Cathie E. Guzzetta, Shelia D. Bunton, Linda A. Prinkey, Anita P. Sherer, and Patricia C. Seifert

Appendix C—Holistic Nursing Assessment Tool 399
Pamela Potter Hughes

Index 407

Foreword

It is with pleasure that I add some thoughts of my own to those of the fine authors of this book: Barbara Montgomery Dossey, Lynn Keegan, Cathie E. Guzzetta, and Leslie Gooding Kolkmeier. We are living in the midst of two distinct cultural movements and this book responds to both. One is techno-medicine, with its materialistic, reductionistic views of man and nature (and therefore of health and illness) on the analogy of a machine, something like a sophisticated supercomputer set amidst other supercomputers. This is still the dominant model, both in the medical community and the general public. The other model, holistic and integrative, offers what amounts to a philosophical revolution, so radical a repositioning of claims as to who we are that it has been termed a paradigm shift. This paradigm—of which this book is a welcome expression—forges a new picture of ourselves and our universe. It weaves a story of the interconnectedness of all beings, postulates the presence of as yet uncharted and powerful but infrequently harnessed forces in nature and ourselves which we can learn to harness for altruistic purposes, and draws daring inferences for our lives.

In 1979, a few years after the emergence of Kunz and Krieger's concept of Therapeutic Touch—when this revolution in human self-image first surfaced in a serious way among health professionals—I published "Philosophical Foundations and Frameworks for Healing." I felt then and continue to feel that the many diverse activities in holistic health are all united by a common bond—the Healing Hypothesis I called it—which provides them with a coherent and plausible philosophical framework. The Healing Hypothesis differs from the mechanistic-reductionistic one and instead urges that we are part of a vitalistic, alive, dynamic universe which is lawful, orderly, intelligent and—most daring—compassionate. The Healing Hypothesis postulates states of matter that range from the dense and stable forms studied in physics and chemistry to states so rarified and inward that they lie in dimensions unimaginable to the ordinary mind. These dimensions—akin to what cosmologists today call hyperdimensional space—do not "prove" the Healing Hypothesis. But they all share a basic common denominator with it, the assertion that certain features of reality cannot be understood within ordinary philosophical frameworks or assumptions. I therefore believe that The New Science, although it does not prove the Healing Hypothesis, is highly compatible with it. Nothing within it rules it out (as old mechanistic science might have done). By analogy, the Healing Hypothesis postulates the reality of a new dimension of space. Like other modes of hyperspace, it is inaccessible to the senses and hence can be neither experienced nor proven through them. Its reality is required, however, by those involved in meditation and healing.

In order to do its work, contemporary science requires hyperdimensional mathematical space. *Healing* requires hyperdimensional, inner, spiritual space. That they are assumed at this point and not yet proven by conventional methods of verification may be frustrating to our empirical selves, but such absence of firm proof does not constitute a definitive argument against the Healing Hypothesis. Its status at this moment ranges from a fruitful working principle to a promissory note for the future, to an already-in-progress paradigm that allows serious research to be organized around it. Its most novel feature is the postulated power of *human intentionality*. Nothing quite as diaphanous ("slippery!" its critics would exclaim) exists in present-day science except—much to the despair of its theoreticians—the strange paradoxes and ambiguities of the new physics called quantum mechanics. But if subjectivity can be tolerated in physics—a subjectivity that places the human observer at the center of the experiment—such subjectivity gains respectability and can surely be tolerated in the healing arts. At the very least, it no longer rules out the effect of the observer on the observed and the power of human consciousness as a reality that has objective consequences.

We are living in the midst of a scientific revolution whose philosophical and spiritual meaning is far from clear to most of us. What these new realities imply for our daily lives is barely grasped, and few of us trust ourselves with the sweeping possibilities we sense lie ahead. Yet even at this early state, two practical implications seem warranted: 1) 20th century science and the faintly discernible outline of 21st century science are more compatible with the Healing Hypothesis than was the science of the 17th-19th centuries and 2) just as gravity, electromagnetism, and the strong and weak nuclear forces provide the fundament of 20th century physics, so does *compassion* provide the basic vector force and energy for healing.

This makes no sense within the mechanistic, Cartesian worldview in which we have been brought up and whose premises we rarely question. But if we feel robbed of the stability (or rigidity) of that world, we must remember that we are not alone in our bewilderment. Nature is not obligated to operate in accordance with our clichés, however widely shared they may be. Nothing can better sum up nature's mystery than the bewildered outcry of G.K. Chesterton, which might aptly apply to those who first surveyed quantum mechanics in the early part of this century: "I have seen the truth, and it makes no sense!" No sense, that is, when forced into our old habits and assumptions.

The assumption that our thoughts and feelings—especially when consciously focused and projected—affect others forms the basis of the Healing Hypothesis and is one of the most radical challenges to the mechanistic world-view. The concept of a psychological and spiritual action-at-a-distance—though it has become associated with the New Age—is rooted in the wisdom traditions of India and Greece, dating back some 5000 years. What is new is the re-emergence of this tradition in modern dress, a synthesis of the ancient esoteric traditions with the laws of 20th century science.

Beyond this, what is new and unprecedented is the widespread accessibility of spiritual and altruistic practices that were once the prerogative of the few. That thousands of credentialed health professionals have chosen to take the initiative and responsibility for these new modalities is as startling as it is welcome. By contrast with the ancient traditions, it signals the shift from theocracy to democracy. Beyond this, it announces a shift as well from the exclusive concern with the so-called "objective" dimension of health care that has been our compulsory canon throughout most of this century. Instead, the holistic focus insists that we must *supplement*—but not supplant—modern techno-medicine with something else: something that is subtle, inward, and as fully real as the conventional tools of medicine. That something is the *human factor*, at once subjective and objective: caring, empathy, and compassion. Let us be clear. These are subjective in that they originate with the nurse or healer. They are deemed objective in two distinct ways: 1) they have consequences for both self and other and 2) most important, their ultimate power is postulated to have its origin beyond the human healer. What makes healing possible and authorizes it is the orderly power of an infinite universe.

These sweeping assumptions entail a spiritual dimension (though not, I believe, religion as conventionally conceived). As the authors of this book make clear, being a healer for others necessarily involves us in a measure of self-healing, greater integration, and in rare instances, self-transformation. Ideally, this entails spiritual growth for both healer and patient. A corollary principle also applies. Healing is hampered by the negative affects: resentment, anger, hatred, envy, jealousy, anxiety, self-pity, fear—i.e., a down-beat outlook on self, others and the universe. These states render us passive and hence less effective to deal with our lives. But the negative affects, alas, are pervasive in our current fragmented culture.

It is therefore heartening that the holistic and healing tradition that entered the nursing community in the early 1970s with Therapeutic Touch and other modalities continues to flourish in the 1980s. That spiritual ideas continue to flow into practical areas such as nursing is a sign of hope and commitment to our common humanity. It provides the counter-force to the inhumanity, indifference, depersonalization, and increasing commercialization of all too much of our present health care system. It thereby alters our image of who we are and who we can become.

Stated simply, holistic health care, its growing adherents, and thus the four dedicated authors of this book all argue for the primacy of love as a force for change. The nurse-healer is the ancient *therapon* who ministers to others through skills and presence. This is a model of interaction far removed from the isolation and abandonment that many of us in our greedy post-industrial world fear even above dying. The modern nurse-healer is a new model of being, a hybrid of scientific skill and spiritual commitment. The nurse's inward journey is charted by compassion and motivated by the desire to diminish suffering. As such, her or his journey can never be construed as solipsistic or narcissistic (by contrast with some other aspects of the New Age and the basis of much of the criticism against it). To unleash the power of love upon a world in pain seems to me an unassailable ideal.

This book glows with the trust in the creative power of compassion. Its publication should be welcomed with pleasure and gratitude by all of us who are committed to healing ourselves, our fellow creatures, and the fragile planet on which we live and whose survival depends on our awakening to its undeniable inner unity. Healing thus construed has both a personal and a cosmic dimension. Through it, we harmonize our lives with the life-affirming forces of the universe itself.

Renée Weber, PhD
Professor of Philosophy
Rutgers University

Preface

Holistic Nursing: A Handbook for Practice is the essence of contemporary nursing. We are indebted to the American Holistic Nurses' Association for their support of this work. Our book on holistic nursing helps guide the contemporary nurse in today's challenging role. We define a holistic approach as body-mind-spirit process of living. The purpose of our book is threefold: (1) to explore the unity and relatedness of nurses, clients, and all aspects of being; (2) to expand an understanding of healing and the nurse as healer; and (3) to develop different strategies to strengthen the whole person.

Is it correct for the contemporary nurse to think in terms of "nurse healer" and "nurse healing?" Initially, these phrases may evoke uncomfortable images, and you may feel a bit awkward or have difficulty thinking of yourself as a healer. But keep an open mind. First of all, healing is something that we can all claim. We are all born with healing potential. Take, for example, the bodymind wisdom in wound healing or the renewed healing that occurs after a wonderful holiday. This healing potential has many levels that we must first recognize and then learn to develop.

We define *nurse healer* as one who facilitates another person's growth toward wholeness (body-mind-spirit) or who assists with recovery from illness or transition to peaceful death. *Healing* is the process of bringing parts of oneself (physical, mental, emotions, spirit, relationships, and choices) together at deep levels of inner knowing, leading to an integration and balance, with each part having equal importance and value. This process is also referred to as self-healing or wholeness.

Allow yourself to explore these ideas of healing as they are developed in Units I, II, and III and then integrated throughout Unit IV. To expand your thinking as healers, each chapter begins with Nurse Healer Objectives and ends with Nurse Healer Reflections, which enable the reader to answer or begin a process of answering specific questions related to the healing potential.

For more information on the American Holistic Nurses' Association write to:

American Holistic Nurses' Association
401 Lake Boone Trail
Raleigh, N.C. 27607
(919) 787-5181

Our book is intended for students, practitioners, educators, and researchers who desire to expand their knowledge of holism, healing, and spirit. The book contains beginning, intermediate, and advanced concepts and interventions. Therefore, the reader can approach this book as a guide for learning basic content or for exploring advanced concepts. The philosophical and conceptual frameworks are presented at a beginning to an advanced level.

This holistic approach is developed by incorporating ideas of perennial philosophy, natural systems theory, and a nursing process framework. The information presented within the book may be of additional interest to the nurse because it incorporates the following:

- American Holistic Nurses' Association Standards for Holistic Nursing Practice
- theory and literature review of each topic
- nursing diagnoses established by the North American Nursing Diagnosis Association including wellness nursing diagnosis
- guidelines for integration of holistic interventions divided into four areas: before, beginning, during, and closing the session
- both basic and advanced strategies/interventions
- client case studies in the acute care and outpatient settings
- research and directions for future research

Throughout the book we use the word *bodymind* for it is the most accurate expression of body-mind-spirit responses and experiences of being human. Each chapter begins with Nurse Healer Objectives to direct your learning in theoretical, clinical, and personal areas. Each chapter has a glossary of definitions, for easy reference. The term *patient* is used for acute care settings, and the term *client* is used in the outpatient settings. Although the term "patient" usually implies dependency, we view patients as co-participants in all phases of care. The challenge is to integrate all concepts in this text in clinical practice. As clinicians, authors, educators, and researchers, we have successfully used these bodymind concepts and interventions from the critical care unit to home health to the classroom.

Our book is divided into four units. Unit I presents the philosophical concepts that help the reader explore what occurs when the nurse honors, acknowledges, and deepens the understanding of inner knowing and wisdom. This unit helps the reader expand concepts relevant to healing and reaching human potential that have direct application to clinical practice and personal life.

Unit II provides the knowledge base for understanding the history and future of healing. It lays the foundation for understanding the psychophysiology of bodymind healing. Unit III addresses the importance of the nursing process and the use of the Unitary Person framework to guide holistic assessment and formulation of nursing diagnoses. It provides information related to wellness, values clarification, and motivation. Guidelines for holistic research are also explored.

Unit IV provides comprehensive information on modalities to strengthen the whole person through nursing interventions and treatments for nursing diagnoses. Each chapter begins with specific definitions, theory, research, and general explanations specific to the topic. The rest of each chapter in Unit IV is organized according to the nursing process and includes nursing assessment parameters, nursing diagnoses, client outcomes, and outcome criteria for each intervention; guidelines for the nurse starting to use each of the interventions; specific ''how tos'' for implementing each intervention; scripts; and evaluation.

Interventions are both basic and advanced. Interventions designated as *basic* are those that the nurse can learn without additional training. Interventions designated as *advanced* require additional training. Each chapter then presents case studies that illustrate how to use the interventions in clinical practice, as well as how to integrate several interventions. This information is followed by Directions for Future Research specific to each topic. This section presents suggested research questions that are timely and in need of scientific exploration in nursing. In concluding each chapter, Nurse Healer Reflections are offered to nurture and spark a special self-reflective experience of bodymind and the inward journey toward self-discovery and wellness.

Holistic Nursing: A Handbook for Practice helps nurses embark on an inward journey toward self-transformation and learn to identify the growing capacity for change and healing within themselves and clients. It is this inward journey that permits the rebirth of a compassionate power to heal ourselves and facilitate healing within others. As we move toward understanding our own bodymind and helping others with their journey we give up separation of healer and healing. Once again we return to the roots of nursing where healer and healing were understood.

We hope that you find this book exciting. We encourage you to be continual students with us. We are still in a process of learning and being challenged. We have never had a greater opportunity in nursing. The profession of nursing and our paradigmatic assumptions about health and illness are undergoing radical changes. These changes will assist us in capturing our essence to emerge as true healers.

Barbara Montgomery Dossey
Lynn Keegan
Cathie E. Guzzetta
Leslie Gooding Kolkmeier

Acknowledgments

With heartfelt thanks to William Burgower, Editorial Director, Aspen Publishers, Inc., for sharing the vision with us of the magnificent potential of holistic nursing. Mr. Burgower is one of those rare individuals who has an intuitive understanding of nurse healing. To him we are deeply indebted.

And to our families—Larry Dossey; Gerald, Catherine, and Genevieve Keegan; Philip, Angela, and Philip C. Guzzetta; and Jim, Catherine, and Jennifer Kolkmeier—who, through their patience and love, are a part of the unity that nurse healing is all about.

Reviewers

Dolores M. Alford, RN, MSN, FAAN
Anna C. Alt-White, RN, PhD
Deborah J. Antai-Otong, RN, MS, CS
Kay Avant, RN, PhD
Chris Baker, RN, MSN, CS
Laurie Collard, RN, BS, MS
JoAnn Cheek Cole, BSN, MSN
Imelda Clements, RN, PhD
LaVerne Gallman, RN, PhD
Barbara Giordano, RN, MS
Sue Hamby, RN, PhD
Dorothea Hover, RN, EdD
Christine Ashley Kessler, RN, MN, CS
Janet A. Moll, RN, MS, GNP
Nancy A. Moeller Sanchez, RN, MS, CS
Frances Mayo, PhD
Tuni Miller, RN, BS
Gay Morris, RN, MS
Colleen K. Norton, RN, MSN, CCRN
Mary Elizabeth O'Brien, RN, PhD
Linda Ohler, RN, MSN, CCRN
Trish Roche, RN, BSN
Charles Schunior, RN, BSN, MA
Hilary Straub, RN, MS
Eileen Stuart, RN, MS
Jane White, RN, DNSc, CS
Elizabeth Hahn Winslow, RN, PhD
Barbara J. Woods, PhD
Michelle Zimmerman RN, MA, CS

unit **I**

The Inward Journey

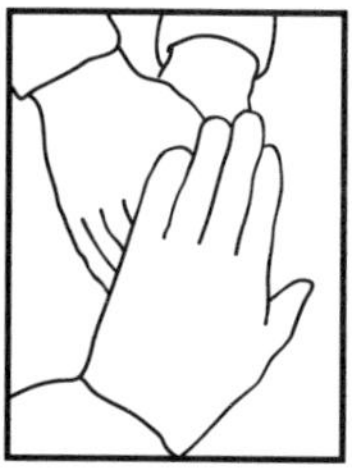

If our natural does not become truer, no amount of supernatural will remedy it. . . . Unless Paradise is established on Earth, it will never be anywhere. For we take ourselves everywhere we go, even into death, and so long as this "stupid" second is not filled with heaven, no eternity will ever be lit with any star.

The transmutation must take place in the body and in everyday life; otherwise no gold will ever glitter, here or anywhere else, for ages of ages.

What matters is not to see in pink or green or gold, but to see the truth of the world, which is so much more marvelous than any paradise.

Satprem

Source: Satprem, *The Mind of the Cells* (New York, New York: Institute for Evolutionary Research, 1982).

chapter **1**

Holism and the Circle of Human Potential

Barbara Montgomery Dossey and *Lynn Keegan*

> It is up to us, each one of us, to take responsibility for making the changes in our lives that will enable us to contribute to the well-being of the whole. If we aspire to optimum health either individually or collectively we must learn to pay attention to all aspects of physical, emotional, mental, existential, and spiritual well-being. Effective self-healing depends on taking all of these into account.[1]
>
> *Frances Vaughan*

This chapter guides the nurse in use of self-assessments, exploring the circle of human potential, and how to begin moving toward improving and maximizing our human potentials. Affirmations are introduced for the purpose of suggesting ways to change perceptions and beliefs so that we may acknowledge our possibilities.

Each of us has the requisite capacity for achieving balanced integration of our human potentials: physical, mental, emotions, spirit, relationships, and choices. We must also strive to learn more about how to gain access to inner wisdom and intuition and apply it in our daily lives. As we take responsibility for making effective choices, then the necessary changes occur in our lives. This then places us in the position to clarify our life patterns, purposes, and processes.

Actualizing human potentials means first recognizing and then accepting all the potentials of our being, even those we wish to change. Developing our potentials requires a willingness to assess where we are in our life, to develop an action plan for change, and then to evaluate where we are with this lifelong process.

NURSE HEALER OBJECTIVES

Theoretical

1. List the six parts of the circle of human potential.
2. Define biodance.

Clinical

1. Identify specific areas in each potential that can help you increase and maximize your effectiveness in clinical practice.
2. Increase daily your conscious attention to recognizing feelings, environment, relationships, and life patterns and processes in your practice.
3. Use the self-assessment tools and the circle of human potential as interventions with clients.

Personal

1. Tabulate your score in each area of the circle of human potential.
2. Establish areas you wish to focus on in order to create changes and choices that lead to new health behaviors.
3. Become aware of how you gain access to or block inner healing.

DEFINITIONS

Biodance: the endless exchange of the elements of living things with the earth itself; it proceeds silently, giving us no hint that it is happening; a dance—animated, purposeful, disciplined—in which every living organism participates.

Healing Awareness: conscious recognition and focusing of attention on sensations, feelings, conditions, and facts dealing with needs of oneself or clients.

Healing: a process of bringing parts of oneself (physical, mental, emotions, spirit, relationships, and choices) together at deep levels of inner knowing leading toward an integration and balance, with each part having equal importance and value; may also be referred to as self-healing or wholeness.

Holism: the view that an integrated whole has a reality independent of and greater than the sum of its parts.

Nurse Healer: one who facilitates another person's growth and life process toward wholeness (body-mind-spirit connections) or who assists with recovery from illness or transition to peaceful death.

Process: the continual changing and evolution of one's self through life; the reflection of meaning and purpose in living.

Psychophysiologic: the quality of body-mind-spirit as a single integrated entity.

Transpersonal Self: the experience that transcends or goes beyond personal individual identity and meaning; includes purpose, meaning, values, and unification with universal principles.

Transpersonal View: the state that occurs with a person's life maturity whereby the sense of self expands.

IN SEARCH OF THE WHOLE PERSON

The whole person is one who seeks the inward journey of understanding the complexities of life. *The inward journey is a path toward self-discovery*. As we proceed on the path, we discover new meaning, understanding, and purpose in living, which can be referred to as *radical aliveness*.[2] Radical means "root," the support or foundation, the fundamental basis or basic principle. When we move on the path of radical aliveness, we are challenged to go to the core or root of aliveness, a state beyond the ordinary. This means exploring our potential and who we are. We should focus on studying people who activate healthy potentials for they provide us with far more insight about human potentials than investigation of those with psychophysiologic disabilities.[3]

Holism is a philosophy that views everything in terms of patterns of organization, relationships, interactions, and processes that combine to form a whole. Wholeness can be present when one has high levels of wellness and also when one has known disease/disability or is in the process of dying. Wholeness is a process and is present when we view ourselves as an open living system in a tapestry of relationships and events. Our actions have an effect on our body-mind-spirit. Because of the holistic aspect of our being, each dimension has a direct effect on the other, as shown in Figure 1-1.

SELF-ASSESSMENTS

In order to maximize our potential, it is important to assess where we are in each aspect of our being: physical, mental, emotions, spirit, relationships, and choices.[4] Take some time to complete the following self-assessments to help you more clearly identify where you are now (Figs. 1-2 to 1-7 and Exhibit 1-1).

The six areas of the circle of human potential are now developed to increase our understanding of how to integrate our human potentials. This understanding will help guide the nurse in use of the self-assessments and circle of human potential as nursing

	BODY	MIND	SPIRIT
BODY	body body	mind body	spirit body
MIND	body mind	mind mind	spirit mind
SPIRIT	body spirit	mind spirit	spirit spirit

Figure 1-1 Body-Mind-Spirit Interrelationships. *Source:* Reprinted from *Self Care: A Program To Improve Your Life* by L. Keegan and B. Dossey with permission of Bodymind Systems, © 1987.

PHYSICAL

Where I am now	Almost Always	Some-times	Almost Never	How I Want It To Be
Assess my general health daily	2	1	0	
Exercise 3 to 5 times a week for 20 minutes	2	1	0	
Eat nutritious foods daily	2	1	0	
Play without guilt	2	1	0	
Practice relaxation daily	2	1	0	
Energy level is effective for daily activities	2	1	0	
Do not smoke	2	1	0	
Drink in moderation	2	1	0	
Have regular physical and dental check-ups	2	1	0	
Balance my work life with personal life	2	1	0	
Physical Score				

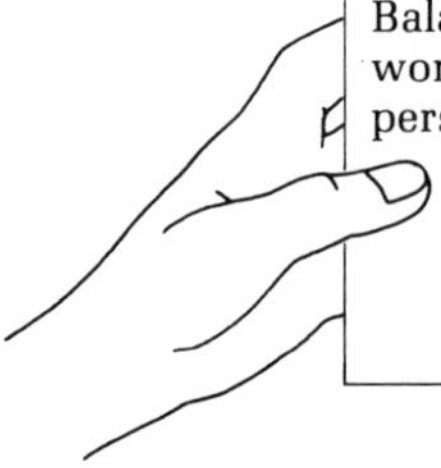

Figure 1-2 Physical Self-Assessment. *Source:* Reprinted from *Self Care: A Program To Improve Your Life* by L. Keegan and B. Dossey with permission of Bodymind Systems, © 1987.

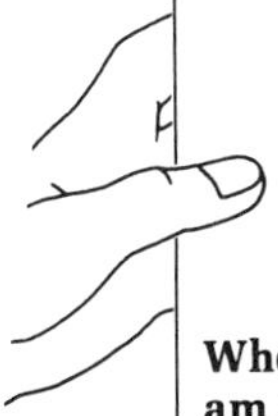

MENTAL

Where I am now	Almost Always	Some-times	Almost Never	How I Want It To Be
Am open and receptive to new ideas and life patterns	2	1	0	
Read a broad range of subjects	2	1	0	
Am interested in and knowledgeable about many topics	2	1	0	
Use my imagination in considering new choices or possibilities	2	1	0	
Prioritize my work and set realistic goals	2	1	0	
Enjoy developing new skills and talents	2	1	0	
Ask for suggestions and help when I need it	2	1	0	
Mental Score				

Figure 1-3 Mental Self-Assessment. *Source:* Reprinted from *Self Care: A Program To Improve Your Life* by L. Keegan and B. Dossey with permission of Bodymind Systems, © 1987.

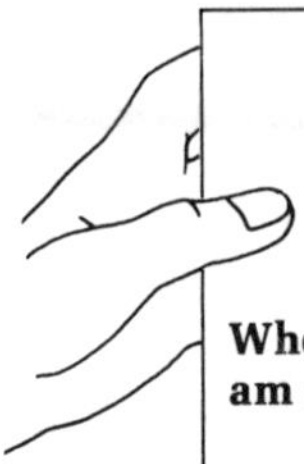

EMOTIONS

Where I am now	**Almost Always**	**Some-times**	**Almost Never**	**How I Want It To Be**
Assess and recognize my own feelings	2	1	0	
Have a nonjudgemental attitude	2	1	0	
Express my feelings in appropriate ways	2	1	0	
Include my feelings when making decisions	2	1	0	
Can remember and acknowledge most events of my childhood including painful as well as happy ones	2	1	0	
Listen and respect the feelings of others	2	1	0	
Recognize my intuition	2	1	0	
Listen to inner self-talk	2	1	0	
Emotions Score	☐			☐

Figure 1-4 Self-Assessment of Emotions. *Source:* Reprinted from *Self Care: A Program To Improve Your Life* by L. Keegan and B. Dossey with permission of Bodymind Systems, © 1987.

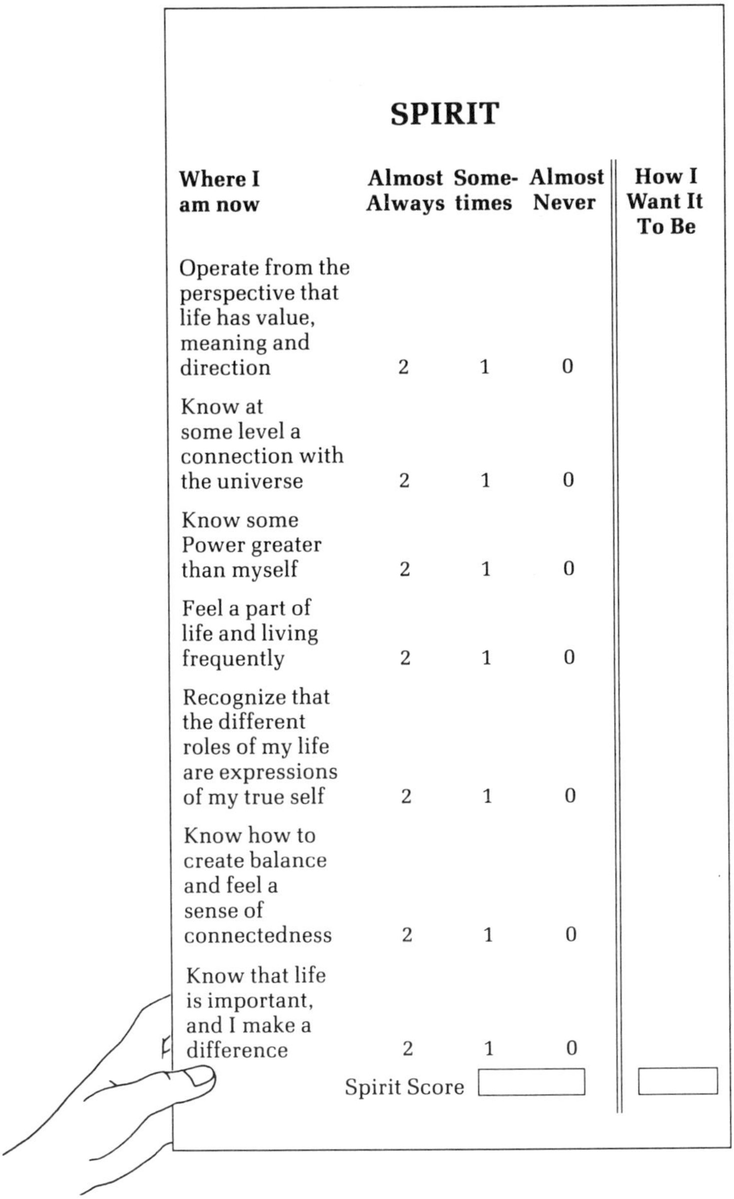

SPIRIT

Where I am now	Almost Always	Some-times	Almost Never	How I Want It To Be
Operate from the perspective that life has value, meaning and direction	2	1	0	
Know at some level a connection with the universe	2	1	0	
Know some Power greater than myself	2	1	0	
Feel a part of life and living frequently	2	1	0	
Recognize that the different roles of my life are expressions of my true self	2	1	0	
Know how to create balance and feel a sense of connectedness	2	1	0	
Know that life is important, and I make a difference	2	1	0	
Spirit Score				

Figure 1-5 Spirit Self-Assessment. *Source:* Reprinted from *Self Care: A Program To Improve Your Life* by L. Keegan and B. Dossey with permission of Bodymind Systems, © 1987.

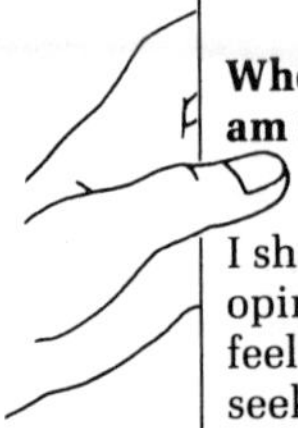

RELATIONSHIPS

Where I am now	Almost Always	Some-times	Almost Never	How I Want It To Be
I share my opinions and feelings without seeking the approval of others or fearing outcomes	2	1	0	
Create and participate in satisfying relationships	2	1	0	
Sexuality is part of my relationship	2	1	0	
Have a balance between my work and family life	2	1	0	
Am clear in expressing my needs and desires	2	1	0	
Am open and honest with people without fearing the consequences	2	1	0	
Do my part in establishing and maintaining relationships	2	1	0	
Focus on positive topics in relationships	2	1	0	
Relationships Score			☐	☐

Figure 1-6 Self-Assessment of Relationships. *Source:* Reprinted from *Self Care: A Program To Improve Your Life* by L. Keegan and B. Dossey with permission of Bodymind Systems, © 1987.

CHOICES

Where I am now	Almost Always	Some-times	Almost Never	How I Want It To Be
Manage my time to meet my personal goals	2	1	0	
Am committed and disciplined whenever I take on new projects	2	1	0	
Follow through and work on decisions with clarity and action steps	2	1	0	
Am usually clear on decisions	2	1	0	
Take risks	2	1	0	
Can accept circumstances that are beyond my control	2	1	0	
Take on no more new tasks than I can successfully handle	2	1	0	
Recognize shortcomings of people and events for what they are	2	1	0	
Choices Score				

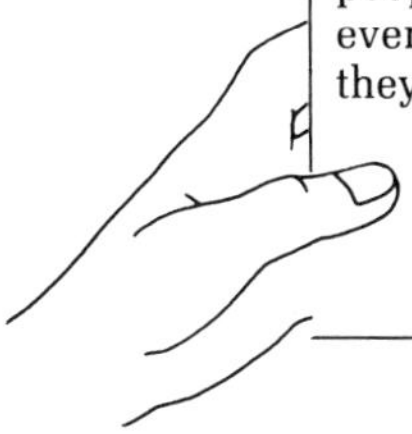

Figure 1-7 Self-Assessment of Choices. *Source:* Reprinted from *Self Care: A Program To Improve Your Life* by L. Keegan and B. Dossey with permission of Bodymind Systems, © 1987.

Exhibit 1-1 The Meaning of the Tallied Scores

Scores of 14 to 20

Congratulations! Your score shows that you are aware of the important areas of your life. You are using your knowledge to work for you by practicing good life patterns that reflect health and balance. As long as you continue with high scores, you will be maximizing your human potential. You are a good model of health to family and friends. Since your score is high in this area move to other areas where your scores are low and identify areas for improvement.

Scores of 10 to 13

Your life patterns in this area are good, but there is room for improvement. Reflect on the "Sometimes or Almost Never," answers. What could you do to change your score? Even the slightest change can make a difference to improve the quality of your life.

Scores of 6 to 9

Your life stressors are showing. You need more information about these important life areas and what changes you can make. Read on to obtain guidance.

Scores of 0 to 5

Your life is full of unnecessary stress. You are not taking good care of yourself. You need to take some time and learn the principles of self-care.

When you finish this exercise you have a composite picture not only of where you are now, but where you want to go. ENJOY THE JOURNEY!

The following sections of this book will guide you through understanding more about your human potentials.

Source: Reprinted from *Self Care: A Program To Improve Your Life* by L. Keegan and B. Dossey with permission of Bodymind Systems, © 1987.

interventions. These same six areas may also be referred to as the whole person wheel[5] and healing the whole person.[6]

CIRCLE OF HUMAN POTENTIAL

The dance of life involves many possibilities. All of our human potentials are constantly interacting. As seen in Figure 1-8, the circle of human potential is comprised of six areas: physical, mental, emotions, spirit, relationships, and choices.

A circle is an ancient symbol of wholeness. The circle in this model has six separate but equally important parts. Together they comprise bodymind, the single integrated entity of one's total psychophysiologic experience. One is not more important than the other. When any one part is incomplete the entire circle loses its completeness because all parts create the whole. It is when we become aware of our strengths in each area, as

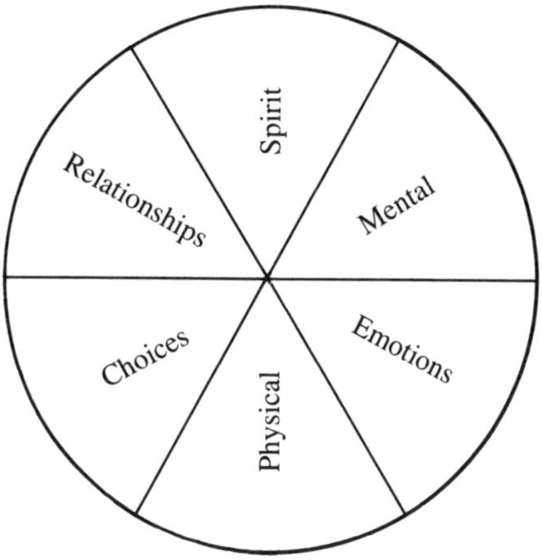

Figure 1-8 Circle of Human Potential. *Source:* Reprinted from *Self Care: A Program To Improve Your Life* by L. Keegan and B. Dossey with permission of Bodymind Systems, © 1987.

well as of our weaknesses, that we begin to move to our highest capabilities and live in accordance with our philosophy of life.

All people are complex feedback loops. As we become aware of these feedback loops we are able to understand our bodymind connections. Our bodies are constantly in a state of change of which we are unaware. Life is a *biodance,* the endless exchange of all living things with the earth that involves all living organisms.[7] It not only exists as we live, but as we die. We do not wait until death to exchange with the earth, for we are *constantly returning* to the universe while *alive*. In every living moment a portion of our 10^{28} atoms in our body return to the world outside.[8] This is another idea of wholeness, which explains why the notion of "boundary" begins to appear as an arbitrary idea, rather than a physical reality.

The purpose of completing the human potential self-assessments is to direct one's healing awareness, bringing balance and direction to all aspects of our being. Healing awareness is the innate quality with which all people are born. It must be developed in order to be actualized to the fullest. Healing is recognizing our feelings, attitudes, and emotions. These feelings are not isolated; our thoughts and emotions are literally translated into body changes. This occurs because images cause internal events through mind modulation that simultaneously affects the autonomic, endocrine, immune, and neuropeptide systems. This healing quality is exemplified by the placebo, the healer who resides within.[9] Everyone has the potential and choice to tap into this innate healing potential. When we acknowledge our bodymind relationships true healing can occur. Self-healing can become blocked in times of stress and crisis or even moment by moment in our daily routine. Therefore, it is necessary for us to continually assess and reassess our wholeness.

Physical Potential

Common biologic experiences that all humans share are birth, gender, growth, aging, and death. The human being has basic biologic needs for food, shelter, and clothing. Once these are met, there are many ways to seek health and wholeness of our physical potential. Physical health is more than the absence of pain and symptoms. Physical potential is influenced by many elements. The major ones are general physical awareness of proper nutrition, exercise, relaxation, and balance between work and play.

Recently, many people have been obsessed with these elements and have failed to recognize that they are not separate or more important than the other potentials. Health is present when there is a balance. As we assess biologic needs, we must also take into consideration our *perceptions* of these areas because our consciousness plays a major role in health and physical potential. Many illnesses have been documented as being stress-related. It is when we assess and reassess our levels of stress that we maximize our potential.

Our body is a gift to nurture and respect. As we nurture ourselves, we increase our uniqueness in energy, sexuality, vitality, and capacity for language and connection with our other potentials. This nurturance strengthens our self-image, which causes several things to happen: (1) Our bodymind responds in a positive and integrated fashion, (2) we become a role model with a positive influence on others, and (3) we actually enhance our general feeling of well-being. It is impossible to gain strengths or empowerment without these changes being manifest and influencing the lives of other people.

Mental Potential

Mental potential involves our thought processes, beliefs, and values. Early in our lives we are told what to think, how to behave, and what to value. As we mature and gain life experience, different shifts occur in our thinking, our behavior, and in our values. Conflicts develop when we do not take the time to sort out our new perceptions and discard old beliefs and values that no longer fit.

Our challenge is to create accurate perceptions of the world through our mental potential. It is through our logical as well as nonlogical mental processes that we become interested in a broad range of subjects that help us expand our full appreciation of the many great pleasures in life. We should increase our awareness of how we use both logical and intuitive thought and increase our skills to create better simultaneous integration of both ways of knowing.

With such interventions as the relaxation response and meditation we learn to participate with *active attention* to thought processes. When this occurs, we increase the experience of learning how to be present in the moment. It is during these moments that we let go of our critical inner voice that is constantly judging and in self-dialogue. These are the moments when we are attuned to expanding our mental knowing.

As we increase our openness and receptivity to information and suggestions, mental growth can occur. Every aspect of our life is a learning experience and becomes part of a lesson in changing. There is no end to what we can learn for the human brain has an unlimited potential to learn new ways of being and thinking if we are willing to tap it.

Emotions Potential

Emotions potential involves our willingness to acknowledge the presence of feelings and value them as important, and the ability to express them. Emotional health implies the choice and freedom we have to express love, joy, guilt, fear, and anger. When we express these emotions, they can give us immediate feedback about our inner state that may be crying out for a new way of being.

Emotions are feelings—our inner and outer responses to the events in our lives. It is when we confront both positive and negative intense emotions that true healing occurs. When we do not confront our emotions various degrees of chronic anxiety, depression, worry, fear, guilt, anger, denial, or repression result. One of the greatest challenges we have is to acknowledge, own, express, and understand our emotions. We are living systems constantly exchanging with our environment. All life events affect our emotions and general well-being. Some events may cause fear. When this occurs we must not run and hide as if these feelings did not exist. Each of us must know our fears just as we know our calmness. As we face our fears, then we come to understand their meaning.

As we become more balanced in living, we allow our humanness to develop. We reach out and ask for human dialogue that is meaningful. Increasing this potential allows for spontaneity and a positive healthy zest for living to emerge. We must be aware and take responsibility for expression that allows spirit and intuition to flower.

Learn to assess your verbal expressions, as well as your nonverbal expressions, such as voice patterns, posture, gait, general appearance, and facial expressions. Connect your thought processes with your emotions. Is there a consistent harmony between them? When you recognize the disharmony, acknowledge to yourself that this causes dissonance and there must be more that needs to be expressed.

Emotions are gifts. Frequently, a first step toward releasing a burden in a relationship is to share deep feelings with another. When we bury emotions, we lose part of ourselves. There is no such thing as a good or bad emotion; each is part of the human condition. Emotions exist as the light and shadow of the self; thus we must acknowledge all of them. They create the dance of life, the polarity of living. The only reason we can identify the light is because we know its opposite, the shadow. When we see the value in both types of emotions, then we are in a position of new insight and new understanding, and we can make effective choices. As we increase our attention to bodymind interrelationships, we can focus on the emotions that move us toward wholeness and inner understanding.

Spirit Potential

Throughout history there has been a quest to understand the purpose of human life experience. Humankind is incomplete unless the human condition for transcendence evolves (see Chapters 2 and 3 for discussion of transpersonal development). Spirit comes from our roots—the universal need to understand the human experience of life on earth. Where did we come from? Where are we going? What is our purpose? Why do good and evil exist? What occurs after death? Who or what put this life form together? The answers to these questions may or may not be found in organized religion. Religion involves a group of people who have similar beliefs about the above questions.

Spirit involves the development of our Higher Self—the transpersonal self. The experience of transcendence is described as a feeling of oneness, inner peace, harmony, and wholeness and connection with the universe. The meaning and joy that flow from developing this aspect of our human potential are vital, enabling one to have a transpersonal view. Some of the ways we may come to know this transcendence are through prayer, meditation, organized religion, philosophy, science, poetry, music, inspired friends, and group work.

Spirit, as with the other potentials, does not develop without some attention. We must acknowledge its value. Every day, with each of our experiences, we must acknowledge our spirit potential that is essential to developing a healthy belief system. It is through our belief system that we shape our perception of the world. Our perceptions will influence whether we have positive or negative experiences. Even through the pain of a negative experience, we have the ability to learn. Pain can be a great teacher. On the other side of the experience is new wisdom, self-discovery, and the chance for making new choices based on wisdom.

Relationships Potential

Healthy people live in intricate networks of relationships and are always in search of new, unifying concepts of the universe and social order.[10] Human beings need to explore and develop meaningful relationships. A healthy person simply cannot live in isolation. Who composes most people's networks? If we look closely at our networks, it is easy to see that in a given day we interact with many people—immediate family, extended family, colleagues at work, neighbors in the community, and numerous people in organizations. Because we spend half or more of our awake time with colleagues at work, we must support and nourish these relationships. We must also extend the concept of network to include our nation and planet Earth. Now as we approach the 21st century, each of us must take an active role in developing networks of relationships to further global concerns for world peace.

Our relationships have different levels of meaning—from the superficial to feeling deeply connected. The challenge in relationships is to extend ourselves and to learn how to exchange our feelings of honesty, trust, intimacy, compassion, openness, and harmony.

When sharing life processes, true interchange between ourself and others must occur. It is only when we increase our awareness and intention that we open up for more of the above qualities to occur with our family, friends, work colleagues, clients and community at large. As we increase our network from one person to another, we extend our boundaries because one contact leads to many more.

It is essential that we identify the cohesiveness in our relationships, as well as the disharmony. We must be aware of the impact that we have on clients, family and friends. When people come together, something always happens, for life is participation. By our attitudes and healing awareness orientation of concern for self and others, we can affect the outcome of all our encounters.

Choice Potential

People have enormous capacity for choices in their lives. These choices can be conscious or unconscious. Balanced lives result when we use skills of making effective choices: discipline, persistence, goal setting, priorities, action steps, knowing our options, and recognizing our perceptions. There is no one way to accomplish anything. At all times we must be open to new knowledge and new skills for living. We must be active participants in daily living, not passive recipients hoping that life will be good to us.

Each of us is responsible for assessing our values and desires. No one else can make decisions for us. When we do not exercise our ability to make choices, the beliefs and values of others are imposed on us and we never reach our highest potential.

Choice involves taking risks. We may make some mistakes along the way, but we also gain experience. Choice involves taking a stand on issues, because not to do so is ambivalent behavior that keeps us stuck.

Continuing to develop clarity in life enables us to follow through on meeting goals. A simple process for changing behavior to enable following through on goals is to learn how to change perception. Take an inventory of all the "shoulds," identify them, and change them in your mind to "I could, and I have a choice."[11] An example would be "I should be more loving" to "I could be more loving, and I have a choice." We create more effective choices when we take the time to not be judgmental and to release fears and guilt. We can all change and it is a skill of awareness to acknowledge that we are worth the effort.

Affirmations

Affirmations are strong, positive statements acknowledging that something is already so. Affirmations can help us change our perceptions and beliefs. If we believe an affirmation to be true, then our perceptions selectively reinforce it because we change our *self-talk*. Our mind is constantly engaged in active thought processing. We are in *constant dialogue* with ourselves at all times. In fact, the person we talk to the most in a day is ourselves. Self-talk even operates in our dreams while we sleep. What are we reinforcing moment by moment? If our thoughts are hopeful and optimistic, our body responds with confidence, energy, and hope. If, on the other hand, negative thoughts dominate, our body responds with tightness, uneasiness, and an increase in breathing, blood pressure, and heart rate.

Affirmations are statements we select to affirm our intentions and choices. Affirmations help us[12]:

- identify what is true for us, and then the truth can manifest in behavior
- increase our clarity of goals, which helps us exercise our options
- assume more responsibility for our actions, thoughts, beliefs, and values

- increase our empowerment
- envision a new way of being
- clarify goals, actions, and assist with self-evaluation

Affirmations for *each* human potential are now listed. The purpose of these affirmations is to acknowledge our possibilities. As you read them you may *change* them in any way you wish to make them more personal. If when you read any of the affirmations you feel *resistance,* simply notice the hesitation or reluctance and *allow* it to be present.

PHYSICAL

- I assess my general health daily.
- I exercise 3 to 5 times a week for 20 minutes.
- I eat nutritious food daily.
- I play without guilt.
- I practice relaxation daily.
- I have energy levels effective for daily activities.
- I do not smoke.
- I drink in moderation.
- I have regular physical and dental check-ups.
- I balance my work life with my personal life.

MENTAL

- I am open and receptive to new ideas and life patterns.
- I read a broad range of subjects.
- I am interested in and knowledgeable about many topics.
- I use my imagination in considering new choices or possibilities.
- I prioritize my work and set realistic goals.
- I enjoy developing new skills and talents.
- I ask for suggestions and help when I need it.

EMOTIONS

- I assess and recognize my own feelings.
- I have a nonjudgmental attitude.

- I express my feelings in appropriate ways.
- I include my feelings when making decisions.
- I can remember and acknowledge most events of my childhood including painful as well as happy ones.
- I listen and respect the feelings of others.
- I recognize my intuition.
- I listen to inner self-talk.

SPIRIT

- I operate from the perspective that life has value, meaning, and direction.
- I know, at some level, a connection with the universe.
- I know some power greater than myself.
- I feel a part of life and living frequently.
- I recognize that the different roles of my life are expressions of my true self.
- I know how to create balance and a sense of connectedness.

RELATIONSHIPS

- I share my opinions and feelings without seeking the approval of others or fearing outcomes.
- I create and participate in satisfying relationships.
- I allow sexuality to be a part of my relationships.
- I have a balance between my work and my family life.
- I am clear in expressing my needs and desires.
- I am open and honest with people without fearing the consequences.
- I do my part in establishing and maintaining relationships.
- I focus on positive topics in relationships.

CHOICES

- I manage time to meet my personal goals.
- I am committed and disciplined whenever I take on new projects.
- I follow through and work on decisions with clarity and action steps.
- I am usually clear on decisions.

- I take risks.
- I can accept circumstances beyond my control.
- I take on no more new tasks than I can successfully handle.

SUMMARY

Each area of our human potential affects our whole being. The challenge for each of us in our personal life and clinical practice is to strive to integrate all our human potentials. When we assess our human potentials and decide how we want our lives to be, we move on the inward journey toward self-discovery. If one area of our human potential is left undeveloped, one has the feeling that things are not as good as they could be. However, when one strives to develop all areas, a sense of wholeness emerges, and one's self-worth increases and life goals are actualized. Being alive becomes more exciting, rewarding, and fulfilling. Even when frustrations arise, the whole person is able to recognize choices and decrease the blocks.

DIRECTIONS FOR FUTURE RESEARCH

1. Determine if there is an increase in obtaining client outcomes if the nurse uses the circle of human potential as assessment tools and as a nursing intervention.
2. Evaluate if the nurse's self-esteem increases when the concepts of the circle of human potential and affirmations for daily living are used.
3. Determine if the client's self-esteem increases when the concepts of the circle of human potential and affirmations are taught.
4. Evaluate changes in behavior and perceived quality of life when clients are guided in learning awareness skills in regard to their human potentials.

NURSE HEALER REFLECTIONS

After reading this chapter, the nurse healer will be able to answer or begin a process of answering the following questions:

- What is my *process* when I assess my circle of human potentials?
- Am I *consciously aware* of the daily opportunity to manifest my own human potentials?
- What can I do to *increase* my *conscious awareness* of *fully* participating in living?
- How do I *feel* when I used the word healer to *describe* myself?
- What is my *inner awareness* when I acknowledge my healing potential?

NOTES

1. Frances Vaughan, *The Inward Arc* (Boston: Shambhala Publications, Inc., 1986), p. 22.
2. Richard Moss, *The Black Butterfly: An Invitation to Radical Aliveness* (Berkeley, CA: Celestial Arts, 1986), p. 2.
3. Roger Walsh and Deane Shapiro, "In Search of a Healthy Person" in *Beyond Health and Normality,* ed. Roger Walsh and Deane Shapiro (New York: Van Nostrand Reinhold Inc., 1983), p. 7.
4. Lynn Keegan and Barbara Dossey, *Self Care: A Program to Improve Your Life* (Temple, TX: Bodymind Systems, 1987), p. 12–18.
5. Sharon Wegscheider, *Another Chance* (Palo Alto, CA: Science and Basic Books, 1981), p. 33.
6. Frances Vaughan, *The Inward Arc*, p. 9.
7. Larry Dossey, *Space, Time and Medicine* (Boston: Shambhala Publications, Inc.,1982), p. 87.
8. Ibid., p. 76.
9. Norman Cousins, *Anatomy of an Illness as Perceived by a Patient* (New York: W.W. Norton, 1979), p. 69.
10. Jacob Needleman, *A Sense of the Cosmos* (New York: Doubleday, 1975), p. 162.
11. Frances Vaughan, *The Inward Arc*, p. 72.
12. Ibid., p. 71.

SUGGESTED READINGS

Ferrucci, Piero, *What We May Be*. Los Angeles. J. P. Tarcher, 1982.

Kunz, Dora, *Spiritual Aspects of the Healing Arts*. Wheaton, IL: The Theosophical Publishing House, 1985.

Remen, Naomi, *The Human Patient*. New York: Doubleday, 1980.

Trungpa, Chogyam, *Shambhala: The Sacred Path of the Warrior*. Boston: Shambhala Publications, Inc., 1984.

Welwood, John, *Awakening the Heart*. Boston: Shambhala Publications, Inc., 1983.

RESOURCES

Self-Care: A Program to Improve Your Life (3-Part Guided Program: 100-page book, 40-minute relaxation and imagery audio cassette tape, and affirmation cards containing 47 affirmations). All in a deluxe bookshelf binder. Excellent program for professionals and clients. Write Bodymind Systems, 910 Dakota Drive, Temple, Texas, 76504.

chapter 2

The Transpersonal Self and States of Consciousness

Barbara Montgomery Dossey

> Synchronizing mind and body is not a concept or a random technique someone thought up for self-improvement. Rather, it is a basic principle of how to be a human being and how to use your sense perceptions, your mind, and your body together.[1]
>
> *Chogyam Trungpa*
> *Buddhist teacher and scholar*

This chapter provides the nurse with the foundations for healing—both healing self and facilitating healing in others. The experience and steps of learning about our inner personal growth and the meaning of states of consciousness are discussed. As we mature we exercise the human capacity to go beyond individual identity and evolve to our highest potential, the transpersonal self. Understanding the dimensions of the transpersonal self is a major force leading to our ability to enhance healing in our self and others. Yet, knowing states of the transpersonal self is not an end point, but a continuing, never-ending process.

NURSE HEALER OBJECTIVES: THE TRANSPERSONAL SELF AND STATES OF CONSCIOUSNESS

Theoretical

1. State the definition of the transpersonal self.
2. Compare and contrast the different states of consciousness.
3. State the definitions of psychophysiologic self-regulation and the relaxation response.

1. Recognize how you operationalize nursing as a human science.
2. Integrate the information in this chapter into your daily practice.

3. Begin to recognize your inner bodymind awareness during your workday, particularly noticing the shifts from tension to relaxation as you evoke the skills of psychophysiologic self-regulation.

Personal

1. Schedule time each day to shift into states of deep relaxation.
2. Set aside quality quiet time to recognize your inner wisdom and creativity.
3. Use a relaxation and imagery exercise and allow an image to appear of your transpersonal self that represents the qualities that you value.

DEFINITIONS

Altered State of Consciousness (ASC): a shift in a person's subjective experience from a usual state of awareness; may be induced by daydreams, dreams, deep relaxation, meditative practice, pharmacologic agents including anesthesia, sudden psychophysiologic shifts (blood loss, anoxia, dehydration etc.).

Meditation: the inward focusing of attention in order to reach a relative pure experience of the self that allows an opening to transpersonal states.

Optimal State of Consciousness (OSC): the state in which one masters the ability to achieve psychophysiologic self-regulation (PPSR).

Perennial Philosophy: historical recordings of humanity's quest for a divine reality and the universal need to understand the purpose of human life experience and what happens after death. This spans all major cultures and ages and can be found within all major spiritual traditions.

Psychophysiologic Self-Regulation (PPSR): the process whereby a person is able to induce varying states of relaxation in order to balance right and left hemispheric function. With disciplined practice one is able to shift into deep states of relaxation.

Relaxation Response (RR): a hypometabolic process of decreased sympathetic nervous system arousal whereby one experiences calmness and relaxation. With disciplined practice deep states of relaxation may be achieved, and one may experience a transcendent state of oneness, unity, and a universal connection with a Higher Power.

Spirituality: a broad concept that encompasses values, meaning, and purpose; one turns inward to the human traits of honesty, love, caring, wisdom, imagination, and compassion; existence of a quality of a higher authority, guiding spirit, or transcendence that is mystical; a flowing, dynamic balance that allows and creates healing of body-mind-spirit; may or may not involve organized religion.

Transcend: to raise one's ordinary state of consciousness above control at a lower material level; a willingness to be aware, moment by moment, of what is true in both inner and outer experience; becoming conscious of one's wholeness, complete in each moment.

Transpersonal Self: the experience that transcends or goes beyond the personal individual identity; includes purpose, meaning, values, and unification with universal principles; synonymous with spirituality.

Usual State of Consciousness (USC): the distinct psychophysiologic state in which one spends the majority of one's daily waking hours.

FOUNDATIONS FOR HEALING

A Human Science

We have a human science when we evoke states of healing and healer. In Weber's eloquent framework for foundations of healing, the *universal healing power,* not the healer's personal energy, accomplishes the healing. The *healer* is like a channel, passively yet paradoxically with discernment, permitting the cosmic energy to flow unobstructedly through his or her own energy fields into those of the *healee*. The healer must be aware of the disturbances in the healee's wholeness at the higher levels. It is the healer who constitutes the link between the universal and the particular; his or her role is analogous to an electrical transformer capable of stepping down the source, in this case the prodigious cosmic energy, into a form used by our bodymind systems.[2]

A human science is based upon[3]:

- a philosophy of human freedom, choices, and responsibility
- a biology and psychology of holism (nonreducible persons connected with others and nature)
- a theory of origins, methods, and limits of knowledge (epistemology) that allows not only for practical experience (empirics) but also for advancement of esthetics, ethical values, intuition, and process discovery
- a branch of metaphysics that deals with the nature of being/reality (ontology) of space and time
- a context of interhuman events, processes, and relationships
- a scientific world view that is open

If we are to operationalize nursing as a human science, we must understand the idea of the person, nursing, and human care. Three areas to focus on are (1) being-in-the-world, (2) the self, and (3) a phenomenal field.[4] The person is viewed as *being-in-the-world,* possessing the spheres of body-mind-spirit. These spheres influence one's concept of self. The *self* indicates the perceptions of "I" and relationships to others. Another level of self is the Higher self, the spiritual self that rises above ordinary waking consciousness. A *phenomenal field* is the individual's frame of reference that can be known only to the person. This phenomenal field (a person's subjective reality) influences how a person responds in any given situation. It involves many levels of consciousness, such as awareness, perceptions of self, self-to-others, body sensations, thoughts, values, feelings, beliefs, and hopes. So when nurse and client come together two phenomenal fields come together. Both are in a process of being, becoming, and developing transpersonal understanding.

Transpersonal Human Care and Caring Transactions

We can speak of transpersonal human care and caring transactions as the professional, ethical, scientific, esthetic, caring, and personalized giving-receiving behaviors and responses between two people (nurse and other) that allow for contact between the subjective world of persons (through physical, mental, and spiritual routes).[5] The nurse and client come together sharing a phenomenal field of their individual uniqueness, which creates an event of caring as seen in Figure 2-1.

The dynamics of the human caring process involve nurse, client, and the phenomenal field of each person. The human caring process thus has a transpersonal dimension. That transpersonal dimension is an intersubjective human-to-human relationship in which the person of the nurse affects and is affected by the person of the other. Both are fully present in the moment and feel a union with the other. They share a phenomenal field that becomes part of the life history of both and are co-participants in becoming in the now and the future. Such an ideal of caring entails an ideal of intersubjectivity, in which both persons are involved.

This coming together can be done in a mechanical manner in which the nurse or client responds without acknowledging the other or recognizing each other's potentials. Or, the nurse and client can come together with a presence of caring that involves actions and choices by both.[6]

The Path toward Spirituality

In this modern age of change, people are searching for how to create new perceptions for their life, as well as to find wholeness and spirituality; they need guidance in their transformation.[7] In order to deal with the spiritual dimension more effectively, the nurse should be aware of the following complex factors that shape one's world view and influence the nurse's ability to help clients with spiritual issues:[8]

- *Pluralism:* nurses and clients each have a vast array of beliefs, values, meaning, and purpose
- *Fear:* the nurse may exhibit confusion about his or her own beliefs and values, confidence in ability to handle situations, and invading client's privacy
- *Awareness of own spiritual quest:* the nurse may be contemplating meaning, purpose, hope, and presence of love in his or her own life
- *Confusion:* the nurse's conflicts between religious and spiritual concepts
- *Basic attitudes:* the nurse's belief system about illness, aging, and suffering

As the nurse becomes more aware of these areas that affect the spiritual dimension the nurse and client can be in dialogue without using traditional religious language to share and express their spiritual dimension. The nurse can encourage the client to explore the following six questions[9]:

1. What do I feel good about?
2. With whom do I feel most free to "be myself"?
3. What is the hardest thing about my illness (or current dilemma) for me and my family?
4. What helps me—"from within myself and from outside"?
5. What worries me the most?
6. What am I afraid of?

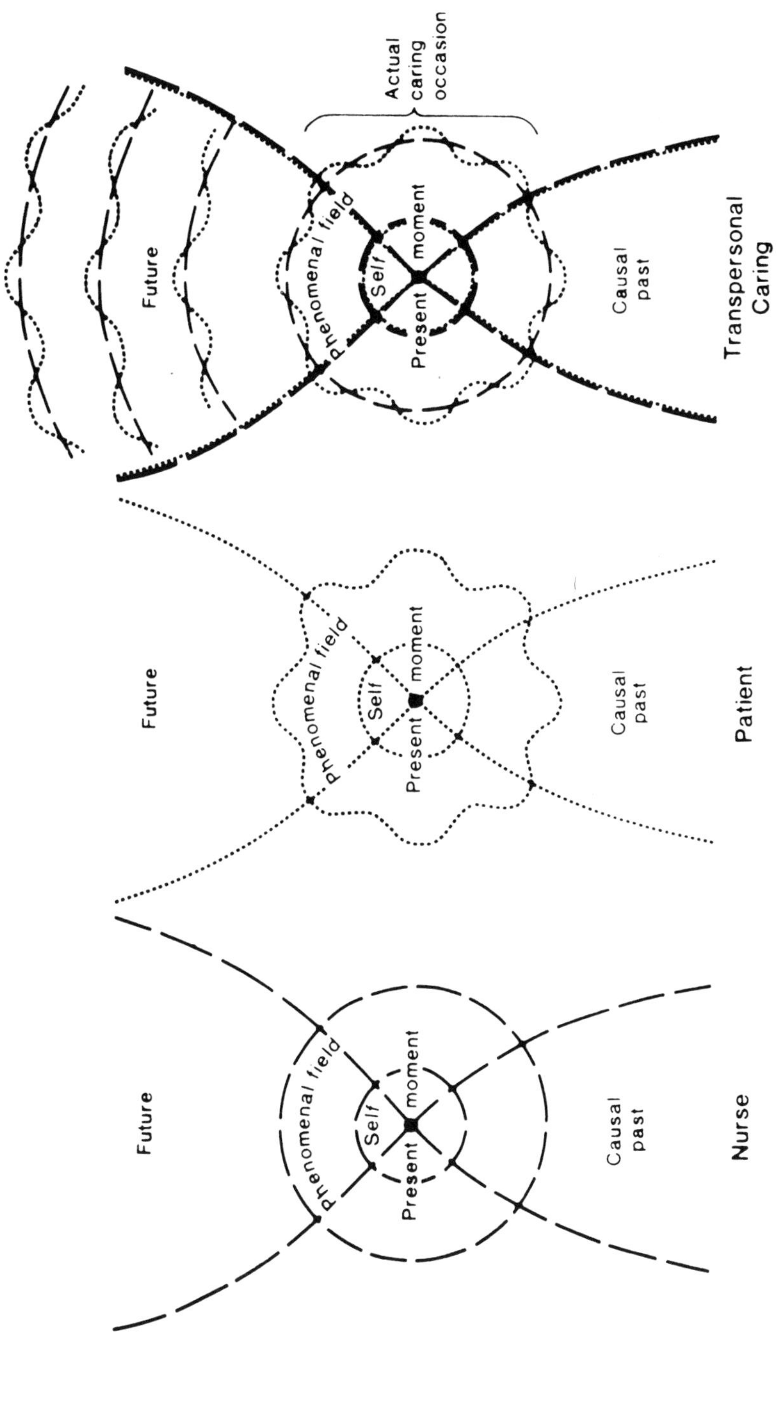

Figure 2-1 Dynamics of the Human Caring Process. *Source*: Reprinted from *Nursing: Human Science and Human Care—A Theory of Nursing* by J. Watson, p. 59, with permission of Appleton & Lange, © 1985. Illustration by Melvin L. Gabel, University of Colorado Health Sciences Center, Biomedical Communications Department.

Many variables determine the dialogue between the nurse and client, such as where the nurse and client are on their inward journey, each one's ability to listen actively and reflect, and the level of trusting relationship that has been established. The following 11 questions are posed to help the nurse listen actively and reflect:[10]

1. What is sacred to this person?
2. For what/whom will this person make sacrifices?
3. How does this person personally perceive God's response? Is God stern? capricious? angry? benevolent?
4. What is trustworthy? In what/whom is trust placed?
5. Is life for this person mostly giving or mostly demand?
6. Does the person have a sense of belonging—to a primary group? to the family? to the universe?
7. Is this life marked by playfulness? caution? grimness? creativity? fear? joy?
8. What brings joy? What brings satisfaction?
9. Does this person feel he or she makes a difference? Is there a sense of mission and purpose?
10. Does the person view him- or herself as a responsible agent in the situation or as a victim or martyr?
11. Does the person see the potential for taking an active role in changing the situation?

Exhibit 2-1 offers guidelines to help clients understand the transpersonal self.[11]

Exhibit 2-1 Guidelines for Helping Persons Experience Their Own Spirituality

1. Know yourself as a spiritual being. What gives your life meaning? What is especially frightening?
2. Remember that being aware of the presence of God does not depend on being able to define or describe God.
3. Remember that each person is the expert about one's own path. It is then that we can explore their uniqueness.
4. Understand spiritual assessment as an ongoing process within the context of a relationship.
5. Be aware that the need to be with and to bear painful feelings is as significant and important as the need to do and to do for persons experiencing spiritual distress.
6. Help the person and yourself find goals, hope, and pleasure for the present moment.
7. Encourage reminiscing and share in life review, a process during which persons remember and often resolve or understand old pain and conflicts from a new perspective.
8. Allow persons to grieve for themselves and those around them.
9. Know that by being present we can decrease the separation and aloneness which persons often fear.
10. Remember and know that you are helping a person toward wholeness—in the moment—now—even when pain and limitation are part of the moment.

Source: Reprinted from "Dealing with Spiritual Concerns of Clients in the Community" by M. Burkhardt and M.G. Nagai-Jacobson, American Holistic Nurses Association Annual Conference, June 1987.

THE TRANSPERSONAL SELF

Perennial Philosophy

Throughout history there has been a quest and universal need to understand the purpose of human life experience and what happens after death. This body of knowledge is perennial philosophy—*philosophia perennis.*[12] Roots of perennial philosophy are found in all traditional lore from the most primitive cultures to the most highly developed. The first recordings of perennial philosophy date from more than 25 centuries ago. There are three major themes of perennial philosophy:[13]

1. the metaphysics that recognizes a divine Reality substantial to the world of things and lives and minds
2. the psychology that finds in the soul something similar to, or even identical with, divine reality
3. the ethics that places the human being's final end in the knowledge of the immanent and transcendent Ground of all being—the thing is immemorial and universal

If we look at the writings of perennial philosophy, human beings are described as being part of a whole, a part of the totality of the universe.

The Great Chain of Being

To be their best, humans must strive toward healthy psychophysiologic wholeness in the areas of physical, mental, emotional, and spiritual health, relationships and choices. In order to reach wholeness humans must understand the relationship of self with the universe and their existential identity. *Existential identity* means the ability to come to terms with the finite nature of existence, the acceptance of our ego limitations, and the willingness to face things as they appear in our life without denying that they exist. In perennial philosophy, the many levels of consciousness are referred to as the Great Chain of Being (Figure 2-2). In different versions of the Great Chain, the levels of consciousness range from 3 to 20 or more.

Each level in the Great Chain transcends but includes its predecessor(s). Each higher level contains functions, capacities, or structures not found on, or explainable solely in terms of, a lower level. The higher level does not violate the principles of the lower level; it simply is not exclusively bound to or explainable by them. The highest transcends but includes the lower, and not vice-versa, just as a three-dimensional sphere includes or contains two-dimensional circles, but not vice-versa.[14] Thus, our consciousness increases as we learn to become more aware of our different levels of existence. All levels are available to us if we allow openness at each level.[15] A person's wholeness and healing are determined by awareness of all levels. Absolute spirit is that which transcends everything and includes everything.

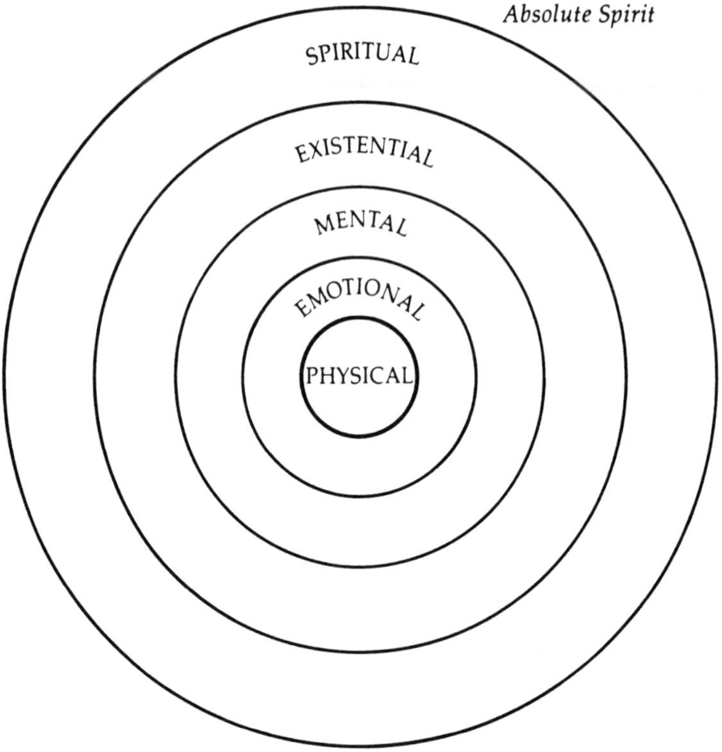

Figure 2-2 The Great Chain of Being. *Source:* From *The Inward Arc* by Frances Vaughan, © 1985. Reprinted by arrangement with Shambhala Publications, Inc., 300 Massachusetts Ave., Boston, MA 02115.

The Inward Arc

When a person reflects on the inner dimension of self, a process referred to as the *inward arc,* this conscious journey toward wholeness evolves toward self-transcendence.

In Figure 2-3, the outward arc of personal ego development precedes the inward arc of transpersonal spiritual awakening. Self-consciousness arises during healthy human development. As the self continues to develop and mature, different self-concepts, identities, and life experiences are understood that lead toward the conscious journey of the inward arc, the inner understanding. The psyche has many layers of consciousness. As one moves more inward, seeking inner knowledge along with personal understanding, one experiences the Absolute that is composed of higher-ordered wholes and integrations. Basic structures of the psyche are not replaced, but become part of the larger unity. The ultimate part of the journey is awakening, or enlightenment to the knowledge that one is part of the whole.

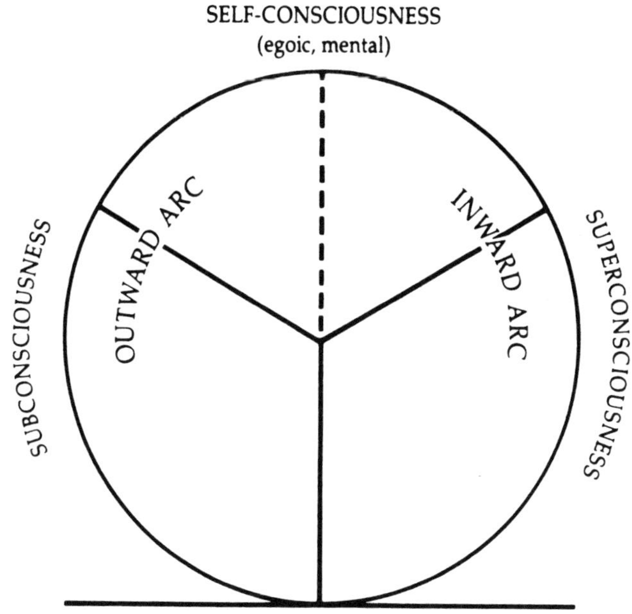

Figure 2-3 The General Life Cycle. *Source:* From *The Inward Arc* by Frances Vaughan, © 1985. Reprinted by arrangement with Shambhala Publications, Inc., 300 Massachusetts Ave., Boston, MA 02115.

Healing Awareness

This transpersonal model helps us understand healing awareness, our ability to discipline ourselves to be present in the moment and understand the meaning of the moment. Several ways to acquire this ability are by developing our skills through relaxation and imagery practice and various meditative disciplines that allow inner silence and the presence of inward focusing. These skills can be practiced any place and any time. What surfaces with this state of being present in the moment is a noninterfering attention that allows natural healing to flow.[16]

The message is the same whether delivered by saints, sages, or mystics whether it is Taoist, Hindu, Islam, Buddhist, or Christian. At the bottom of one's soul is the soul of humanity itself, a divine, transcendent soul, leading from bondage to liberation, from enchantment to awakening, from time to eternity, from death to immortality.[17]

Healing awareness requires authenticity. Authenticity implies consistency between *inner experience* and *outer expression* and *congruence* between *beliefs* and *behaviors*.[18] Perception and beliefs tend to be mutually reinforcing; that is, if a person believes something to be true, then the perception will selectively reinforce it. Much unhealthy living occurs because people do not operate from a state of *authenticity*.

When we operate from authenticity, there is harmony in our behaviors, thoughts, and feelings. When nurses model healing awareness, consciously or unconsciously, the experience is translated and is evoked in clients and others. Clients learn more from what nurses do and their persona than what nurses teach or say. When operating from authenticity we are in a better position to act with intention and clear purpose and to have the freedom for creating choices that can empower our lives. If authenticity is not present, a perceptual internal conflict exists that manifests as anxiety, burnout, and confusion about living and may result in symptoms that can lead to illness.

Patanjali-Derived Psychophysiologic Principle

The transpersonal can be seen as a self-induced (autogenic) movement toward greater health—physical, mental, emotional, and spiritual.[19] This transpersonal framework is based on the Patanjali system of yoga where everything in the cosmos consists of mind and its modification.[20] This framework also incorporates concepts from theosophy, Buddhism, Hinduism, Sufism, American Indian philosophy, Christian mysticism, Islam, Judaism, and modern transpersonal synthesis. The reader is referred to the work of Green and Green for specific references and detail.

Patanjali was a yogi mystic who may have lived from 900-800 B.C., though some think that he lived as long as 8,000-10,000 years ago.[21] When Patanjali's ancient works are read today, they seem amazingly current. In fact, his works have been used as a basis for a school of psychotherapy.[22]

Usually we are dominated by rational thought and the information given to us by our senses. Patanjali's techniques advocate stilling the mind and its endless chatter. This process of stilling the mind is expressed in the following way by one of the great spiritual doctrines, the Katha Upanishad.[23]

> When the five senses are stilled, when the mind
> Is stilled, when the intellect is stilled,
> That is called the highest state by the wise.
> They say yoga is this supreme stillness
> In which one enters the unitive state,
> Never to become separate again.*

Patanjali believed that *all the body is in the mind, though not all of the mind is in the body*. This theory implies that every cell of the body is a cell of the mind. If we consider this view, it is possible that a person who visualizes white cells as stronger than cancer cells may literally command certain cells in the body to change. A person with a fractured bone can focus on the specifics of bone healing and recover days to weeks faster than a person with the same fracture who does not participate in the visualization. The body is in and influenced by the mind. Chapter 12 explores further the use of imagery and bone healing.

Green and Green have paraphrased the Patanjali-derived psychophysiologic principle as follows[24]:

> Every change in the physiologic state is accompanied by an appropriate change in the mental-emotional state, conscious or unconscious; and con-

---

*Reprinted by permission from *The Upanishads*, translated by Eknath Easwaran, Copyright 1987, Nilgiri Press, Petaluma, California.

versely, every change in the mental-emotional state, conscious or unconscious, is accompanied by an appropriate change in the physiological state.

When this psychophysiologic principle is linked with volition, it is called psychophysiologic self-regulation. Psychophysiologic training can ''open'' the normally closed door in the brain that leads to awareness of normally unconscious processes in the spectrum of being.[25] The remainder of this chapter explores states of consciousness and psychophysiologic self-regulation in order to develop strategies to enhance healing in the modern sense.

STATES OF CONSCIOUSNESS

In order to know how nurse-client interactions can consistently promote healing, we must consider states of consciousness. This discussion focuses on exploring consciousness and the state of totality—being aware of one's own feelings, thoughts, and attention to stimuli in the immediate surroundings.

Altered States and Usual States of Consciousness

In the past, nurses have used the term ''states of consciousness'' to describe pathologic or altered states of consciousness (ASC) resulting from drug manipulation, metabolic derangements, psychotic states, posttraumatic head injuries, or anoxia. However, when we speak of ASC, we must include not only those above-mentioned states but also daydreaming, dream states, deep relaxation, and meditative practices. In other words, ASC involves healthy natural states, as well as the traditionally recognized pathologic states. Usual states of consciousness (USC) are the ordinary states of waking consciousness in which people spend most of their working hours.

Left and Right Hemispheric Function

Consciousness involves left and right hemispheric functioning. It is important to understand that one hemisphere is not more important than the other and that hemispheric differentiation has been oversimplified. It is inaccurate to say that someone is either right or left brain, because all activities involve both hemispheres simultaneously.[26] It is true, however, that the left and right hemispheres do have specialized functions. The left hemisphere is more involved in logical, analytic thought processing than the right hemisphere. The right hemisphere is more adept at nonlogical, nonanalytical thought processing and spatial tasks than the left hemisphere.

Yet, the hemispheres work together at all times. When we say that a person is ''being very intuitive,'' most of us are implying that the person is really ''right brain.'' This is not the whole picture. When a person has a hunch or a flash of insight, it is the left hemisphere that processes and synthesizes the activities that precede the intuition. Nurses must not deny their intuition and just focus on scientific principles, but consciously use both ways of knowing in order to practice the art and science of nursing.

Additionally, the right hemisphere is not entirely nonanalytical. Think of some of the spatial activities in which the right hemisphere specializes, such as pattern recognition; analysis of mazes, maps, and diagrams; and handling of geometric forms. Left hemisphere reasoning skills also use spatial activities. For example, nurses use visual-spatial skills when solving the problem of malfunctioning intravenous lines. Visually and spatially, they see the line setup while thinking through the normal line flow in relation to stopcocks and then to the insertion site. If no external malfunctions are found, they then visualize the line from the insertion point under the skin to the catheter position and think about possible internal blocked sites.

Another example of the right and left hemispheres working together occurs when a nurse walks down the hall after leaving a person's bedside and intuitively feels that something is not right. While continuing to walk away from the room, the nurse thinks about objective data, such as no change in physical assessment findings and vital signs within the normal range, but a strong intuitive sense draws the nurse back to the bedside now to see this person in a state of cardiac arrest.

We think of emotions as right brain, but any nurse has seen how a client in emotional pain can logically explain the character and etiology of pain. Another example is the nurse who is in pain explaining the pain logically to another person. Emotions have components of both right and left hemispheres. We go back and forth with both hemispheres in all activities, and we must learn to honor both ways of knowing. Let's now explore ways to achieve psychophysiologic self-regulation.

Psychophysiologic Self-Regulation and the Relaxation Response

Psychophysiologic self-regulation (PPSR) is the skill of inducing a state of balance of left and right hemispheric functioning. It reduces the dominant left hemisphere activity and evokes the relaxation response. The *relaxation response (RR)* is a *hypometabolic state of decreased sympathetic nervous system arousal in which one feels a sense of calmness*. With disciplined practice a person can achieve deep states of relaxation in which one senses a connection with the whole.[27]

The process of PPSR may be described as having three parts: (1) body and inner self-awareness, (2) relaxation and visualization, and (3) making effective choices. These parts are not separate, but are part of the whole process leading one to optimal states of consciousness (OSC) where one is able to master the ability to achieve deep states of relaxation. OSC creates a state of increased inner awareness of calmness and quietness. Therefore, bodymind self-awareness and making effective choices become more accessible.

PPSR has many uses. For example, clients can be taught how to control acute and chronic pain, hypertension, Raynaud's syndrome, tension, or migraine headaches, asthma, acne, irritable bowel syndrome, acute anxiety, stage fright, and phobias. The "how tos" of integrating PPSR as nursing interventions are developed in Chapters 11–13.

Another use of PPSR is in athletic performance where the athlete can improve performance without actually doing the sport. Training to combine hemispheric functioning is referred to as visual-motor behavioral rehearsal (VMBR). VMBR enables the athlete to go into a deeply relaxed state and then rehearse in the imagination the event step by step.

Skills To Evoke Optimal and Altered States of Consciousness

Learning specific PPSR skills enhances nurse healing and being a nurse healer. The theory behind these skills can be learned by reading books on the subject and attending seminars. However, the actual skills are learned from practice and personal experience for which there is no substitute. They are best learned in a quiet environment free of distractions and in a comfortable position. In order for OSC or natural ASC to occur more frequently the following skills must be learned[28,29]:

- attaining an inward focus of attention
- being aware of alterations in perception of linear time—past, present, and future
- being able to let go of judging events as good or bad
- controlling one's state of awareness, rather than a guide or therapist controlling the person's awareness
- attaining a relaxed inner calmness that may be goal or nongoal directed
- merging awareness and consciousness activity as a unit

A person can achieve OSC and PPSR through many strategies: biofeedback, imagery, relaxation, meditation, prayer, music therapy, playing the piano, jogging, keeping a diary or journal, and dreaming. By employing these strategies new perspectives are gained. One is able to release the notion of separateness and experience body-mind-spirit integration, thereby envisioning the whole. Doing so places one in an optimal state, a state of conscious inner presence needed to reach higher potentials.

This text develops the theory and practice of strategies that involve shifting the nurse and client's states of consciousness inward. These states may be active or passive. An active goal-directed state occurs in hypnosis when one is given a suggestion to change behavior or illness. Passive nongoal-directed states occur with relaxation training. The purpose of achieving these states is to become aware of new realities and different ways to understand and relate to these new perceptions.

SUMMARY

Nurse healing is possible when the nurse is attuned every day to the continuous discovery about inner wisdom and awareness of one's being. Nurses must strive to explore and acknowledge inner wisdom as a first step on the journey toward wholeness. The ideas of bodymind connections are not new, but have been recorded for over 5,000 years. What is new is that science (psychoneuroimmunology and certain areas within biology, physics, engineering, and other fields) is providing data that confirm bodymind connections.

DIRECTIONS FOR FUTURE RESEARCH

1. Formulate studies that incorporate PPSR and determine which interventions work best in which setting.

2. Validate the defining characteristics for the nursing diagnosis—spiritual distress—as formulated by the North American Nursing Diagnoses Association (refer to Chapter 6).
3. Measure the outcomes of nursing interventions when dealing with clients in spiritual distress.
4. Evaluate modes of integrating concepts of psychophysiologic self-regulation in nursing curriculum, inservice education, and seminars.
5. Determine holistic guidelines and therapies to help clients be in harmony with the changes that occur throughout the life span.
6. Determine whether client outcomes differ when clients interact with nurses who practice self-healing techniques compared to interaction with nurses who do not use self-healing techniques.

NURSE HEALER REFLECTIONS

After reading this chapter the nurse healer will be able to answer or begin a process of answering the following questions:

- Do I find *meaning* and *purpose* in my life?
- How do I *define* spirituality?
- How do I feel when I observe the *contents* of my consciousness?
- When I use the word *Guiding Force, Higher Power, God,* or *Absolute,* what kind of link with a universal wholeness do I experience?
- What occurs in my consciousness when I *focus* my awareness on one stimulus at a time?
- What is my experience when I allow myself to move into a *natural altered state of consciousness* through deep relaxation or meditation?
- What is my *internal awareness* when I experience that *felt shift* of being present in the moment?

NOTES

1. Chogyam Trungpa, *Shambhala: The Sacred Path of the Warrior* (Boston: Shambhala Publications, Inc., 1984), p. 51.
2. Renee Weber, ''Philosophical Foundations and Frameworks for Healing'', in *Spiritual Aspects of the Healing Arts,* ed. Dora Kunz (Wheaton, IL: The Theosophical Publishing House, 1985), p. 38.
3. Jean Watson, *Nursing: Human Science and Human Care* (Norwalk, CT: Appleton-Lange, 1985), p. 16.
4. Ibid., pp. 54–55.
5. Ibid., p. 58.
6. Ibid., p. 59.
7. Lynn Brallier, *Successfully Managing Stress* (Los Altos, CA: National Nursing Review, 1982), pp. 249–280.
8. Margaret Burkhardt and Mary Gail Nagai-Jacobson, ''Dealing With Spiritual Concerns of Clients in the Community,'' *Journal of Community Health Nursing* 2, no. 4 (1985): 193.

9. Ibid., p. 195.
10. Ibid., p. 195.
11. Ibid., p. 196.
12. Aldous Huxley, *The Perennial Philosophy* (New York: Harper Colophon Books, 1945), p. vii.
13. Ibid., p. vii.
14. Ken Wilbur, *Quantum Questions* (Boston: Shambhala Publications, Inc., 1984), pp. 15–16.
15. Ibid., pp.1–60
16. Lawrence LeShan, *How To Meditate* (New York: Bantam, 1972), p. 4.
17. Ken Wilbur, *No Boundary* (Boston: Shambhala Publications, Inc., 1979), p. 138.
18. Frances Vaughan, *The Inward Arc*, (Boston: Shambhala Publications, Inc., 1985), p. 21.
19. Elmer Green and Alyce Green, ''Biofeedback and Transformation,'' in *Spiritual Aspects of the Healing Arts*, ed. Dora Kunz (Wheaton, IL: The Theosophical Publishing House, 1985), pp. 145–162.
20. Ibid., p. 150.
21. Charles Johnson, *The Yoga Sutras of Patanjali: The Book of the Spiritual Person* (Albuquerque, NM: Brotherhood of Life, 1983), p. 4.
22. Ken Wilbur, ''The Evolution of Consciousness,'' in *Beyond Health and Normality*, ed. Roger Walsh and Deane Shapiro (New York: Van Nostrand Reinhold Company, 1983), pp. 338–369.
23. Eknath Easwaran, *The Upanishads* (Petaluma, CA: Nilgiri Press, 1987), p. 96.
24. Elmer Green and Alyce Green, ''Biofeedback and Transformation,'' p. 150.
25. Ibid., p. 152.
26. Charles Tart, *Waking Up: Overcoming the Obstacles to Human Potential* (Boston: Shambhala Publications, Inc., 1987), pp. 3–18.
27. Herbert Benson, *The Relaxation Response* (New York: Morrow and Company, 1975), p. 23.
28. Lawrence LeShan, *How To Meditate*, p. 2.
29. Errol Korn and Karen Johnson, *Visualization: The Uses of Imagery in the Health Professions* (Homewood, IL: Dow Jones-Irwin, 1983), p. 45.

SUGGESTED READINGS

Firman, John, and Vargui, James, ''Personal and Transpersonal Growth: The Perspective of Psychosynthesis,'' in *Transpersonal Psychotherapy*, ed S. Boorstein. Science and Behavior Books, Inc.

Hampden-Turner, Charles. *Maps of the Mind*. New York: Collier Books, 1981.

Lovejoy, Arthur. *The Great Chain of Being*. Cambridge, MA: Harvard University Press, 1964.

White, John. *The Highest States of Consciousness*. New York: Anchor Books, 1972.

Wilbur, Ken; Engler, Jack; and Brown, Daniel. *Transformations of Consciousness*. Boston: Shambhala Publications Inc., 1986.

Wilbur, Ken. *The Spectrum of Consciousness*. Wheaton, IL: The Theosophical Publishing House, 1977.

chapter 3

Nurse As Healer: Toward the Inward Journey

Barbara Montgomery Dossey

> The spiritual element in human nature must be recognized and cultivated if all the powers of the human soul are to act together in perfect balance and harmony. There can never be any real opposition between spirituality and science, for one is the complement of the other. Every advance in knowledge brings us face to face with the mystery of our own being.[1]
>
> *Max Planck*
> *Physicist*

This chapter shares essential elements of the principles of healing, being a healer, and the path toward the inward journey. Nurses have the unique opportunity of being present to guide people in understanding *meaning* in their life, whether it be through wellness instruction, acute situational crisis intervention, chronic illness management, or the transition to death. This is *healing*—being present to guide and help the client in making connections of body-mind-spirit. The clearest way to understand this interaction is through the concept of *nurse healing* where the nurse serves as a *healer*. And the fundamental principle one follows to become a healer is skillfully bringing together inner resources of knowledge and intuition. The nurse healer must identify the individual inward journey of self—his or her own woundedness, the life polarities, and the purposes and meaning in life.

NURSE HEALER OBJECTIVES: NURSE AS HEALER

Theoretical

1. Assess the presence of nurse healer characteristics in your life and clinical practice.
2. Compare the two dimensions of growth.
3. Integrate the information in Chapter 1 and 2 with this chapter.

Clinical

1. Identify real versus pseudo-listening with clients and colleagues.
2. Assess your skills as a guide and decide if there are areas you wish to improve in regard to guiding.
3. Identify which nurse healer characteristics you wish to increase.

Personal

1. Learn techniques to become centered and integrate the experience in your daily life.
2. Acknowledge what your inner feelings are when you are fully present with yourself, your friends, and family.
3. Acknowledge the purpose and meaning in your life.
4. Decide on ways to increase the ritual of inner healing in your life.

DEFINITIONS

Centeredness: fine tuning of sensitivity to life's inner and outer patterns and processes; recognizing a state of balance of self and allowing the process of intuition to unfold.

Guide: one who helps others discover and recognize insights and healing awareness on their life journey.

Healing: a process of bringing parts of oneself (physical, mental, emotions, spirit, relationships, and choices) together at deep levels of inner knowing, leading to an integration and balance, with each part having equal importance and value. This may also be referred to as self-healing or wholeness.

Intention: readiness to focus and move forward with purpose in action and personal growth.

Intuition: perceived knowing of things and events without the conscious use of rational processes.

Life Potentials: the activities and pursuits of your daily experience that weave into your life, allowing creative resources to come forward.

Love: being open to feelings that allow understanding and awareness of the goodness of people, events, and things.

Meditation: the inward focusing of attention that creates an awareness of being; done for the purpose of reaching a relatively pure experience of the self and allowing an opening to transpersonal states.

Nurse Healer: one who facilitates another person's growth and life processes toward wholeness (body-mind-spirit) or who assists with recovery from illness or with transition to death.

Play: activities done in a spirit of fun, rather than for goal achievement.

Polarities: the contrast of opposite qualities, forms, tendencies, and powers, such as health and illness.

Relationships: one, two, or more nonjudgmental people with whom you share your interests, successes, and failures; people who facilitate and accelerate the process of reaching your life potentials.

Relaxation: letting go of physical and emotional tension and allowing your conscious awareness to recognize this state; learning to quiet the mind in order to listen to all the answers to life that reside within all of us.

Resolution: willingness to experience and face your fears and worries; devoting time to open space within yourself to understanding the wisdom that occurs when joining with these life events.

Self-Responsibility: the ability to respond to correct choices and activities that lead to integration of body, mind, and spirit.

Self-Care: activities that one initiates and performs on one's behalf to maintain wholeness and well-being.

Transpersonal: referring to experiences and meaning that go beyond individual and personal uniqueness; involves one's purpose, values, and beliefs.

Transpersonal Self: the sense of self that goes beyond the ego and "I" that does not identify itself as a single isolated individual.

Wounded Healer: concept derived from Greek mythology, specifically the myth of Chiron, which suggest that even the greatest healers have inherent weaknesses and fallibility that should be recognized by the healer.

TOWARD THE INWARD JOURNEY

Nurse As Healer

What does healing mean? What does a healer do in healing? Is there anything that you do in a day that constitutes healing and being a healer? What is healing in the modern sense? Let us develop the root of these words and incorporate their true meaning into our daily nursing practice.

The root word of healing and healer is "hale," which means to facilitate movement toward wholeness or to make whole on all levels—physical, mental, emotional, social, and spiritual. As sophisticated as our modern medical system is, there are no criteria for what constitutes healing. In fact, it often seems that there are two different sets of criteria for the evaluation of healing. One set of criteria looks at "the numbers" of biologic data; the other set is more subjective and assesses the experience of the client "feeling stronger" or "feeling better."

If we use the root word in the true sense, healing incorporates both sets of criteria. The either/or—that is either a body problem or an emotional problem—is a false dichotomy. There is no such thing for "bodymind" is a single integrated entity. To change body or mind is to change the other simultaneously.

What does a healer recognize about healing and interactions with others? A healer is aware of the importance of a ritual and of understanding the other person's belief system. A healer enlists the consciousness of the other person during the interaction. A healer recognizes that consciousness operates not only within a person, such as when he or she thinks about emotional conflicts or uses relaxation and imagery for pain control, but also operates between and among individuals—between nurse-client and among nurse-client-family-colleagues.

Contemporary nurses are broadening their experience of themselves as healers. By paying increased attention to their philosophy, values, and beliefs about the profession, nurses empower themselves to recognize their unique qualities. As this recognition of their unique qualities evolves, caring grows and the true philosophy and science of caring emerges in their nursing practice.

Reflect for a moment on the characteristics of a nurse that facilitate healing in self, clients, and others. Exhibit 3-1 lists these qualities. The clearer we become about knowing ourselves, the clearer we will be in relating to other people, with the outcome being more meaningful relationships. The highest form of knowing is loving,[2] so as we learn to love ourselves, the more closely we are attuned to our intuition and self-healing. Chapter 6 explores intuition further.

Nurse Healer As Guide

A nurse healer is a *guide* who uses the art of *guiding* to help others discover and recognize new health behaviors, make choices, and discover insights about how to cope effectively. A guide helps a person explore purpose and meaning in life. Guiding is a special art and intervention that nurses may use at all times. The purpose of guiding is to bring to the present moment a client's fullest potential. This process helps the client be in congruence with his or her inner resources, decrease stress, and enhance self-direction toward balance and harmony.

A nurse healer guides the client in developing all areas of human potential. The client is offered the knowledge of the inner journey of self-discovery, but the nurse as guide does not assume to know what is the best course for the client.[3] Clients must make their

---

Exhibit 3-1 Characteristics of a Nurse Healer

Aware that self-healing is a continual process
Familiar with the terrain of self-development
Recognizes weaknesses and strengths
Open to self-discovery
Continues to develop clarity about life's purposes to keep us from acting mechanical and feeling bored
Aware of present and future steps in personal growth
Models self-care in order to help self and clients with the inward process
Aware that his or her presence is equally important as technical skills
Respects and loves clients regardless of who or how they are
Offers the client methods for working on life issues
Guides the client in discovering creative options
Presumes that the client knows the best life choices
Listens actively
Empowers clients to recognize that they can cope with life processes
Shares insights without imposing personal values and beliefs
Accepts what clients say without judging
Sees time with clients as being there for them client, to serve and share

own choices. As clients seek guidance and help with life possibilities and dilemmas, the nurse as a guide knows some of the hazards and precautions that occur with lifestyle changes and can only suggest new options. The nurse has no way of knowing what each experience holds for a person, for moment by moment, the contrast of polarities, such as health and illness, joy and sadness, are always present in one's life. The nurse and client are both constantly confronted with their woundedness as portrayed by the Greek mythological figure, Chiron. This myth is an excellent example of the fundamental polarity of health and illness. It is a reminder that we should acknowledge our woundedness and that self-healing is a continual life process.

The Wounded Healer: The Myth of Chiron

Chiron was a centaur, half man and half horse, who was skilled in healing. Along with other centaurs, Chiron was invited to the cave of Heracles. Pholos, also a centaur, had delivered a jar of wine to Heracles. The scent of the wine intrigued the other centaurs, and they began to drink. Because they were unaccustomed to drinking, they became intoxicated and began to fight. During the battle, one of the arrows shot by Heracles hit Chiron in the knee. Heracles tended Chiron's wound by following the instructions of Chiron, the wounded healer. The point of the arrow had been dipped in the poison of the hydra; thus the wound was incurable. Chiron, an immortal, could not be cured but could not die. From his cave, Chiron taught many heroes his great knowledge of healing. One of the students he taught was Asclepius, who gained knowledge of the healing herbs and the power of acknowledging one's woundedness.

We are all wounded. No one has total freedom from stress or illness, although many try to hide from this fact. Yet, the more we hide from our woundedness, the more we set ourselves up for psychophysiologic symptoms that may lead to illness.

One of the major obstacles in understanding how both wellness and illness are a fact of our existence and how illness is as necessary as wellness is the way we perpetuate the myth that the darker side can be ignored. Let us begin to explore light and shadow and how it can enhance or retard healing.

The Light and Shadow

The dance of human life is a matter of polarity, the light and the shadow. Polarity *implies* difference, like the North and South poles. Just as a magnet cannot be a magnet without opposites, so does human existence require polarities. Without the shadow we have no concept of the light. Contrast is essential in every aspect of our life. Think of a few of the polarities of daily experience with which we are familiar: happiness and sadness, strengths and weaknesses, resolution and conflict, elation and depression. Another example of this contrast is wellness and illness. The only way that we have a concept of personal wellness is to have at some point in our life a first-hand experience with illness or major life stressors.

Particularly in Western culture, emphasis is placed throughout our lives on the high peaks, with the dark side—the shadow—being ignored. One of the major obstacles to understanding our wholeness is this inability to recognize our darker side. The human psyche does not cope well with the polarity, for the ego loves clarity.[4] Yet, it is when we repress the polarity that it is taken into our unconscious and causes psychophysiologic disturbances.[5]

When a major stressor, disaster or illness occurs, the easiest course is to repress the meaning of the darkness. Over time the failure to understand this meaning becomes a futile spiral. At some point we must address the shadow side of life because it is always present. There is a part of us that always needs healing—the wounded healer—yet we find it easy to ignore this woundedness. We must learn to sense our limitations, as well as to recognize our strengths. All great healers acknowledge their inherent weakness and fallibilities.

When a client and nurse come together with both denying their woundedness, the outcome of care is mechanical at best. Neither the client nor the nurse is able to use their inner wisdom on their own behalf to activate self-healing. Both have devalued this innate potential. Inner healing does not flow from the nurse to the client. The nurse cannot give inner healing to the client, for it already exists within the client. Rather, the nurse acts as a *facilitator* to evoke the client's process of inner healing. Healing occurs when the client and the nurse *both* acknowledge the polarity of light and shadow and use it to move toward balance and harmony.

As the best of both traditional and holistic practices merge, much of the work that remains to be done will be to learn the art of healing and being a healer and to work on the self, our imperfect, fallible self.[6] We must recognize our polarity, our weaknesses and strengths, and acknowledge our inadequacies. It is only then that we know a powerful part of our being and allow new strengths to be born. It is the use of self, in a loving and compassionate way, that provides us with our most powerful instrument for healing.[7]

Centering

Centering is the state achieved when one moves within oneself to an inner reference of stability. It is a sense of self-relatedness that can be thought of as a place of inner being, a place of quietude within where one can feel truly integrated, unified, and focused.[8] Centering has been described as the source of our conscious awareness of our involvement in life. It is a personal space apart from either involvement or the consequent reaction to that involvement.[9]

To be *centered* implies a quality and essence of being present in the moment. Centering is a skill that is learned by *daily practice* of at least 15-20 minutes of solitude to quiet the inner dialogue and body simultaneously. This can be achieved through practice of the relaxation response and other relaxation interventions and of various meditative disciplines.

When we develop the skills and awareness of centering, our ability to become more sensitive to our life patterns and processes increases. We act more frequently with purposeful *intention*. We have a greater ability to be with our state of *resolution;* that is, we are more willing to experience and face our fears and worries. Centering allows us to devote more time to be silent within. This quality of inner silence lets us understand more of the wisdom that we gain access to when we acknowledge our polarities in life. Our *love* flows naturally, for we are open to the expressions of nonjudgmental love. When this quality is integrated in our life we are more consistently available for meaningful *relationships*.

One can achieve a state of *basic vulnerability* through meditation. This basic vulnerability is a space where we release the outer shell or facade of our role.[10] Ordinarily we identify the self we know from an awareness of our different roles and our constant stream of thoughts and feelings. In meditation we learn to fall into the space between the successive moments of trying to grasp onto ideas and feelings. It is in this space that we open to being with others in a different way.[11]

Centering and meditation allow us to help ourselves and clients enter into the *place of conflict*.[12] We are able to see the polarity that resides in the concept of conflict. The only way we can identify conflict is by recognizing its opposite, which is resolution. As we become centered we are able to organize inner energy and balance it with the incoming energy of people and events.

Our basic work as professionals is to become full human beings and to inspire full human-beingness in other people who feel starved about their lives.[13] When we are centered, we experience wholeness, which vibrates and radiates from us. We have the ability to help others begin to appreciate whatever it is that is in the present moment, regardless of how overwhelming it might seem.

Real versus Pseudo-Listening

Any communication process has three components. These are: (1) a sender of the message, (2) a receiver of the message, and (3) the content of the material.

In order for us to understand others, we must listen actively. Being quiet while someone else is talking is not equivalent to real listening. The key to real listening is *intention*.[14] Intention occurs when we focus with someone in order to move with purpose in our responses and interventions. This can lead others or ourselves toward effective action steps or forward in personal growth. Real listening occurs when we have the intention to understand someone, enjoy someone, learn something, or want to give help to someone.

Good listening is achieved by the ability of the nurse to quiet the inner dialogue. Good listening has an enormous quality of *nowness*. Nowness is the ability to throw away intellectualizations when the client goes off in an unexpected direction.[15] How often when counseling a client who is intent on telling a part of his or her story, the nurse will stop the flow of the story and bring the client back to a certain point which then blocks the client's insight. Often we get too intent on a personal view of what we think should be happening in a session, because we start our own inner dialogue of analysis and intellectualization. We must continue to develop the skills of listening with intent. As we increase this process of nowness, it allows the client also to move to a state of nowness that provides a place of inner wisdom to emerge. Questioning, and listening, that does not structure the answers, except minimally, is a great art.[16]

At times, we all lapse into pseudo-listening when we try to meet the needs of others. Begin to recognize any of the following events that indicate when you are meeting your own needs and not listening actively to others. These are signs of pseudo-listening:[17]

- silence as you buy time preparing your next remark
- listening to others so that they will listen to you
- listening only to specific information while deleting the rest
- acting interested when you are not
- partially listening because you do not want to disappoint another person
- listening in order not to be rejected
- searching for a person's weaknesses in order to take advantage of them
- identifying weak points in dialogue so that you can be stronger in your response

We must continue to learn how to be with clients. The *first focus* is to learn to listen actively to *what is going on with the client*. The *second focus* is to enable the client to *live in what is, not to avoid it, to let it be*.[18]

Active listening skills promote effective communication in several ways. They clarify the message. The receiver of the message can verify nonverbal messages communicated through body language or by what is not said by the sender of the message. The receiver is also able to gather additional information that can help with interventions. Active listening facilitates a greater acceptance of the sender's thoughts and emotions. Thus, the receiver of the message can help the sender choose the most effective behaviors that lead toward health and wholeness.

Working with Others

As we engage in holistic nursing and embark on our inward journey for self-change, the following principles should guide our work with clients and self[19]:

- *What we communicate by word, act, attitude, and setting will affect our potential for change*. Everything affects our clients—our choice of words, our presence with silence, our greeting, and our personal surroundings.
- *What we believe is important*. Our beliefs affect our self-image which in turn affects our actions. It also influences our capacity for self-healing. Our beliefs are conveyed to our clients.
- *Perceive yourself and your client as whole*. You and the client are whole and not a portion of disturbance or pathology. Perceive the cancer patient as a person with cancer. Release the label. We encourage pathology when we focus primarily on it and not on the client's healing potential.
- *The practitioner needs to be self-experienced*. We cannot guide clients down new paths to new experiences if we do not know the path from experience. The more we know from experience, the more we know that change is possible.
- *Every part is connected to every other part, and every part in the system affects every other part*. We form a network in which everyone participates. There is no such thing as an independent observer. Nurse and client are always creating change in one another.

- *Consider the whole setting*. Clients are asked to consider changing life patterns. Look at all the client's life potentials—physical, mental, emotional, spiritual, relationships, and choices. It is only when we consider the whole client and the significant others that we have a chance at directing the client toward wholeness.
- *Teaching competence is the basis for change*. Teach in such a manner that the client cannot fail. Help the client with realistic goals that can be measured. Attaining success directly affects beliefs.
- *Develop and support a positive self-image*. One must accept and like oneself if change is to occur.
- *Encourage learning without judgment*. To develop skills that are necessary for change, it is helpful to allow all learning experiences to occur without judgment. For example, a person with migraine headaches should be encouraged to "attend to the process," and not to blame him- or herself for the headache symptoms. Encourage the client to accept the headaches while learning stress management skills to decrease the headache pattern.
- *Acknowledge all changes, however slight*. Each change leads to another. Each slight change is progress.
- *Reframe experiences positively*. Our internal thoughts are very changeable. Instead of the saying "the glass is half empty," reframe it by saying "the glass is half full." The reframe allows bodymind to respond with new possibilities.
- *New skills must be practiced*. Learning is an ongoing process. Involve friends and family in the learning. The new skills must be integrated into all aspects of life.
- *Fear of failure leads to failure*. Fears become our prophesies. Negative anticipation creates tension and leads to failure.
- *Be present oriented*. Consciously stay in the present moment. Change takes place in the present, not in the past or future.*

The practice of meditation by the therapist creates the possibility to activate true healing. True healing occurs when the therapist is *empty of personal needs*, especially the need to be a good therapist or to have the right technique or say the right thing. The metaphor of "psychotherapeutic materialism" is helpful.[20] This refers to the things that get in the way of self-healing. Presence in the moment allows the release of the guilt and frustration of "I don't have time to do the important teaching that I should be doing" or "If only I had time to be with the client." Learning the skills of *being fully present* in the moment allows the nurse to be able to spend 5 to 10 focused minutes with a client and share ideas that may be a marked turning point in the client's self-healing. For example, spending a few moments teaching a client breathing and relaxation techniques to decrease anxiety may be the beginning of self-discovery that can lead to awakening his or her healing potential. This period of focused intention with the person may be as valuable or more valuable than an hour of counseling.

**Source:* Adapted from *Spiritual Aspects of the Healing Arts* by E. Peper and C. Kushel, pp. 132–137, with permission of Theosophical Publishing House, © 1985.

Purpose

The nurse healer recognizes that the inward journey involves purpose in all aspects of life. *Purpose* implies the conscious direction and flow of a person's inner visions toward maximizing human potential. Increasing purpose in one's life can be achieved along two dimensions of growth—the *personal* and the *transpersonal*—as seen in Figure 3-1.[21] The integrative path of life weaves its way between the two dimensions.

In Figure 3-1, the personal growth is represented on the horizontal axis and the transpersonal growth by the vertical axis. The curved line between the two is life's path toward transcendence, which is never a straight line. The transpersonal self, the star in the upper right-hand corner, is the point where individuality (personal dimension) and universality (the transpersonal) join.

The personal dimension of growth concerns meaning and integration of our personal existence. This dimension—possessing logical and analytical thought and being self-motivated, and goal-oriented in one's professional and personal life—is what is most valued in Western culture. The transpersonal dimension is less recognized and valued in Western culture. However, it is just as important. This dimension concerns the ultimate meaning and purpose of the universal existence of humanity.

We should also consider a third dimension of human growth, the *interpersonal* dimension, which is part of the other two dimensions.[22] In the personal dimension one

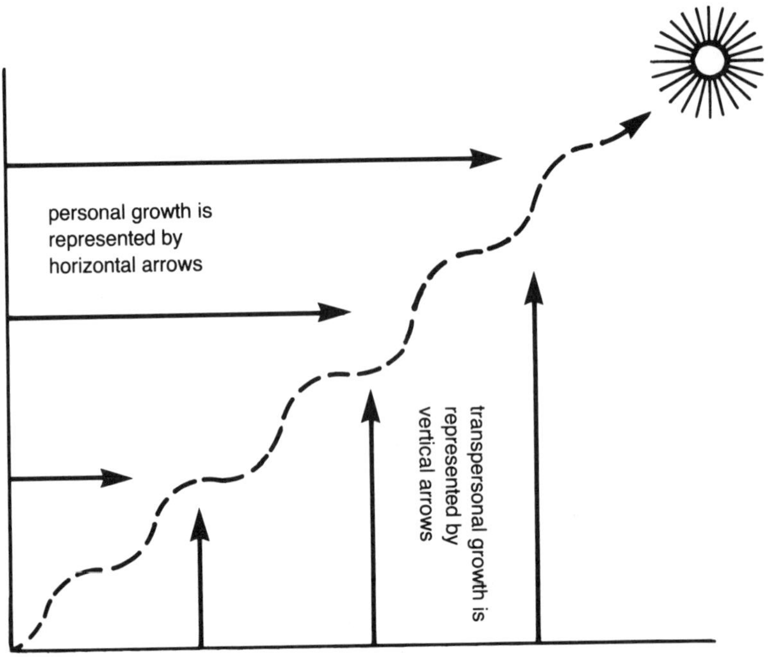
personal growth is
represented by
horizontal arrows
transpersonal growth is
represented by
vertical arrows

Figure 3-1 Two Dimensions of Growth. *Source:* Reprinted from *The Unfolding Self* by M. Brown, p. 16, with permission of Intermountain Associates for Psychosynthesis, © 1983.

develops the basic social skills of communication, courtesy, and friendship that are requisite for survival with others. Then as we begin to develop along the transpersonal dimension, we become aware of our basic interdependency, the essential merging with the other. The merging of the interpersonal with the other two dimensions allows us to have balanced supportive relationships with family, friends, community, and clients. It also allows the depth necessary in meaningful relationships. Without the interpersonal dimension, our relationships would be at best unenlightened and superficial.

As nurses integrate their personal and transpersonal dimensions, four identifiable characteristics have the potential for being manifested in their life and work:[23]

1. the capacity for responsibility and choice in the moment and in life as a whole
2. true preference for living in accordance with one's purpose and regarding as less valuable those aspects of life that distract or conflict
3. the capacity to accept the limitations of one's life and responsibility and a willingness to be in the world just as it is
4. a sense of having a destiny, a meaning, and overall purpose in life

Meaning

This discussion addresses four questions: What is meaning? Why should we seek out meaning? What do we do with it? How do we keep it?

Meaning is seen as *differences*—contrast, novelty, and heterogeneity—and is necessary for the healthy function of human beings. We should seek out meaning because our life seems fuller and richer when it *means* something positive for us. Take away the important meaning of our lives and it is not worth living. The more we understand about meaning in life, the more we are able to empower ourselves to recognize more effective ways to cope with life and to learn more effective methods of working on life issues. In doing this, we create richer meaning in our daily lives. This attention to meaning allows us to be more effective with clients in teaching them about meaning.

When we believe meaning is absent, our bodies become bored; bored bodies become the spawning ground for depression, disease, and death.[24] Failure of meaning has become a cliché. Professions, personal lives, even entire cultures are said to suffer from a breakdown of meaning. Although at times it seems that meaning may be absent from our lives and our universe; in fact, such a thing is not possible, even in principle.[25]

Our existence is awash with meaning, and it is only a matter of which meaning we shall choose. And the choices are crucial. Nowhere is this more important or apparent than in health and illness. It is clear from the wealth of scientific data that it is impossible to separate the mental and the physical parts of our being. The importance of meaning can no longer be ignored for it is directly linked with mind modulation of all body systems that influence states of wellness or illness. The following true case study is a rather spectacular example of how meaning can surface in the life of an individual and be a matter of life or death.[26]

Halloween and Helplessness: The Importance of Meaning and Health

A unique tale is that of a 50-year-old man who for a year had multiple abscesses of his right breast. These had required incision and drainage over a

> period of some 8 months, which kept him out of work for an appreciable amount of time. He finally agreed to go to the hospital and had a mastectomy in August. He had no previous history of cardiovascular disease, but the evening after his surgery and recovery from anesthesia he developed a myocardial infarction. Following this he did quite well in recovering from his infarction in the hospital and at home. According to his wife, however, he was increasingly depressed and particularly upset that he was not able to return to work. In late October, he had become "not angry," she said, but just "feeling he couldn't do anything about it" when a group of local youngsters blew up a firecracker, damaging their mailbox on the night of Halloween. Three days later his wife persuaded him to take their first stroll in his convalescence into the garden of their home in the hope of cheering him up a little. They walked into the back garden and noted for the first time that an arborway, which he had built early that summer and of which he was very proud, had been sprayed with tar paint. The patient apparently just looked at this while his wife expressed her anger. The patient then said he did not feel well and wanted to return to the house. He got 20 yards, as far as the kitchen side door, and collapsed. As he did so she asked him whether he was having any pain to which he replied, "No." He died within 5 minutes. The wife added the fact that she was so relieved that they had not gone further out into the back yard where they had a new trailer, which had also been spray-painted as a Halloween prank.
>
> Because it was unusual for a man to have a mastectomy, I asked whether having a mastectomy was of any particular significance to this man. To this his wife replied, "It's strange you should ask that question." She then stated that her sister had died 2 years before on November 12 with a carcinoma of the breast after mastectomy. This man's death actually occurred on November 3. His wife then indicated that on November 3, one year before, the patient's sister, who had had a carcinoma of the breast and a mastectomy, had died. Also on November 12, one year ago, his older and favorite brother had dropped dead of a myocardial infarction.*

This unfortunate man's plight illustrates how disturbed meanings can erupt in one's physical health. He was overwhelmed with a sense of failure, impotence, impasse, and helplessness—all those feelings that make up the "no exit" syndrome. He could not express his outrage, but kept those feelings bottled up inside. It is possible, of course, for persons to have a calm inner acceptance of life's events, but that is not what this man felt. He was simply overpowered and beaten down, and as his world continued to collapse he gave up. And not only did his world collapse, so did he. All meaning gone, all emotions absent, there was no reason to live any longer.

His death is also a classic example of what has been called the "anniversary phenomenon," in which something dreadful occurs at some yearly increment from the death of a significant person in one's life.[27] It seemed that this man was living out the fate of others he cared about—two women who had mastectomies at the same time of year, and his favorite brother who had died a year earlier, also from a heart attack.

Source: Adapted from *Archives of Internal Medicine,* Vol. 129, pp. 725–731, with permission of American Medical Association, © 1972.

Because meanings and emotions go hand in hand, is it strange that the meanings we perceive could affect the body? Or that the body could affect our emotions and our meanings? These connections are so intimate that we must think of bodymind as a single integrated unit.

What are the lessons here? How can we keep meaning in our life?

- We should simply pay more attention to the meanings we perceive in life. Easy to say, yes, but more difficult to do. It's much easier to concentrate on the cholesterol level, the blood pressure, diet, vitamin intake, body weight, and having the annual physical exam. But if we really believed that we could die not only from *heart* failure but from *"meaning failure"* as well—as the above case strongly suggests—perhaps we would be more attentive to the meanings we create in our lives.
- Wellness and illness are vastly more complex than we have heretofore believed. Wellness is not a matter of simply covering the bases physically, for we know that there is no clear separation of the physical and the mental. This recognition places much more responsibility on each individual and less on the physician for one's health. No prescriptions can be written for meaning; each of us has to attend to our own meanings in the way that is best for us. Routinely, we should assess and evaluate our human potentials (Chapter 1) to keep meaning in our life.
- We should be leery of anyone who proclaims that any particular problem is "all physical" or "all mental." These simplistic statements cannot be defended any longer in modern medical science. Those who make such claims cannot even tell us what it is they mean by "the physical" or "the mental," for the dividing line between them has become increasingly thin.
- There is good news here—positive perceptions and meanings can actually increase the level of our health, all other factors being equal. It would be wrong to believe that meanings can only bring havoc. They can be as therapeutic as a medication or a surgical procedure.
- We should recognize science for the information that it can give us and understand that the true meaning of wellness and life is in our evolving process of expanding our consciousness.[28]

Meanings matter. When the time comes for your next annual physical examination, keep this fact in mind: It isn't just the body that needs the checkup; one's personal life meanings need to be checked from time to time too.

SUMMARY

Being a nurse healer is a journey that allows the nurse an opportunity to explore the inner dimensions of personal and transpersonal growth. True nurse healing requires attention to identifying one's woundedness and the polarities, the purpose, and the meaning in life. This attention can be enhanced by learning to move to a place of centeredness in order to be present with intention. Quieting the mind places nurses in the best position to develop skills of active listening. Learning about the inward journey opens many unique opportunities to be with self, clients, and others. The nurse can guide and facilitate the client to increase inner awareness and self-understanding and learn new skills that provide great opportunities for reaching one's human potentials. Awareness of healing and healer allows a presence where nurse-client interactions take on new dimensions.

DIRECTIONS FOR FUTURE RESEARCH

1. Conduct qualitative studies that examine the interactive variables that identify the characteristics of nurse healers.
2. Evaluate if nurses who meditate or practice some form of relaxation response have more empathy, caring, and job satisfaction.
3. Test guidelines to help the nurse increase the skill of active listening.
4. Evaluate tools that guide the nurse in recognizing intuition.

NURSE HEALER REFLECTIONS

After reading this chapter the nurse healer will be able to answer or will begin a process of answering the following questions:

- How do I *feel within* when I use the word *healer* to describe myself?
- Do I *acknowledge* my *strengths* and *weaknesses*?
- Do I *recognize* that self-healing is a *continual* process?
- What do I experience when I become *centered*?
- Do I listen *actively*?
- How do I *know* that I am listening actively?
- Do I *acknowledge* my intuition?
- How do I *experience* myself as a guide?
- What are my *unique qualities* of guiding?
- What is my *purpose* on the inward journey?
- What *rituals* can I add to my life for *healing awareness*?
- What are my *best strategies* for *moving toward* the inward path?
- Do I acknowledge the *meaning* in my life process?

NOTES

1. Max Planck, *Where Is Science Going?* (New York: W.W. Norton and Company, 1932), p. 37.
2. Margaret Newman, *Health As Expanding Consciousness* (St. Louis: C.V. Mosby Company, 1986), pp. 71–72.
3. Molly Brown, *The Unfolding Self* (Los Angeles, California: Psychosynthesis Press, 1983), p. 20–23.
4. Larry Dossey, *Beyond Illness* (Boston: Shambhala Publications, Inc., 1984), pp. 173–207.

5. Jerome Frank, "Mind-Body Relationships in Illness and Healing," *Journal of the International Academy of Preventive Medicine* 2, no. 3 (1975): 46–59.
6. Janet Quinn, "The Healing Arts in Modern Health Care," in *Spiritual Aspects of the Healing Arts*, ed. Dora Kunz (Wheaton, IL: The Theosophical Publishing House, 1985), p. 123.
7. Ibid., p. 124.
8. Dolores Krieger, *The Therapeutic Touch* (Englewood Cliffs, NJ: Prentice-Hall, Inc., 1979), p. 35.
9. Ibid., p. 36.
10. John Welwood, "Vulnerability and Power in the Therapeutic Process," in *Awakening the Heart*, ed. John Welwood (Boston: Shambhala Publications, Inc., 1983), p. 149.
11. Ibid., p. 152.
12. Richard Heckler, "Entering the Place of Conflict," in *Awakening the Heart*, ed. John Welwood (Boston: Shambhala Publications, Inc., 1983), pp. 176–182.
13. Chogyam Trungpa, "Becoming a Full Human Being," in *Awakening the Heart*, ed. John Welwood (Boston: Shambhala Publications, Inc., 1983), pp. 126–131.
14. David Brandon, "Nowness in the Helping Relationships," in *Awakening the Heart*, ed. John Welwood (Boston: Shambhala Publications, Inc., 1983), pp. 140–147.
15. Ibid., pp. 143–145.
16. Ibid., p. 142.
17. *Active Listening Sheet* (Dallas: Dallas Diagnostic Association, 1986).
18. Diane Shaimberg, "Teaching Therapists to Be With Clients," in *Awakening the Heart*, ed. John Welwood (Boston: Shambhala Publications, Inc. 1983), pp. 163–175.
19. Eric Peper and Casi Kushel, "A Holistic Merger of Biofeedback and Family Therapy," in *Spiritual Aspects of the Healing Arts*, ed. Dora Kunz (Wheaton, IL: The Theosophical Publishing House, 1985), pp. 125–144.
20. Karl Sperber, "Psychotherapeutic Materialism," in *Awakening the Heart*, ed. John Welwood (Boston: Shambhala Publications, Inc., 1983), p. 74.
21. Molly Brown, The Unfolding Self, p. 21.
22. Ibid., p. 21.
23. Ibid., p. 23.
24. Larry Dossey, *Space, Time, and Medicine* (Boston: Shambhala Publications, Inc., 1982), p. 150.
25. Larry Dossey, *Recovering the Soul: A Scientific and Spiritual Search* (New York: Bantam, 1989).
26. W. A. Green, Sidney Goldstein, and Arthur J. Moss, "Psychosocial Aspects of Sudden Death," *Archives of Internal Medicine* 129 (May, 1972): 725–731.
27. George Engel, "A Life Setting Conducive to Illness: The Giving-Up-Given-Up Complex," *Annals of Internal Medicine* 69, no. 2 (1968): 292–300.
28. Margaret Newman, *Health As Expanding Consciousness*, p. 3–4.

SUGGESTED READINGS

Hanh, Thich Nhat. *The Miracle of Mindfulness*. Boston: Beacon Press, 1976.

Laurie, Sanders, and Tucker, Melvin. *Centering*. New York: Destiny Books, 1978.

Suzuki, Shunryu. *Zen Mind, Beginner's Mind*. New York: Wheatherhill, 1970.

Trungpa, Chogyam. *Shambhala: The Sacred Path of the Warrior*. Boston: Shambhala Publications, Inc., 1983.

Underhill, Evelyn. *The Essentials of Mysticism*. New York: Dutton, 1960.

Unit **II**

Conscious Journey toward Wholeness

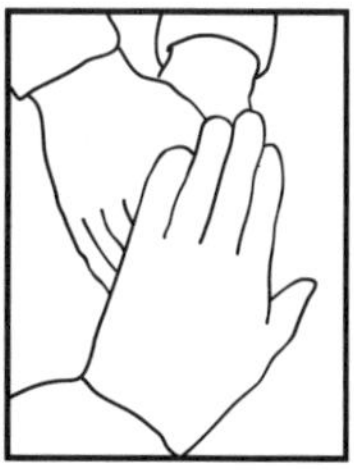

The spacetime view of health and disease tells us that a vital part of the goal of every therapist is to help the sick person toward a reordering of his world view. We must help him realize he is a process in spacetime, and not an isolated entity who is fragmented from the world of the healthy and adrift in flowing time, moving slowly toward extermination. To the extent that we accomplish this task we are healers.

Larry Dossey

Source: Larry Dossey, *Space, Time and Medicine* (Boston: Shambhala Publications, Inc., 1982).

chapter **4**

The History and Future of Healing

Lynn Keegan

The use of history is to give value to the present hour and its duty.

Ralph Waldo Emerson[1]

This chapter explores the history and future of healing, its art and science, and the emerging combination of the best from antiquity with the marvels of modern technology. There is an old saying that those who do not learn from history are doomed to repeat it. The art of healing requires more than techniques and a cognitive knowledge base. It also requires an understanding of who we are and how we have evolved. As we approach the 21st century we have the opportunity to blend the tradition and knowledge of all cultures in recorded time with modern technology to create the finest and most sophisticated healing for the future.

The practice of holistic health is a relatively recent development in our Western health care system, even though the concept has been around for thousands of years. The word "holistic" comes from the Greek root "hale" meaning whole. Holistic health is a system of care that is directed toward the integration and balancing of body, mind, and spirit. The goal of holistic health is to help the total person, rather than just to treat a disease. Ancient philosophers explored the holistic concept. As long ago as 200 B.C., Chinese philosophers believed that when one treats a disease, one must first treat the mind; there are no diseases—only people with diseases.[2] Holistic health is a reminder of the unity of all life and the essential oneness of all systems.[3]

NURSE HEALER OBJECTIVES: THE HISTORY AND FUTURE OF HEALING

Theoretical

1. Explore what cultures from antiquity have contributed to the healing arts and sciences.

2. Understand the concept of Cartesian dualism.
3. Study the evolution of holism.
4. Examine the projections for the future of healing.

Clinical

1. Attempt to understand the health agency you work in from a historical perspective.
2. Consider your agency in a futuristic perspective.

Personal

1. Consider the meaning of viewing your current situation from a historical perspective.
2. Consider how your practice mode of today will fit into the 21st century.

DEFINITIONS

Atomism: the idea that all matter is made up of basic building blocks, the smallest of which is the atom. These can be separated and studied in their most minute form. Matter and spirit are separate entities.

Paradigm: a framework of thought.

Reductionism: the idea that all the workings of human beings are accounted for by behavior of the constituent parts of the body—the atoms and electrons that make up substance.

Shamans: wise, gifted individuals who serve as healers and pivotal figures in the rites of passage in their cultures.

Shamanic culture: a culture in which the shaman serves as healer and as a philosopher/priest who is privy to the supernatural.

Telematics: the term applied to new information technologies; involves the interrelationship of computers, telecommunications, and diagnostic science.

HEALING IN ANTIQUITY

From the dawn of humankind, people have been fascinated by the healing process. The healing arts have always attracted the most creative and intellectually curious among us. And from the very earliest times, healers have used their creative force to explore and utilize everything that their time and culture afforded them to augment the still-mysterious healing process. Table 4-1 provides a chronology of healing in ancient times.

Table 4-1 Chronology of Healing in Antiquity

Event	*Date*
Drawings and carvings signifying the recognition of the cyclic nature of time	35,000 B.C.
Cave depictions of shamanic activities	20,000 B.C.
Necropsy (study of the dead and practice of mummification) in Egypt	3,000 B.C.
Egyptian literature on healing and magic	2,000 B.C.
Scientific classification and writings by Hippocrates in Greece	500 B.C.
The Yellow Emperor's Classic of Internal Medicine: contents included anatomy, physiology, hygiene, acupuncture, and moxibustion	200 B.C.
Rg-Veda: contents included philosophy and healing consciousness of India	200 B.C.
The Materia Medica of Shen-nung: contents included description of 365 pharmaceutical drugs	200 A.D.

Primitive Cultures

People living in primitive cultures were closely tied into natural law, thus having a close affinity to the animal and plant kingdoms. Because of this intimacy with nature, people ascribed to all life forms the same qualities that they had. They believed that all natural objects—rocks, rivers, trees, wind, and animals—were alive and possessed a spirit or soul. This belief in animism profoundly affected the development of the practices related to the treatment of maladies.

Because the cause of illness might be due to spiritual woes, many cures were attempted through spiritual intervention. Consequently, a great body of tribal lore developed that included incantations, rites, rituals, and spells. The primary goal was to manipulate the body in such a fashion to make it an unpleasant place for evil spirits, thereby ridding the body of the cause of the illness.

As this magical lore accumulated, it became too complex to be easily understood by the ordinary tribespeople, so individuals with special insight were selected to devote their time to mastering and interpreting the spiritual realms to the others. The possession of life-giving powers granted these "medicine men and women" or "shamans" a place of prestige and set them above the ordinary person. Thus, the esoteric position of the healer and his or her devotion to the pursuit of the alleviation of pain and suffering began.[4]

Role of the Shaman

The word "shaman" is derived from the Russian word "saman." In primitive times the shaman was the artist, dancer, poet, clown, and curer. He or she was generally gifted in most of the entertaining talents. In addition, the shaman could relate to guardian spirits from whom power and knowledge was gained. Shamans use rituals—drums, chanting, fasting, and sleeplessness—to slip into a dream-like state where vivid imagery experiences and contact with the spirit world is said to exist. Thus, the shaman, as well as being a healer, served and still serves in some areas of the world as a philosopher/priest who participates in supernatural reality.[5]

Shamanic practice uses entertainment and spiritual talents to move in and out of special states of consciousness for the purpose of helping others (see Chapter 5). Unlike some other mystics, shamans do not seek enlightenment for its sake alone, but for the specific purpose of healing or in some manner aiding the community. They follow a circular path, moving in and out of other realms of consciousness and returning each time with new knowledge and power for use in healing.

Shamanism is the oldest method of healing. Archaeological evidence suggests that shamans first practiced as long as 20,000 years ago.[6] In the Les Trois Freres cave in France is found a painting thought to represent a shaman. Ancient carvings and paintings from the Paleolithic period depict shamans in what is now England. What is striking is that shamanistic practices are remarkably consistent in all countries and cultures. The similarity may exist because shamanism worked, and through trial and error, the same techniques for healing were adopted by diverse populations. Viewed from another perspective, the ancient way is so powerful and taps so deeply into the mind that one's usual cultural belief systems and assumptions become irrelevant in the face of a healing mode that works.

The purpose of shamanic intervention is spiritual development. Healing is of a spiritual nature and may or may not result in an extension of life. Disease has its origins and gains its meaning from the spirit world. The very purpose of life is to advance into the visionary realms of the spirit and to achieve balance in all things. To lose one's soul is the most tragic thing that can happen as it would eliminate any meaning from life either here or in the hereafter. Consequently, much of shamanistic healing is directed toward the nurturance and preservation of the soul.

Illness in the modern sense is regarded as something that happens to the body from without. The healer is expected to remove it or protect the body from it. In contrast, in the shamanistic system the problem is not perceived as something external, but rather the loss of personal power that has permitted the intrusion, be it a foreign body, bacteria, or an evil spirit. Thus, a shaman first works to strengthen the power of the sick person, and then second, combats the illness-producing agent.

Even though the shaman relates to the spiritual realm, no distinction is ever actually made between body, mind, and spirit. In reality, body is mind, and mind is spirit. Even as they move into spiritual planes shamans believe that spirit is always in matter. In this system body-mind-spirit are considered both part of each other and separate from each other, much as the living flora is both part of and separate from the earth and sky.

Much of the shamanistic lore is so foreign to contemporary health care that it has been dismissed as untenable for 20th century sophisticated, civilized, humankind. Yet, many shamanistic practices continue to thrive alongside mainstream medical thought. The current widespread interest in these practices reflects a longing for a more humanistic, spiritual aspect to our modern health care delivery systems.

Ancient Greece

In ancient Greece, institutions dedicated to healing arose. There were as many as 200 of these temples, which were called Asclepions after the god of healing, Asclepius.

These centers that existed for approximately a thousand years from 700 B.C. to 300 A.D. had complete systems of mythology, symbolism, priest healers, and a method of healing that incorporated all the knowledge of the era. When an ill person sought healing, total immersion in a physical, mental, and spiritual healing environment followed. Dreams, drama, music, art, laughter, massage, bathing, and rest were used, along with herbs and the basic surgical treatments available during that period.[7] By 500 B.C. Hippocrates had catalogued many methods of scientific treatment. The 57 volumes that survived of his writings were divided into many of the same subspecialty categories that we use today. The method of inquiry and scientific practice was at its height during the Grecian era before the Western world began its long dark descent through the Middle Ages.

The Hippocratic Oath, which is an ethical code of honor, has been and continues to be taken by many physicians upon graduation from medical school. This code is a dedication to the mythical foundation of medicine. Even in today's technological world, the new physician takes the oath that begins, "I swear by Apollo the physician, by Asclepius, and Hygeia and Panacea and all the gods and goddesses, making them my witnesses, that I will fulfill according to my ability and judgement this oath and this covenant: . . . ."[8]

The Far East

Healing in Far Eastern cultures, both in ancient times and the present, focuses upon the movement of life energy, which is called *ch'i,* along a system of unseen, but recognized meridians. It is these meridians that contain the acupuncture and acupressure points. Ch'i is affected by how the opposing energies called *yin* and *yang* are ordered. The yin and yang are fundamentally female and male energies with many attributes accorded to each. When the flow between yin and yang is blocked, illness occurs. One of the treatments for illness is the insertion of acupuncture needles in one or more of the hundreds of points along the meridians for the purpose of stimulation and restoring the flow of the ch'i energy.

The development of medicine in China was based on the following applied sciences: orbisiconography (functional relationships within the body), sinarteriology, (the natural channeling of ch'i energy through meridians of the body), pharmaceutical agents, change in climatic environment, and immunology. The sciences of organic anatomy, histology, and biochemistry were not developed because they did not fit into their theoretical framework of healing. The Chinese treated illness according to how the patient's energy flowed in relation to the energy of the universe.[9]

Ayurvedic System in Ancient India

Ayurveda, the Indian Hindu system of healing developed more than 2,000 years ago, is concerned with eight principal branches of medicine. These branches include pediatrics, gynecology, obstetrics, ophthalmology, geriatrics, otolaryngology, general medicine, and surgery.[10] Each ailment is addressed according to theories of the five elements (ether, air, fire, water, and earth), the body humors, the body tissues, the body excretions, and the trinity of life: body, mind, and spiritual awareness.

To understand healing from this perspective one must realize that it is primarily the inward search and quest for soul growth that is important. The theory of reincarnation affects every aspect of life, including the treatment of illness and the acceptance of death.

One of the primary approaches utilized in the Vedic system is Yoga. Yoga is the science of union with the Divine and with truth.[11] Its purpose is to help the individual achieve longevity, rejuvenation, and self-realization. Yoga deals with the unfoldment of human consciousness with the goal of reaching total enlightenment. Yoga, which can be practiced in a variety of ways, is done in order to speed up the natural evolution of the individual. When left on his or her own without the discipline of Yoga, an individual would more slowly evolve through the inevitable suffering that is a condition of earthly life.

It was through the Indian healing system that Western culture gained knowledge of chakras. *Chakras* are unseen energy fields consisting of vortices of energy that can be activated by concentration or meditation. The chakras, like the Oriental meridians, can become stagnant or blocked, giving rise to illness. There are seven major chakras located along the anterior human body from the top of the head to the base of the spinal column. In contrast to Western healers who tended to do something to someone else to alleviate sickness, the Vedic Indians learned to activate the chakra energy centers for self-healing. However, they too had knowledge of herbs and roots and had rudimentary understanding of anatomy and physiology.[12]

Early Christian Period

From the time of Christ well into the 1600s, healers were imbued with a holy or mystical aspect as they practiced their art. From the third to the twelfth century, the Catholic Church served as the authority in health care, as well as doctrinal concerns. Christian healers derived this orientation from the New Testament, which suggests not only the presence of God in all matter but also encouraged them to see the image of Christ in every man.

In the Gospel of John is found this passage, "All things were made through Him, and without Him was nothing that has been made. In Him was life, and the life was the light of men." Of those who believed in His name, John wrote, "Who were born not of blood, nor of the will of the flesh, nor the will of man, but of God. And the word was made flesh, and dwelt among us." These and other passages speak to the intertwining of the flesh and the spirit—the bond of body-mind-spirit.

The very origins of the nursing profession were based on these early Christian concepts. Early in the development of the Christian church, widows were recognized as being specially selected to care for the poor. The title of widow did not necessarily refer to a woman whose husband had died, but was used as a designation of respect for age. Paul clearly stated the qualifications for this title as one who was pious, devoted in hospitality, anxious to relieve the afflicted, and was at least 60 years old. The later addition of the vow of chastity led to the absorption of the widows into the community life of the nuns. These religious orders laid the groundwork for charitable and nursing work. Indeed, it was the "widow" Fabiola who established the first Christian hospital in Rome in 390 A.D.[13]

For a thousand years following the birth of Christ, it was monastic orders made up both of men and women who, based on the concept of Christian charity and its imagery of the presence of the spirit in the body of man, made a particular virtue of what were called the corporal works of mercy. These works of mercy nourished the spirit through the care of the body. The orientation of healers during this 1,000-year period was totally holistic; it incorporated into every healing process an interlinking of body, mind, and spirit even to the point of considering some diseases as caused by the presence of evil spirits and treating these maladies by exorcism. From our modern view we can see both the error in this thought process, as well as its inherent symbolic wisdom.

As the Christian church, which was the foundation of our Western society developed, interest grew in a scientific approach to learning and a method and system of thought referred to as scholasticism began. Such thinkers as Albertus Magnus, Thomas Aquinas, and Duns Scotus Erigena began to systematize learning. They returned to ancient roots of Greek philosophy and superimposed upon those concepts the redeeming aspects of Christianity.

Between 1265 and 1272, Aquinas wrote a summary of these studies known as the *Summa* (summary). In this work he states clearly that humans in their natural state, in this life, are an inseparable synthesis of spirit and body. He thus verbalized the concept that had been intuitively acted upon for the past 1,000 years.

Aquinas took the ancient knowledge of pagan and Arabic civilizations and showed that their wisdom was consistent with Christianity and that Christianity could add a new dimension to their reality. He opened the minds of his contemporaries not only to the philosophy of the ancients and the Arabic world but also to their science, mathematics, and medicine. It was this acceptance of the Arabic culture that brought us our modern numerologic system (Arabic numerals), concepts of quantification, and eventually the emergence of empiricism, the scientific method, and modern technology.

The Enchanted World

The view of nature that predominated before the dawn of the Scientific Revolution (early 1600s) was that of an enchanted world. Everything was seen as wondrous and alive. The cosmos was a place of belonging. As a member of this cosmos one was not an alienated observer, but rather a direct participant in its drama. One's personal destiny was bound up with nature's destiny, and this known relationship gave meaning to life. This "participating consciousness" involved merger with one's surroundings and being part of a psychic wholeness. This wholeness was lost with the emergence of the modern scientific era.[14] It is this very concept of psychic wholeness that holistic healers are now reconstructing.

SCIENTIFIC REVOLUTION

Cartesian Dualism

Many scholars date the beginning of the Scientific Revolution to the work of the 17th-century philosopher Rene Descartes. Descartes began with the premise that the mind must be able to know the world. In order to do so, one must first eliminate all previously held belief systems and medieval thought patterns. Descartes believed that his new system based on skepticism and methodical order would allow thinkers to achieve clarity and truth. This line of thought, however, brought him to a depressing conclusion: There was nothing at all of which one could be certain.[15]

Descartes' world-changing theory was that the human being's activity as a thinking being is purely mechanical. Thinking confronts the world as a separate object. The problem to be studied is broken down into its component parts and studied "atomistically." Problem solving and knowing reduce the object of study into its smallest parts and then sum the results to reach conclusions. The object and the observer are therefore two distinct entities.

In his scholarly work, *Principles of Philosophy* (1644), Descartes wrote that the clear and logical linking of ideas leads to the conclusion that the universe is no more than a vast machine, wound up by God to tick forever. This machine consists of two basic entities, matter and motion. Spirit, in the form of God, hovers on the outside of the universe, but plays no direct part in it. The human being can know all there is to know by way of reason, and mind and body, subject and object, are radically disparate entities.

To Descartes, the mind-body split was true of all perception and behavior. It was this duality of thinking, the heart of the Cartesian paradigm, that broke the body-mind-spirit connection and paved the way for the evolution of reductionist thinking. The new healer was taught to be purely rational and "clear thinking" in approach.

Descartes' philosophy did much to hasten the emergence of the scientific secular world. In the 18th century the well-known German poet Johann Schiller (1759-1805) wrote of the "disgodding" of nature. Later in the 19th century, sociologist Max Weber (1864-1920) described the "disenchantment" of the world. Each concluded that the history of the West was the progressive removal of mind and spirit from phenomenal appearances. Most other scholars deepened the separation of mind and body, and the new science bore all the hallmarks of Descartes' thinking.

The New World View

By the 19th century the Cartesian approach was well integrated into the healing arts. Both physicians and nurses followed scientific curricula and worked diligently to serve the sick using their best atomistic approaches. The religious communities, which educated many nurses, continued to embody a spiritual approach in their practices.

Holistic health care in the early years of American history suffered a serious setback. The complexities of the evolution of an agrarian to an industrialized society coupled with the cities' burgeoning immigrant population left little time for holistic health concerns. Early American nurses waged battles with sanitation, basic hygiene, and immunization to combat the serious physical health problems of the era. Again with the exception of the hospitals run by religious orders, less and less attention was given to the mental and spiritual aspects of healing.

In the late 19th and first half of the 20th centuries, the increasing division between the healers (doctors and nurses) and increasing specialization within the medical field pushed the concept of whole body healing farther and farther into the recess of the past. The more specialized and technical delivery systems became, the less attention was given to the spiritual aspect of care. With the exception of the isolated work of a few healers, by the 1960s the pendulum had swung the limit away from holistic health care. Illness was perceived as a strictly pathophysiologic event, with the cure being completely allopathic (based on treatment using remedies producing effects opposite from those produced by the disease being treated).

The work of the isolated few, however, kept the concept of wholeness alive. The term "holistic health" was introduced in South Africa in 1926 by Prime Minister Jan Smuts. He theorized that nature tends to bring things together to form whole organisms and that the determining factors in nature and evolution are wholes and not their constituent parts.[16]

The first scientifically trained nurse recognized for her holistic orientation was Florence Nightingale. In her book, *Notes on Nursing* (1859), she shared the essence of her knowledge and wisdom. Some of her deceptively simple ideas are implemented in current-day practices. She called attention to the natural antidotes to disease: fresh air, the reparative importance of quiet in the hospital, good lighting, and a properly managed environment.[17] Not only was she remembered for the theory she generated but also for her political activism and the pursuit of a cause greater than herself. She was truly concerned with the body, mind, and spirit of the sick. Nightingale in her life behavior and thinking startled those about her by living her human potential. She dared to move beyond the accepted customs of her day, thereby leading her peers, not always with their approval, to higher levels of thinking and performance.[18]

It was, however, during the second half of the 19th century when scientific curricula were gaining ascendancy that the gradual decline and ultimate dissolution of the feminine influence on medicine occurred. As the scientific content of nursing curricula increased, the feminine qualities of nurturance, intuition, and empathy decreased. These qualities were seen as threats and impediments to the progression of the new scientific order.[19]

Reawakening of Holistic Health Care

The reawakening of whole person thought related to health and illness probably began in New York in the 1940s. It was here that Flanders Dunbar, a psychiatrist at Columbia Presbyterian Medical Center, did pioneer work in psychosomatic medicine.[20] In her clinical studies she analyzed the relationships among personality type, stress, and physical illness in over 1,600 patients over a period of 12 years. These patients suffered from cardiovascular disease, diabetes, fractures, allergies, and gastrointestinal disease. In each type of malady, Dunbar found certain personality characteristics typical of the majority of patients suffering from that particular disorder. Case histories revealed that the stressful emotional situations that patients experienced shortly before illness onset included moving to a new home, neighborhood, or town; death of a close friend or relative; a recent marriage; marital problems and poor sexual adjustment; problems with in-laws; increased family size; and problems with a job, job change, or job loss.

It was information gleaned in the early psychosomatic studies that led another pioneer to the exploration of the related phenomenon of the psychophysiology of stress. Hans Selye developed the theory of stress based upon what he termed the general adaptation syndrome (GAS)[21] (see Chapter 5).

Although Flanders Dunbar's work in the 1940s was sometimes criticized as speculative and nonscientific, it was expanded on by two researchers in the 1960s. Building on Dunbar's stressful emotional situation categories, Holmes and Rahe in 1967 developed a 43-item questionnaire that elicited information on the occurrence of significant life events during the previous year. Each item was given a point value. The researchers predicted that when the point value reached a certain level there was an increased likelihood that a physical illness would soon occur. This questionnaire has been used in many studies to document the relationship between the occurrence of the stresses of significant life events and the onset of illness or disease. Findings generated by a revised version of the tool revealed that, the more change individuals underwent, the more likely they were to become sick. Thus, a correlation between lifestyle and the onset of illness was established.[22]

Ethical Code for Nurses

At the same time as the above correlative studies were being conducted, the American Nurses' Association was developing a code of ethics for the profession. This *Code of Ethics,* which was adopted by the professional association in 1950, is periodically revised. The present *Code,* although remaining prescriptive, depends more on the nurse's accountability to the client rather than the physician, which is where the evolving nurse healer's accountability truly lies. The 11-point *Code* is shown in Exhibit 4-1.

Wellness Paradigm

In the early 1960s the concept of wellness was first addressed by Halpert Dunn, who is known as the founder of the wellness movement in this century. His now-classic definition of "high-level wellness" was "an integrated method of functioning which is oriented toward maximizing the potential of which the individual is capable within the environment where he is functioning."[23] Wellness is an ongoing process toward higher potential, not a static goal, and high-level wellness is a feeling of being "alive to the tips of the fingers, with energy to burn, tingling with vitality."[24] Health professionals tend to focus on disease, rather than wellness or prevention, because it is easier to fight against sickness than to fight for a condition of greater wellness.

It was the Canadian government that made the first public and political statement about whole health. In 1974 the Canadian Ministry of Health and Welfare released a publication entitled, *A New Perspective on the Health of Canadians.*[25] This important document presented the epidemiologic evidence for the significance of lifestyle and environmental factors on health and illness. The report called for a host of health promotion strategies and presented evidence that health status would improve only when people began to assume more responsibility for their own health. When circulated in the United States this document became the impetus for American political action.

In 1976 the U.S. Senate Select Committee released a landmark report on nutrition and human needs. *Dietary Goals for the United States* revealed the link between diet and disease and called for sweeping changes in American food consumption patterns.[26] This report paved the way for changes in the ways Americans eat.

Exhibit 4-1 Code for Nurses

1 The nurse provides services with respect for human dignity and the uniqueness of the client unrestricted by considerations of social or economic status, personal attributes, or the nature of health problems.

2 The nurse safeguards the client's right to privacy by judiciously protecting information of a confidential nature.

3 The nurse acts to safeguard the client and the public when health care and safety are affected by the incompetent, unethical, or illegal practice of any person.

4 The nurse assumes responsibility and accountability for individual nursing judgments and actions.

5 The nurse maintains competence in nursing.

6 The nurse exercises informed judgment and uses individual competence and qualifications as criteria in seeking consultation, accepting responsibilities, and delegating nursing activities to others.

7 The nurse participates in activities that contribute to the ongoing development of the profession's body of knowledge.

8 The nurse participates in the profession's efforts to implement and improve standards of nursing.

9 The nurse participates in the profession's efforts to establish and maintain conditions of employment conducive to high quality nursing care.

10 The nurse participates in the profession's effort to protect the public from misinformation and misrepresentation and to maintain the integrity of nursing.

11 The nurse collaborates with members of the health professions and other citizens in promoting community and national efforts to meet the health needs of the public.

Source: Reprinted from *Code for Nurses with Interpretive Statements*, p. 3, with permission of American Nurses' Association Inc., © 1976.

The number and scope of holistic practitioners began to increase in the late 1970s. These practitioners—nurses, physicians, and nontraditionally prepared practitioners—began to integrate a wellness lifestyle as a major factor in the health process. New techniques were tried and new ways explored. Major emphasis was placed on four dimensions: nutrition, physical awareness, stress reduction, and self-responsibility. Out of this new practice, literature and research emerged that helped influence the way Americans conceptualized health and healing.

Ferguson, in her now-classic book, *The Aquarian Conspiracy,* quickened the interest of many when she wrote that a tremendous social transformation is taking place.[27] This transformation embodies a new sense of spirituality and a mind evolution that encompasses consciousness raising. Individuals are developing an increased interpersonal awareness of their own body-mind-spirit connection, as well as that interrelationship in others. When individuals develop a new awareness of the body-mind-spirit connection, they focus their attention on a search for patterns and causes of their symptoms. They develop a new body-mind perspective and seek additional ways to prevent the occurrence of illness. Individuals take more responsibility for developing and maintaining a state of wellness.

Ferguson contrasts the old and new paradigms of medicine in Table 4-2.

As new theory and practice literature emerged, scientific studies were undertaken to document some of the suppositions underlying holistic concepts. The findings of one of the most extensive scientific investigations were published in 1982 as The Multiple Risk Factor Intervention Trial (MRFIT).[28] This study was an outgrowth of a recommendation to do this research from the National Heart and Lung Institute. It was a randomized primary prevention trial to test the effect of a multifactor intervention program on

Table 4-2 Comparison of Old and New Paradigms of Medicine

Old Paradigm of Medicine	*New Paradigm of Medicine*
Treatment of symptoms	Search for patterns, causes
Specialized	Integrated, concerned with the whole patient
Emphasis on efficiency	Emphasis on human values
Professional should be emotionally neutral	Professional's caring is a component of healing
Pain and disease as wholly negative	Pain and disease may be valuable signals of internal conflicts
Primary intervention with drugs, surgery	Minimal intervention with appropriate technology, complemented with full armamentarium of noninvasive techniques (psychotechnologies, diet, exercise).
Body seen as machine in good or bad repair	Body seen as dynamic system, a complex energy field within fields (family, workplace, environment, culture, life history)
Disease or disability seen as entity	Disease or disability seen as process
Emphasis on eliminating symptoms, disease	Emphasis on achieving maximum body/mind health
Patient is dependent	Patient is (or should be) autonomous
Professional is authority	Professional is therapeutic partner
Body and mind are separate; psychosomatic illnesses seen as mental; may refer to psychiatrist	Bodymind perspective; psychosomatic illness is the province of all health care professionals
Mind is secondary factor in organic illness	Mind is primary or co-equal factor in all illness
Placebo effect is evidence of power of suggestion	Placebo effect is evidence of mind's role in disease and healing
Primary reliance on quantitative information (charts, tests, dates)	Primary reliance on qualitative information, including patient reports and professional's intuition; quantitative data an adjunct
Prevention seen as largely environmental: vitamins, rest, exercise, immunization, not smoking.	Prevention synonymous with wholeness: in work, relationships, goals, body-mind-spirit

Source: Adapted from *The Aquarian Conspiracy: Personal and Social Transformation* by M. Ferguson, pp. 246–248, with permission of Jeremy P. Tarcher, Inc., © 1980.

mortality from coronary heart disease (CHD) in 12,866 men aged 35 to 57 years at high risk for CHD. The findings, from a 7-year follow-up period, were that men in special intervention programs consisting of counseling for cigarette smoking, stepped-care treatment for hypertension, and dietary advice for lowering blood cholesterol levels had a lower mortality rate than their control group counterparts. This major, broad-based study awakened the scientific community to the importance of education and prevention and opened the doors for numerous ongoing scientific investigations.

Modern Holistic Health Movement in Nursing

Modern holistic nurses prepare to assume more responsibility for total health care by learning new knowledge and skills organized around the basic life processes of self-responsibility, caring, stress management, lifestyle, communication, and change. Nurses began developing literature in the holistic arena at the same time as their physician and lay counterparts in the late 1970s and early 1980s.

In 1980 the American Holistic Nurses' Association was formed. This organization was the first to bring whole person healing back into mainstream American nursing. Its purpose is to promote the education of nurses and the public in the concerns and practice of health of the whole person. Through this organization nurses have once again taken up the role of healer and seek to tighten the loosened threads of body, mind, and spirit.

In the late 1980s the majority of nursing educators are scientifically oriented, yet easily become frustrated because they cannot effect cures quickly enough. However, we really have no reason to become impatient with science when we consider that it is really less than two centuries old. Ninety percent of all the scientists the world has ever produced are still living now.[29]

If we are to continue to evolve into wholeness we must be based in empiricism, but must also take into account those ineffable, immeasurable, nonmaterial, and spiritual values that have motivated our predecessors in their search for truth. As Larry Dossey stated in his book, *Beyond Illness,* "Let us acknowledge that we are the sons and daughters of the earth, and that we do have access to its tools."[30] The world of empiricism has yielded valuable insight that should continue to be used, but our efforts must be blended with an understanding of the higher level of spirit. Our objective now is to learn from the past to help restore a balance, for true science combines the philosophical sciences with the natural sciences. In this way we may return to our ancient roots in which all healing professions are based. We must search for ends and goals and become truly teleologic in our approach to truth and value, finding ultimately that they are the same reality.

THE FUTURE OF HEALING

> "The future belongs to those who can regain at a higher level the old sense of balance and belonging between man and nature."
>
> *Unknown*

Thomas Kuhn, a science historian and philosopher, resurrected the term "paradigm" from the Greek word "paradigma" (meaning pattern) in his 1962 landmark book, *The*

Structure of Scientific Revolutions.[31] Kuhn believed that every dominant paradigm eventually exceeds the limits of its methodology and ceases to become effective. When this occurs a shift to a new paradigm occurs.

Today, we are functioning at the end of one paradigm and the beginning of a new one. Our present health care delivery system is at the end of its effectiveness. Wildly expensive medical care has made little progress against catastrophic illness while at the same time becoming more impersonal and more intrusive.[32] In contrast, the new paradigm sees humankind as embedded in nature. It promotes and supports the autonomous individual in a decentralized society. We are at the threshold of awakening as stewards of all our resources, both inner and outer. As this paradigm shift advances, emphasis for both the individual and society will be placed on achieving maximum wellness.

Healing and Consciousness

Arguelle, author and visionary historian, believes those living in the future may have little need of health care professionals.[33] By then individuals will have awakened to learning how to care for themselves better and will consequently have less need for present-day invasive care. Not only will people take more responsibility for self-care but in the future there will be more knowledge of how to harness the environment, nutrition, and other factors to foster health and reduce illness.

Kaiser, a health care futurist, thinks that an individual's degree of consciousness development will play a vital role in how care is rendered.[34] Clients will have the opportunity to learn to use consciousness skills to alter their bodymind responses. Those who become skilled in these techniques will be segregated on acute and subacute care units by consciousness ability, as well as by diagnoses. It is likely that clients with well-developed biofeedback skills or other bodymind capabilities will be treated with less invasive techniques and will instead be offered more subtle treatments.

Schindler, another health care futurist, in describing life in the 23rd century to the organization, Nurses and Physicians for Social Responsibility, sees the last decade of the 20th century as humanity's "evolutionary turning point."[35] Humanity can achieve a new vision by (1) giving up the "victim mind" mentality that perpetuates despair and sabotages vision, (2) growing up on a species-wide basis, and (3) outgrowing the need to always be right. As we grow toward these new perspectives the necessary societal changes will occur.

Societal Changes

Demographic Changes

Perhaps the most significant change here will be the vast number of old-old (those over 85 years of age). The dramatic increase in this population will significantly affect the type, location, and quality of elder care services.

Technology

The vast increase in the sophistication and complexity of technology will continue as we move into the 21st century. The development of telematics and biotechnology will also continue.

> These technologies include machines and communication systems, bringing together video, computers, and satellites; networks, management systems, and artificial intelligence. There will be advances in the information technologies used in data bases, which will be clinical, epidemiological and environmental and will concern individuals and communities. Artificial intelligence will lead to highly sophisticated clinical and administrative decision making. Other systems will lead to management of complex machines.[36]

To realize the speed with which changes will occur just consider that, as recently as 1970, computer chips did not even exist. Today, there are more of them than people on the face of the earth.[37]

Change in Societal Self-Image

The model of society as a complex organism will gain strength, leading to the design of health care communities as living, organic, integrated wholes. New types of healing centers will be created. Because of the emerging orientation to combine the sacred and the secular many of these centers will have the potential to become the new holy places of our society. Visualize healing centers filled with once and future myths, the wisdom of the family-oriented society, the ancient algorithms of the heart, and all combined with the latest in medical technology.

Holistic Ethics

Because many aspects of future health care delivery will be based on the decisions that we make now, it is important that nurses examine future healing activities from an ethical perspective. A new framework for ethical decision making using a holistic approach has recently emerged.

Holistic ethics embraces both traditional and the masculine/feminine historical perspectives, but it transcends both by taking into account the unity of being.[38] The holistic view of humanity is one of self-realization, placing the highest value on the development of the individual to attain higher levels of awareness. It is within this framework that a unique moral viewpoint arises. The relationship of the act to the universal "I" becomes the new categorical imperative of the holistic practitioner. Evolution of consciousness and actions should be directed toward positive ends. It should be directed at the "good" of humanity as perceived by a contemplation of the reality of being, beginning with the individual and his or her own self-realization within a universal context.

Healing Sites

Acute Care Settings

The hospital as we know it today will dramatically change. It will be a setting of multiple intensive care units that offer highly specialized, technological care. Clients with very complex conditions requiring sophisticated medical interventions will come to the acute care setting for short periods of time.

Robots will play an important role in the acute care setting.[39] Robot models now being tested will read x-ray films, assist in the operating room, deliver meals and medications to the bedside, fill prescriptions, take vital signs, and complete other labor-intensive tasks. Simple outpatient problems will be treated by robots as they perform limited physical examinations and diagnose common ailments.[40] Serious problems will be referred to specialist robots that will be programmed to perform much of the work that medical specialists do today.

Subacute Care Settings

Because there will be shorter stays and less care given in the acute care setting, a greater variety of subacute facilities will develop. These facilities will include hospices, rehabilitation centers, halfway houses, client education facilities, laboratories, child care centers, and health-wise recreation facilities. Dignified communities for the elderly will also evolve. Nurses will work with this population to help them feel wanted, needed, and useful. New elder roles, such as surrogate grandparents in child care centers or companions or counselors to the more severely ill, will emerge. Elders may even take clients into their homes for rehabilitative care.

The subacute facilities will be more involved with the nurturing and care of the client's body, mind, and spirit. Interventions will include music, imagery, touch, play, and the like. Centers of healing will re-emerge. Nurses will both practice and teach the interventions discussed in this text.

The hospice concept, first developed by Dr. Cecily Saunders in England in the late 1960s, will finally become fully operational in this country during the next decade. Issues regarding payment coverage, as well as ethical issues, will be resolved by legislation, thereby allowing the full development of hospice centers.

Mother Theresa, with her work in developing hospices in India and Nepal, has done important groundwork in modeling a more enlightened approach to death and care of the dying. Health care professionals will acknowledge and value the death and dying period as a meaningful time of transition.

Renewal Centers

The future will see a renaissance of healing and renewal centers reminiscent of the Asclepion centers in ancient Greece. These healing centers will contain all the elements of antiquity, but in addition, will house and utilize new-age technology. They will use such devices as flotation tanks, quadraphonic sound, light and color therapy, and sophisticated motivation, relaxation, and teaching therapies. Clients will be able to choose from a variety of touch therapies, prevention classes, lifestyle assessment, and recharging content in motivational classes. Stress, a hallmark of the 1980s, will be tempered, if not eradicated, in those who avail themselves of these centers.

Imagine future healing centers being planned as parts of ecologic systems, with health care professionals given special time to act as patient advocates or even chaplains. When this occurs the sacredness and wholeness of the healing mission will be revived.

The day of the "cure" is almost over. We will soon move from the medical model to a new model. Nurses in the future will focus on how to "heal" those who cannot be cured.

Expanded Role of the Nurse

The future for nurse healers is bright. An increase in primary nursing and the case management method in acute care settings is already occurring.[41] In the future, there will be fewer nurses making more money and they will have more freedom, yet more accountability. Many nurses will set up and run their own independent businesses within established health care corporations. Nursing will come into its own by organizing services by nursing diagnoses. Nurses will become the new healers of society and will combine the role and functions of the church, school, and counselors of today.

Aydelotte predicts that future nurses will work within a health care system that is divided into four branches.[42] The first branch will be concerned with health promotion, health education, self-help, and health evaluation. A second branch will manage chronic disease. The third branch will be concerned with trauma and severe illnesses. The fourth branch will concentrate on the care of the frail elderly, the physically limited, and the dying.

Individuation and Specialization

True holism represents a universal view in which facts and value become inseparable and in which subject and object become aspects of the same process.[43] The distinction between ourselves and others becomes blurred. The future of the health profession will lie in what we do together and as part of this organism even though we are specialized. What we can do together is far greater than what we could achieve if we operated as individuals.

Our specialization as health professionals cannot be just technical. It must, as we evolve, reflect our cultural, ethnic, ecologic, and spiritual milieu.

> We are at the threshold of a new age in which we may advance or recede. If we are to advance we need a radical transformation of our society back to a spiritual orientation to our universe and all reality.[44]

SUMMARY

Healing has evolved through many eras and cultures into the current intertwining of the best of Western empiricism and Eastern mysticism.

The future of healing holds promise for disease prevention by modeling and teaching healthy lifestyles, the avoidance of unnecessary drugs and chemical manipulation, and maximizing potentials by learning new skills. Nurses will teach the exploration of inner environments and offer new and alternative treatments to those who desire them. This will be done when we ultimately recognize that many diseases arise in response to a disturbed physical, mental, or spiritual environment.

DIRECTIONS FOR FUTURE RESEARCH

1. Develop historical descriptive studies of healers from antiquity.
2. Develop valid and reliable tools to test the effectiveness of some of the healing techniques from antiquity.
3. Continue to compare and contrast allopathic and holistic healing modalities.

NURSE HEALER REFLECTIONS

After reading this chapter, the nurse healer will be able to answer or begin a process of answering the following questions:

- How does the *knowledge* of the *history* of healing affect my current practice?
- Who are the *shamans* in my life?
- What *healing arts* from antiquity can I use in my life to increase my effectiveness in self-healing and to help others in my role as healer?
- What can *I* look forward to in the future?
- Will there be a *place for me* to *practice* in 2010?

NOTES

1. W. Gurney Beham, *Putnam's Complete Book of Quotations* (New York: G.P. Putnam's Sons, 1927): 132a.
2. Margo M. Griffin, "A Holistic Approach to the Health Care of the Elderly Client," *Journal of Gerontological Nursing* 6, (April 1980): pp. 193–196.
3. Edward Bauman, et al., *The Holistic Health Handbook* (Berkeley, CA: And/Or Press, 1981), p. 17.
4. R.H. Shyrock, *The History of Nursing: An Interpretation of Social and Medical Factors Involved* (Philadelphia: W.B. Saunders Co., 1959), p. 1ff.
5. Jeanne Achterberg, *Imagery in Healing* (Boston: New Science Library, 1985), pp. 10–51.
6. Ibid., p. 15.
7. John A. Sanford, *Healing and Wholeness* (New York: Paulist Press, 1977), pp. 42–62.
8. Tom Beauchamp and James Childress, *Principles of Biomedical Ethics* (New York: Oxford University Press, 1979), p. 280.
9. Dolores Krieger, *Foundations for Holistic Health Nursing Practices: The Renaissance Nurse* (Philadelphia: 1981), p. 36.
10. Vasant Lad, *Ayurveda* (Santa Fe, NM: Lotus Press, 1984), p. 13.

11. Ibid., pp. 18–19.
12. Dolores Krieger, *Foundations for Holistic Health Nursing Practice: The Renaissance Nurse,* p. 59.
13. Patricia M. Donahue, *Nursing: The Finest Art* (St.Louis: C.V. Mosby Co., 1985), p. 110.
14. Morris Berman, *The Reenchantment of the World* (Ithaca, NY: Cornell University Press, 1981), p. 16.
15. Ibid., p. 32.
16. Susan McKay, ''Wholistic Health Care: Challenge to Health Providers,'' *Journal of Allied Health* 9 (August, 1980): 194–201.
17. Florence Nightingale, *Notes on Nursing* (New York: Dover Publications, Inc., 1969), p. 1ff.
18. Mary-Charlotte Shealy, ''Florence Nightingale 1820-1910: An Evolutionary Mind in the Context of Holism,'' *Journal of Holistic Nursing* 3, no. 7 (Spring 1985): 4–6.
19. Jeanne Achterberg, *Imagery in Healing,* p. 7.
20. Flanders Dunbar, *Psychomatic Diagnosis* (New York: Paul B. Haeber, Inc., 1945), p. 1ff.
21. Hans Selye, *The Stress of Life* (New York: McGraw Hill, 1956), p. 1ff.
22. Thomas H. Holmes and Richard Rahe, ''The Social Readjustment Rating Scale,'' *Journal of Psychosomatic Research* 11 (1967): 213–218.
23. Halpert Dunn, *High Level Wellness* (Arlington, VA: R.W. Beatty Co., 1961), pp. 5–6.
24. Ibid., p. 2.
25. Mark LaLonde, *A New Perspective on the Health of Canadians* (Ottawa: Government of Canada, 1974), p. 1ff.
26. Senate Select Committee Report, *Dietary Goals for the United States* (Washington, DC: U.S. Government Printing Office, 1976), p. 1ff.
27. Marilyn Ferguson, *The Aquarian Conspiracy* (Los Angeles: J.P. Tarcher, Inc. 1980), p. 1ff.
28. ''Multiple Risk Factor Intervention Trial,'' *Journal of the American Medical Association,* 248 (September 24, 1982): 1465–1477.
29. Paulos Mar Gregorios, *Science for Sane Societies* (New York: Paragon House, 1987), p. 57.
30. Larry Dossey, *Beyond Illness* (Boston: New Science Library, 1984), pp. 180–181.
31. Thomas S. Kuhn, *The Structure of Scientific Revolutions* (Chicago: University of Chicago Press, 1962), p. 1ff.
32. Marilyn Ferguson, *The Aquarian Conspiracy,* p. 29.
33. John-Alexis Viereck, ''Earth Speaks: The Great Return,'' *Meditation,* Summer 1987, p. 6.
34. Leland R. Kaiser, ''The Next Frontier: Computer and Robotic-Enhanced Health Care,'' *Group Practice Journal* 35 (November/December 1986): 11.
35. ''Physicians' Group Prescribes Prevention for War,'' *Leading Edge* 4 (April 2, 1984): 4.
36. Myrtle K. Aydelotte, ''Nursing's Preferred Future,'' *Nursing Outlook* 35 (May/June 1987): 115.
37. Irma E. Goertzen, ''Making Nursing's Vision A Reality,'' *Nursing Outlook* 35 (May/June 1987): 122.
38. Gerald Keegan and Lynn Keegan, ''A Holistic Concept of Ethics,'' submitted for publication, 1987.
39. Leland R. Kaiser, ''The Next Frontier: Computer and Robotic-Enhanced Health Care,'' *Group Practice Journal,* p. 6.
40. Ibid., p. 10.
41. Karen Zender, ''Entrapreneur/Intrapreneur: Choices for Nurses.'' Paper presented at the Texas Nurses' Association Annual Conference, Houston, Texas, 1986.
42. Myrtle K. Aydelotte, ''Nursing's Preferred Future,'' *Nursing Outlook,* p. 118.
43. Gerald T. Keegan, ''Reflections on a Healing Philosophy,'' *Rosicrucian Digest* 60 (1982): 10–12.
44. Gerald Keegan and Lynn Keegan, ''Spirituality and the Technological Crisis,'' *Healing Currents* 11, no. 2 (1987): 26–28.

chapter 5

The Psychophysiology of Bodymind Healing

Barbara Montgomery Dossey

> I am going to suggest that neuropeptides and their receptors form an information network within the body. Perhaps this suggestion sounds fairly innocuous, but its implications are far reaching. I believe that neuropeptides and their receptors are a key to understanding how mind and body are interconnected and how emotions can be manifested throughout the body. Indeed, the more we know about neuropeptides, the harder it is to think in the traditional terms of a mind and a body. It makes more and more sense to speak of a single integrated entity, a ''*bodymind*.''[1]
>
> *Candace B. Pert*
> *Chief, Section on Brain Chemistry*
> *National Institute of Mental Health*

This chapter describes new scientific discoveries that provide a scientific foundation for bodymind interrelationships. It also addresses their exciting implications for the practice of holistic nursing. The tenets of natural systems and information theory are presented as a theoretical base for bodymind healing. This scientific information validates what nurse healers have always intuitively understood: The bodymind is a single integrated unit. The reader is referred to general physiology textbooks for an overview of the nervous system, neuron transmission, and general adaptation syndrome.

NURSE HEALER OBJECTIVES: THE PSYCHOPHYSIOLOGY OF BODYMIND HEALING

Theoretical

1. Explain the concepts of bodymind.
2. Discuss natural systems theory.

3. Discuss information theory.
4. Explain the placebo effect.
5. Discuss state-dependent learning.

Clinical

1. List four ways to enhance the placebo effect.
2. Discuss two ways to integrate a natural systems view into your clinical practice.
3. Acknowledge fragmentation in your clinical practice and use stress management skills to decrease tension.

Personal

1. Assess how your mind and body communicate every day with attitudes, tension, relaxation, and images.
2. Begin to learn methods to gain access to and reframe state-dependent memory to move toward bodymind healing.

DEFINITIONS

Bodymind: state of integration involving body, mind, and spirit.

General Adaptation Syndrome (GAS): activation of the hypothalamic-pituitary-adrenal axis in response to varying degrees of stress that simultaneously affect all body systems.

Information Theory: a mathematical model that helps explain many of the connections between consciousness and bodymind healing.

Limbic-Hypothalamic System: the major anatomic connecting link between the body and mind.

Mind Modulation: the natural process by which thoughts, feelings, attitudes, and emotions—neural messages—are converted in the brain into neurohormonal "messenger molecules" and sent to all body systems—autonomic, endocrine, immune, and neuropeptide. Mind modulation facilitates health or dis-health.

Natural System Theory: a model of psychobiologic unity and the interconnectedness of natural structures in the universe with a key characteristic of information flow.

Neuropeptides: messenger molecules produced at various specific sites throughout the body to transmit bodymind patterns of communication.

Neurotransmitters: chemicals that facilitate nerve transmission in the body.

Placebo: an inert substance that is taken in the form of medication or treatment to evoke a particular response; it can also be a belief or a ritual, such as a special ceremony or the wearing of a ritual piece (i.e. copper bracelet) to cure a joint problem.

Placebo Response: the healing, improvement, or recovery that a person experiences following the administration of a placebo; a person's expectation and belief are always factors in outcome of therapy and contribute to this response.

Receptors: sites on cell surfaces that serve as points of attachment for various types of messenger molecules.

Reframe: the technique of identifying undesired behavior and taking the responsibility to add or substitute more creative alternatives to replace the undesired behavior.

State-Dependent Learning: a person's psychophysiologic state at the time of the experience; all memories are dependent and limited to the state in which they were acquired.

NATURAL SYSTEMS THEORY, INFORMATION THEORY, AND TRANSDUCTION

Natural Systems Theory

Natural systems theory, which is derived primarily from the work of von Bertalanffy,[2,3] provides us with a model of psychobiologic unity. It provides a way of visualizing the interconnectedness of natural structures in the universe. The theory is complex, but has relevance to the health care professions (Figure 5-1).

In brief, as seen in Figure 5-1, natural structures of vastly different sizes from the level of subatomic particles all the way to the biosphere each possess definite characteristics at each level and are governed by similar principles of organization. The components of the hierarchy of natural systems also share similar characteristics.[4] Therefore, if one knows about the behavior of one component, one automatically knows about the behavior of all the others. Knowledge about molecules provides knowledge about tissues, organ systems, families, species, as well as all the other components that comprise the hierarchy of natural systems.

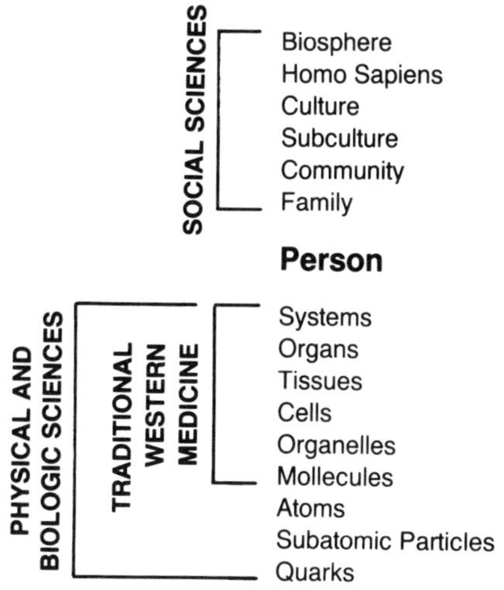

Figure 5-1 The Pattern of Natural Systems Components that Make Up Human Beings

A key characteristic of the hierarchy of natural systems is *information flow*. Information flows everywhere and is omnidirectional. Regardless of where the information originates, it spreads up and down the hierarchy. Each level can be involved, or the information flow can involve giant feedback loops that may bypass whole levels.[5] Either way, information flow has a domino effect, as the whole system is affected by information originating at any point in the system. This concept has important implications for our views of health and disease.

The traditional view of disease usually stops at the level of the organ, although it may proceed to the level of the person as shown in Figure 5-1. However, the natural systems approach gives us a more accurate way of viewing disease. Disease can result from a disturbance from the subatomic level to the suprapersonal. Health can be seen as the harmonious interaction of all the components of the natural systems hierarchy, whereas disease results when a force disturbs or disrupts the structure of the natural systems themselves.[6]

Information Theory

Information theory was developed in the late 1940s as a mathematical model for the emerging communication technologies.[7] In 1960 Black first used information theory as a conceptual base for connecting mind and biologic life.[8] Information theory appears to be capable of unifying biologic, psychological, and physiologic phenomena in a framework that helps explain many of the connections between consciousness and bodymind healing. All of the interventions described in this text are an attempt to facilitate bodymind communication by converting ideas, words, sensations, sounds, beliefs, and expectations into psychophysiologic events leading toward healing.

How is consciousness projected into various bodyparts? The bodymind can be seen as an integrated system, a *network,* with the mind being the information flow among all the body parts that holds the network together.[9] In this view, the mind is composed of information that has a physical substrate; body and the brain are composed of another immaterial substrate involving information flow, which is that process we call consciousness.

Transduction

Transduction is the conversion or transformation of energy or information from one form to another.[10] Body and mind comprise an integrated information system, and biologic, psychological, and anthropological processes can be understood as different forms of information transduction.[11] To illustrate this concept, two examples of information transduction are now given.

Energy transduction occurs when a nurse helps decrease a person's high level of anxiety before a procedure. The nurse guides the person in a relaxation and imagery exercise that involves being relaxed during the procedure, as well as visualizing the procedure going well. The suggestions are the process of transforming the idea into an act of relaxation. For example, the person is guided in relaxed abdominal breathing. The auditory nerve perceives the spoken words, and the message is sent to the motor center where it is relayed to the cortical center. The brain carries out the act of relaxed breathing as soon as it is formulated. This same sequence occurs with all the senses.

Another example of energy transduction occurs during biofeedback. A person thinks and feels relaxation states, and this transduction of information is registered via the biofeedback electrodes on a person's body. The electrodes measure a person's biologic energy in terms of muscle tension, which is then transduced into a measurement displayed on a digital meter.

Mind can be seen as nature's supreme way of receiving, generating, and transducing information.[12] The more improbable an idea or event is, the higher its informational value. Those events that are new—challenging, intriguing, and mysterious—have the highest informational value. New ideas cause bodymind changes; that is, consciousness and neural pathways connect and create information transduction.

The interventions in this text work for two reasons: (1) They facilitate mind-modulation of the autonomic, endocrine, immune, and neuropeptide systems; and (2) they are "novel stimuli" and the bodymind responds to events that have higher informational value. Traditional health care providers have dealt with the familiar hard sciences and have ignored consciousness and intuition or regarded these as less important. The interventions in this text combine proven science and intuitive knowledge. These interventions enable the client to gain information that has high informational value. One gains access to inner strengths when one experiences high informational value. Receiving new information can help people adopt more effective coping styles and strategies to stabilize or improve their quality of life. The body's response to novel information explains some of what is understood about the placebo effect.

PLACEBO EFFECT

The word "placebo" is derived from the Latin word meaning "I will please." A placebo may be an inert substance that is taken in the form of medication, or it can also be a treatment, technique, or ritual. The placebo response occurs if the person improves or if symptoms lessen. A person experiences a change (physical, mental, psychological, or spiritual), although medical science cannot explain scientifically the results, other than "the natural course of the disease or symptom/s."

The placebo response also is affected by one's positive or negative attitudes and emotions toward wellness and healing. Attitudes and emotions move us toward healing or in the opposite direction to the extreme of death. For example, a person may believe that touching or breathing a certain substance will cause a bad response, and indeed the "bad response" occurs. On the other hand, a person might believe that touching something before an event will cause a good response, and indeed the "good response" occurs.

Placebo medications are supposedly unable to cause electrochemical changes in the body. However, when a person gets better or symptoms disappear or lessen following a placebo medication, electrochemical changes *have* occurred within the body. When the client receives a placebo medication or treatments with the belief that they will help, the psychoneuroimmunologic responses and the way the medication is metabolized within the body are different than if the person dreads the medication or treatment.[13] The placebo response is evidence that a suggestion can be translated into changes at the cellular level. Each person has remarkable power and wisdom to effect bodymind changes; the challenge is to enhance this ability. One can think of the placebo as the healer that resides within. However, this innate wisdom can become blocked by negative stress, denial, or depression.

Many researchers and clinicians believe that a placebo stimulates an innate, automatic bodymind communication by using a person's resources to reduce anxiety and fear and by incorporating cultural beliefs and expectation of healing. A review of carefully controlled experimental research studies using a double-blind design concluded that there is a consistent 55 percent placebo response of the therapeutic effect for all the analgesic drugs studied.[14–16] This finding suggests a communication link between the mind and body. Many researchers believe that the limbic-hypothalamic system is the anatomic structure responsible for the placebo response.

The nurse's attitude has a marked influence on drug, treatment, and expectation effectiveness. Therefore, the nurse should perform all nursing interventions with awareness of eliciting the placebo response in clients. Placebos provide pain relief and can serve as a bodymind healing factor because clients' beliefs and expectations directly influence treatments, procedures, and recovery from illness. They need to be informed how medications work, not only for correct use and safety but also to enhance the drug effect via the placebo response. Though not clearly understood, client faith in the medication directly influences the placebo response.

To elicit the placebo response in clients, the nurse should follow these guidelines[17]:

- Avoid using placebos to determine if a person's pain is real or "in the person's imagination."
- Avoid using placebos to determine pain severity.
- Avoid using placebos to judge a person's personality, suggestibility, or psychopathology.
- Avoid assuming that the psychological reactions occurring after a drug is given must be due to the drug. Side effects may be due to the placebo response.
- Avoid dispensing medication as though it were a mundane chore.

STATE-DEPENDENT LEARNING

What is learned and remembered is dependent on one's psychophysiologic state at the time of the experience and is referred to as *state-dependent learning*. Our memories are state-dependent because they are dependent upon and limited to the state in which they were acquired.[18] Thoughts that we experience in our daily routines are habitual patterns of state-dependent memories joined together by associative connections.

State-dependent learning plays a major role in mind-body healing and hypnosis, although most learning theories do not integrate memory and bodymind relationships. However, in his review of the state-dependent learning literature from 1855-1987, Rossi does connect it with discoveries of molecular biology and psychoneuroimmunology. Four integrated hypotheses can be made about the relationship of memory to bodymind relationships.[19]

1. The limbic-hypothalamic system is the major anatomic connecting link between mind and body.
2. State-dependent memory, learning, and behavior processes encoded in the limbic-hypothalamic and closely related systems are the major information transducers between mind and body.
3. All methods of mind-body healing and therapeutic hypnosis operate by gaining access to and reframing the state-dependent memory and learning systems that encode symptoms and problems.
4. The state-dependent encoding of mind-body symptoms and problems can be reached by psychological as well as physiologic approaches—and the placebo response is a synergistic interaction of both.

Within the limbic-hypothalamic system are patterns of both positive and negative emotions. The fundamental task for each healer is to help activate a person's psychophysiologic resources to evoke painful memories that need to be healed, along with joyful experiences, memories of health and general well-being, creative work, and effective coping patterns. In gaining access to the raw material of one's inner resources, these imagery patterns can be reframed into patterns that may modulate positive changes at the biochemical levels within the cells. Let us now explore where these brain centers are and how modulation occurs.

WHERE ARE THE BRAIN CENTERS?

The brain, according to the traditional way of viewing it, is located in the skull. Current thinking, however, holds that brain centers are found throughout the body.[20] The greatest resistance to the idea that information is stored throughout the brain and body comes from the stubborn insistence that specific brain regions control specific physiologic and psychological functions. A more accurate way of understanding brain function is to use the model of a hologram.

A hologram is a specially processed photographic record that provides a three-dimensional image when a laser is beamed through it. If any part of it should be destroyed, any of the remaining parts is capable of reconstructing the whole image.[21] The brain operates like a hologram. This model does not contradict the traditional model, but adds to it a new method of considering how information is transmitted, stored, and received.

By viewing brain centers in a holographic manner, one can see their omnipotent influence on psychophysiologic function.[22] This concept is important when challenging belief systems about health and illness. If people do not believe they have the conscious ability to effect a physical change with their imagination, they may never try to do so. They will not sort through memories and patterns of past experience and will continue to keep responding in the same manner indefinitely.

There are conflicts between the traditional neuroanatomic model and information theory and mind modulation. If we are to use bodymind interventions effectively, it is important to review these conflicts.

These elements of the traditional neuroanatomic model contradict current data on brain functioning[23]:

- Memories do not seem to be stored in any single area, but rather in multiple overlapping areas. Loss of specific memory is related more to the amount of brain damage than to location and damage.
- The ability to remember that is lost initially, when the brain is damaged by gunshot wounds, tumors, or cardiovascular accident (stroke), often returns, even though specific neural regeneration is not believed to be possible.
- Paranormal events, which involve receiving, processing, and sending information in ways that do not conform to our understanding of energy transfer, are not explainable by the current knowledge of neuronanatomy. This includes the transpersonal healing imagery typically related with shamanic work and with psychic or metaphysical healers.
- Such phenomena as phantom limb sensations, persistent phantom pain, and "auras" extending beyond the corporal self (as seen in Kirlian photographs) call into question the storage of body image, as well as what constitutes physical boundaries of the body.
- If only one bit of information is processed per second by the brain, 3×10^{10} nerve impulses per second would be required by the current model of memory storage—an inconceivable amount of neural activity.
- The mechanisms of consciousness, or the ability of the brain to consider itself or create or retrieve images, elude description in terms of the sheer knowledge of structures and their function as presented in the anatomic models.

To further understand the new information of mind modulation, the channels of bodymind communication via the autonomic, endocrine immune, and neuropeptide systems are now discussed. Credit is given to Rossi for the title of mind modulation as it relates to these systems.

MIND MODULATION OF THE AUTONOMIC NERVOUS SYSTEM

Mind modulates the biochemical functions within the major organ systems through the autonomic nervous system as shown in Figure 5-2. The process of mind modulation of cellular activities by the autonomic nervous system has three stages[24]:

1. Images and thoughts are generated in the frontal cortex.
2. Images and thoughts are transmitted through the state-dependent memory learning and emotional areas of the limbic-hypothalamic system to the neurotransmitters that regulate the organs of the autonomic nervous system branches.
3. The neurotransmitters—norepinephrine (sympathetic branch) and acetylcholine (parasympathetic branch)—initiate the information transduction that activates the biochemical changes within the different tissues down to the cellular level. Neurotransmitters act as messenger molecules. They cross the nerve cell junc-

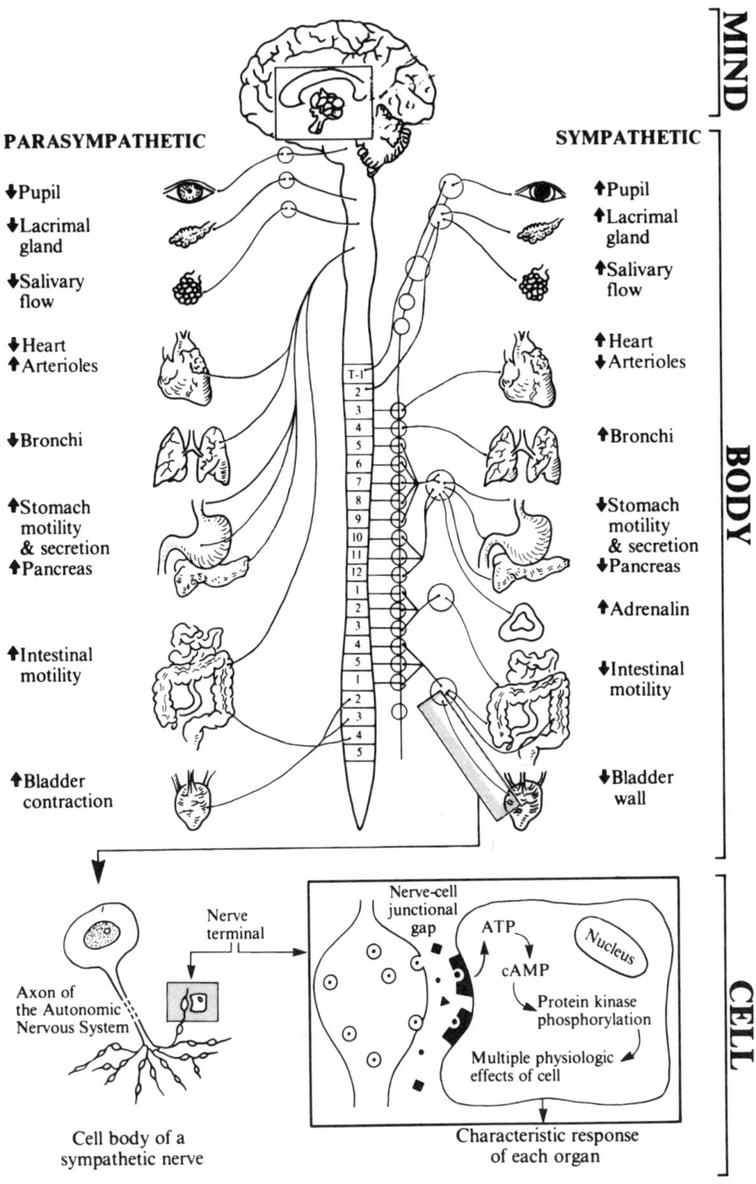

Figure 5-2 Bodymind Communication: Mind Modulation of the Autonomic Nervous System and Its Two Branches, the Sympathetic and the Parasympathetic, down to the Cellular Level. *Source:* Reproduced from *The Psychobiology of Mind-Body Healing* by Ernest Lawrence Rossi by permission of W.W. Norton & Company, Inc. Copyright © 1986 by Ernest Lawrence Rossi.

tional gap and fit onto receptors found in the cell walls, thus changing the receptor molecular structure. This causes a change in cell wall permeability and a shift of such ions as sodium, potassium, and calcium. The basic metabolism of each cell is also changed by a series of hundreds of complex activations of cell enzymes that are the second messenger system.

These three stages give us a better understanding of how different behavioral therapies work. When clients are taught to use relaxation, imagery, music therapy, or hypnosis, their sympathetic response to stress is reduced and the calming effects of the parasympathetic system take over. Exhibit 5-1 lists some of the areas of mind modulation of blood flow to various body parts and body cells that have occurred by using these interventions.

MIND MODULATION OF THE ENDOCRINE SYSTEM

The endocrine system is responsible for the secretion of hormones and the regulation of these hormones throughout the body, as seen in Figure 5-3. Stimulation of the senses results in activation of specific hormones. Research into how hormones, sensation, and perception are integrated with thought and behavior has found that hormones released by sensory stimulation act to modulate the strength of memory of the sensory experience. In addition, central modulating influences on memory in the limbic system interact with influences of the peripheral hormones.[25]

The central concept of neuroendocrinology is neurosecretion: the transduction of information of the limbic-hypothalamic system into somatic processes of the body via the pituitary and endocrine system.[26] Thoughts from the limbic system excite or inhibit the neural impulses of the cerebral cortex and are converted into pituitary regulation by

Exhibit 5-1 Mind Modulation of Blood Flow to Various Body Parts and Body Cells

- Warming and cooling different parts of the body for treatment of different types of headaches
- Controlling blushing and blanching of the skin
- Stimulating the enlargement and apparent growth of breasts in women
- Stimulating sexual excitation and penile erection
- Ameliorating bruises
- Controlling bleeding in surgery
- Minimizing and healing burns
- Producing local skin inflammation similar to previously experienced burns
- Ameliorating congenital ichthyosis
- Aiding coagulation of blood in hemophiliac patients
- Ameliorating hypertension and cardiac problems
- Ameliorating Raynaud's disease
- Enhancing the immune function

Source: The Psychobiology of Mind-Body Healing by E.L. Rossi, p. 110, W.W. Norton & Company, Inc., © 1986.

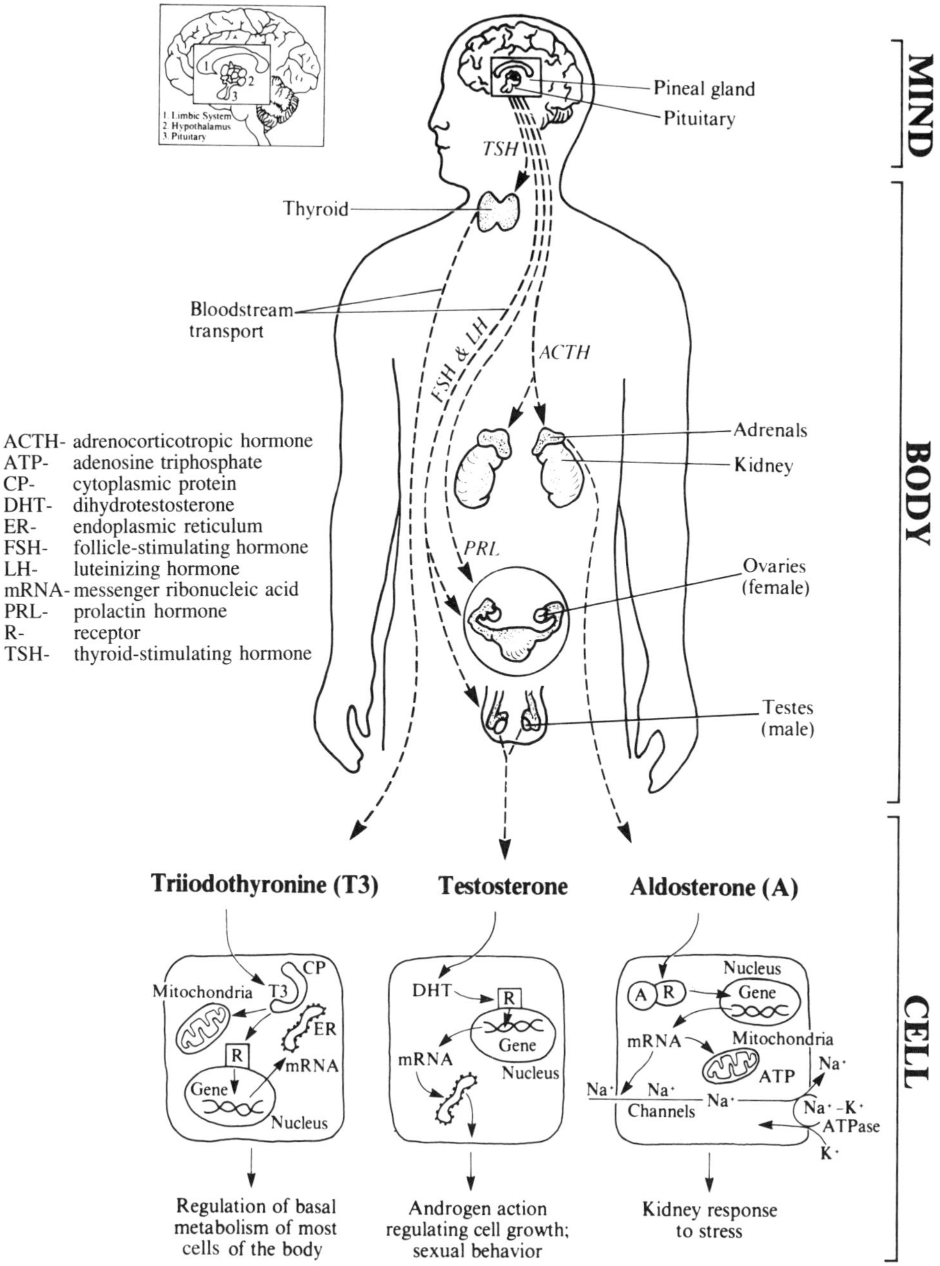

Figure 5-3 Bodymind Communication: Mind Modulation of the Endocrine System, with Three Examples at the Cellular Level of the Mind/Gene/Molecule Connection. *Source:* Reproduced from *The Psychobiology of Mind-Body Healing* by Ernest Lawrence Rossi by permission of W.W. Norton & Company, Inc. Copyright © 1986 by Ernest Lawrence Rossi.

the influence of the hypothalamus. This understanding is the basis for the inclusion of psychobiology as a branch of information theory.[27] This information gives scientific support to the importance of right brain hemisphere exercises that help a person tap into self-healing.

The most recent discoveries in the field of endocrinology are the pituitary hormones—*endorphins* and *enkephalins,*—that influence modulation of stress, pain, perception, addictions, appetite, learning and memory, and work and sports performance, to name a few areas.[28] Exhibit 5-2 lists some of the hormones that act on the cell receptors of the brain and body.

The endorphins are so new that they do not yet have a physiologic classification. The endorphin system may represent a new division of the autonomic nervous system.[29] Endorphins have been discovered throughout the body—in the brain, spinal cord, and the enteric system (gastrointestinal tract). The enteric tract, which is responsible for the internal regulation of the stomach and intestines, is considered by some researchers to be a third branch of the autonomic nervous system.[30] This may explain why people feel their emotions in their gut.

Exhibit 5-2 Hormones That Have Bodymind Function

Corticotropin Releasing Factor (CRF): A hypothalamic hormone that mediates pituitary release of ACTH, which stimulates the adrenal cortex to release cortisol into the bloodstream.

New Data: Receptor sites for CRF and ACTH in brain cells that can mediate stress-like behaviors and such psychological variables as attentiveness, memory, and learning have been identified.

Cholecystokinin (CCK): A hormone that is active from the throat to the small intestines, which modulates gall bladder contraction, the pancreatic enzyme, and motility of the gastrointestinal tract.

New Data: CCK receptor sites are found in the brain. This is important information for therapies for obesity because it suggests a psychobiologic route by which mind may modulate appetite. CCK also may mediate the so-called gut feelings.

Insulin: A hormone secreted by the pancreas that affects carbohydrate metabolism by increasing the uptake of glucose by cardiac, muscle, liver, and adipose tissue.

New Data: Insulin receptor sites are located in the brain. This indicates that insulin modulates eating behavior by direct effects on cerebral capillaries.

Gonadotropin-Releasing Hormone (GnRH): A hormone released by the hypothalamus that stimulates the release of pituitary hormones, such as gonadotropin,luteinizing hormone (LH), and follicle-stimulating hormone (FSH), which stimulate growth and regulate sexual processes.

New Data: When receptors in the brain of rats are activated by GnRH, they show sexual posturing.

Vasopressin or Antidiuretic Hormone (ADH): Hormone released from the posterior pituitary when it receives appropriate posterior signals from the hypothalamus. Vasopressin regulates kidney action, water balance, and urine flow.

New Data: ADH also acts as a vasoconstrictor in blood flow regulation, especially the splanchnic circulatory system. With cell receptor stimulation, vasopressin has been found to enhance memory and learning. A relationship has been demonstrated between circadian rhythms and ADH levels in cerebrospinal fluid. Thus, memory and learning may be related to fluctuations in ADH's access to many different types of brain tissue.

Sources: The Journal of Immunology, Vol. 135, No. 2., pp. 820-826, Plenum Press, © 1986; *The Psychobiology of Mind-Body Healing* by E.L. Rossi, p. 128., W.W. Norton & Company, Inc., © 1986.

Other scientists feel that endorphins are not a branch of the autonomic system but are definitely part of the endocrine system. In support of this stance they note that the major biosynthesis of one of the major endorphins (beta-endorphin) and enkephalins (meta-enkephalin) occur in the same mother molecule as the adrenocorticotropic hormone (ACTH) in the anterior pituitary.[31] They are both released in response to stress and circadian and ultradian rhythms.

All of the body's major systems—the autonomic, endocrine, immune, and neuropeptide systems—are communication channels whereby the person's thoughts and images activate the genetic material and cellular structures to reorganize according to new information to help a person toward healing.

THE MIND-GENE CONNECTION

Genes are in dynamic equilibrium with cellular metabolism. Changes in the genetic material are modulated by the messenger molecules, the hormones and neurotransmitters. The transduction of information in the mind-gene process has three stages[32]:

1. Stage 1 involves the frontal cortex. Images and life experiences from the frontal cortex are encoded into the state-dependent memory of the limbic-hypothalamic system.
2. Stage 2 involves transduction. The state-dependent memory is transduced by the hypothalamus into the hormone-releasing factors that regulate the pituitary gland. This sets up a cascade of hormones that then affect the entire endocrine system.
3. Stage 3 occurs at the cellular level where hormones are stimulated or pass directly to the cell nucleus that activates the mind-gene process.

These three stages can be illustrated by reviewing the action of the adrenal hormone, aldosterone. In response to psychophysiologic stress (Stage 1), aldosterone is secreted and acts at many sites. Within the cytoplasm of the renal tubule cells, a specific receptor protein binds with aldosterone, carrying it to the genes to produce new proteins (Stage 2). These new proteins promote sodium reabsorption from the tubules and potassium secretion, the "sodium-potassium pump," within a brief 45-minute period (Stage 3).[33]

MIND MODULATION OF THE IMMUNE SYSTEM

The immune system is the third major regulatory system of the body. In the new discipline of psychoneuroimmunology (PNI), researchers investigate how the brain affects the body's immune cells. The brain sends signals along nerves to enhance defenses against infection and make the body fight more aggressively against disease. Figure 5-4 illustrates mind modulation of the immune system.

Researchers have identified actual psychophysiologic mechanisms whereby the hypothalamus can change both cellular and humoral immune activity in its anterior and posterior nuclei. Receptor sites, located on the surfaces of the T and B lymphocytes, have the ability to activate, direct, and modify immune function. They are described as

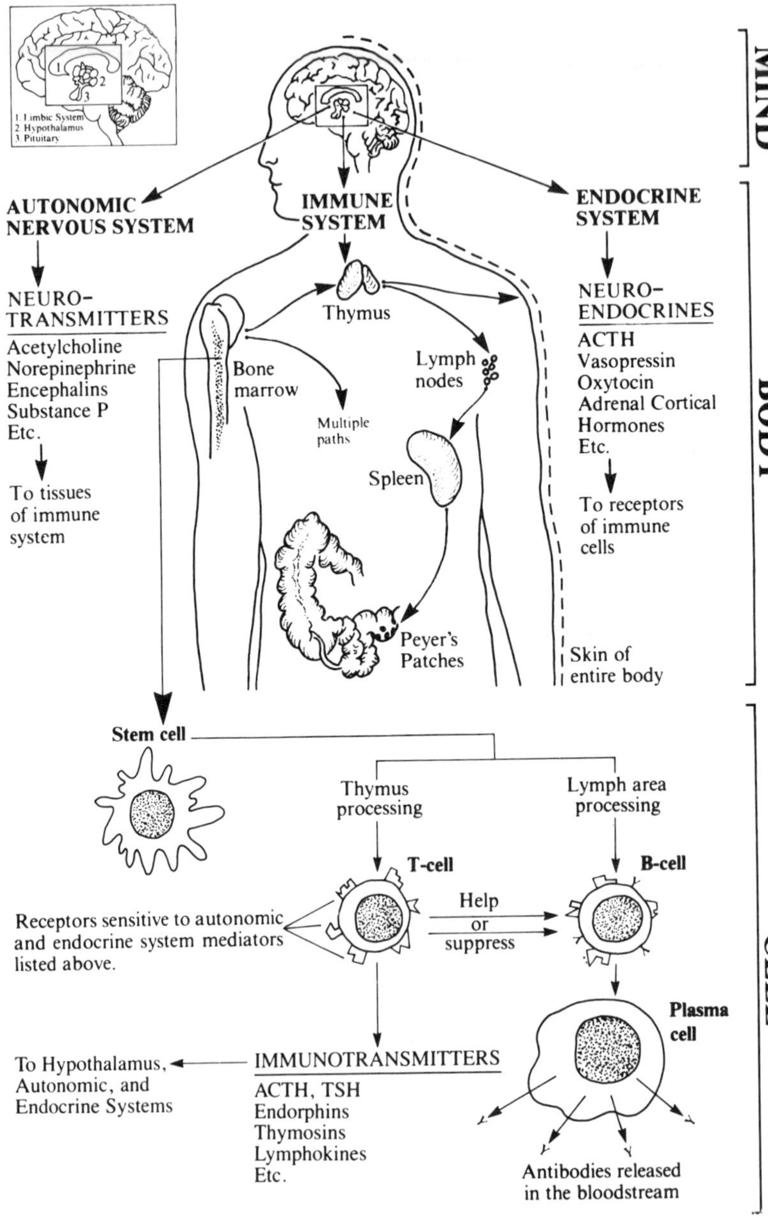

Figure 5-4 Bodymind Communications: Mind Modulation of the Immune System by Neurotransmitters of the Autonomic Nervous System and Hormones of the Endocrine System That Communicate with the Immune System; the Immunotransmitters That Communicate with These Systems Are Shown. *Source:* Reproduced from *The Psychobiology of Mind-Body Healing* by Ernest Lawrence Rossi by permission of W.W. Norton & Company, Inc. Copyright © 1986 by Ernest Lawrence Rossi.

being like locks (the receptors) and keys (neurotransmitters) that open and turn on the activity of each system.

None of the body systems is separate from the other, for images and stressors perceived by the person's mind are transduced to the messenger molecules—the neurotransmitters of the autonomic nervous system and the hormones of the endocrine system. Recent evidence from PNI researchers shows that there is a bidirectional information circuitry operating between the immune system and the autonomic and endocrine systems. It is also known that the three systems can modulate the activity of each other.[34]

Six types of experimental data provide support for mind-modulating influences of the immune system.[35]

1. The neuroanatomic and neurochemical evidence for the innervation of lymphoid tissue (bone marrow, thymus, spleen, tonsils, Peyer's patches, lymph nodes, etc.) by the central nervous system. This means that mind by way of the central nervous system has direct neural access for modulating all these organs of the immune system.
2. The observations that inhibiting or stimulating the hypothalamus changes immunologic reactivity and, conversely, that activation of an immune response in the body results in measurable changes within the hypothalmus. Because the hypothalamus is regulated by higher brain centers (via connections with the limbic cortex), these intercommunications between the immune system and hypothalamus may be open to mind modulation.
3. The findings that lymphocytes bear receptors for hormones of the endocrine system and neurotransmitters of the autonomic nervous system. Therefore, all the mind-modulating effects of the autonomic and endocrine systems may be communicated to the immune system as well. This conclusion is also supported by the next point.
4. Evidence that alterations in hormone and neurotransmitter function modify immunologic reactivity and, conversely, that elicitation of an immune response is accompanied by changes in hormonal and neurotransmitter levels.
5. Data documenting the effect of behavioral interventions, including conditioning on various parameters of immune function.
6. Experimental and clinical studies in which psychological factors, such as stress and depression, have been found to influence the onset of disease processes.

Researchers are able to demonstrate that people can be taught to modulate the immune system with certain biobehavioral interventions. For example, persons with cancer can be taught to reframe how they imagine their cancer cells. Instead of visualizing the cancer cells as strong and invading healthy body structures, they are taught to visualize them as weak and confused. These relaxation and imagery interventions seem to work, because they facilitate the inner healer, the innate wisdom that resides within a person. In Chapter 12 references and a detailed discussion of the imagery process are provided.

MIND MODULATION OF THE NEUROPEPTIDE SYSTEM

Neuropeptides and their receptors are one key to understanding the bodymind interconnections and how emotions are experienced throughout the body. Figure 5-5 shows focal areas of the neuropeptide communicating system.

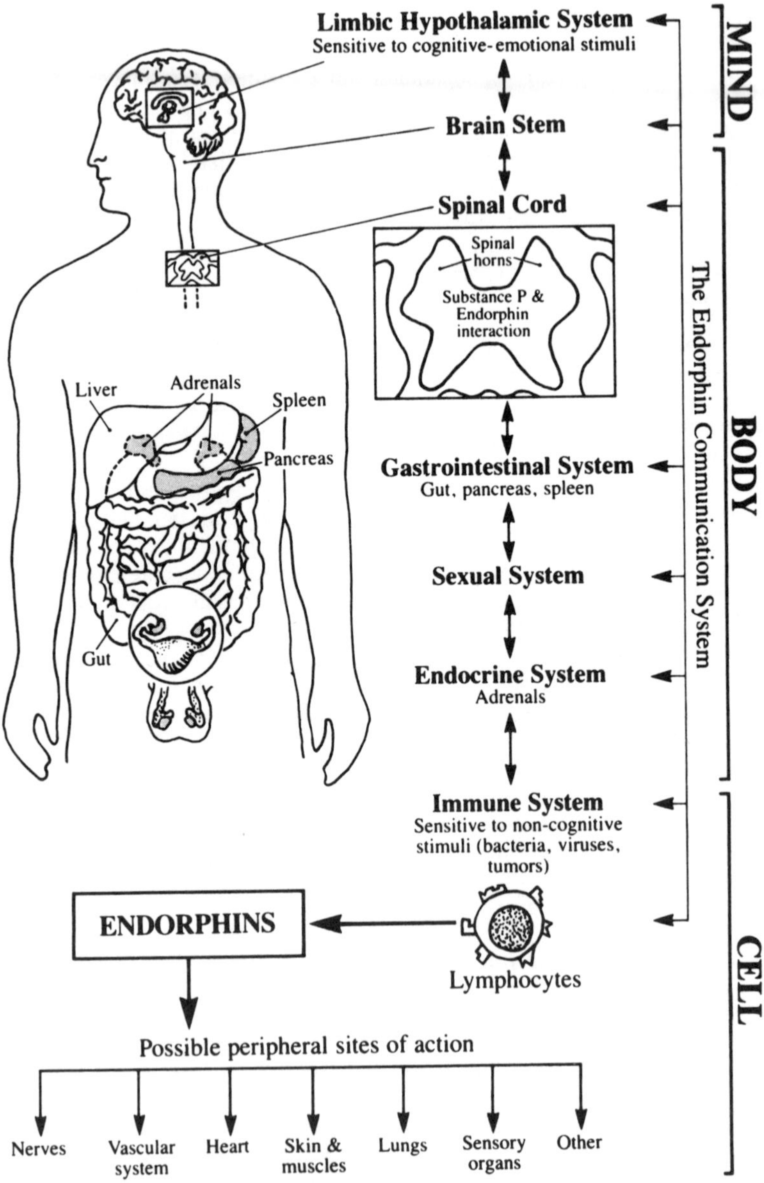

Figure 5-5 Bodymind Communication: The Nodal or Focal Areas of the Neuropeptide Communication System, with the Endorphin Neuropeptide in Bodymind Regulation Indicated. *Source:* Reproduced from *The Psychobiology of Mind-Body Healing* by Ernest Lawrence Rossi by permission of W.W. Norton & Company, Inc. Copyright © 1986 by Ernest Lawrence Rossi.

Neuropeptides are amino acids produced in the brain, and when they lock into their receptor sites (distinct classes of recognition molecules), they can facilitate or block a response.[36] Beta endorphin was the first neuropeptide discovered. It is called a neuropeptide because it is produced in brain nerve cells and consists of peptides. Beta endorphins have also recently been found in the pituitary and the gonads.[37] Approximately 50-60 additional neuropeptides have been discovered that are as specific as beta endorphin. These neuropeptides come directly from the body's DNA. It is now known that neuropeptides are located and circulate throughout the body. The information transfer occurs due to the specificity of the receptor sites found in the body.

Pert refers to the communication of the neuropeptide system as the "informational substrate."[38] The autonomic, endocrine, and immune systems, which form a complex bidirectional network of communication, are the channel carriers for the neuropeptides, the messenger molecules responsible for connecting body and emotions. The neuropeptides integrate all of these systems.

The receptor sites for the neuropeptides can be seen as the keys to the biochemistry of emotions. The limbic system regulates the emotions and the body physiology. When Pert and her team began mapping opiate receptor sites with radioactive molecules, they found that the limbic system had 40 times the number of opiate receptor sites than any other area of the brain.[39]

Traditionally hormones were thought to be produced only by glands and not nerve cells. New mapping techniques, which locate the site of action of neuropeptides through radioactive labeling, have recently detected hormones in the brain.[40]

These new data have changed our view of the neuropeptides. Insulin was thought to be produced by the pancreas and to flow from the pancreas to specific receptor sites. Now it is known that it is produced and stored in the brain and that insulin receptor sites are present in the brain. Angiotensin receptors are found not only in the kidney but also in the brain. The release of the neuropeptide angiotensin leads to behaviors that increase water consumption and water conservation.

Other receptor sites, called *nodal* points, have been found outside of the brain.[41] Nodal points are located in places that receive significant emotional modulation; for example, the dorsal (back) horn of the spinal cord. The dorsal horn is where sensory information comes in and is transmitted to and processed by the brain.

The cells of the immune system travel around and interact with the neuropeptides. Monocytes, the scavenger cells that ingest foreign substances, are also responsible for wound healing and tissue repair mechanisms.[42] In addition, monocytes have receptor sites for opiates and other neuropeptides. Every neuropeptide receptor located by mapping has been found on human monocytes.[43] Monocytes circulate in the body, communicating with T and B cells, identifying foreign substances, and locating areas needing repair. These monocytes not only have receptor sites but they can also make neuropeptides. This means that these monocytes make the chemicals that control mood and tissue integrity. Thus, we see the anatomy and physiology of bodymind connections.

The gut is another example of bodymind connection. The enteric nervous system operates the gastrointestinal system in a semi-independent manner. The entire tract from the esophagus to the anus is lined with cells containing neuropeptides and receptor sites. When people say that they have a "gut feeling" it can now be demonstrated that this emotion indeed resides in the gut.[44]

Currently, neuropeptide research is focused in the following six areas:[45]

1. limbic-hypothalamic locus of neuropeptide activity
2. brainstem and spinal cord locus of neuropeptide activity
3. immune integration by the neuropeptides
4. endocrine system integration by the neuropeptides
5. enteric nervous system
6. sexual system and neuropeptide activity

WHAT NEXT?

New data from the neurosciences are rapidly emerging, and we must use this information to guide our theory, diagnoses, clinical practice, and the development of new forms of therapy. It is becoming clearer that we have the ability within our bodies for the brain, endocrine, and immune systems to talk to each other. This new information helps us understand how visualization and hypnosis works via information transduction, information theory, and mind modulation with the different body systems. The therapies are grounded in science. We must continue to refine the processes and techniques for specific modulation of bodymind symptoms.

These new data invalidate Western idea of consciousness residing within the brain.[46] Rather, consciousness can be projected to various body parts—the brain, the glands, and the immune, enteric system and sexual systems. Bidirectional communication exists for each of these areas and their organs.

Questions and speculations yet to be answered include:

- Can the mind survive the physical death of the brain?
- Where does the information go after the destruction of the molecules and the tissue mass that composed it?

Because matter can neither be created nor destroyed, it is possible that biologic information flow may not disappear at death, but rather is transformed into another form. No scientist can say this is impossible, because no mathematical formula has unified gravitational field theory with matter and energy.[47]

According to Dossey,

> We will never achieve the validation of our spiritual intuitions by scrutinizing monocytes, neuropeptides, and receptor sites. What we will achieve is an expanded view of what it means to be human. The point that we will continue to emphasize is that the physiological and the spiritual are not equivalent, and if we ignore the difference between these two domains it will be at the risk of our spiritual impoverishment.
>
> These scientific insights are important signposts pointing to the nonlocal nature of consciousness. They get the mind out of the brain and into the body at large. Any science that helps us toward this understanding—which is con-

tained in the sublimest visions of the most acute seers of our race—deserves, I would submit, our deepest respects."*

SUMMARY

This chapter has explored the scientific data on the psychophysiology of bodymind healing. Mind modulation of the autonomic, endocrine, immune, and neuropeptide systems was reviewed. The ideas of natural systems theory and information theory were also developed as a theoretical basis for bodymind healing. This information gives nurses insight into why placebos and the techniques in this text are enhanced when performed from a natural systems frame of reference.

DIRECTIONS FOR FUTURE RESEARCH

1. Examine the scientific basis for study of client behavior and evaluation of nursing care specific to the stress response.
2. Investigate effective ways for nurses and clients to learn to modulate stress.
3. Evaluate learning strategies in order to teach clients how to gain access to, reframe, and use their own unique inner repertoire of psychophysiologic resources that can ultimately lead to bodymind healing.

NURSE HEALER REFLECTIONS

After reading this chapter, the nurse healer will be able to answer or begin a process of answering the following questions:

- What do I *experience* and *understand* about myself on days when I am *"going with the flow"* or when I am *"out of sync?"*
- Do I *listen* to the *inner wisdom* of my own *human factors* daily?
- When do I *allow* time for *self-reflection* in order to increase my *creativity* and *spirituality*?
- In what ways do I *recognize* my *bodymind connections*?
- How can I be *aware* of and *expand* my view of what it *means* to be human?

**Source*: Keynote Address, First Annual Conference on Aids, Medicine, and Miracles. "Aids: A Transpersonal Perspective," Boulder, CO, March 5, 1988.

NOTES

1. Candace Pert, "The Wisdom of the Receptors: Neuropeptides, the Emotions, and Bodymind," *Advances* 3, no. 3 (Summer 1986): 8–16.
2. Larry Dossey, *Space, Time and Medicine* (Boston: Shambhala Publications, Inc., 1982), pp. 98–101.
3. Ludwig von Bertalanffy, *General Systems Theory* (New York: George Braziller, Inc., 1968), pp. 1–20.
4. Ervin Lazlo, *The Systems View of the World* (New York: George Braziller, Inc., 1972), pp. 42–37.
5. Larry Dossey, "Care Giving and Natural Systems," *Topics In Clinical Nursing* 3, no. 4 (January 1982): 24–25.
6. Howard Brody, "The Systems View of Man: Implications for Medicine, Science, and Ethics," *Perspectives in Biology and Medicine* 17, no. 1 (1973): 71–92.
7. C. Shannon and W. Weaver, *The Mathematical Theory of Communication* (Urbana, IL: University of Illinois Press, 1949), pp. 1–20.
8. S. Black, *Mind and Body* (London: William Kimber, 1969), pp. 1–34.
9. Candace Pert, "The Wisdom of the Receptors: Neuropeptides, the Emotions, and Bodymind," p. 14.
10. Ernest L. Rossi, *The Psychobiology of Mind-Body Healing,* p. 36.
11. Ibid., p. 34.
12. Ibid., p. 23.
13. Jeanne Achterberg, *Imagery In Healing* (Boston: Shambhala Publishers, Inc., 1985), pp. 48–87.
14. Ernest L. Rossi, *The Psychobiology of Mind-Body Healing,* p. 18.
15. Ibid., p. 16.
16. F. Evans, "Expectancy, Therapeutic Instruction, and the Placebo Response," in L. White, B. Tursky, and G. Schwartz, eds., *Placebo: Theory,* R
17. S. Perry and G. Heidrich, "Placebo Responses: Myth and Matter," *American Journal of Nursing* 81, no. 4 (April, 1981): 720.
18. Ernest L. Rossi, *The Psychobiology of Mind-Body Healing,* pp. 36–37.
19. Ibid., p. 55.
20. Larry Dossey, *Meaning and Medicine: A Doctor's Tales of Breakthrough and Healing* (New York: Bantam Books, 1991): pp. 190–191.
21. Karl Pribram, *Languages of the Brain* (Monterey, CA: Brooks/Cole Publishing Co., 1971): pp. 5–11.
22. Jeanne Achterberg, *Imagery and Healing,* p. 134.
23. Jeanne Achterberg, *Imagery and Healing,* p. 131.
24. Ernest L. Rossi, *The Psychobiology of Mind-Body Healing,* p. 107.
25. J. McGaugh, "Preserving the Presence of the Past: Hormonal influences on memory storage," *American Psychologist* 3, no. 2 (1983): 163–164.
26. Ernest L. Rossi, *The Psychobiology of Mind-Body Healing,* p. 104.
27. Ibid., p. 104.
28. J. Davis, *Endorphins* (New York: Dial Press, 1984): pp. 26–31.
29. Candace B. Pert, "The Wisdom of the Receptors: Neuropeptides, the Emotions, and Bodymind," p. 11.
30. Ibid., p. 14.
31. Ibid., p. 12.
32. Ernest L. Rossi, *The Psychobiology of Mind-Body Healing,* p. 130.
33. Ibid., p. 132.
34. Candace B. Pert, " The Wisdom of the Receptors: Neuropeptides, the Emotions, and Bodymind," p. 14.
35. Ernest L. Rossi, *The Psychobiology of Mind-Body Healing,* pp. 153–154.
36. Jeanne Achterberg, *Imagery and Healing,* p. 46.
37. Candace B. Pert, "The Wisdom of the Receptors: Neuropeptides, the Emotions, and Bodymind," p. 14.

38. Ibid., p. 14.
39. Ibid., p. 11.
40. Ernest L. Rossi, *The Psychobiology of Mind-Body Healing*, p. 182.
41. Ibid., p. 184.
42. Jeanne Achterberg, *Imagery and Healing*, pp. 161–172.
43. Candace B. Pert, "The Wisdom of the Receptors: Neuropeptides, the Emotions, and Bodymind," p. 14.
44. Ibid., p. 14.
45. Ernest L. Rossi, *The Psychobiology of Mind-Body Healing*, pp. 183–189.
46. Candace B. Pert, "The Wisdom of the Receptors: Neuropeptides, the Emotions, and Bodymind," p. 16.
47. Ibid., p. 16.

SUGGESTED READINGS

Achterberg, Jeanne, and Lawlis, G. Frank. *Bridges of the Bodymind*. Champaign, IL: Institute of Personality and Ability Testing, 1980.

Achterberg, Jeanne, and Lawlis, G. Frank. *Imagery and Disease*. Champaign, IL: Institute of Personality and Ability Testing, 1984.

Ader, Robert. *Psychoneuroimmunology*. New York: Academic Press, 1981.

Dembroski, Theodore M.; Schmidt, Thomas H.; and Blumchen, Gerhard. *Biobehavioral Bases of Coronary Heart Disease*. Basel, Switzerland: Karger, 1983.

Haskell, Robert, "Cognition and Dream Research," *The Journal of Mind and Behavior* 7 (1986): 131–161.

Hornig-Rohan, Mady, and Locke, Steven. *Psychological and Behavioral Treatments for Disorders of the Heart and Blood Vessels: An Annotated Bibliography*. New York: Institute for the Advancement of Health, 1985.

Locke, Steven. *Psychological and Behavioral Treatments for Disorders Associated with the Immune System: An Annotated Bibliography*. New York: Institute for the Advancement of Health, 1986.

Locke, Steven, and Hornig-Rohan, Mady. *Mind and Immunity: Behavioral Immunology: An Annotated Bibliography*. New York: Institute for the Advancement of Health, 1983.

unit **III**

Theory and Practice of Holistic Nursing

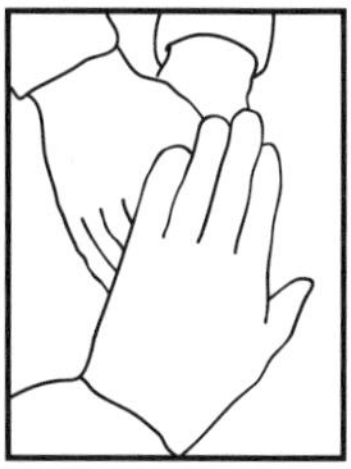

We put thirty spokes together and call it a wheel;
But it is on the space where there is nothing that the usefulness of the wheel depends.
We turn clay to make a vessel;
But it is on the space where there is nothing that the usefulness of the vessel depends.
We pierce doors and windows to make a house;
And it is on these spaces where there is nothing that the usefulness of the house depends.
Therefore just as we take advantage of what is, we should recognize the usefulness of what is not.

Lao Tsu

Source: Lao Tsu, *Tao Te Ching* (New York: Vintage Books, 1972).

Nursing Process and Standards of Care

Cathie E. Guzzetta

> The human care process between a nurse and another individual is a special, delicate gift to be cherished. The human care transactions provide a coming together and establishment of contact between persons: one's mind-body-soul engages with another's mind-body-soul in a lived moment. The shared moment of the present has the potential to transcend time and space and the physical, concrete world as we generally view it in the traditional nurse-patient relationship.[1]
>
> *Jean Watson, RN, PhD, FAAN*
> *Professor and Dean*
> *University of Colorado Health Science Center*

This chapter discusses each step of the nursing process as the link between the nursing process, theory, and standards of care is explored from a holistic perspective. In addition, this chapter provides the basis for understanding the nursing process content found within each chapter in Part IV and guides the reader in operationalizing the steps involved in providing holistic nursing care.

NURSE HEALER OBJECTIVES

Theoretical

1. Define the term "nursing process."
2. Outline the steps of the nursing process.
3. Discuss how conceptual models of nursing guide the nursing process.
4. Discuss how standards of care are incorporated into the nursing process.
5. Contrast the old and new paradigms of the nursing process.

Clinical

1. Analyze the assessment tool you are using in clinical practice to determine whether the tool is based on a nursing point of view.

2. Identify whether you are using Taxonomy I for the current classification of accepted nursing diagnoses.
3. Incorporate wellness diagnoses into your client problem lists.
4. Carry out the nursing process by incorporating the Standards for Holistic Nursing and Person-Centered Caring.

Personal

1. Learn to develop and trust your intuitive thinking processes when assessing clients.
2. Notice the impact of intuitive thinking in both your professional and personal life.
3. Explore your own beliefs and values regarding concepts of holistic nursing.
4. Write down specific examples of how you practice holistic nursing when providing care at each step of the nursing process.

DEFINITIONS

Intuition: immediately knowing about something without consciously using reason.

Nursing Diagnosis: cluster of signs/symptoms describing actual or potential health problems that nurses, because of their education and experience, are licensed and able to treat.

Nursing Process: steps used to fulfill the purposes of nursing; includes assessment, diagnosis, client outcomes, plans, intervention, and evaluation.

Paradigm: a model for conceptualizing information.

Standards of Care: criteria developed to define and establish the scope of nursing practice.

Taxonomy I: a classification schema for the organization of the accepted list of nursing diagnoses based on the nine human response patterns of the Unitary Person Framework.

Unitary Person Framework: framework created by the North American Nursing Diagnosis Association to guide the identification and development of nursing diagnoses.

NURSING PROCESS

In 1967 the nursing process was conceptualized as having four steps: assessment, planning, implementation, and evaluation.[2] Today, the nursing process has been incorporated into academic and clinical settings throughout the United States for the purpose of providing quality nursing care to maintain the client's health, maximize the client's resources, or return the client to a state of health. Since 1967, the nursing process has become more complete and comprehensive to include six steps:

1. client assessment
2. nursing diagnoses
3. client outcomes

4. therapeutic care planning
5. implementation of care
6. evaluation

The nursing process is a client-centered process *guided* by a holistic framework. In contrast to the traditional paradigm in which nursing practice was divided into distinct parts of assessment, diagnoses, interventions, and evaluations, the holistic framework views nursing practice as a process of pattern recognition. In this process there is a continuous flow of actions and movement that merge together.

For years leaders of the nursing profession have recommended that a conceptual model of nursing be used to guide the steps of the nursing process.[3] There are many conceptual models of nursing, such as Roy's adaptation model,[4] Rogers' unitary man model,[5] King's systems model,[6] Orem's self-care model,[7] Watson's human care model,[8] or Newman's health as expanding consciousness model.[9] As nurses become more familiar with these models and test them in clinical practice, they tend to choose a model that is realistic, useful, and in concert with their values and philosophy of nursing.

Because the choice of a model to guide practice is so individual, we have not chosen any one particular nursing model for this book. We did not want to reduce the clinical applicability of the material found in this book by limiting the information to one model. Rather, the nursing process information contained in Chapters 9–17 can be guided by any one of the nursing models. That is, the concepts, propositions, assumptions, and wording of a particular model will direct the specific assessment, diagnosis, outcome, plan, intervention and evaluation phases of the nursing process. The overall framework (model) we have chosen to guide the development of this book is the holistic framework (see Chapter 1).

HOLISTIC ASSESSMENT

A holistic assessment evaluates the client's total state of being. The client's biopsychosocial patterns are assessed in order to identify an overall pattern of interrelationships. One analyzes and synthesizes the relationships that exist between and among the human response patterns of individuals. These human response patterns are not isolated responses, such as biologic or psychologic alterations. As viewed within a holistic framework, they reflect a synthesis of the processes that represent the integrated whole person. Changes that occur in one response pattern always influence changes in other dimensions.

Developing Holistic Assessment Tools

A holistic assessment not only evaluates the client's physical responses but also various psychologic, socioeconomic, cultural, and spiritual responses. Is the client depressed? Does the client view him- or herself as basically well or ill? What support systems exist for the client? What is the client's spiritual state? How does this illness affect the client's financial responsibilities? How is illness perceived in this client's culture? How has the client dealt with past crises? What coping mechanisms were used?

We ask these questions and others during our assessment. Each fragment of information is placed in perspective, synthesized, and interrelated to formulate conclusions regarding the client's state of being.

If nurses truly wish to perform holistic assessments, they must collect all of the data that are necessary to draw conclusions adequately about the client's state of being. You need to ask yourself, "Am I collecting all the necessary data?" Think about the assessment questions asked in the preceding paragraph. Why were those questions asked? What human response patterns are assessed by asking such questions? How would you interrelate the data formulated from those questions? Most important, what questions are *missing* that are necessary to assess the whole client adequately?

Now, turn your attention to the assessment tool *you* use in clinical practice. Visualize the assessment you do and the questions you ask. Does your assessment tool cover pertinent demographic data, chief complaint, history of present and past illnesses, review of systems, and physical examination? Are specific psychosocial and cultural questions included at the beginning and/or end of the tool? Is the tool familiar, easy to use, and beneficial in collecting pertinent data necessary to assess clients?

In reality, most assessment tools traditionally used in clinical practice are nothing more than a medical data base.[10] Because medicine is guided by the biomedical model, its assessment tool and its questions reflect an attempt to assess, diagnose, and treat disease. Nurses using some variation of a medical data base cannot, despite their best intentions, collect the necessary data for a holistic assessment. The data are not collected from a holistic framework nor from a nursing point of view. Data collected from a tool guided by the biomedical model assist one in interrelating physiologic information, but provide no direction for interrelating physiologic responses to the other human response patterns manifested by the whole client.

There is no doubt that the addition of psychologic, socioeconomic, and cultural questions to many assessment tools is an attempt to gather more information for a holistic assessment. Ask yourself, however, "Who decided that those questions should be included? Why were they included? And what is missing?"

The use of a nursing model/framework to guide the assessment is not only logical but fundamental to a holistic assessment. A conceptual model (framework) of nursing that is grounded in a holistic approach provides the concepts, assumptions, and wording necessary to develop a holistic nursing data base. The nurse uses the model to determine what areas need to be assessed, what data should be collected, and what assessment parameters might be missing. The model also provides direction for how data from one response pattern are interrelated to another. When nursing models are used to develop assessment tools, nurses can feel confident that they are assessing clients from a nursing and holistic point of view.

Nursing assessment is done for the purposes of synthesizing data, drawing conclusions, and formulating nursing diagnoses. One reason why nurses are having problems formulating nursing diagnoses is because we are using inappropriate assessment tools.[11] If a biomedical data base is used for assessment, it should not be surprising that nursing diagnoses are difficult to identify because the data are not collected from a nursing point of view. Conversely, when a holistic model is used to guide the assessment phase, nursing diagnoses are readily identified.

Opening Our Receptivity

Assessment is an ongoing process that is used to evaluate changes that occur over time. With each encounter we incorporate new information that helps explain interrelationships and validates previously collected data and conclusions. All isolated data are important, but the key to a holistic assessment is to discover the overall pattern and interrelationships of the responses.

At the core of assessment is the nurse-client relationship. This relationship involves an omnidirectional flow of information. In order to be open to information flow, it is necessary to understand how our personal beliefs, values, and prejudices affect our assessment (see Chapter 7). To achieve a holistic assessment we must not permit our prejudices and beliefs to limit our awareness.[12] Rigidity in our beliefs introduces a barrier to the flow of information and can separate us from our clients. As we transcend beliefs and prejudices, we view the world perceptively. We become open to our clients, and we learn to listen with focused intention.

Intuitive Thinking

Assessing clients holistically not only involves observation and evaluation of data from a rational, analytic, and verbal (or left brain) mode. Nurses also must be aware of and open to a nonverbal, intuitive (right brain) mode of processing data. Unfortunately in nursing we have not placed much value on "soft" data that cannot be measured and validated through scientific methods. Historically in nursing, intuitive perceptions have been seen as opposing the empirical, factual knowledge base of practice.[13] Intuitive feelings have been credited with minimal value and have elicited negative reactions. I admit that I have been among the many to share such a reaction. During the assessment classes taught to critical care nurses, I remember saying "We can no longer allow intuition to influence our assessments. We must develop technical expertise in our (physical) assessment. We must be able to justify our conclusions based on quantifiable data."

The idea that only quantifiable data are important in science is changing (see Chapter 8). Scientific exploration involves not only analytical thinking but also a qualitative yet undefinable process that scientists use to organize fragmented findings into meaningful wholes.[14] This undefinable process is called intuition, the *tacit dimension,* which is fundamental to all knowing.[15] It is a process whereby we know more than we can explain.

Intuitive perception allows one to immediately know about something without consciously using reason.[16] Clinical intuition has been described as a "process by which the nurse knows something about a client which cannot be verbalized or is verbalized poorly or for which the source of the knowledge cannot be determined."[17] It is a "gut feeling" that something is wrong even if there are no hard data to support that feeling. Intuition does not conflict with analytical reasoning.[18] Rather, it is simply another dimension of knowing. When analytic thinking and intuitive perception are used during assessment, we use our whole brain to collect and analyze data.

Some exciting "hard" data have recently emerged in the nursing literature to support the idea that intuitive processes are a valid means of conscious knowing and are necessary and desirable to quality client care.[19,20] The intuitive experiences of 15 neonatal intensive care nurses were recently reported.[21] Tape recordings from subject interviews and researcher field notes were analyzed qualitatively to discover emergent themes that influenced intuitive thinking. The first factor (theme) that was discovered related to the characteristics of the nurse. Intuitive thinking was identified in the most experienced and technically proficient nurses. The second factor was a feeling, caring, and loving relationship when providing day-to-day ongoing care to a particular infant. The third factor involved perceiving the infant's cues. Although such cues were physiologic (i.e., color, activity, movement, tone, and posture), most were not easy to quantitate. The fourth factor involved relating present perceptions to past experience. The nurses described a kind of déjà vu experience whereby they were, at some level, able to link previously experienced events to a present perception.

Another study reported the intuitive perceptions of 41 female nurses who were working in several agencies.[22] Seventy-five incidents that involved intuition were analyzed. The analysis revealed that intuition functions both as a process and a product. The intuitive process involves a nurse-patient encounter in which cues, feeling, and past experience become integrated with the current event. The intuitive product is something concluded as in the form of knowing or doing something or both.[23] In the majority of intuitive incidents, information emanated from "feeling" cues. Data on the validity of the judgments made on the basis of intuition were available for 81 percent of the events. Of the judgments, 92 percent were categorized as correct, indicating that the cues intuitively perceived by the nurse were useful in deciding on a particular course of action.

Certain conditions or attributes facilitate intuitive thinking.[24] Direct client contact and nursing experience are two factors that have been identified in the research.[25] Another factor is self-receptivity or the ability to be open and vulnerable. The nurse must be emotionally able to receive information and must have the desire to "tune in." Personal and emotional problems reduce receptivity. The nurse's energy level is a related factor that influences his or her readiness to receive, perceive, and interpret information. Intuitive thinking is reduced when energy is low, as in times of illness or stress. Self-confidence is the last factor identified as facilitating intuitive experiences. Self-confidence enables the nurse to believe in the validity of his or her intuitive experience. This confidence is reflective of what the nurse knows and the decisions to be made without experiencing any major discomfort regarding the lack of objective data.[26]

Therefore, the value of intuitive perception in nursing must be brought to our conscious awareness and viewed as a desired outcome of practice.[27] We must recognize that there are multiple ways of knowing and assessing clients and that intuition is a part of the nursing process. Assessment and decision making are not solely guided by objective information. Intuitive thinking involves a caring nurse-client relationship. It involves experience and energy that permit us to be open and receptive to the subtle cues and feelings that occur between two human beings. It involves the confidence to acknowledge and act upon new levels of (intuitive) knowledge.

Intuitive thinking must be cultivated in nursing. Although we cannot directly teach feelings, we can teach the skills necessary to recognize subjective data and to verbalize feelings, cues, and decisions.[28] (Refer to Chapters 2 and 3 on "Knowing" and Chapter 15 for a "Focusing Exercise" to expand intuitive skills). We can attempt to evaluate systematically the usefulness of the cues in making correct decisions. We can emphasize the value of such thinking in nursing and continuing education. We can share intuitive experiences with students and colleagues. We can support nurses who have experienced intuitive events and encourage them to review and analyze the process. We can provide inexperienced nurses with subtle repeated cue patterns that will assist them in recognizing intuitive information, thereby increasing their confidence about interpreting the cues and acting on their decisions.[29]

NURSING DIAGNOSES

Before the nursing diagnosis movement, problem identification was viewed as the weak link in the nursing process. Since 1973, however, the nursing diagnosis process has grown and has come to be accepted in clinical and academic settings and within our textbooks, journals, standards of care, and nurse practice acts. Even the definition of nursing from the American Nurses' Association (ANA) Congress for Nursing Practice incorporates nursing diagnosis; nursing is defined as "the diagnosis and treatment of human responses to actual or potential health problems."[30] Thus, problem identification is now seen as a clear and distinct step of the nursing process.

A nursing diagnosis can be defined as a "cluster of signs and symptoms describing actual or potential health problems (state-of-the-client) which nurses, because of their education and experience, are licensed and able to treat."[31] After nursing diagnoses are identified and prioritized, they become the basis for directing the remaining steps of the nursing process.

North American Nursing Diagnosis Association

Although problem identification has always been an important function of nursing practice, little effort was made to standardize the terminology used. The North American Nursing Diagnosis Association (NANDA) was formed to define, explain, classify, and research summary statements about health problems related to nursing. NANDA has worked to standardize the labels for client problems, facilitate communication, and enhance research so that specific client outcomes and nursing interventions can be developed for each diagnosis.[32] Although the nursing diagnosis movement is still in its infancy, many important developments have emerged that have advanced nursing practice. As the movement continues to be validated by clinical practice and scientific research, it has the potential for enhancing the quality of client care and identifying those problems and activities that are unique to nursing.

Nursing Diagnostic Process

The nursing diagnostic process uses the Problem-Etiology- Signs/Symptoms (P-E-S) format:[33]

- **P** *problem:* a brief statement of the client's actual or potential health problem; the "state-of-the-patient"

- **E** *etiology:* the probable cause of the problem or factors related to its development
- **S** *signs and symptoms:* the specific client behaviors (defining characteristics) observed in the assessment that lead nurses to believe that the client has a specific problem

The problem and etiology are connected by the phrase "related to," thereby forming the *diagnostic statement* e.g., "severe anxiety related to acute and sudden illness."

Problem

The problem should be an actual or potential health problem. It should be stated clearly and concisely so that it is easily understood. The problem indicates what needs to be changed to achieve a healthier state, and it should be used to direct client outcomes.[34] The accepted list of nursing diagnoses developed by NANDA includes client problems that nurses encounter (see Taxonomy I). When possible the specific problems and wording of the problems as developed by NANDA should be used to enhance standardization and communication. (See Appendix A for NANDA Qualifiers.)

Etiology

The etiology refers to the probable cause of the actual problem. The cause should be stated concisely in a few words and be easily understood. Because the etiology helps identify what is maintaining the problem or what is preventing the client from moving to a healthier state, it therefore guides the plan of care.[35]

Signs/Symptoms

The nurse must first assess the client's signs/symptoms and subtle cues, synthesize and analyze the data, draw conclusions, and then formulate nursing diagnoses.[36] Signs and symptoms for many of the diagnoses have been tentatively identified to differentiate among various diagnoses.[37–39] In some cases, the lists of associated signs/symptoms are incomplete, and in most cases they have not been validated by research. If a list of the signs/symptoms associated with a particular diagnosis is not available to help validate the presence of a particular diagnosis, then nurses should use their education and experience when assessing a particular patient to determine if the signs/symptoms observed do demonstrate an actual or potential health problem.

Impact of Unitary Person Framework

The Unitary Person Framework was created by NANDA to guide the development and identification of nursing diagnoses.[40] Its primary focus is the health of the unitary person. The unitary person is conceptualized as an open system in mutual interaction with the environment. An open system is characterized by *negentrophy*, a process by which the unitary person has the potential to develop continuously toward increasing complexity and diversity.[41] Negentrophy can be seen in individuals as they progress through developmental stages and through the life-span. Individuals and their roles, function, structure, and services all have the potential to become more diverse and complex. Unitary person is also viewed as a four-dimensional energy field characterized by a unique pattern and organization. The unique pattern and organization of each person are manifested by nine human response patterns (Exhibit 6-1).

Underlying the Unitary Person Framework is the assumption that health is valued by both the nurse and the client. Health signifies a pattern of energy exchange that enhances the integrity of the person to move towards life's potential. Health is manifested by the nine human response patterns that are interrelated and reflective of the whole person.[42] The nine human response patterns provide an assessment framework for pattern recognition. The nurse collects data in terms of these nine human response patterns to search for the underlying pattern of the relationships.[43]

Taxonomy I

Taxonomy I (Exhibit 6-2) was developed recently from the Unitary Person Framework by NANDA to enhance the development of nursing diagnoses.[44] Its classification schema is based on the nine human response patterns of the Unitary Person Framework. All nursing diagnoses approved by NANDA have been placed under one of the nine categories (Exhibit 6-1). Diagnoses are then placed within various lower-level categories depending on their degree of specificity. To enhance the clarity of the system, items were added and are identified by parentheses. The number signs were added to emphasize the provisional and incomplete status of the system.[45] Taxonomy I replaces the old alphabetical system that was used for the accepted list of nursing diagnoses which itself will be tested and revised. (See Appendix B for Unitary Person Assessment Tool: A Prototype.)

Wellness Diagnoses

From a holistic perspective, the accepted list of nursing diagnoses has been criticized because it is limited to identifying only client problems. It has been recommended that the list be expanded to include statements related to health, wellness, and strengths. If we assess and diagnose only problems and omit health qualities and strengths, then we are assessing only part of the total person.[46]

Exhibit 6-1 Nine Human Response Patterns of Unitary Person

1. EXCHANGING:	a human response pattern involving mutual giving and receiving
2. COMMUNICATING:	a human response pattern involving sending messages
3. RELATING:	a human response pattern involving establishing bonds
4. VALUING:	a human response pattern involving the assigning of relative worth
5. CHOOSING:	a human response pattern involving the selection of alternatives
6. MOVING:	a human response pattern involving activity
7. PERCEIVING:	a human response pattern involving the reception of information
8. KNOWING:	a human response pattern involving the meaning associated with information
9. FEELING:	a human response pattern involving subjective awareness of information

Exhibit 6-2 NANDA Nursing Diagnosis Taxonomy I

1. EXCHANGING: A human response pattern involving mutual giving and receiving.
    - 1.1 Alterations in Nutrition
        - 1.1.1 (Cellular)
        - 1.1.2 (Systemic)
            - 1.1.2.1 More Than Body Requirements
            - 1.1.2.2 Less Than Body Requirements
            - 1.1.2.3 Potential for More Than Body Requirements
            - 1.1.2.4 #########
    - 1.2 (Alterations in Physical Regulation)
        - 1.2.1 (Immune)
            - 1.2.1.1 Potential for Infection
            - 1.2.1.2 #########
        - 1.2.2 Alteration in Body Temperature
            - 1.2.2.1 Potential
            - 1.2.2.2 Hypothermia
            - 1.2.2.3 Hyperthermia
            - 1.2.2.4 Ineffective Thermoregulation
            - 1.2.2.5 #########
    - 1.3 Alterations in Elimination
        - 1.3.1 Bowel
            - 1.3.1.1 Constipation
            - 1.3.1.2 Diarrhea
            - 1.3.1.3 Incontinence
        - 1.3.2 Urinary Patterns
            - 1.3.2.1 Incontinence
                - 1.3.2.1.1 Stress
                - 1.3.2.1.2 Reflex
                - 1.3.2.1.3 Urge
                - 1.3.2.1.4 Functional
                - 1.3.2.1.5 Total
            - 1.3.2.2 Retention
        - 1.3.3 (Skin)
            - 1.3.3.1 #########
            - 1.3.3.2 #########
    - 1.4 (Alterations in Circulation)
        - 1.4.1 (Vascular)
            - 1.4.1.1 Tissue Perfusion
                - 1.4.1.1.1 Renal
                - 1.4.1.1.2 Cerebral
                - 1.4.1.1.3 Cardiopulmonary
                - 1.4.1.1.4 Gastrointestinal
                - 1.4.1.1.5 Peripheral
            - 1.4.1.2 Fluid Volume
                - 1.4.1.2.1 Excess
                - 1.4.1.2.2 Deficit
                    - 1.4.1.2.2.1 Actual
                    - 1.4.1.2.2.2 Potential
            - 1.4.1.3 #########
        - 1.4.2 (Cardiac)
            - 1.4.2.1 Decreased Cardiac Output
            - 1.4.2.2 #########

Exhibit 6-2 continued

1.5 (Alterations in Oxygenation)
    1.5.1 (Respiration)
        1.5.1.1 Impaired Gas Exchange
        1.5.1.2 Ineffective Airway Clearance
        1.5.1.3 Ineffective Breathing Pattern
    1.5.2 #########
1.6 (Alterations in Physical Integrity)
    1.6.1 Potential for Injury
        1.6.1.1 Potential for Suffocating
        1.6.1.2 Potential for Poisoning
        1.6.1.3 Potential for Trauma
    1.6.2 Impairment
        1.6.2.1 Skin Integrity
            1.6.2.1.1 Actual
            1.6.2.1.2 Potential
        1.6.2.2 Tissue Integrity
            1.6.2.2.1 Oral Mucous Membrane
            1.6.2.2.2 #########
            1.6.2.2.3 #########
        1.6.2.3 #########

2. COMMUNICATING: A human response pattern involving sending messages
2.1 Alterations in Communication
    2.1.1 Verbal
        2.1.1.1 Impaired
        2.1.1.2 #########
        2.1.1.3 #########
    2.1.2 (Nonverbal)
2.2 #########
2.3 #########
    2.3.2 #########
    2.3.3 #########

3. RELATING: A human response pattern involving establishing bonds
3.1 (Alterations in Socialization)
    3.1.1 Impaired Social Interaction
    3.1.2 Social Isolation
    3.1.3 #########
3.2 (Alterations in Role)
    3.2.1 (Role Performance)
        3.2.1.1 Parenting
            3.2.1.1.1 Actual
            3.2.1.1.2 Potential
        3.2.1.2 Sexual
            3.2.1.2.1 Dysfunction
            3.2.1.2.2 #########
            3.2.1.2.3 #########
        3.2.1.3 (Work)
    3.2.2 Family Processes
    3.2.3 #########
3.3 Altered Sexuality Patterns
3.4 #########

Exhibit 6-2 continued

4. VALUING: A human response pattern involving the assigning of relative worth
    - 4.1 Alterations in Spiritual State
        - 4.1.1 Distress
        - 4.1.2 #########
        - 4.1.3 #########
    - 4.2 #########
        - 4.2.1 #########
        - 4.2.2 #########

5. CHOOSING: A human response pattern involving the selection of alternatives
    - 5.1 Alterations in Coping
        - 5.1.1 Individual
            - 5.1.1.1 Ineffective
                - 5.1.1.1.1 Impaired Adjustment
                - 5.1.1.1.2 #########
            - 5.1.1.2 #########
        - 5.1.2 Family
            - 5.1.2.1 Ineffective
                - 5.1.2.1.1 Disabled
                - 5.1.2.1.2 Compromised
            - 5.1.2.2 Potential for Growth
            - 5.1.2.3 #########
        - 5.1.3 (Community)
    - 5.2 (Alterations in Participation)
        - 5.2.1 (Individual)
            - 5.2.1.1 Noncompliance
            - 5.2.1.2 #########
            - 5.2.1.3 #########
        - 5.2.2 (Family)
        - 5.2.3 (Community)

6. MOVING: A human response pattern involving activity
    - 6.1 (Alterations in Activity)
        - 6.1.1 Physical Mobility
            - 6.1.1.1 Impaired
            - 6.1.1.2 Activity Intolerance
            - 6.1.1.3 Potential Activity Intolerance
            - 6.1.1.4 #########
        - 6.1.2 (Social Mobility)
            - 6.1.2.1 #########
            - 6.1.2.2 #########
    - 6.2 (Alterations in Rest)
        - 6.2.1 Sleep Pattern Disturbance
        - 6.2.2 #########
    - 6.3 (Alterations in Recreation)
        - 6.3.1 Diversional Activity
            - 6.3.1.1 Deficit
            - 6.3.1.2 #########
        - 6.3.2 #########
    - 6.4 (Alterations in Activities of Daily Living)
        - 6.4.1 Home Maintenance Management
            - 6.4.1.1 Impaired
            - 6.4.1.2 #########

Exhibit 6-2 continued

- 6.4.2 Health Maintenance
- 6.4.3 #########

6.5 Alterations in Self-Care
- 6.5.1 Feeding
  - 6.5.1.1 Impaired Swallowing
  - 6.5.1.2 #########
  - 6.5.1.3 #########
- 6.5.2 Bathing/Hygiene
- 6.5.3 Dressing/Grooming
- 6.5.4 Toileting

6.6 Altered Growth and Development
- 6.6.1 #########
- 6.6.2 #########

7. PERCEIVING: A human response pattern involving the reception of information

7.1 Alterations in Self-Concept
- 7.1.1 Disturbance in Body Image
- 7.1.2 Disturbance in Self-Esteem
- 7.1.3 Disturbance in Personal Identity
- 7.1.4 #########

7.2 Sensory/Perceptual Alteration
- 7.2.1 Visual
  - 7.2.1.1 Unilateral Neglect
  - 7.2.1.2 #########
- 7.2.2 Auditory
- 7.2.3 Kinesthetic
- 7.2.4 Gustatory
- 7.2.5 Tactile
- 7.2.6 Olfactory

7.3 (Alterations in Meaningfulness)
- 7.3.1 Hopelessness
- 7.3.2 Powerlessness
- 7.3.3 #########

8. KNOWING: A human response pattern involving the meaning associated with information

8.1 Alterations in Knowledge
- 8.1.1 Deficit
- 8.1.2 #########
- 8.1.3 #########

8.2 (Alterations in Learning)
- 8.2.1 #########
- 8.2.2 #########

8.3 Alterations in Thought Processes
- 8.3.1 (Confusion)
- 8.3.2 #########
- 8.3.3 #########

9. FEELING: A human response pattern involving the subjective awareness of information

9.1 Alterations in Comfort
- 9.1.1 Pain
  - 9.1.1.1 Chronic
  - 9.1.1.2 (Acute)
  - 9.1.1.3 #########
- 9.1.2 (Discomfort)

Exhibit 6-2 continued

9.2 (Alterations in Emotional Integrity)
- 9.2.1 Anxiety
- 9.2.2 Grieving
  - 9.2.2.1 Dysfunctional
  - 9.2.2.2 Anticipatory
  - 9.2.2.3 #########
- 9.2.3 Potential for Violence
- 9.2.4 Fear
- 9.2.5 Post-Trauma Response
  - 9.2.5.1 Rape Trauma Syndrome
    - 9.2.5.1.1 Rape Trauma
    - 9.2.5.1.2 Compound Reaction
    - 9.2.5.1.3 Silent Reaction
  - 9.2.5.2 #########
- 9.2.6 #########
- 9.2.7 #########

9.3 #########

Source: North American Nursing Diagnosis Association, St. Louis, Missouri, 1986.

Health-oriented statements can be developed in terms of strengths. A strength diagnosis is made when clients have positive resources and support that permit them to draw physical or emotional energy to establish lifestyles and habits that foster wellness.[47]

Strength diagnoses can include such statements as "appropriate individual coping related to regular relaxation exercises and supportive family structure." Other health-oriented diagnoses are outlined in Exhibit 6-3. To include health-oriented diagnoses, a

Exhibit 6-3 Health-Oriented Diagnoses

Adequate health maintenance
Effective individual coping
Adequate support systems
Functional grieving
Regular elimination
Adequate nutrition
Controlled pain
Maintenance of independence
Adequate self-care
Effective coping
Active role in health maintenance
Active participation in decision making
Effective stress reduction activities
Compliance with health regimen
Effective home maintenance management
Effective health maintenance
Adequate self-concept, body image, self-esteem, role performance, or personal identity
Adequate socialization
Adequate activity tolerance
Adequate diversional activities

revised definition of nursing diagnosis has been recommended, wherein nursing diagnoses are defined as "conclusions (strengths and problems) that describe human responses to actual or potential health concerns and practices."[48]

Because nursing has a commitment to wellness, health-oriented diagnoses can be used to measure the impact of health promotion interventions. Interventions in this book help reduce the need for illness-related care and emphasize wellness, health maintenance, and illness prevention.

CLIENT OUTCOMES

After nursing diagnoses are identified, goals are set that direct the plan of care. Goals, developed in terms of specific and concisely stated client outcomes, are written for each diagnosis.

A client outcome is a direct statement of the desired end that the client will reach in a specified time frame. It addresses the maximum level of wellness that is realistically attainable for the client.[49] One or more client outcomes are written for each problem. Outcome criteria are then developed that describe the specific tools, tests, or observations that will be used to measure whether the client outcome has been achieved.

Outcome criteria must be measurable and may include the following categories[50,51]:

- what should or should not occur in the client's status
- the level at which some change should occur
- what clients should verbalize about what they know, understand, or feel about the situation
- specific client behaviors or signs/symptoms that are expected to occur as a result of intervention
- specific client behaviors that are expected to occur as a result of adequate management of the environment

If outcomes are to be achieved, they must be established by the client with the assistance of the nurse and family. The client must be motivated and want to change in order to establish healthy patterns and behaviors.

PLAN

In the holistic approach to the nursing process, it is during the planning stage that the client and family are helped to repattern their behaviors to achieve a healthier state. The planning process identifies interventions that will achieve long- and short-term goals (client outcomes). The plan is developed in terms of nursing orders, which are the specific actions that the nurse performs to help the client solve problems and achieve effective client outcomes.[52] Nursing orders direct the implementation of care.

It has been recommended that the nurse choose interventions based on five criteria[53]:

1. Criterion 1 reflects the characteristics of the nursing diagnosis; that is, whether the nurse aims intervention at the etiology, signs/symptoms, or at potential problems.
2. Criterion 2 deals with an evaluation of the research base that validates the effectiveness of the intervention, its clinical significance, and the nursing control associated with the intervention.
3. Criterion 3 involves the feasibility of implementing the intervention in terms of the other diagnoses and their respective priorities, and the cost and time involved with the intervention.
4. Criterion 4 concerns the acceptability of the intervention to the client in terms of their own goals and priorities related to the treatment plan.
5. Criterion 5 involves the nursing competency necessary to implement the intervention successfully.[54]

IMPLEMENTATION

When guided by a holistic framework, nurses approach the implementation phase with an awareness that (1) clients are active participants in their care, (2) nursing care should be performed with purposeful, focused intention, and (3) the client's humanness is an important factor in implementation.

Within the holistic framework, anything that produces a physiologic change will cause a corresponding psychologic alteration. Conversely, anything that produces a psychologic change will cause a corresponding physiologic alteration. Thus, when a nurse encounters a client, be it for the purpose of talking to the client, touching the client, or taking a blood pressure, such an exchange produces psychophysiologic changes. The event changes the physiology and the consciousness of both the nurse and the client. Many nurses go through nursing school without ever learning that human emotions can be translated into physiologic responses. Many nurses also never learn that the greatest tool/intervention for helping and healing clients is the therapeutic use of self.[55] So often we touch clients or perform some procedure without any conscious awareness of the enormous impact the event could have on the client if it were a purposeful, centered activity.

Within a holistic framework, nurses incorporate modalities that assist clients to make bodymind connections. These modalities are thoroughly discussed in Unit IV. By incorporating self-regulation modalities into practice, along with traditional modes of therapy, nurses become holistic healers.

EVALUATION

Data about the client's biopsychosocial status and responses are continuously collected and recorded throughout the nursing process. The information is related to the nursing diagnoses, the outcome criteria, and the results of the nursing action. The goal of evaluation is to determine if successful client outcomes have been achieved and to what extent. The nurse, client, family, and other members of the health team are involved in the evaluation process. Together, they synthesize the data from the evaluation to determine successful repatterning behaviors toward wellness. During the evaluation, one would hope to see a higher level of client awareness regarding previous patterns, insight into the interconnections of all dimensions of the client's life, and the benefits of repatterning behaviors. For example, does the client have some insight that his or her current job and level of stress have a direct impact on the current illness state? Periodic evaluation and re-evaluation of client outcomes are necessary because of the dynamic nature of human beings and the frequent changes that occur during illness and health. Outcomes may be effectively achieved, or new client outcomes may need to be developed and the plan of care revised. Factors facilitating the achievement of effective outcomes or preventing solutions to problems should be evaluated.

STANDARDS OF CARE

Within each step of the nursing process, process standards have been written to designate quality client care. Many subspecialty organizations have developed their own standards of care. For example, the ANA Division on Medical Surgical Nursing and the American Heart Association Council on Cardiovascular Nursing have developed Standards of Cardiovascular Nursing Practice[56] that should be used when caring for clients with cardiovascular dysfunctions. Many of the standards developed from subspecialty groups are physiologically based or disease-centered. Such standards are useful when dealing with the physiologic domain, but they do not provide detailed criteria for nursing practice standards within the psychosocial and spiritual domains, nor do they provide standards that direct holistic care.

Standards for Holistic Nursing

In 1986, the American Holistic Nurses' Association developed Standards for Holistic Nursing[57] (Exhibit 6-4). These standards define and establish the scope of holistic nursing practice. They are based on the philosophy that nursing is an art and a science that has as its primary purpose the provision of services that strengthen individuals to achieve the wholeness inherent within them. The concepts of holistic nursing then are based on broad and eclectic academic principles. Holistic concepts incorporate a sensitive balance between art and science, analytic and intuitive skills, and the ability and knowledge to choose from a wide variety of treatment modalities to promote balance and interconnectedness of body, mind, and spirit.[58]

By definition, holistic nursing can be practiced by any nurse in any setting. The Standards for Holistic Nursing provide the criteria by which to measure the quality of holistic nursing care rendered to clients. Because the Standards for Holistic Nursing have been developed based on the universal language of the nursing process, they easily may be synthesized and combined with other more physiologically based standards. For example, the Standards of Cardiovascular Nursing are based on the nursing process and include standards for assessment, diagnoses, outcome criteria, plans, interventions, and evaluations when caring for the cardiovascular client. The Standards for Holistic Nursing could easily be combined with the Standards of Cardiovascular Nursing within each step of the nursing process to ensure not only quality physiologic care but also

Exhibit 6-4 Standards for Holistic Nursing

STANDARD I

The collection of data about the patient is a holistic, humane, systematic, continuous process. These data are communicated to appropriate persons, recorded, utilized, and stored in a retrievable and accessible system.

Data are obtained by observation, interview, physical examination, review of records and reports, and consultation. Priority of data collection is determined by the mental, emotional, physical, and spiritual condition of the patient.

Assessment Factors:

1. Health data are derived from a nursing data base which includes but is not limited to:
   a. The patient's perceptions and expectations which are related to health care services;
   b. Current medical diagnosis and therapy;
   c. Environmental, occupational, and recreational information as it relates to the patient's habits;
   d. Spiritual information;
   e. Mental and emotional responses;
   f. Information about previous use of health services and health history;
   g. Assessment of function and status in the following areas:
      —cardiovascular and respiratory
      —gastrointestinal
      —fluid and electrolyte balance
      —kidney and bladder
      —neuromuscular
      —sensory
      —integumentary
      —sexuality and reproductive
      —metabolic regulation
      —sleep, rest, comfort
      —immunological and hemopoietic
   h. A summation of patterns and perceived causes of previous and current health problems
2. Health data are collected by appropriate methods.
3. Health data collection is complete and ongoing.
4. Health data are seen as integrated, concerned with the whole patient, and the patient's system (family, workplace, lifestyle, etc.).
5. Disease or disability is included as a process; pain and disease are included as valuable signals of internal conflicts.
6. An emphasis on patient's values is included.
7. The patient's preferred name is noted.

STANDARD II

Nursing diagnosis is derived from health status data. Nursing is a concise statement identifying the patient's actual or potential health problems and limitations which nurses are able to treat. It is not a summary of all abnormalities.

Assessment Factors:

1. The nursing diagnosis is based upon the identifiable data, such as qualitative data, patient reports, and professional *intuition*; included is the recognition of the individual's unique responses to each situation.
2. Health status deviation(s) is determined by comparing the identified data to established norms and/or the patient's previous condition.

Exhibit 6-4 continued

3. Nursing diagnosis is consistent (as far as possible) with current knowledge.
4. Nursing diagnosis may be developed for individuals in any of the following phases of illness: acute, chronic, intermittent, potential.
5. The nursing diagnosis provides the basis for nursing orders and should include the etiology or probable cause to ensure an appropriate treatment plan.
6. The nursing diagnosis includes mind as primary or co-equal factor in all illness.
7. The body is seen in diagnosis as a dynamic system, a complex energy field within fields (family, workplace, environment, culture, life history).

STANDARD III

Goals for holistic nursing care are formulated. A goal is the end state toward which nursing action is directed.

Assessment Factors:

1. Goals are derived from nursing diagnosis and are assigned appropriate priority.
2. Goals are stated in terms of observable outcomes.
3. Goals are formulated by the patient, his family, health personnel and significant others, with adequate information having been given to all persons concerned.
4. Goals are congruent with the patient's present and potential physical and behavioral patterns and are made with the intent of placing the body and mind in such a state, internally and externally, that they can heal themselves.
5. Goals are attainable through available human, community, and material resources, including such resources with which the patient may feel more comfortable.
6. Goals are achievable within an identifiable time frame.
7. Goals include minimal intervention with appropriate technology, complemented with full use of non-invasive, natural techniques (diet, massage, etc.).
8. Emphasis includes achieving maximum body-mind health.
9. When establishing goals, the patient is to be considered as an autonomous being who is being assisted.

STANDARD IV

The plan for holistic nursing care prescribes nursing actions to achieve the goals. The plan for nursing care describes a systematic method to meet the goals.

Assessment Factors:

1. The plan includes priorities for nursing actions.
2. The plan includes a logical sequence of actions to attain the goals.
3. The plan is based on current scientific knowledge and all identifiable data found in the assessment (includes nursing intuition).
4. The plan incorporates available and appropriate resources (human, material, community, and environmental controls).
5. The plan is implemented.
6. The plan reflects the consideration of the "Patient's Bill of Rights."
7. The plan specifies the following:
   - what is to be done
   - how to do it
   - when to do it
   - where to do it
   - who is to do it
   - what results are expected

Exhibit 6-4 continued

8. The plan is developed with and communicated to patient, family, significant others, and health care professionals as appropriate.
9. The plan is realistic and achievable.
10. The plan is documented in the patient's permanent record.

STANDARD V

The plan for holistic nursing care is implemented. The plan must be applied to achieve goals.

Assessment Factors:

1. Nursing actions are documented by written records, observations of performance, and/or patient report(s) of nursing actions.
2. Nursing actions are consistent with the plans for nursing care.
3. Nursing actions are implemented with an attitude of caring for the whole person.
4. Actions are implemented with an attitude of working with the patient as a therapeutic partner.
5. Nursing actions are performed with safety, skill, and efficiency.
6. Nursing actions reflect consideration of the individual's and family's dignity, beliefs, values, and desires.
7. Nursing actions include, but are not limited to:
   - educating family and patient
   - discussing patient/family rights with them
   - involving patient/family in decision making
   - providing privacy
   - ensuring confidentiality
   - making interdisciplinary resources available
   - respecting patient/family coping behaviors without making value judgments
   - facilitating patient/family support systems
   - continuing contact with family if patient dies
   - supporting patient/family as a unit
   - providing direct care
   - delegating tasks and supervising others
   - referring the individual to other professionals for specialized services
   - coordinating the efforts of health team members
   - maintaining a body-mind-spirit perspective in all health care settings
   - continually striving for high-level wellness in own life as a role model

STANDARD VI

The plan for holistic nursing care is evaluated. Patient response is compared with observable outcomes which are specific goals.

Assessment Factors:

1. Current data about the patient are used to measure progress toward goal achievement.
2. The patient, family, health personnel, and significant others contribute to the evaluation of goal achievement.
3. Patient/family willingness and ability to participate in and adjust to altered lifestyles are considered during the evaluation.
4. The degree of goal achievement is communicated by the nurse to the patient, family, significant others, and health personnel, and vice versa.

Exhibit 6-4 continued

5. The individual demonstrates ability to cope with alterations in lifestyle.
6. The individual is able to achieve or modify goals to attain high quality of life.
7. The placebo effect is evidence of mind's role in disease and healing and therefore evaluated as a valid healing event.

STANDARD VII

Reassessment, reordering priorities, new goal setting, and revision of the plan for nursing care are a continuous process. The steps of the nursing process are used concurrently and recurrently.

Assessment Factors:

1. Reassessment is directed by goal achievement and/or new data (from patient, family, health care personnel).
2. Ongoing documentation is consistent with the time frame specified in the goals.
3. Current goals are consistent with evaluation of the patient's progress.
4. The individual's response to nursing action is compared with the outcome stated in the goals.
5. New plans are developed and initiated in conjunction with patient and family.

Source: Reprinted from *Standards for Holistic Nursing* with permission of the American Holistic Nurses' Association, 401 Lake Boone Trail, Raleigh, N.C. 27607, © 1987.

quality holistic nursing care to this client population. Thus, the Standards for Holistic Nursing could be incorporated into all subspecialty standards of care.

Standards for Person-Centered Caring

To complement and enhance the Standards for Holistic Nursing, the Standards for Person-Centered Caring were developed in 1980 by a nurse, Ann Paulen, at the University of Wisconsin Hospital, in Madison[59] (Exhibit 6-5). These standards, which can be incorporated into the nursing process, illustrate how nurses can implement natural systems theory and the human factor in providing care. They reflect a concern that nursing care be individualized and nurturing to human beings. The standards also address the essence of the therapeutic nurse-client relationship and help clarify what is meant by the concept of "treating the client like a whole person."

The standards are useful as a tool for teaching students and new staff during orientation. They specify the expected levels of care, desired client and family outcomes, and the expected nursing activities that comprise person-centered caring. Since these standards are *person*-centered, rather than *disease*-centered, they can be applied across client populations. With little effort they can be incorporated into physiologically based standards and can be used in any setting where caring nurses deliver holistic nursing care.

Exhibit 6-5 Standards for Person-Centered Caring

I. Humanness
   A. Standard
      The patient's and family's humanness is respected.
   B. Outcome criteria
      The patient and family—
      1. feel they are treated like human beings
      2. describe ways in which their own values and life style are considered
      3. feel their rights are being upheld
      4. state that they are considered in care planning, decision making, and information giving
      5. state they are addressed by preferred names.
   C. Process criteria
      The nurse—
      1. considers patient/family values and/or life style, e.g., activities important to patient/family
      2. notes the name the patient prefers.

II. Family
   A. Standard
      The patient and family are treated as a unit.
   B. Outcome criteria
      The patient and family—
      1. state that their relationship is supported
      2. state they they have the information they want/need
      3. state that they participate in care as desired.
   C. Process criteria
      The nurse—
      1. supports the patient and family as a unit, e.g., flexible visiting hours, participation in care
      2. counsels/teaches/informs the family as well as the patient
      3. continues contact with the family if a patient dies.

III. Rights
   A. Standard
      The patient's and family's rights are upheld.
   B. Outcome criteria
      The patient and family—
      1. feel they are treated as human beings
      2. state they receive the information wanted and needed to make decisions
      3. feel involved in decision making to the extent desired
      4. feel supported when either accepting or rejecting the treatment plan/recommendations
      5. feel comfortable with the confidentiality of personal information
      6. state that their privacy is considered
      7. state that resources desired are made available to them.
   C. Process criteria
      The nurse—
      1. discusses the patient's/family's rights with them
      2. provides information to the patient/family
      3. involves the patient/family in decision making as they desire
      4. provides for patient/family privacy
      5. ensures confidentiality of information
      6. makes interdisciplinary resources available.

IV. Coping
   A. Standard
      The patient's and family's coping skills are respected.
   B. Outcome criteria
      The patient and family—

Exhibit 6-5 continued

1. feel that their own way of adapting to health/illness is respected by staff
2. state that their support systems are facilitated, e.g., religion, visits with family/friends.

C. Process criteria
The nurse—
1. respects patient/family coping behaviors without making value judgments
2. facilitates patient/family support systems.

V. Choice
A. Standard
The patient's control over his/her own life (and death) is facilitated.
B. Outcome criteria
The patient—
1. feels s/he is treated as a partner in own health care
2. states s/he has sufficient information on which to base decisions
3. states s/he is involved in decision making to the extent desired.

C. Process criteria
The nurse—
1. treats the patient as a partner in his/her own health care
2. provides information to the patient
3. involves the patient in decision making.

VI. Comfort
A. Standard
The patient's symptoms are managed to the patient's and family's satisfaction
B. Outcome criteria
The patient and family—
1. feel that reports of alterations in comfort level are accepted without value judgment
2. feel that their suggestions for modifying physical and emotional comfort are sought and considered
3. feel satisfied with the management of symptoms.

C. Process criteria
The nurse—
1. assesses symptoms, e.g., pain, anxiety, sleeplessness, loneliness
2. considers patient/family input in planning and evaluating symptom management
3. uses creative problem solving techniques to relieve symptoms
4. evaluates the efficacy of interventions.

VII. Continuity
A. Standard
Continuity of caring is fostered.
B. Outcome criteria
The patient and family—
1. feel that ongoing health/illness care can be compatible with their own values and life style
2. state that they have the information and resources needed for continuing health care
3. feel that they have developed an adequate relationship with some member(s) of the health care system
4. feel secure in knowing who to contact with questions/concerns.

C. Process criteria
The nurse—
1. collaborates with the patient/family to individualize plans for ongoing health/illness care
2. plans for ongoing follow-up (including bereavement counseling)
3. informs the patient/family about community resources.

Source: Reprinted with permission from author from *Standards for Person-Centered Caring* by A. Paulen, University of Wisconsin Hospital, 1980.

SUMMARY

The nursing process was discussed within a holistic framework. During the assessment phase data are collected from a nursing point of view that incorporates both analytic and intuitive thinking. The nursing diagnosis phase of the nursing process has been influenced by recent developments within the nursing diagnosis movement. Client outcomes, plans, interventions, and evaluations are related to client participation, motivation, and acceptance for changing health patterns and behaviors. Standards of care are closely linked to the nursing process. The content from this chapter guides the nursing process sections within each chapter in Unit IV.

DIRECTIONS FOR FUTURE RESEARCH

1. Determine whether incorporating Standards for Holistic Nursing positively affect subjective and objective client outcomes.
2. Determine whether incorporating Standards for Holistic Nursing improve nurse work satisfaction and turnover.
3. Evaluate the correctness of intuitive judgments in terms of its usefulness for making decisions for a variety of client populations.
4. Evaluate the effectiveness of a program designed to enhance intuitive thinking among nurses, i.e., one that includes these elements—theory, sharing experiences, reviewing and analyzing the event, participating in focusing exercises, providing repeated cue experiences, providing consultation for recognizing and interpreting cues, and building confidence regarding the value of the experience.

NURSE HEALER REFLECTIONS

After reading this chapter, the nurse healer will be able to answer or will begin a process of answering the following questions:

- How am I able to *remove* my life's prejudices during the assessment of my clients?
- Do I *value* the significance of intuitive thinking?
- Do I *feel confident* with my intuitive decisions?
- How can I *cultivate* my intuitive processes?
- How do I *react* when clients indicate they are not motivated to change health patterns and behavior?
- How do I *feel* when I incorporate principles of holistic nursing into my delivery of care?

NOTES

1. Jean Watson, *Nursing: Human Science and Human Care* (Norwalk, CT: Appleton-Century-Crofts, 1985), p. 47

2. Helen Yura and Mary Walsh, *The Nursing Process: Assessing, Planning, Implementing, Evaluating* (New York: Appleton-Century-Crofts, 1984), p. 1ff.
3. Barbara M. Dossey and Cathie E. Guzzetta, ''Person-Centered Caring and the Nursing Process,'' in *Cardiovascular Nursing: Bodymind Tapestry,* ed. Cathie E. Guzzetta and Barbara M. Dossey (St. Louis: C.V. Mosby, 1984), pp. 61–76.
4. Calistra Roy, *Introduction to Nursing: An Adaptation Model* (Englewood Cliffs, NJ: Prentice-Hall, 1976), p. 1ff.
5. Martha Rogers, *Introduction to the Theoretical Basis of Nursing* (New York: Davis, 1969), pp. 39–121.
6. Imogine King, *Towards a Theory of Nursing* (Boston: Little, Brown and Co., 1981) pp. 10–106.
7. Dorothea Orem, *Nursing Concepts of Practice* (New York: McGraw-Hill, 1980), p. 1ff.
8. Jean Watson, *Nursing: Human Science and Human Care,* p. 47.
9. Margaret A. Newman, *Health as Expanding Consciousness,* pp. 107–134.
10. Cathie E. Guzzetta and Marguerite Kinney, ''Mastering the Transition from Medical to Nursing Diagnosis,'' *Progress in Cardiovascular Nursing* 1, no. 1 (October/November 1986): 41–44.
11. Cathie E. Guzzetta, Shelia D. Bunton, Linda A. Prinkey, Anita P. Sherer, and Patricia C. Seifert, ''Unitary Person Assessment Tool: Easing Problems with Nursing Diagnoses,'' *Focus on Critical Care* 15, no. 2 (April 1988): 12–24.
12. Dolores Krieger, *Foundations for Holistic Health Nursing Practice* (Philadelphia: J.B. Lippincott Co., 1981), pp. 150–155.
13. Constance E. Young, ''Intuition and Nursing Process,'' *Holistic Nursing Practice* 1, no. 3 (May 1987): 54.
14. Michael Polanyi, *Personal Knowledge* (New York: Harper & Row, 1958), p. 1ff.
15. Michael Polanyi, *The Tacit Dimension* (New York: Anchor Press, 1966), p. 4.
16. Barbara D. Schraeder and Dorothy K. Fisher, ''Using Intuitive Knowledge in the Neonatal Intensive Care Nursery,'' *Holistic Nursing Practice* 1, no. 3 (May 1987): 47.
17. Constance E. Young, ''Intuition and Nursing Process,'' p. 52.
18. Carl Jung, *Psychological Types* (New York: Harcourt, Brace, 1959), p. 78.
19. Constance E. Young, ''Intuition and Nursing Process,'' p. 52.
20. Barbara D. Schraeder and Dorothy K. Fisher, ''Using Intuitive Knowledge in the Neonatal Intensive Care Nursery,'' pp. 45–51.
21. Ibid., pp. 45–51.
22. Constance E. Young, ''Intuition and Nursing Process,'' pp. 52–62.
23. Ibid., p. 57.
24. Ibid., p. 59.
25. Barbara D. Schraeder and Dorothy K. Fisher, ''Using Intuitive Knowledge in the Neonatal Intensive Care Nursery,'' pp. 45–51.
26. Constance E. Young, ''Intuition and Nursing Process,'' p. 60.
27. Patricia L. Gerrity, ''Perception in Nursing: The Value of Intuition,'' *Holistic Nursing Practice* 1, no. 3 (May 1987): 63–71.
28. Constance E. Young, ''Intuition and Nursing Process,'' p. 61.
29. Ibid., p. 61.
30. American Nurses' Association Congress for Nursing Practice: *Nursing: A Social Policy Statement,* (Kansas City, MO: ANA, 1980).
31. Marjory Gordon, ''Nursing Diagnosis and Diagnostic Process,'' *American Journal of Nursing* 76 (1976): 1298.
32. Audrey M. McLane, *Classification of Nursing Diagnosis: Proceedings of the Seventh Conference* (St. Louis: C.V. Mosby Co., 1987), p. 507
33. Mi Ja Kim and Derry Ann Moritz, *Classification of Nursing Diagnoses: Proceedings of the Third and Fourth National Conferences* (New York: McGraw-Hill, 1982), p. 340.

34. Ibid., p. 340.
35. Ibid., p. 340
36. Ibid., p. 340.
37. Mi Ja Kim, Gertrude K. McFarland, and Audrey M. McLane, *Pocket Guide to Nursing Diagnoses* (St. Louis: C.V. Mosby Co., 1986), p. 1ff.
38. Marjory Gordon, *Manual of Nursing Diagnoses* (New York: McGraw-Hill, 1982), p. 1ff.
39. Audrey M. McLane, *Classification of Nursing Diagnoses, Proceedings from the Seventh Conference,* pp. 478–507.
40. Calista Roy, "Framework for Classification Systems Development: Programs and Issues," in *Classification of Nursing Diagnoses: Proceedings of the Fifth National Conference,* ed. Mi Ja Kim, Gertrude K. McFarland, and Audrey M. McLane (St. Louis: C.V. Mosby Co., 1984), pp. 26–33.
41. Ibid., p. 29.
42. Ibid., pp. 26–33.
43. Margaret A. Newman, *Health as Expanding Consciousness,* pp. 73–75.
44. Phyllis B. Kritek, "Development of a Taxonomic Structure for Nursing Diagnoses: A Review and Update," in *Classification of Nursing Diagnoses: Proceedings of the Sixth Conference,* ed. Mary Hurley (St. Louis: C.V. Mosby Co., 1986) pp. 23–38.
45. Audrey M. McLane, *Classification of Nursing Diagnoses: Proceedings of the Seventh Conference,* pp. 469–473.
46. Sue Popkess-Vawter and Norma Pinnell, "Should We Diagnose Strengths: Yes," *American Journal of Nursing* 87, no. 9 (September 1987): 1211–1216.
47. Karin Martens, "Let's Diagnose Strengths, Not Just Problems," *American Journal of Nursing* 86, no. 2 (February 1986): 192–193.
48. Sue Popkess-Vawter and Norma Pinnell, "Should We Diagnose Strengths: Yes," p. 1216.
49. Cynthia Flynn Capers and Rosemary Kelly, "Neuman Nursing Process: A Model of Holistic Care", *Holistic Nursing Practice* 1, no. 3 (May 1987): 23.
50. Gloria M. Bulechek and Joanne C. McCloskey, "Nursing Interventions: What They Are and How to Choose Them," *Holistic Nursing Practice* 1, no. 3 (May 1987): 43.
51. Barbara M. Dossey and Cathie E. Guzzetta, "Person-Centered Caring and the Nursing Process," p. 64.
52. Ibid., p. 64.
53. Gloria M. Bulechek and Joanne C. McCloskey, "Nursing Interventions," p. 40.
54. Ibid., pp. 40–42.
55. Dolores Krieger, *Foundations for Holistic Health Nursing Practice,* p. 201.
56. American Nurses' Association Division on Medical-Surgical Nursing Practice and American Heart Association Council on Cardiovascular Nursing, *Standards of Cardiovascular Nursing Practice* (Kansas City, MO: ANA, 1981), p. 1ff.
57. American Holistic Nurses' Association, *Standards for Holistic Nursing* (Springfield, MO: American Holistic Nurses' Association, 1987), pp. 1–10.
58. Ibid., pp. 1–10.
59. Ann Paulen, "Standards for Person-Centered Caring" (Madison: University of Wisconsin Hospital, 1980).

SUGGESTED READINGS

Barnum, B.J. "Holistic Nursing and the Nursing Process." *Holistic Nursing Practice* 1 (May 1987): 27–35.

Henderson, V. "Nursing Process: A Critique." *Holistic Nursing Practice* 1 (May 1987): 7–18.

Hughes, C.; Blackburn, S.; and Waryo, M. "On Masking Among Clients." *Topics in Clinical Nursing* 8 (April 1986): 83–89.

La Monica, E. *The Nursing Process: A Humanistic Approach*. Menlo Park, CA: Addison-Wesley, 1979.

Paterson, M. "Time and Nursing Process," *Holistic Nursing Practice* 1 (May 1987): 72–80.

chapter 7

Wellness, Values Clarification, and Motivation

Barbara Montgomery Dossey and Cathie E. Guzzetta

> We are responsible for the effects of our actions; and we are also responsible for becoming as aware as we can of these effects.[1]
>
> *Rollo May*

This chapter guides the nurse in expanding concepts of wellness, exploring the factors that facilitate motivation toward wellness, and assessing the impact of values clarification on wellness. Wellness is one's philosophy of living where there is awareness of purpose, meaning, and unique striving toward reaching human potentials. During all of our lives we are in a process of moving toward wellness. The concepts of wellness apply to the person who is dying, ill, or disabled, as well as to the highly motivated healthy individual. When people are under varying degrees of stress or illness, they can lose their appreciation for life's purpose and meaning. It is at these times that the nurse healer facilitates the journey toward understanding the wellness process.

NURSE HEALER OBJECTIVES

Theoretical

1. Define wellness.
2. Explain the steps in values clarification.
3. Explain the human motivational model.

Clinical

1. Identify four action steps that will increase your state of wellness in the workplace.
2. List the benefits of modeling wellness at work.

3. Work together with a colleague to write a contract on supporting each other to incorporate wellness behaviors at work.
4. Discuss a client's health beliefs and social support to determine which of the four categories most closely represent the client's characteristics.
5. Based on your assessment of the above client, identify and implement the appropriate strategies for motivating lifestyle changes.

Personal

1. Identify four wellness goals and then the behaviors and actions steps necessary to accomplish these goals.
2. Record in a journal your steps toward wellness.
3. Compare your beliefs/attitudes about self-care and wellness to the ideas presented in this chapter.
4. Identify one of your beliefs/attitudes about wellness. Using the values clarification process, check your belief/attitude with the seven value clarification steps. Determine what steps you still need to consider so that your belief/attitude can become a value to guide your behavior.

DEFINITIONS:

Hardiness: individual characteristics of stress-resistant individuals who possess certain attitudes, beliefs, and a sense of control over all aspects of their lives.

Motivation: the internal spark or desire necessary for a person to be committed to change, set goals, or succeed.

Self-Image: all of the perceptions and behavioral traits that a person may or may not exhibit that set the boundaries for what a person can and cannot do.

Self-Responsibility: the ability to respond to correct activities, choices, attitudes, and values that lead to integration of body-mind-spirit.

Values Clarification: a process whereby one becomes more aware of how life values and beliefs are established and how these values and beliefs control one's life or boundaries to achieve a high degree of wellness.

Wellness: one's philosophy of living whereby one is in the process of moving toward an increased awareness of reaching human potentials and the journey toward transpersonal self.

CONTEMPORARY NURSING

Remarkable changes are occurring in today's health care arena. Basic assumptions that our culture has traditionally held regarding health care are changing as a paradigmatic shift is underway. Perhaps the most significant change in thought concerns responsibility for health. Long thought to be the responsibility of the physician, today we recognize that health care has its roots in the individual. The shifting tides of thought about health care challenge us to expand our awareness about healing, as well as our role as healers.

Increased emphasis on preventive health and wellness is essential to help cut skyrocketing health-care costs and to add to the quality of human life. Because there are 2.1 *million* practicing nurses in the United States,[2] they are in a key leadership position—by virtue of both training and numbers—to teach healthy lifestyles to the public. Nurses across the country are placing more emphasis on prevention and wellness in their own lives. Not only are they teaching self-care, self-responsibility, and choices that lead toward health but they are also becoming increasingly recognized as powerful role models for the message they bring.

An increasing number of methodologically sound and scientifically convincing research studies support the notion that a person's psychologic state can actually produce a body illness. Today we know that emotions, attitudes, and thoughts are intimately connected with the expressions of human health, as well as of illness and distress. We know that disease states themselves generate changes in our mental lives that, in turn, affect the disease state, producing a spiral of events that defies any ultimate distinction between body-mind-spirit. If our minds can produce body illness, can our minds also be used to prevent illness, diminish complications, and promote healing? The answer is yes. The mind not only plays a negative role but also has the potential to affect health, illness, and healing potential positively and powerfully. To illustrate this concept we use the word bodymind, which means a single integrated entity.[3]

In the future clients will be taught to use their own consciousness as a bodymind-altering technology.[4] They will be segregated on hospital units according to new criteria: those who have well-developed consciousness skills and those who do not. In these two groups, the nursing care needs, the complications that can be expected in their illness, speed of recovery, and general prognosis will be vastly different. Technological advances as implemented by cold and sophisticated machinery will continue to create an even greater demand for "high touch" skills. Nurses will continue to add to the human dimension of care by the intentional use of therapeutic touch and by teaching and facilitating the use of bodymind capabilities through relaxation, imagery, music therapy, and biofeedback. In the past, these therapies have been left to chance and ascribed to the "bedside manner" of the nurse. Today nurses are beginning to employ these skills consciously, purposefully, and with a high order of discipline.

TOWARD WELLNESS

Wellness is a state and presence of being alive. Because we are an illness culture that has focused on not "being sick," we have not realized the total picture of wellness. Yet, health is not synonymous with wellness. Health is more a state of education and the pursuit of excellent health behaviors, such as weight management, exercise, and smoking cessation. Wellness involves not only performing the actual health behaviors but also a shift in thinking. Wellness is that continual process of evolution through life whereby the individual increases awareness, purpose, quality of life, uniqueness in all areas of human potential (Chapter 1), and movement toward the transpersonal self (Chapters 2 and 3). The terms "wellness" and "holistic" are interchangeable. Wellness involves motivation and values clarification. Values clarification helps a person act from authenticity; that is, actually living what one believes.

Many people are changing parts of their lives by exercising and eating better, but despite these changes, life is still not as good as it could be. The question asked by many is, "What can I be doing differently? I have a good job, family, extra money to spend, but life just is not satisfying." For example, it is not doing the running that is important, but also experiencing the joy of running; it is not the self-denial of nonnutritious foods, but the experience of the joy of health-giving-receiving of food.

Basic assumptions about wellness provide a foundation from which nurses can teach themselves and others the steps toward wellness. All individuals are assumed to:

- possess an innate healing ability
- exhibit qualities of life with purpose and meaning, even if they are critically ill
- have the capacity for self-reflection
- be in varying degrees of the wellness process
- be searching for answers about life process
- have the capacity for assessing, implementing, and evaluating areas of life that reflect the direction toward wellness
- have the capacity for change and taking risks

Nurses help themselves and others assess and identify areas of their life that will assist them to move toward wellness and improve their quality of living. As nurses teach, it is important to focus on the individual and to pay attention to inner discipline, stamina, and determination. Most people are not able to sustain new health behaviors because the culture in which they spend most of their time—home, the workplace, and community—does not support them in change. Unless the culture—in the home, workplace or community—supports a person in preventive health behaviors, regardless of how hard one tries, it is difficult to maintain life style pattern changes due to barriers and obstacles. If nurses are to be models of wellness, it is mandatory that they learn stress management skills and apply them in their own lives so that they can teach clients effectively. Stress management courses should include the information in this text, along with cognitive restructuring, assertiveness training, dealing with aggressive people, and giving and receiving negative feedback (see Suggested Reading).

Modeling Wellness, Self-Responsibility, and Self-Image

Nurses must first identify their own state of wellness and model a wellness lifestyle if they are to be effective teachers. Wellness is an evolving process that does not just happen. It requires self-assessments in all areas of human potential, as well as investigation of one's values and beliefs. Pause for a moment and reflect on these questions about your state of wellness:

- Do you see wellness as a fluctuating state over which you have control?

- Do you see your health as affected and determined by family, friends, job, and environment?
- Do you think that you can learn new wellness behaviors?
- Is the responsibility for staying well yours or someone else's?

Self-responsibility for wellness resides within each of us. What are the key elements in your wellness program? Do these elements include all areas of the circle of human potential as discussed in Chapter 1? It is through these areas that we focus on maximizing wellness. In planning a wellness program we must develop and incorporate four basic and critical factors: (1) a good self-image, (2) a positive attitude, (3) self-discipline, and (4) integration of body-mind-spirit. Each person will develop and incorporate these factors in his or her own unique way.

Self-image means that we view ourselves as good and well human beings. We must continue to develop keenly all of our senses and see ourselves as well in all respects—physical, mental, emotional, spiritual, and in our relationships, and making choices. A *positive attitude* means that we like and respect ourselves in all that we do. To thrive in this life, we have to learn to respect our body-mind-spirit. We also have to teach ourselves *discipline*. Discipline embodies the idea of being calm and consistently following positive wellness patterns, such as relaxation, exercise, play, and good nutrition. *Body-mind-spirit integration* means that we see ourselves as a whole, not as separate from the rest of our community. We must learn how to be more humane to ourselves. We are part of a whole universe, and we must see this relationship in terms of interacting wholes that are more than the sum of the parts. We must feel a keen sense of balance and relatedness between who we are, where we are, and how we interact with everyone.

Application of the wellness model to our own lives can assist us in feeling whole and inspired about life. To apply the model, we need to take the following steps:

- search for patterns and causes of stress and anxiety, as well as those of good feelings and emotions
- emphasize our human values
- assess any pain and disease as valuable signals of internal conflict, not as being totally negative
- place emphasis on achieving maximal body-mind-spirit wellness
- view our own body-mind-spirit as all co-equal factors, with one element never being more important than the others

Mission in Life

Reflect on your philosophy of life. Does your present life situation reflect your philosophy? To live more fully, we must have a *worthy personal mission*. A personal mission is a *survival technique*. One of the ways to survive, stay well, and feel whole is to know who we are and what we care about doing and to spend time effectively doing what it is that we care about. We need to determine what the beautiful threads are that weave our life tapestry together—the special and important areas, the people, places, and pleasures. We need to concentrate on developing the best in us, not on continually piecing the worst together. Our lives are not fixed for there is only one *permanent dance* that we can count on and that is *change*. We have an abundance of wellness choices in our lives, and we must exercise our ability to make choices that move us toward our best.

Problem solving is another way to increase wellness and identify our life mission. Following these ten steps can help you see a new way to deal with all levels of stress[5]:

1. Define overall needs, purposes, and goals.
2. Define problems.
3. Analyze capabilities/constraints and interest groups.
4. Specify an approach to problem solving.
5. State behavioral objectives and performance criteria.
6. Generate alternative solutions.
7. Analyze alternatives.
8. Choose the best alternative by decision action.
9. Implement and control decision rules.
10. Evaluate the effectiveness of decision action.

We can use problem-solving steps to clarify our perceptions. What are your current perceptions of stress? Because perception is an intellectual and cognitive process, you can pinpoint the stimuli that trigger negative defensive reactions, and you can develop effective coping strategies to use. Be aware of the internal and external factors that govern stress. Internal factors are past experiences, already existing behavior patterns, and heredity. Some external factors are environment, family, work, relationships, drugs, and alcohol.

Changing and Taking Risks

Changing and taking risks are an important part of life. Often when people do not change, they conclude they do not have the willpower to change. *Willpower* is a myth that does not lead to insight that effects long-lasting lifestyle changes. Rather, we should think in terms of *skillpower*. Skillpower implies new information and skills that lead to changes in lifestyle patterns. Change is a process of learning about our capacities through opening up to some new ways of being. Change implies flexibility and that lifestyle habits do not have to be permanent. Experiment. Notice what occurs when you try new ways of relating with friends, family, and colleagues, as well as new ways of eating, exercising, and playing. Changing detrimental or risky habits is essential for well-being. The more we choose effective lifestyle patterns, the better we learn the change process. The more we risk at changing lifestyle, the more consistently we select positive changes because the fear of changing is lessened.

Hardiness

Individuals who are said to possess "psychologic hardiness" have certain characteristics that make them almost resistant to illness[6]:

- openness to change
- perception that problems do not exist—there are only challenges
- feeling of involvement in what they are doing
- sense of personal power and control over life events
- thrive on challenges
- commitment to goals, work, family, and friends
- perception of body and mind as an integrative system

In addition researchers have found that "psychologically hardy" individuals demonstrate involvement in self-improvement programs and consistently utilize stress management, relaxation, and imagery techniques in their daily lives.

Work Spirit

Despite the complaints that we hear about the stressors of work, there are healthy persons who can teach us a great deal about the health of work and the workplace. These individuals exhibit something called "work spirit." People with work spirit possess these seven qualities[7]:

1. abundant energy and always appear to be "on a roll" or "in a flow state"
2. sense of purpose
3. creative and nurturing
4. different sense of time
5. sense of higher order and oneness
6. positive open state of mind
7. full sense of self

Can you imagine having these qualities at work? Work spirit is related to increased effectiveness, productivity, and individual satisfaction, which contribute to positive results in the workplace. It is also directly related to how much responsibility one is willing to take to change the course of one's life. Work spirit is fostered by (1) self-knowledge about human potentials; (2) self-care with attention to exercise, nutrition, play, relaxation, and stress management strategies; and (3) selflessness; that is being unself-consciously engrossed in the outcome of work tasks and projects, rather than worrying about what others think about how one is performing.[8]

Organizations can increase individual work spirit by having an identified purpose that can be shared and articulated by the worker. When this purpose is clearly communicated, supervisors or managers recognize individual strengths and talents and channel creative energy toward the organizational goals. Those organizations that offer praise, rewards, and encourage risk taking while not punishing for mistakes also increase individual work spirit.

Individuals with work spirit exhibit *synergy;* that is, they are involved in discovering common threads when there appears to be nothing but opposites and conflicts in situations.[9] They work with self and others to produce greater results. These people exhibit hardiness. They can make shifts in thinking and can release old mindsets. They understand that patterns and processes in any project create the whole, rather than focusing on isolated parts. They value input from colleagues, seek meaningful relationships, and also praise co-workers' talents and resources. They focus on win/win situations.

Individuals who have low levels of work spirit can create *dysergy* in the workplace; that is, they focus on an isolated action that promotes one function, but impedes the progress of another person or the group working together.[10] These individuals tend to work alone or evoke unnecessary competition among colleagues. They exhibit poor communication skills, aggressiveness, and insecurity, and they emphasize win/lose outcomes and reject meaningful interaction from co-workers.[11]

In order to integrate the previously discussed concepts of wellness and to become more aware of how to motivate self and others to make sustained changes toward wellness, the values clarification process is now discussed.

VALUES CLARIFICATION

A value is an affective disposition about the worth, truth, or beauty of a thought, object, person, or behavior. Values are important because they influence our decisions, behavior, and our nursing practice. They give direction and meaning to life[12] and guide behavior and conduct. They provide us with a frame of reference by which to integrate, explain, and evaluate new thoughts, experiences, and relationships.[13]

Individuals possess both personal values and professional values, which at times may be in conflict. When an individual has a strong personal value that directly conflicts with a professional value confusion, frustration, and dissatisfaction result.[14] A nurse has the right, however, not to participate in any activity or experience that violates personal values.[15]

Beliefs and attitudes are related closely to values. *Attitudes* are feelings toward a person, object, or idea that include cognitive, affective, and behavioral elements.[16] *Beliefs* are a subclass of attitudes. The cognitive factors involved in beliefs have less to do with facts and more with feelings; they represent a personal confidence or faith in the validity of some person, object, or idea.[17]

Values have a more dynamic dimension than attitudes because they possess motivational characteristics (see section on Human Motivational Model), in addition to the cognitive, effective and behavioral elements. Although both attitudes and values influence the outcomes of behaviors, individuals have more attitudes than they do values.[18]

Values are important in guiding our actions and professional practice. Usually, when confronted with a situation, we can take a variety of alternative actions. When choosing among alternative actions, it is important to focus on values so that the best alternative can be chosen.[19]

Traditionally, values have been transmitted by moralizing, modeling, a laissez-faire attitude, explaining, manipulation, and a reward/punishment approach.[20] In the 1960s, a *values clarification* approach was developed by Raths.[21] Values clarification is a dynamic process that emphasizes our capacity for intelligent self-directed behavior. Critical thinking is used to assist us in finding our own answers to a variety of questions or concerns.[22] There is no attempt to create a "correct" set of values because no one set of values is appropriate for all individuals.[23] Rather, the process of values clarification helps us become more internally consistent by achieving a closer fit between what we do and what we say.

The three steps in values clarification are choosing, prizing, and acting. When one values something, one[24]:

1. Chooses: (a) freely
   (b) between alternatives
   (c) after carefully evaluating the consequences of each alternative
2. Prizes: (a) is proud of the alternative chosen
   (b) affirms the choice publicly
3. Acts: (a) incorporates the choice into one's behavior
   (b) repeats the choice

First, the person must *choose* the value freely and not because someone else's beliefs or values have been imposed on them. The person must also choose from alternatives and understand the consequences of the decision. The next step is to *prize* and cherish the decision and be willing to affirm or communicate publicly the choice. The last step in the valuing process is to *act* which implies an action oriented process.[25] These steps are translated into what one values by a behavioral change that is consistent and repeated over time.

These three steps serve as the criteria by which we can determine whether we hold a particular value. A true value is present when it meets all of the criteria, although they may not necessarily occur in the order discussed above.[26] Many of our feelings, goals, and beliefs do not meet all of the criteria. Such beliefs are termed value *indicators*.[27] Individuals tend to have more value indicators than values.

Value indicators can become values if the individual is motivated to undergo the values clarification process. Consider, for example, your beliefs about wellness. Do you value exercise and proper nutrition? Use the values clarification process to check your beliefs about wellness according to the three steps discussed above. Then ask yourself what steps you need to consider more carefully so that this belief can become a value to guide your behavior.

Values clarification is a critical component of successful client education.[28] We know that our teaching is not always effective in changing client behaviors. This may be because we often ignore the important first step of the teaching process—determining what the client values and wants to know. What the nurse values as important in promoting successful outcomes is frequently not what the client values. It may be important, for example, to examine clients' values about their own health. Do they value prevention of complications or avoidance of recurrent illness? Nurses can assist clients in examining their values in terms of their alternatives. They can help clients discuss the consequences of their choices and choose an alternative behavior that is consistent with their values. They can also support clients in consistently incorporating the valued behavior over time. Positive health behavior outcomes are then likely to occur because the client has made the decision to change based on internally consistent values. An example of values clarification follows.

Case Study

Mr. B.Z. is a 49-year-old man who was admitted to the coronary care unit with a diagnosis of acute myocardial infarction. He was executive vice-president of a large company. Following admission, the patient was stable and had no major complications. On the second day of his hospital stay the patient was found lying in his hospital bed with his briefcase open, surrounded by papers, writing a report, and requesting a telephone in his room. The nurse handled the situation as follows:

Nurse: It sure looks like you have a lot of work.

Patient: Yes, I have so many deadlines this week, I cannot believe it. I really do not have time to be here. I sure hope they can get that telephone installed in here for me.

Nurse: It seems that your work is very important to you. I certainly can understand deadline problems. Could we take just a minute to discuss some other things that are important to you right now?

Patient: Sure. Getting better and out of here are important to me, and having the energy to deal with the demands of my job. This better not happen to me again.

Nurse: Tell me what you know about preventing another heart attack.

Patient: Well, I know I am going to have to lose some weight and get some regular exercise. I'm not sure how I will fit that into my schedule, though.

Nurse: Do you think that the heavy demands of work had anything to do with this illness?

Patient: Well . . . I know a lot of stress can make people sick. I've got to admit that I have had a stressful couple of months at work. Yes, I suppose all of that didn't help.

Nurse: You've told me that your work is important to you. You've also told me that preventing another heart attack is important. You have said that it will be important to lose weight, exercise, and perhaps reduce some of your daily stress. If you were willing to begin to work on one of these areas, which area would you choose?

Patient: I guess learning to deal with stress.

Nurse: That is a great place to start. There are many techniques that can be used to reduce stress levels that can have a profound impact on your mind, as well as a positive effect on your body. If you are willing, I'd like to take a few minutes now and guide you in a relaxation technique that can be of help to you right now and later after your discharge. Would you be willing to try this with me?

Patient: Sounds good. I'm willing to try. I suppose I should have thought about this stuff a long time ago.

Values influence our motivation to act, the health services we choose, and the way we perceive health concepts. A motivational model is now discussed to integrate the previously discussed concepts of wellness and values.

HUMAN MOTIVATIONAL MODEL

Let us now direct our attention to motivation and identify what makes a person set goals and embark upon behaviors that move toward wellness. Motivation is present when there is that spark or desire to improve one's present position. Imagination is also a prequisite of motivation, for one must be able to answer the question, ''What do I really want?'' Discipline and determination must also be engaged. The following four-element motivational model of what is called a person's ''subjective motivational state'' guides the nurse in better understanding motivation.[29] The model as seen in Figure 7-1 represents the person's subjective experience. The four elements do not represent unconscious processes (unnoticed bodily states) or the objective reality of the person's world view/perceptions. The first and second elements contain half-circles that represent the symbol of the T'ai Chi t'u, the intermingling of two opposites to form a harmonious whole.[30]

The first element represents the person's concept of ''things as they are,'' including the conceptual map of him- or herself and the world. The ''little yin'' *(a)* represents the person's raw experience of felt urges and sensations. The dashed triangle *(b)* that surrounds the yin represents the person's interpretation and identification of those sensations; that is, what those mean to the person. This triangle is represented by dashed rather than solid lines to indicate that identification and interpretation are less solid than the underlying experience. For example, consider a nurse under significant stress who is experiencing recurrent severe headaches. There is no denying that the recurrent severe headaches are real. However, if the nurse fails to connect the stress with the headaches, the identification and interpretation of the headache as being a stress-related headache may be in error. Before the nurse will choose intentional behaviors to change the headache pattern, he or she has to identify a change in behaviors as needs and desires. This is a common example of how people have the capability to repress, ignore, or misinterpret messages from their bodymind.

The second element represents the person's concept of ''things as they might be'' or future alternatives. This vision usually includes other people and things. People frequently think of both the present and the future in terms of people and things; they tend to think of the future as a given over which they have little control which creates confusion. This confusion is visually represented in the second element as the small dashed ''yang'' *(a)* to illustrate the less solid potential experiences of satisfaction or dissatisfaction, and the solid triangle *(b)* to represent potential satisfiers, such as the perfect job, the perfect family and mate, or the fast car and beautiful home.

The third element of this model represents the person's concept of strategies or the means of bridging the gap between ''things as they are'' and ''things as they might be.'' For example, if the desire of the nurse in the example above is to improve professional status, but full-time work is essential to achieve that goal, some alternatives might be starting an exercise program, developing strategies with mate and children about sharing household responsibilities, or choosing to start a stress management course to learn relaxation and time management skills.

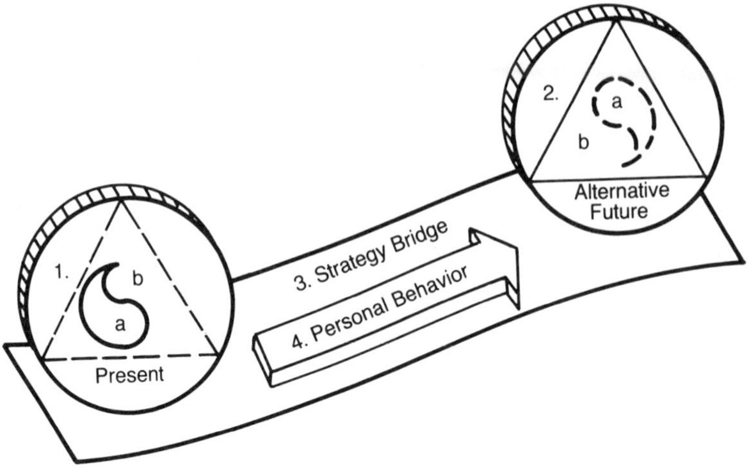

Figure 7-1 Model of Subjective Motivational State. The four-element motivational model has four parts that are represented as 1) "things as they are," 2) "things as they might be," 3) possible strategies, and 4) person's concept of possible actions and behaviors. The discrepancy between 1 and 2 represents the "motivational gap" that is necessary for new health behaviors to be elicited and sustained. *Source:* Reprinted from *Synergic Power: Beyond Dominance and Permissiveness* by J. Craig and M. Craig, p. 26, ProActive Press, © 1979.

The fourth element blends into the third element and represents the person's concept of his or her ability to carry out selected strategies of the third element or getting the satisfactions/satisfiers of the second element. To continue the above example, the nurse might decide that the real desire to start an exercise program is present and sharing of household responsibilities with family is also possible. However starting a stress management course is not feasible at the present time.

When all four elements are present then the person can recognize the discrepancy between the first two elements, which is referred to as a motivational gap.[31] It is at this point that the person experiences a tension and wishes to eliminate the discrepancy. The four elements are said to be "properly in tune" when the last three elements fall into place behind a first element that contains a strong, unambiguous need or want. When a motivational gap is generated, motivated behavior will normally follow. However, when one or more of the elements is totally missing, a motivational gap is not generated and the person *will not* change behavior.

Some of the known circumstances that will block motivated behavior are[32]:

- self-doubts and fears of unknown consequences that can override a person's desire for fulfillment or learning of new health behaviors

- belief that prior commitments or high priority projects leave little time for learning or implementing new behaviors
- perception of the person who is starting new skills that the new behaviors are too distasteful
- previous failures in changing behavior
- lack of confidence in the ability to implement new strategies
- cultural beliefs that discourage the new behavior
- lack of support from family, co-workers, or other groups

Many people do not recognize to what degree their culture conditions their beliefs and attitudes. They often feel helpless, burdened with power struggles and role responsibilities, and have a pervasive sense that they cannot really do anything to change the state of existing problems. Herein lies the challenge for the nurse. As people begin to develop clarity about their beliefs and values they are then in a better position to identify the life areas producing obstacles to change and to rename them as challenges. How effective the nurse will be in motivating clients to see their life challenges depends in large part on the degree to which the nurse models wellness and health behaviors.

Motivating Lifestyle Change: Strategies

Two factors that significantly influence a client's motivation to change are his or her health attitudes and beliefs and social support.[33] The Health Belief Model (HBM) identifies specific attitudes and beliefs that influence people to choose preventive health behaviors and comply with medical regimens.[34] According to this model, motivation to change behavior depends on the perception of the reward being greater than the perceived cost and perceived barriers. The HBM examines these major factors in determining compliance[35]:

- the health and willingness of the client to accept medical recommendations
- the client's subjective estimate of his or her susceptibility, vulnerability, and extent of bodily harm
- the interference of the client's social roles
- the client's perception of the efficacy and safety of the proposed regimen

The HBM focuses on the client's perceptions, rather than those of the health care worker. However, the HBM alone does not predict or screen persons who are at risk for noncompliance.[36]

People are more likely to choose healthy behaviors and comply with medical regimens if they have adequate social support.[37] Social support is defined as "resources provided by other persons,"[38] where affection, feelings of belonging, emotional support, and actual material goods are experienced.[39] To some degree, the individual's intention to perform a given act depends on that person's beliefs about what others expect to happen in that situation.[40]

Based on the relationship of health beliefs and attitudes and social support to facilitate compliance, four categories of individuals can be identified[41]:

1. Category 1: individuals who have positive health beliefs and attitudes and adequate social support
2. Category 2: individuals who have negative health beliefs and attitudes but adequate social support
3. Category 3: individuals who have positive health beliefs and attitudes but absent or negative social support
4. Category 4: individuals who have negative health beliefs and attitudes and absent or negative social support

The choice of strategies to facilitate compliance is then determined by the category to which the client belongs.

To determine to which category the client belongs, the nurse must first assess the client's health beliefs and attitudes regarding "risky" behavior, e.g., smoking, high stress, improper diet, lack of exercise, or failure to take hypertensive medication. This assessment must evaluate the following factors[42]:

- the client's general beliefs regarding health
- the client's willingness to seek health care advice
- the client's willingness to accept health care advice
- the client's perception of the seriousness of the risky behavior and its consequences
- the client's perception of susceptibility and vulnerability to the consequences of the behavior
- the client's perception of the risks, benefits, and degree of interference that the new behavior will have on current roles

Likewise, social support must be assessed in terms of the physical, emotional, and material support that the person receives, as well as the behavioral expectation that the support group places on the person in relation to the risky behavior and the newly advised activities.[43]

Individuals in category 1 perceive that their illness is serious and that their therapy will be helpful. Teaching efforts should be structured and developed to facilitate affective, cognitive, and psychomotor learning. Attention must be paid to matching the information presented with the person's coping style and locus of control.[44] The most important points should be discussed first and then repeated. The information, which should be presented clearly and concisely, should be discussed in logical categories. Any printed materials should be aimed at the reading level of the learner.

To accommodate different coping styles, those persons who use denial should be given basic survival information, whereas those who cope by focusing on the problem should be given detailed information.[45] Those persons who are internally controlled (i.e., who believe that what they do will affect their outcomes) should be given specific instructions on how they can manage or control the situation; those who are externally controlled (i.e., those who believe that their outcomes are determined by others or fate) should have the information presented to them by an authority figure.[46]

Individuals in category 2 have negative health beliefs and attitudes but adequate social support. Strategies for these individuals should focus on consciousness-raising techniques.[47] Nurse-client discussions should be used to explore feelings and beliefs regarding behaviors. Self-help group meetings can be arranged for the client to meet with other individuals with similar problems and concerns. Values clarification is another technique that can be used with the client to explore alternatives for healthy behaviors.

Other strategies that can be used with this group of people include behavior modification techniques.[48] Cues that stimulate healthy behavior should be recommended, and cues that stimulate unhealthy behaviors should be avoided. Temporary, artificial rewards can be suggested to support healthy behaviors. The reward should follow the behaviors and should be as small as possible yet still be rewarding, e.g., taking 30 minutes off to read a good book following the daily exercise program. Clients should be encouraged to identify a list of rewards before attempting the behavior change (see Chapter 11). Keeping a diary and making log entries for several days may be done to identify the cues and consequences of a particular behavior (see Chapter 17).

Individuals in category 3 have positive health beliefs and attitudes but absent or negative social support. Strategies recommended for this group are increase social support and cognitive strengthening.[49] Social support may be increased by providing family and friends with important information and encouraging their involvement with recommended therapy, discussion, or value clarification sessions. Client involvement with community agencies and self-help groups may also be appropriate. Cognitive strengthening may also be used to enhance coping skills. Such techniques may include assertiveness training, relaxation and imagery, and problem-solving and goal-setting approaches.[50]

Persons in category 4 have negative health beliefs and attitudes and absent or inadequate social support. The foot-in-the-door strategy in which minimal behavioral change is required may work with clients in this category.[51] The change is no more than the client can tolerate yet can still successfully accomplish to produce a positive outcome. Regimens should be simplified and basic goals established. Rewards and reinforcement are recommended. A graduated regimen is suggested in which complex behaviors are broken into smaller parts, with clients mastering the subparts before moving on to more complex behaviors. Written rather than verbal contracts are suggested for this group of clients.[52]

WORKSITE WELLNESS

Many worksite wellness programs are now being developed throughout the United States because of (1) the increasing interest of the American population in physical fitness, (2) the escalating health care costs of employees, (3) cumulative research findings documenting the rising health care costs associated with unhealthy employee behaviors, and (4) the effective organization of groups supporting worksite health programs.[53] Worksite wellness programs generally focus on stress management, nutritional education, weight control, exercise/physical fitness, smoking control, high blood pressure control, alcohol and drug control, accident prevention, and early cancer detection.[54] Industries, service agencies, hospitals, universities, and communities are all benefiting from such programs.

Nurses, because of their education and holistic focus, are in an ideal position to develop wellness programs. Ideally, such nurses should have knowledge of current health care practices, existing worksite wellness programs, and marketing and health care reimbursement.[55] They should possess leadership skills and knowledge as well.

The first step in developing a wellness program is to assess the needs of the worksite and the availability of wellness programs in the community. The following questions should be addressed by this assessment[56]:

- Using a health history or risk appraisal assessment form, what are the sociodemographic characteristics of the group, i.e., age, sex, ethnic origin, occupation, education, and residence?
- What conditions or diseases are documented in this group of people? Gather information related to health, weight, lipid levels, blood sugar, blood pressure, and such lifestyle habits as nutrition, exercise, stress, smoking, and use of alcohol and drugs.
- What are the costs of health care insurance premiums, disability benefits, and sick leave for this group?
- What kinds of acute and chronic illnesses are being treated in this group?
- What kind of prevention and wellness needs does this group want to consider?
- What kind of wellness programs does the group believe needs to be developed?
- What community wellness programs are already available for this group?

When developing wellness programs, participating clients should be included in the planning process. The vital roles that family and friends play in the person's ability to participate in wellness activities also should be recognized. Thus, such programs should be developed to include dependents and retired workers.

The evaluation of wellness programs should be considered early in the planning stages. Relevant evaluation outcomes must be identified based on the goals and objectives of the program. The reader is referred to the Life Gains Program and O'Donnell's comprehensive text on workplace wellness.[57,58]

SUMMARY

The nurse who is aware of the wellness model is able to assist the person in investigating the purpose and meaning of an acute crisis, as well as exploring the transpersonal state. A four-element motivational model was presented to help explain why people act as they do. This framework can increase the nurse's awareness of how values and beliefs affect each element of the motivational process. The motivational gap must be present before one will begin to change behavior that moves one toward wellness. Worksite wellness was presented to encourage the nurse to investigate an area in which major health education and implementation must occur.

DIRECTIONS FOR FUTURE RESEARCH

1. Evaluate if nurses who model health exhibit psychologic hardiness and work spirit characteristics.
2. Evaluate whether client outcomes are enhanced when nurses identify the presence of a client's motivational gap.
3. Compare and contrast various strategies for motivating lifestyle changes.

NURSE HEALER REFLECTIONS

After reading this chapter, the nurse healer will be able to answer or begin a process of answering the following questions:

- How do I *feel* when I reflect on my state of wellness?
- What are the *inward feelings* I acknowledge when I become aware of my motivation?
- What is my *self-image*?
- What is my current *quality of life*?
- What do I feel *joyful* about?
- What are my *values* and *beliefs* regarding wellness?

NOTES

1. Rollo May, *Power and Innocence: A Search for the Sources of Violence* (New York: W.W. Norton, 1972), p. 259.
2. Linda Aiken and Carolyn Mullinex, "The Nurse Shortage: Myth or Reality," *New England Journal of Medicine* 317, no. 10, (September 3, 1987): p. 641.
3. Candace Pert, "The Wisdom of the Receptors: Neuropeptides, the Emotions, and Bodymind," *Advances* 3, no. 3 (Summer 1986): 8.
4. Leland Kaiser, "The Next Medical Frontier: Computer and Robotic-Enhanced Health Care," *Group Practice Journal,* November/December, 1986, p. 5.
5. June Baily and Katherine Claus, *Decision Making In Nursing: Tools for Change* (St. Louis: C.V. Mosby Co., 1975), p. 1ff.
6. Suzanne Kobasa, "How Much Stress Can You Survive?," *American Health* 3, no. 7 (1984): 64–77.
7. Connie Zweig, "Work Spirit," *American Way Magazine,* June, 1987, pp. 14–19.
8. Ibid., p.15.

9. Perry Pascarella, "Job Stress: A State of Mind," *Industry Week* (November 1982), p. 92.
10. Ibid., p. 2.
11. Ibid., p. 2.
12. S.B. Simon, L.W. Howe, and H. Kirschenbaum, *Values Clarification: A Handbook of Practical Strategies for Teachers and Students* (New York: Hart Publication Company, 1972), p. 13.
13. Diane B. Uustal, "Values Clarification in Nursing: Application to Practice," *American Journal of Nursing* 78, no. 12 (December 1978): 2059.
14. Shirley M. Steele and Vera M. Harmon, *Values Clarification In Nursing* (New York: Appleton-Century Crofts, 1979), p. 2.
15. Ibid., p. 7.
16. Ibid., p. 3.
17. Ibid., p. 3.
18. Ibid., p. 3.
19. Ibid., p. 5.
20. Diane B. Uustal, "Values Clarification In Nursing," p. 2060.
21. L.E. Raths, M. Harmin, and S.B. Simon. *Values and Teaching: Working With Values in the Classroom* (Columbus, OH: Charles E. Merrill Books, 1966), p. 30.
22. James Z. Wilbering, "Values Clarification," in *Nursing Interventions: Treatments for Nursing Diagnoses,* ed. Gloria Bulechek and Joanne C. McCloskey (Philadelphia: W.B. Saunders Co., 1985), p. 175.
23. Diane B. Uustal, "Values Clarification in Nursing," p. 1260.
24. L.E. Raths, M. Harmin, and S.B. Simon, *Values and Teaching,* p. 30.
25. Diane B. Uustal, "Values Clarification in Nursing," p. 1261.
26. James Z. Wilbering, "Values Clarification," p. 175.
27. Diane B. Uustal, "Values Clarification In Nursing," p. 1261.
28. Ibid., p. 1262.
29. James and Marguerite Craig, *Synergic Power: Beyond Domination and Permissiveness* (Berkeley, CA: ProActive Press, 1979), p. 25.
30. Deborah Bockman and Doris Riemen, "Qualitative versus Quantative Nursing Research," in *Holistic Nursing Practice* 2, no. 1 (November 1987): 74.
31. James and Marguerite Craig, *Synergistic Power: Beyond Domination and Permissiveness,* p. 27.
32. Ibid., p. 28.
33. Polly Ryan, "Strategies for Motivation Life-Style Changes," *The Journal of Cardiovascular Nursing* 1, no. 4 (August 1987): 54–66.
34. M.H. Becker, *The Health Belief Model and Personal Health Behavior* (Thorofare, NJ: Slack, 1984), p. 4.
35. Polly Ryan, "Strategies for Motivating Life-Style Changes," p. 55.
36. Ibid., p. 55.
37. Ibid., p. 55.
38. S. Cohen and S. Symes, *Social Support and Health* (New York: Academic Press, 1985), p. 25.
39. Polly Ryan, "Strategies for Motivating Life-Style Changes," p. 56–57.
40. Ibid., p. 55.
41. Ibid., pp. 54–66.
42. Ibid., p. 57.
43. Ibid., p. 57.
44. Ibid., pp. 57–59.
45. Ibid., p. 59.
46. J. Kerr, "Multidimensional Health Locus of Control, Adherence, and Lowered Diastolic Blood Pressure," *Heart and Lung* 15 (1986): 87–92.
47. Polly Ryan, "Strategies for Motivating Life-Style Changes," p. 59.

48. Ibid., p. 60.
49. Ibid., p. 62.
50. Ibid., p. 62.
51. Ibid., p. 63.
52. Ibid., p. 63.
53. Philip Greiner, ''Nursing and Worksite Wellness: Missing the Boat,'' *Holistic Nursing Practice* 2, no. 1 (November 1987): 53–60.
54. R. Parkison, *Managing Health Promotion in the Workplace* (Palo Alto, CA: Mayfield Publishing Co., 1982), p. 58.
55. Philip A. Greiner, ''Nursing and Worksite Wellness: Missing the Boat,'' p. 58.
56. R. Parkinson, *Managing Health Promotion in the Workplace,* pp. 22–26.
57. Carolyn Chambers Clark, *Wellness Nursing* (New York: Springer Publishing Co., 1986), pp. 296–299.
58. Michael O'Donnell, and Thomas Ainsworth, *Health Promotion in the Workplace* (New York: John Wiley and Sons, 1984), pp. 10–9.

SUGGESTED READINGS

Davis, M., McKay, M., and Eshelman, E. *Relaxation and Stress Management Workbook,* 2nd ed. Oakland, CA: New Harbinger, 1983.

Ellis, Albert, and Harper, Robert. *A Guide to Rational Living*. North Hollywood, CA: Wilshire Books Company, 1975.

Knowles, Ruth, *A Guide to Self-Management Strategies for Nurses*. New York: Springer Publishing Co. 1984.

McKay, M., Davis, M., and Fanning, P. *Messages: The Communication Book*. Oakland, CA: New Harbinger, 1983.

chapter **8**

Research and Holistic Implications

Cathie E. Guzzetta

> Nothing is more important about the quantum physics principle than this, that it destroys the concepts of the world as "sitting out there," with the observer safely separated from it . . . . To describe what has happened, one has to cross out that old word "observer," and put in its place the new word "participator." In some strange sense the Universe is a participatory universe.[1]
>
> *John A. Wheeler*
> *Physicist*

This chapter discusses research methods and problems from a holistic point of view. Nurses have come to realize that the fit between traditional research methods and holistic nursing principles is not always a good one. The shift to the wellness model has redirected research priorities and methodologies to a significant degree. It has also provided us with some exciting challenges.

NURSE HEALER OBJECTIVES

Theoretical

1. Discuss how the wellness model has redirected priorities in nursing research.
2. Compare and contrast qualitative versus quantitative research methods.
3. Identify variables that are related to wellness and illness.
4. Read a qualitative research study in one of the nursing research journals.

Clinical

1. Develop a psychophysiologic tool that will measure the outcomes of self-regulation interventions.

2. Collect data from various clients participating in some form of self-regulation therapy to determine their subjective evaluation of their outcomes.
3. Design a research study based on one of the questions found in the section, "Directions for Future Research," at the end of this chapter.

Personal

1. Set aside some time to learn more about research methods.
2. Attend a research conference.
3. Discuss some of the ideas in this chapter with a nurse researcher.

DEFINITIONS

Heisenberg's Uncertainty Principle: one cannot look at a physical object without changing it.

Qualitative Research: a form of research that studies the context and meaning of interactive variables as they form patterns reflective of the whole.

Quantitative Research: a form of research that embodies the principles of the scientific method, including formulating hypotheses, testing the hypotheses, and rejecting or not rejecting the hypotheses.

Reductionism: breaking down phenomena to their smallest possible part.

WELLNESS MODEL

The framework guiding client/patient care research is shifting from an illness model to a wellness model of health care. The wellness model views individuals holistically as biopsychosocial units who assume responsibility for their own health. It emphasizes the enormous potential possessed by each individual to use the healing potential of his or her own bodymind.

The shift to the wellness model has been supported by research in the fields of chemistry, psychology, neurophysiology, and quantum physics. The hemispheric functions of the brain, voluntary control of the autonomic nervous system, and the production of endorphins in the brain are just a few of the research areas that have provided proof of the bodymind connectedness. Investigations evaluating biofeedback, meditation, Benson's relaxation response, guided imagery, music therapy, progressive relaxation, hypnosis, acupressure/ acupuncture, and therapeutic touch have all concluded that these interventions have the exciting potential to prevent illness and maintain high-level wellness. (Refer to Chapters 9–17, Theory and Research, for references.) In addition, such research has been instrumental in guiding the development of humanistic and holistic approaches to health care. Nurses have the education and ability to add significantly to this body of knowledge. The future challenge and responsibility of nursing is to explore how these findings can be applied to our nursing practice.[2]

HOLISTIC RESEARCH METHODS

Although the scientific method used today has evolved over many centuries, Descartes' teachings in the 17th century did much to advance medical research. Descartes' notion of reductionism in research—the breaking down of every question to its smallest possible part—has been enormously beneficial in isolating causative factors responsible for disease. For example, the physiologic part of an individual can be divided into organs, cells, and biochemical substances and then to molecular, atomic, and subatomic levels. Such an approach is useful for identifying the etiology of disease (e.g., a virus causes acquired immunodeficiency syndrome) and offers direction for studying the cures of disease, e.g., antibodies are used to kill the infection and sterilize the lesions associated with endocarditis.

The scientific or quantitative method was created so that the results obtained in one study could be generalized to other patient populations and replicated in similar studies. The key issue of the quantitative method is its ability to predict and control outcomes. The quantitative method formulates hypotheses by reducing the area of interest to its smallest possible part, tests the hypotheses, and rejects or does not reject the hypotheses.

Biomedical research using quantitative methods abounds as scientists seek to find unknown causes and cures for physiologic (and sometimes psychologic) illnesses. Enormous numbers of personnel and dollars are directed toward finding answers at the molecular level to such problems as the common cold, cancer, acquired immunodeficiency syndrome, essential hypertension, and thyroid disease, to name only a few. Such a reductionistic research approach, however, cannot account for the whole person as an integrated unit.

The success of medical research was a significant factor in establishment of medicine as a scientific profession. This success also heavily influenced the nursing profession to follow closely in medicine's footsteps. Nurses have come to realize, however, that the fit between quantitative methods and holistic nursing practice is not always an ideal one. The central tenet underlying the holistic framework is that the whole is greater than the sum of its parts. Because quantitative methods seek only to find answers to parts of the whole, such a process conflicts with holistic principles.

Therefore, nurses have looked to alternate philosophies of science and research methods that are compatible with investigating humanistic and holistic phenomena.[3,4] Such methods have been termed *qualitative research*. Qualitative research is used to study patterns by investigating the context and meaning of observed patterns. Its scope is holistic, and its methods incorporate interactions of variables.[5]

A holistic approach to research describes all possible variables in the life of an individual who has a specific problem or illness.[6] Collection of such descriptive data can contribute to understanding what combination of variables affects a particular problem or illness. Such a process is used to emphasize the interactive nature of variables, rather than the isolation of one part. In such research it is not necessary for the same variable to affect all individuals in the same way to be significant.[7]

For example, a nurse researcher might study the variables involved in the life of an individual who has coronary artery disease. Data might be collected on childhood lifestyle, dietary patterns, and illness; job stressors; social support; exercise patterns; emotional life changes; smoking and alcohol behavior; spiritual beliefs; and values and attitudes related to wellness. This data would then be analyzed to determine the impact of such variables on the individual's problem and to gain insight on how such variables represent patterns that characterize the individual's pathway to coronary artery disease. When this information is understood the nurse can begin to evaluate other individuals with coronary artery disease to identify similarities and differences. The results can lead to theory development regarding the interactive nature of such variables on the development of the illness. Intervention studies can then be designed to repattern pathways toward wellness.

The quantitative scientific method may be used to identify an isolated cause that is producing the undesired effect. Validating cause and effect is accomplished by isolating parts and using group comparisons and statistical analyses. The quantitative method, however, does not take into account the phenomenologic nature of variables, nor does it consider the characteristics of one individual's pathway to a particular problem. It does not take into account or averages out the unique patterns and interacting variables of one individual.[8] A flaw inherent in the deductive quantitative method is that it does not explain why one individual becomes ill and why another will not. Historically, this issue has been deemed irrelevant because it has never been a concern of the biomedical paradigm.[9]

The very roots of this paradigm have been challenged, however, by current bodymind researchers. The field of psychoneuroimmunology has generated astounding research findings supporting the interactive nature of psychophysiologic variables. There is conclusive evidence that thought and emotions affect the immune system at the cellular and subcellular levels.

It has taken centuries to progress beyond Cartesian dualism and to generate convincing data that refute the idea that the body is separate from the mind. We must realize that currently we are taking part in a revolutionary change in thinking. We must also realize that not all health care professionals understand or accept such change. Many remain tied to the biomedical model and view holistic principles and its corresponding research as unscientific. Consider the following quote from a recent editorial in one of the leading medical journals: "It is time to acknowledge that our belief in disease as a direct reflection of mental state is largely folklore."[10]

The psychophysiologic link between health and illness has been criticized because evidence to support the link has been provided in the form of anecdotes or personal testimonials. "Hard core" researchers who embrace the quantitative method have not placed much value on the "softer" data obtained from qualitative studies. Even when quantitative methods were used to support the link, such studies were criticized because of their retrospective designs, methodologic problems, or lack of tools with psychometric properties.[11]

It is clear that, before the bodymind link is universally accepted, additional research will have to be conducted. Nurses, by virtue of their day-to-day care of the client, are in a unique position to observe, document, analyze, and quantify the interactive relationship of variables on health and illness. The value of qualitative research methods undoubtedly will increase as important bodymind variables are discovered in future studies. The respectability of qualitative research might make rapid gains also if the authors of nursing research texts dedicated more time to this content area and if research journal editors would begin to accept more qualitative studies for publication.[12] Moreover, the results from qualitative studies could supply researchers with a plethora of potential research hypotheses.

The decision to use qualitative versus quantitative methods, however, should not be viewed from an either/or perspective. A strong case has been argued for both methodologies in holistic research.[13] Qualitative research is needed to explore patterns and variables about which little is known. It is also needed to investigate interactive variables, the meaning of which cannot be understood when they are broken down into isolated parts. Quantitative research, on the other hand, is needed to validate new knowledge, identify etiologies, and predict outcomes of nursing interventions. Both approaches, therefore, are needed in holistic research.[14]

IDENTIFYING HOLISTIC VARIABLES

One way to conduct holistic research is to investigate health and illness by clarifying the precise definitions of those two states. Two major factors contributing to the lack of research on healthy individuals are confusion about the health-illness continuum and conflicting definitions of health.[15]

The traditional health-illness continuum asserts that health and illness are linear and opposite states. Such an assertion has complicated theoretical definitions of health and illness because the researcher is artificially forced to derive a definition of health that is opposite to illness.

Illness is defined as a state of being ill that is characterized as unwell, sick, evil, and objectionable.[16] Health is defined as the general condition of the body and mind with reference to soundness, vigor, vitality, and wholeness.[17] Correlates of health include a fullness of life, an openness to environmental interaction, and a sense of self-determination.[18,19] Such definitions encompass the notion that health includes both physiologic and psychologic factors, including enthusiasm, meaningfulness, fullness, and growth in the individual's interaction with the living and nonliving environment. When evaluating definitions of health and illness, it is obvious that they are not opposites, but rather are different states of existence.[20]

Clarifying definitions is essential, therefore, to conducting sound research. The definitions are then operationalized to describe health patterns, and the variables are correlated to predict health behaviors or analyzed to determine the effects of interventions on maintaining or restoring health. For example, if fullness of life is to be studied descriptively, data might be collected on an individual's satisfaction with work, creativity, enjoyment of sexual activities, and hobbies.[21] Correlational studies might include the relationship of fullness of life and a sense of self-determination. From an experimental viewpoint, one might measure the effects of relaxation and guided imagery on desired physiologic outcomes, self-determination, and fullness of life.

EVALUATING HOLISTIC INTERVENTIONS

All of the self-regulation interventions described in this book are in need of further investigation. Many have been used to treat a variety of problems in various settings, but their appropriateness and adequacy in these populations and settings have not been assessed fully. Many early evaluation studies were concerned with discovering whether such interventions "worked" and, as a result, employed an experimental group and a control group to identify differences. Today we need to be asking a more sophisticated question related to these interventions: Under what conditions is the technique the treatment of choice for which particular client/patient with what type of clinical problem?[22] Evaluation studies are needed to determine the usefulness, indications, contraindications, and dangers of one self-regulation intervention as *compared* to another.[23] Moreover, these interventions need to be evaluated not only in terms of treating various illnesses but also from the perspective of maintaining high-level wellness and preventing illness.

The holistic researcher will quickly discover some inherent difficulties when trying to measure the outcome effects of self-regulation interventions. The primary difficulty is that there are no holistic measurement devices or tools that measure holistic therapies.[24] If a self-regulation intervention is believed to affect the individual's bodymind, then it is reasonable to believe that we should be able to measure these bodymind effects. Because Cartesian dualism has heavily influenced our current methods of scientific inquiry, we find too often that we have studied body effects and we have studied mind effects but rarely have we studied the relationship between the two.

A variety of physiologic measurements are available to study the outcome effects of self-regulation interventions. Physiologic measurements are often used in combination to develop a physiologic profile of observed outcomes. They tend to be used by researchers with more confidence than psychologic parameters. This lack of confidence in psychologic measurements in part stems from the view that psychologic data are less reliable and valid than their physiologic counterparts. The author also suspects that many of the psychologic measurement tools currently available are not sensitive indicators of the psychologic outcomes associated with self-regulation interventions. Thus, many tools may not be well suited for this type of research because they are not capable of picking up or demonstrating subtle yet significant psychologic changes that are present. When a psychologic indicator is not found to be significant, it does not disprove necessarily the existence of a significant psychologic effect. It may indicate that (1) the wrong variable was studied, or (2) the psychologic tool used was not sufficiently sensitive to measure its existence.

It is clear that additional tools need to be developed to measure outcomes of holistic interventions. Nurses have the knowledge and ability to contribute significantly to this area. Qualitative research methodologies would be useful in identifying and clustering psychophysiologic interactive outcome variables. Quantitative methods could then be used to develop tools that incorporate these variables to measure the effects of the interventions. Self-regulation therapies influence many psychophysiologic parameters, but they do not necessarily influence the same variables in different individuals. Thus, a number of parameters must be used to evaluate the outcomes of these interventions satisfactorily.[25] Physiologic and psychologic outcomes should be used in combination and their effects correlated as a means of increasing the validity of the findings and discovering bodymind links. In addition, physiologic and psychologic measurements should be combined together in developing various psychophysiologic tools.

Both Morse[26] and Curtis et al.[27] found no physiologic changes when evaluating various forms of self-regulation therapies, but both did report significant positive differences in the subjects' evaluations of these therapies. A rich, promising, and holistic source of data therefore lies within the subjects' own estimate of their behavior and outcomes. Meaning and quality of life are essential tenets of the holistic model. Qualitative methods are well suited to tapping this important source of data.

OBJECTIVITY AND SCIENTIFIC INVESTIGATION

Most researchers accept the universal principle that objectivity must govern scientific inquiry. This belief has been shaken, however, by the Nobel Prize winner, Werner Heisenberg, who studied information obtained from an electron. From his work, Heisenberg's Uncertainty Principle evolved, which states that one cannot look at a physical object without changing it.[28] Thus, objects and clients are changed when we observe them. The holistic researcher realizes the enormous implications of this principle. The researcher does not stand apart from the research or research subject. Because we are a part of nature and not separate from it, we are part of the research that we study. We are not objective observers of the world we study, but rather participants in that world. This participation, in turn, affects the results we obtain through research. Our participation may be a word, an action, a touch, an observation, or simply our very presence. The researcher becomes an integral part of the experiment. The term "nonparticipant observer" in research is therefore meaningless.

Based on his work, Heisenberg also proposed that it is not possible to obtain a complete description of a physical object because, when we describe it, we change it. Because we cannot obtain all the data to describe an object, some information will always be unknown.[29] Research effects are verified by observations. However, if it is impossible to obtain a complete description of a physical object, then some outcomes will be unknown. It is misleading to believe that research can *always* be validated in terms of testable or observational effects. The effects of a certain experiment, whether they are observable or not, will ultimately affect the subject. Thus, it is theoretically possible to build a scientific theory without any observable data.[30]

In addition, certain phenomena related to holistic research may not be accessible to scientific investigation. Some experiences may be ineffable. The individual who experiences certain feelings while using self-regulation interventions may not be able to conceptualize or express them or may be unable to translate or communicate these effects to another. Likewise, the researcher may be unable to interpret the effects because of a lack of experience with these feelings or because our language is limited and inadequate when describing and communicating these phenomena.

SUMMARY

The shift to the wellness model has had some exciting implications for nursing research. Not only has the holistic movement redirected our priorities in nursing research but it also has redefined our methods of scientific investigation.

DIRECTIONS FOR FUTURE RESEARCH

1. What intervention programs are beneficial in promoting wellness behaviors in specific patient populations?

2. What variables do nurses/clients believe are indicators of wellness? Illness?
3. How can self-regulation interventions be combined to enhance efficiency for the individual, e.g., combining Benson's relaxation response with biofeedback or combining music therapy with imagery and progressive relaxation?
4. What is the most effective way to combine self-regulation interventions with traditional modes of therapy to achieve successful client outcomes?
5. Which interventions are most effective for individuals with a specific problem or illness?

NURSE HEALER REFLECTIONS

After reading this chapter, the nurse healer will be able to answer or will begin a process of answering the following questions:

- How do I *feel* about the respectability of qualitative research methods?
- How do I *feel* about the importance of research in advancing holistic nursing practice?
- What is my *role* in participating in nursing research?
- How do I feel when I *realize* that some intervention outcomes can never be measured?

NOTES

1. John A. Wheeler, "Not Consciousness But Distinction Between the Probe and the Probed as Central to the Elemental Quantum Level of Observation," in *Role of Consciousness in the Physical World,* ed. Robert Jahn (Boulder, CO: Westview Press, 1981), pp. 87–111.
2. Patricia Flynn, *Holistic Health: The Art and Science of Care* (Bowie, MD: Brady Co., 1980), pp. 1–8.
3. Margaret A. Newman, *Health as Expanding Consciousness* (St. Louis: C.V. Mosby Co., 1986), pp. 91–96.
4. Mary Cipriano Silva and Daniel Rothbart, "An Analysis of Changing Trends in Philosophies of Science on Nursing Theory Development and Testing," *Advances in Nursing Science* 6, no. 2 (January 1984): 1–13.
5. P. Mullen and D. Iverson, "Qualitative Methods for Evaluative Research in Health Education Programs," *Health Education,* May-June 1982, pp. 11–18.
6. L. Mehl, *Mind and Matter: Foundations for Holistic Health* (Berkeley, CA: Mindbody Press, 1981), p. 74.
7. Carolyn Chambers Clark, *Wellness Nursing: Concepts, Theory, Research and Practice* (New York: Spring Publishing Co., 1986), p. 318.
8. Deborah F. Bockmon and Doris J. Riemen, "Qualitative Versus Quantitative Nursing Research," *Holistic Nursing Practice* 2, no. 1 (November 1987): 71–75.
9. Carolyn Chambers Clark, *Wellness Nursing,* p. 318.
10. Marcia Angell, "Disease as a Reflection of the Psyche," (Editorial), *New England Journal of Medicine* 312 (1985): 1570–1572.

11. Cathie E. Guzzetta, ''The Human Factor and the Ailing Heart: Folklore or Fact?'' (Editorial), *Journal of Intensive Care Medicine* 2, no. 1 (January-February 1987): 3–5.
12. Deborah F. Bockmon and Doris J. Riemen, ''Qualitative Versus Quantitative Nursing Research,'' p. 72.
13. Ibid., pp. 74–75.
14. Ibid., p. 75.
15. Patricia Winstead-Fry, ''The Scientific Method and Its Impact on Holistic Health,'' *Advances in Nursing Science* 2, no. 4 (July 1980): 1–7.
16. *Random House College Dictionary* (New York: Random House 1975).
17. Ibid.
18. *World Health Organization Constitution,* Geneva: World Health Organization, 1960.
19. H. Dunn, *High-Level Wellness* (Arlington, VA: R.W. Beatty Co., 1969).
20. Patricia Winstead-Fry, ''The Scientific Method and Its Impact on Holistic Health,'' p. 2.
21. Ibid., p. 6.
22. D.H. Shapiro, ''Overview: Clinical and Physiological Comparison of Meditation with Other Self-Control Strategies,'' *American Journal of Psychiatry* 139 (1982): 267.
23. American Psychiatric Association, ''Position Statement on Meditation,'' *American Journal of Psychiatry* 134 (1977): 720.
24. M. Garbin, ''Stress Research in Clinical Settings,'' *Topics in Clinical Nursing* 1, no. 1 (April 1979): 91.
25. P. Bohachick, ''Progressive Relaxation Training in Cardiac Rehabilitation: Effects on Psychologic Variables,'' *Nursing Research* 33 (1984): 283–287.
26. D.R. Morse, S. Martin, M.L. Furst, et al., ''A Physiological and Subjective Evaluation of Meditation, Hypnosis, and Relaxation,'' *Psychosomatic Medicine* 39 (1977): 304.
27. W.D. Curtis and H.W. Wessberg, ''A Comparison of Heart Rate, Respiration, and Galvanic Skin Response Among Meditators, Relaxers, and Controls,'' *Journal of Altered States of Consciousness* 2 (1975/1976): 319.
28. Werner Heisenberg, *Physics and Philosophy* (New York: Harper & Row, 1978), p. 42.
29. Gary Zukav, *The Dancing Wu Li Masters: An Overview of the New Physics* (New York: William Morrow & Co., 1979), pp. 111–114.
30. Charles T. Tart, *States of Consciousness* (New York: E.P. Dutton and Co., 1975), pp. 207–228.

SUGGESTED READINGS

Dossey, Larry. *Space, Time, and Medicine*. Boston: Shambhala Publications, Inc., 1982.

Floyd, J.A. ''Research Using Rogers' Conceptual System: Development of a Testable Theorem.'' *Advances in Nursing Science* 5 (January 1983): 37–48.

Lovejoy, N.C. ''Biofeedback: A Growing Role in Holistic Health.'' *Advances in Nursing Science* 2 (July 1980): 83–93.

Lynch, J. *The Language of the Heart*. New York: Basic Books Inc., 1985.

Tinkle, M.B., and Beaton, J.L. ''Toward a New View of Science: Implications for Nursing Research.'' *Advances in Nursing Science* 5 (January 1983): 27–36.

unit **IV**

Strategies to Strengthen the Whole Person

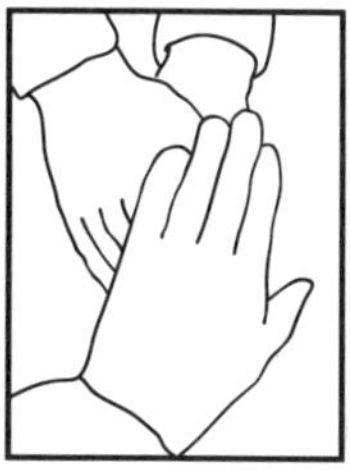

Healing awareness is an available option that can be consciously cultivated. It is a noninterfering attention that allows natural self-healing responses to take place. . . . As healing awareness develops one learns to witness the content, process, and contents of consciousness, without trying to evaluate, control, or modify them. . . . Healing awareness depends on a willingness to acknowledge the truth about oneself at all levels.

Frances Vaughan

Source: Frances Vaughan, *The Inward Arc* (Boston: Shambhala Publications, Inc., 1985).

chapter **9**

Nutrition, Exercise, and Movement: Nourishing the Bodymind

Lynn Keegan

> In large measure joy and vitality can come from eating well, exercising, and creatively moving to the rhythm of life.

This chapter guides the nurse in how to maximize and develop the best of nutrition, exercise, and movement skills both for self and for the client. Continuing the philosophy found throughout this text, nurses are encouraged to develop their own wellness behaviors in order to model these skills and qualities for their clients.

As we approach the 21st century the ancient Greek ideal of a sound mind in a strong, able, body is once again gaining favor. The physical body can indeed be the temple for the mind/spirit. How we care for and nourish it affects not only our general physical well-being but also increases our capacity for actualizing the mental and spiritual capacities.

NURSE HEALER OBJECTIVES

Theoretical

1. Learn the definitions of the terms in this chapter.
2. List the recommended goals set by the U.S. Senate Subcommittee on Nutrition.
3. Develop a plan that combines good nutrition, exercise, and ideal weight.
4. Differentiate among exercise, fitness, and movement.
5. Learn the benefits of exercise.

Clinical

1. Assess your level of nutrition at work that adds to energy levels or depletes it.
2. Develop an awareness of body mechanics both during clinical physical activity and desk work.

3. Employ strategies to improve nutrition, exercise, and movement in your workplace.
4. Consider the ways a nurse serves as a role model during the workday.

Personal

1. Spend time becoming aware of your current eating habits, exercise patterns, and movement activity.
2. Assess your habits in each of the areas, recognizing strengths and weaknesses.
3. Begin to experiment with new patterns in each area.
4. Become increasingly sensitive to nuances of feeling as you gradually refine skills in each area.

DEFINITIONS

Nutrition

HDL: high-density lipoprotein form of cholesterol associated with reduced risk of atherosclerosis.

LDH: low-density lipoprotein form of cholesterol strongly associated with increased risk of atherosclerosis.

Mineral: an inorganic element or compound necessary for human life.

Vitamin: an organic substance necessary for normal growth, metabolism, and development of the body; important in energy transformations, usually acting as co-enzymes in enzymatic systems.

Movement and Exercise

Aerobic Exercise: sustained muscle activity within the target heart range that challenges the cardiovascular system to meet the muscles' needs for oxygen.

Endurance: the period of time the body can sustain movement or exercise.

Fitness: the ability to carry out daily tasks with vigor and alertness, without undue fatigue, and with ample reserve to enjoy leisure pursuits; the ability to respond to physical and emotional stress without an excessive increase in heart rate and blood pressure.

Flexibility: the ability to use a joint throughout its full range of motion and to maintain some degree of elasticity of major muscle groups.

Maximal Heart Rate: the rate of the heart when the body is engaged in intense physical activity.

Movement: changes in the spatial configuration of the body and its parts, such as in breathing, eating, speaking, gesturing, and exercising.[1]

Resting Heart Rate: the rate of the heart when the body is in deep rest.

Strength: the power of muscle groups.
Target Heart Rate: the safe range for the heart during exercise.

THEORY AND RESEARCH

Nutrition and exercise are addressed together in this chapter because both work synergistically to promote high-level wellness behavior. The lack of proper nutrition, exercise, and movement contributes to major risk factors, such as hypertension, hypercholesterolemia, and obesity. How an individual eats also affects exercise abilities and vice versa. The exciting fact is that if one's exercise and nutrition patterns are not as healthy as they might be, both are modifiable when one makes the decision to move toward wellness.

Nutrition

During the past decade nutrition has moved into the forefront as a prominent component in health promotion and disease prevention. We are now aware of the correlation between what we eat and how we feel, bodymind function, and the potential for development of diseases. One impetus for the increased interest came from the U.S. Senate Select Committee on Nutrition of the United States. This committee was appointed in 1976 to study Americans' nutritional habits and to make recommendations for improvement. In 1977 the committee reported that nutrition was the United States' number one public health problem. The general population consumed an unbalanced supply of calories and nutrients, which contributed to disease and multiple minor ailments. The committee adopted these seven dietary goals to be implemented during the remainder of this century[2]:

1. To avoid becoming overweight, consume only as much energy (calories) as expended. Decrease energy intake and increase exercise if overweight.
2. Increase consumption of fresh fruits and vegetables and whole grains to 48 percent of food intake.
3. Reduce consumption of refined and processed sugars to 10 percent of daily intake.
4. Reduce fat consumption to 30 percent of daily intake.
5. Reduce intake of saturated fat to 10 percent of daily intake and take in 10 percent of calories in polyunsaturated fats and another 10 percent in monounsaturated fats.
6. Reduce cholesterol consumption to 300 grams per day.
7. Limit intake of salt to 5 grams per day.

Healthy nutrition is concerned with all aspects of optimizing bodymind potential. The literature abounds with new evidence that what we eat can indeed prevent or even reverse many major diseases, including cardiovascular disease, cancer, and osteoporosis, plus the many minor ailments that plague and weaken our bodies. It is not within the scope of this text to cover all of these findings or recommendations, but rather to point out their existence and lead interested nurses to further investigate this area of self-care and client intervention. The relationship of nutrition to cardiovascular disease, cancer, and osteoporosis is now discussed.

Cardiovascular Disease

Nutrition is the leading public health problem, and heart disease is the leading cause of death. In 1987 some 43,500 Americans suffered from heart or vessel disease, 1,500,000 had a myocardial infarction, and about 550,000 died from cardiovascular disease.[3] The cardiovascular diseases are one of the best examples of how lifestyle factors affect health. New evidence continues to link what we eat to our potential to develop heart disease.

Plaque is progressively built up on arterial walls in large measure due to poor and uninformed eating patterns. There are no early warning signs of plaque build-up. Often the first symptom is a myocardial infarction or cerebral vascular accident. However, we now know that proper diet and a prescriptive exercise program can prevent plaque build-up in many people.

Extensive studies have been done on the relationship between atherosclerosis and elevated blood cholesterol.[4] Many clinicians believe a six-point program (described in a later section) can lower blood cholesterol levels and optimize HDL/LDL ratios, thereby reducing the risk of cardiovascular disease. The goal of this nutritional program is to achieve and maintain total cholesterol levels in a range of 160 mg % to 180 mg %, rather than the current adult average of 235 mg %.

Cancer

Cancer of the colon, breast, lung, mouth, throat, and cervix may all be linked in some degree to what one eats. The sluggish bowel syndrome caused by a high-fat, low-fiber diet allows waste products to sit in the colon and to break down there into potential carcinogens. High-fat intake has been related to breast cancer, but the nature of this relationship is still unknown. Alcohol has been related to cancers of the throat and mouth. And studies have found that women with dysplasia—precancerous cervical cell changes—are more likely to have lower blood levels of vitamin C, beta-carotene, and folate than women without dysplasia.[5]

Osteoporosis

Twenty million American women have osteoporosis. By the age of 65 one out of every four women will have a compression fracture of the spinal vertebrae. To a large extent this disease and the associated complications are due to the decalcification of bones of postmenopausal women. A high-calcium diet is detailed in specific interventions.

Exercise

Exercise is a form of movement that ranges from active physical exercise to subtle motions that are only slightly perceptible. Traditionally, regular exercise programs were thought to be only necessary for athletes in training. We now know that vigorous aerobic exercise is good for everyone. Today less than 1 percent of all the energy used in factories, workshops, and farms comes from human muscles. During the next few years, there will continue to be growth in information and technology occupations that are increasingly sedentary, hence potentially unhealthy.

According to the Gallup polls, participation in exercise nearly doubled from 1961 to 1977 and increased by 27 percent from 1982 to 1984.[6] In a review of national surveys, one study found that approximately 20 percent of adults exercise with the intensity and frequency necessary for cardiovascular benefit, 40 percent are moderately active, and 40 percent are basically sedentary.[7] Thus, even though the number of adults who exercise regularly is increasing, most people are not doing so at the intensity or frequency necessary to obtain maximal health benefits.

Yet, a new paradigm of fitness is emerging (Table 9-1). Its orientation is broader and is focused more on enjoyment. As the new paradigm gains strength it is probable that there will be a continuing increase in both the numbers of people exercising and in those exercising at the level of vigor necessary to achieve a cardiovascular benefit.

Physical activity is positively associated with long life.[8] A variety of clinical trials support the contention that regular participation in physical activity is associated with either delays in the onset of or reduction in the severity of several chronic diseases, including obesity and coronary heart disease.[9]

Movement

Movement has many purposes. Various aspects of movement, such as dance, theatre, and sport, have been used in ritual, celebration, and healing rites since humans were first organized into collective tribes and families. For thousands of years Eastern cultures and philosophical thought have considered symbolic physical motion to be essential for physical and mental well-being. Yoga and Tai Chi are two examples of ancient physical movement forms that are still practiced today to enhance overall health. Movements within each of these disciplines are based on concepts of total concentration, strength, relaxation, and symbolic motion. In Western culture, movement includes dancing, swimming, and sports. In health care, movement is used for a number of therapeutic purposes, including range of motion exercises, water exercises, and specific physical therapy movements for a variety of rehabilitative programs.

Table 9-1 Old and New Fitness Paradigms

Old Fitness Paradigm	*New Fitness Paradigm*
Emphasis exclusively physical	A bodymind integration
Compared self with others	Noncomparative
Regulated calisthenics	Aerobic dance to motivational music; individually paced; build up with technology and feedback machines; motivation and subliminal tapes for individual challenge
Competition with others	Competition with self
Rigorous and punitive	Exhilarating and fun
Muscle building	Health building

Movement ranges from the rapid motions of active dance or acrobatics to the subtle rhythm characterized by breathing or the slow careful movements of Tai Chi. Movement includes posture (the way individuals hold and carry their bodies) and the way groups communicate nonverbally. Exercise is one form of movement. It is the form we give attention to because of its known benefits to health maintenance.

GENERAL EXPLANATIONS: NUTRITION, EXERCISE, MOVEMENT

Bodymind Communication: Nutrition, Exercise, Movement

Physical activity and food consumption have a direct effect on the body, mind, and spirit. In general as one becomes increasingly fit and nutritionally sound, one's body feels more alive and vital. A feeling of well-being that comes from physical health permeates each and every individual activity, enabling the quickest mental thoughts, a better night's sleep, and perhaps easier access to spiritual direction.

Nutrition

In order to follow the dietary goals established by the U.S. Senate Committee on Nutrition, several approaches that simply modify the usual food consumption patterns are recommended. Table 9-2 summarizes these recommendations.

Foods should be as free as possible of chemicals, additives, preservatives, and toxins. The healthiest foods are those subjected to the least processing, such as raw vegetables and fruits, living sprouts, whole grain breads and cereals, brown rice, dry peas and beans, raw unroasted seeds and nuts, and whole soy products. These products also increase the fiber in the diet. Eggs yolks and high-fat dairy products should be taken in moderation. Foods are best eaten raw, poached, steamed, or grilled. Whenever possible high-fat content and/or fried foods should be avoided.

Most people consume 60 percent of their calories from sugar, fat, and alcohol, which contain almost no vitamins or minerals. Fat reduction is a major thrust of healthy eating. Use the following suggestions to guide the client in ways to substitute low-fat for high-fat foods.

- Because many major diseases are linked to high-fat diets, always choose the leanest cut of meat.
- Trim all fat from meat and take the skin off poultry and fish.
- Use meat more as a condiment than as a main course.
- Broil, poach, or steam instead of frying foods.
- Use vegetable oils in moderation.
- Use the nonfat and low-fat varieties of dairy products.

Table 9-2 Dietary Goals and Recommendations

Dietary Goal	*Food Group*	*Recommendation*
Reduce fat	Meat, fish, and poultry	No high-fat meats Trim fat edges from meats Remove skin from poultry
	Eggs	Two egg yolks or less per week, egg whites as desired
	Dairy products	Skim milk, low fat yogurt, cottage cheese, and sherbet
	Fats and oils	Corn, safflower, or sunflower oils and margarines
	Commercial, processed, and fast foods	Limit to 1-2 times/week Buy with nutritional awareness and savvy
Reduce sugar	Soft drinks	Limit or eliminate soft drink consumption
	Fruits and vegetables	Eat fresh fruit or fresh or frozen vegetables
Reduce and maintain ideal body weight to ± 10%	Calories	Consume calories and expend calories to attain and maintain ideal weight
Increase complex carbohydrates (CHO)	Complex CHO—fiber	Increase use of lentils, dried peas, beans, whole grains products, nuts, and seeds
Reduce salt	Salt	Lower use of salt in cooking Eliminate processed foods high in salt
Reduce caffeine	Caffeine	Reduce coffee, tea, and diet sodas to under 2 cups per day
Reduce alcohol	Alcohol	1 ounce or less per day

Nontraditional Foods

The preceding discussion has focused on food intake of traditional American foods. Today, however, new foods are available that both satisfy the palate and meet nutritional goals. Tofu, which is made by curding the milky part of the soybean, is one of the most versatile protein foods in the world. It has been a high-protein staple in parts of Asia for over 2,000 years. It is low in calories, fats, and carbohydrates and contains no cholesterol. Tofu can be prepared and served as a substitute for traditional protein in every kind of food from entree to dessert. Tofu cookbooks are appearing in the marketplace, and once the tastebuds are re-educated the prepared meals taste as good or even better than traditional high fat meals.

Another protein food source introduced from Asia is miso. Miso is a fermented soybean paste with a texture resembling smooth peanut butter or cottage cheese. Like yogurt, it is a living food containing lactobacillus and other healthful micro-organisms.

Yogurt, a traditional Middle eastern food, is becoming increasingly popular. It is high in B vitamins and low in calories. The best yogurt is the low-fat, nonsweetened variety containing live bacteria cultures. The *Lactobacillus acidophilus* culture seems to aid in digestion and is reported to replace intestinal flora lost with long-term use of antibiotics.

Another Asian custom recently introduced to this country is the eating of sprouted seeds. In 2939 B.C., the Emperor of China recorded the use of "health giving sprouts" in a book about plants.[10] Sprouts are high in protein, vitamins, and minerals, yet low in calories. The importance of plant seed sprouts will increase in the future as the population grows and arable land decreases. An acre of land will yield more edible plant food than any other means when the seed harvest is sprouted. For example, an acre of land can produce as much as 385 pounds of alfalfa seed from one pound of seed. If 384 pounds were sprouted for food, the yield would be approximately 3180 pounds of consumable sprouts. Nurses should be cognizant not only of individual food needs but also the food needs of all people of the earth and the needs of the planet itself.

Vitamins and Minerals

Vitamins are as necessary for our health as food and water. Whether or not we obtain all the necessary nutrients from even optimal food consumption patterns is a controversial topic. Arguments both for and against supplementation have not yet resolved the issue. Nurses should therefore explore in depth new advances and controversies in vitamin therapy and supplementation.

Minerals are also necessary for human growth, development, and optimal function. They fulfill the following nine functions:

1. are the essential constituents of all cells
2. form the greater portion of the hard parts of the body (bone, teeth, and nails)
3. are essential components of respiratory enzymes and enzyme systems
4. regulate the permeability of cell membranes and capillaries
5. regulate the excitability of muscular and nervous tissue
6. are essential for regulation of osmotic pressure equilibrium
7. are necessary for maintenance of proper acid-base balance
8. are essential constituents of secretions of glands
9. play an important role in water metabolism and regulation of blood volume

Minerals are divided into two categories: macrominerals, which are needed in relatively large quantities, and trace elements, which are only required in small amounts. Table 9-3 describes the functions, Recommended Daily Allowance (RDA) requirements, and food sources of both macrominerals and trace elements.

Digestion for Energy Production

After food is consumed, it is digested and broken down for energy production. Figure 9-1 illustrates this process.

Exercise

The primary purpose of exercise is to produce the outcome of fitness. The basic components of fitness are flexibility, muscle strength and endurance, and cardio-

Table 9-3 Macrominerals and Trace Elements

Macromineral	*Function*	*Current Recommended Daily Amount*	*Food Sources*
Calcium	Key building blocks for bones and teeth; aids in transmission of nerve messages to the brain, muscle movement, and blood clotting	800 mg	Skim or low-fat milk, low-fat yogurt, sardines, salmon, tofu, broccoli
Sodium	Works with potassium to regulate body fluids; necessary for nerve and muscle function	Not established	Table salt and most processed foods
Potassium	Works with sodium to regulate body fluids; necessary for nerve and muscle function	800 mg	Apricots, blackstrap molasses, broccoli, brussel sprouts, dates, figs, bananas, potatoes, sunflower seeds
Chloride	Aids in regulation of muscle movement	Not established	Seafood, skim milk, lean meat, eggs
Magnesium	Acid-alkaline balance, blood sugar metabolism, protein structuring	300 mg	Bananas, roasted peanuts, low-fat milk, yogurt, brown rice, bone meal, bran
Phosphorus	Bone/tooth formation, cell growth and repair, RNA and DNA involvement	800 mg	Lentils, liver, yogurt, milk, dark-meat poultry
Iron	Hemoglobin production, stress and disease resistance, growth in children	18 mg	Cream of wheat, liver, oysters, red meat, tuna, oatmeal, raisins
Zinc	Burn and wound healing, carbohydrate digestion, prostate gland function, reproductive organ growth and development	15 mg	Oysters, low-fat yogurt, grains, dark-meat poultry, liver, red meat, Brewer's yeast, fish, wheat germ
Fluoride	Strong bones and teeth, prevention of caries by guarding against demineralization of teeth	Not established	6-8 glasses of fluoridated water daily
Copper	Bone formation, hair and skin color, healing processes, hemoglobin and red blood cell formation, mental processes, and emotional states	2-3 mg	Oysters, lobster, liver, grains, avocado, cauliflower, legumes, liver, molasses, nuts, organ meats, raisins
Chromium	Blood sugar level, glucose metabolism	50-200 mcg	Black pepper, cheeses, corn oil

Table 9-3 continued

Macromineral	*Function*	*Current Recommended Daily Amount*	*Food Sources*
Selenium	Antioxidant, DNA and protein synthesis, immune response, membrane integrity	50-200 mcg	Poultry, lean beef, Brewer's yeast, broccoli, fish, onion, tomatoes
Manganese	Enzyme activation, reproduction and growth, sex hormone production	2.5 mg	Bananas, bran, buckwheat, celery, green leafy vegetables, liver, nuts
Iodine	Energy production, body temperature, and growth	150 mcg	Iodized salt, seafood, bread, dairy products

respiratory endurance (Exhibit 9-1). In addition to the components of fitness regular cardiac conditioning produces a number of specific benefits (Figure 9-2).

Before beginning an exercise program, an individual should be encouraged to follow these basic guidelines. By beginning the regimen in a disciplined manner, the chances of maintaining the program are increased.

- Learn about the different types of exercise programs available in your area.
- Consult your doctor or exercise authority. If you are over 35, have never seriously exercised, or have a handicap or chronic illness, obtain guidance to avoid injuries or complications.
- Establish an exercise routine. Choose exercises or sports you will enjoy. Decide on a place and time of day to exercise. Ask a friend to join you or meet some new people at the jogging trail or health club. Create or join an exercise class before, during, or after work. There are endless possibilities.
- Warm up and cool down. Stretching exercises are essential before and after each exercise period.
- Set realistic goals and work toward them. Some benefits of exercise may not be quickly apparent. Be patient. Build up slowly to your long-term goals.
- Evaluate the program on a periodic basis. Determine if you are making progress. If you want to go further, set new goals. Create competition for yourself only if it benefits you. If you have allowed too much competition, exercise may become more of a burden than a joy.

The benefits and rewards of exercise and physical activity start as soon as you begin. Mental and spiritual improvements include beneficial changes in:

- mental attitude toward your work, yourself, and things in general
- ability to cope with stress
- ability to avoid or control mild depression
- improved sleep

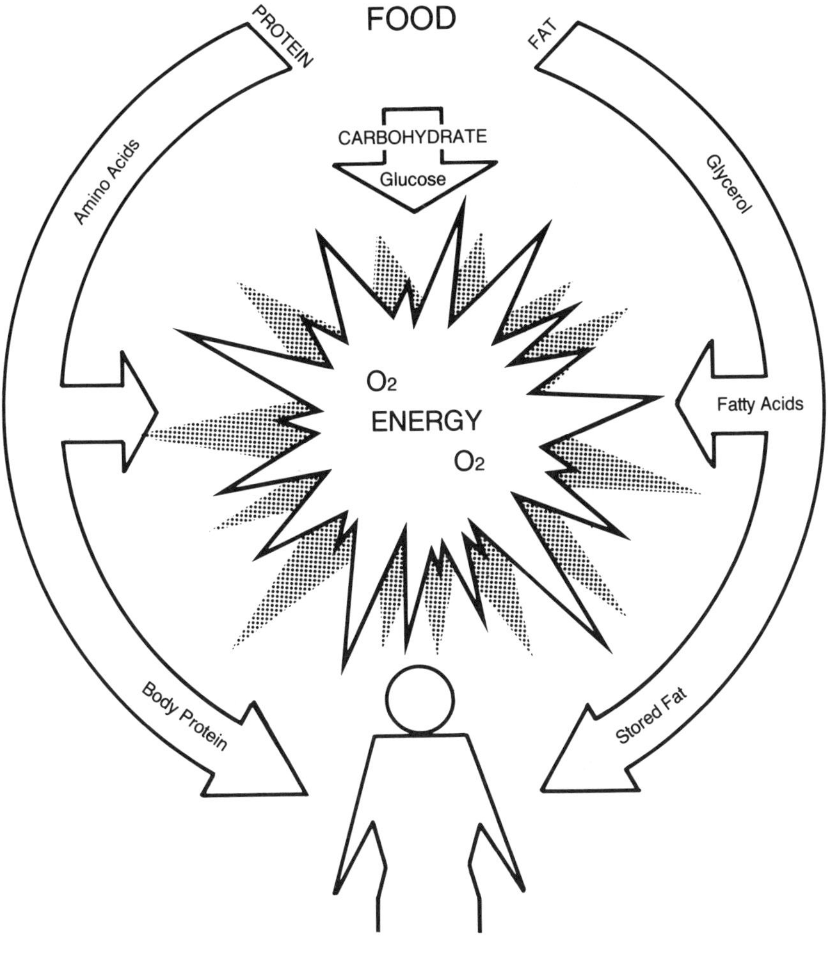

Figure 9-1 Breakdown of Food As It Gets into Body. *Source:* Reprinted from *Self Care: A Program To Improve Your Life*, by L. Keegan and B. Dossey, p. 32, with permission of Bodymind Systems, © 1987.

- improved strength and endurance
- eating less and eating better types of foods
- more youthful appearance and increased vitality
- improved posture
- increased physical stamina as you age

Movement

Movement programs are perhaps the least understood of the three topics of this chapter. Because we all use movement continually, we usually take it for granted.

Exhibit 9-1 The Components of Fitness

Flexibility: the ability to use a joint throughout its full range of motion and to maintain some degree of elasticity of major muscle groups

Importance

1. Provides increased resistance to muscle and joint injury
2. Helps prevent mild muscle soreness if done before and after vigorous activity

Muscle Strength: the contracting power of a muscle

Importance

1. Daily activities become less strenuous as muscles become stronger
2. Strong abdominal and lower back muscles help prevent lower back problems
3. Appearance improves as muscles become firmer

Cardiorespiratory Endurance: the ability of the circulatory and respiratory systems to maintain blood and oxygen delivery to the exercising muscles

Importance

1. Increases resistance to cardiovascular diseases
2. Improves the ability to maintain activity levels
3. Allows for a high energy return for daily activities

However, for many who are handicapped, disabled, or in rehabilitative programs, the design of creative movement plans can make the difference between achieving a partial or full development of their physical potential. Often it is the occupational or physical therapist who designs and teaches movement programs. However, with the increased emphasis on wellness programs, new types of therapists have emerged. Dance therapists and Tai Chi instructors are now more widely utilized, particularly by those seeking high-level wellness. Creative movement programs are taught in group sessions, at wellness centers, or in continuing education classes.

Creative movements, including dance, Tai Chi, and other expressive movements, are health-promoting behaviors that are appropriate for a variety of populations and age groups. Movement as a nursing intervention can be employed with independent, active people, as well as with those with mobility deficits.[11] Dance, which is one of the major movement therapies, places emphasis on the holism of human beings.[12] In dance, one can externalize concepts created in the mind, thus making another bodymind experience possible.

NURSING PROCESS

Assessment

In preparing to use nutrition, exercise, and movement interventions with clients, assess the following parameters:

- the client's current eating habits, food preferences, and nutritional needs
- the client's alcohol, caffeine, and high fat consumption

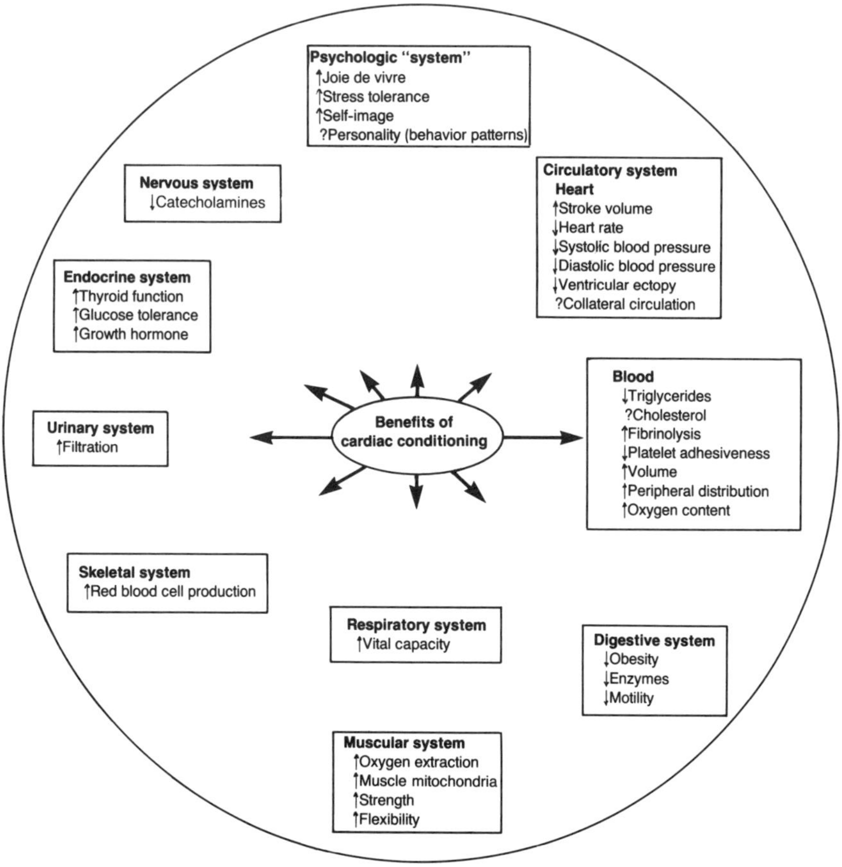

Figure 9-2 Benefits of Cardiac Conditioning. *Source:* Reproduced by permission from *Cardiovascular Nursing: Bodymind Tapestry* by C. Guzzetta and B. Dossey, The C.V. Mosby Company, St. Louis, © 1984.

- the client's financial and religious restrictions, as well as habit patterns formed during childhood
- the client's nonverbal movement patterns and known restrictions for/of movement limitations
- the client's desirable body weight and caloric needs
- the client's motivation, desire, and ability to make the necessary lifestyle changes in the areas of nutrition, exercise, and movement

Nursing Diagnosis

Nursing diagnoses compatible with the interventions described in this chapter and that are related to the nine human response patterns of unitary person are as follows:

• Exchanging:	Alterations in nutrition Alterations in circulation Alterations in oxygenation
• Choosing:	Alterations in coping
• Moving:	Physical mobility Sleep pattern disturbances Alteration in activities of daily living
• Perceiving:	Disturbance in body image Disturbance in self-esteem Hopelessness Powerlessness
• Knowing:	Knowledge deficit
• Feeling:	Pain Anxiety Grieving

Client Outcomes

Table 9-4 guides the nurse in client outcomes, outcome criteria, and evaluation for the use of nutrition, exercise, and movement as nursing interventions.

Table 9-4 Nutrition, Exercise, and Movement Interventions

Client Outcomes	*Outcome Criteria*	*Evaluation*
The client will be motivated to improve nutrition, exercise, and/or movement program.	1. The client will do own personal self-assessment. 2. The client will participate with the nurse in developing goals and action plans. 3. The client will follow through on the action plans and work with the nurse on evaluation and reformulation of new goals.	1. The client completes a self-assessment form. 2. The client participates with the nurse to develop a personalized program. 3. The client meets with the nurse for program evaluation.
The client will demonstrate knowledge of healthful nutrition, exercise, and movement patterns.	1. The client will contribute to discussions about his or her program. 2. The client will learn more about healthful behaviors as he or she works with the nurse.	1. The client participates in the session discussion. 2. The client demonstrates new knowledge.

Plan and Interventions

Before the Session

- Create an environment in which the client feels comfortable to discuss the needs of his or her physical body from a nutritional and physical movement perspective.
- Clear your mind of other client or personal encounters in order to be fully present when meeting with the client.
- Gather input data forms and teaching charts.
- Prepare all necessary assessment equipment.
- Prepare handouts or between-session worksheets to give to client during the session.

Beginning the Session

- Take and record the necessary physical assessment data, i.e., height, weight, skinfold thickness measurements, body contour measurements, blood pressure, etc.
- Guide the client as he or she discloses past habit patterns that affect eating or exercise behavior.
- Have the client write down typical foods consumed and consumption patterns and/or review food diary that client brought to session.

During the Session

- Review with the client current weekly exercise patterns.
- Be alert to psychologic clues that may relate to overeating behavior or extremes (anorexia and bulemia).
- Following data collection, work with the client to develop an individualized nutrition, exercise, and movement program.
- Make certain that teaching is at the intellectual and emotional level to which the client can best relate.

Closing the Session

- Have client identify options that you have presented that best fit with his or her own lifestyle.
- Work together to write down goals and target dates.
- Give client specific affirmations to use to support these goals.
- Give handout material to reinforce the teaching.
- Plan for follow-up sessions.

Special Interventions

Nutrition

Nurses can employ intervention teaching in almost every area of nursing care. Clients who are hospitalized because of acute illness are often interested in doing anything to prevent a recurrence. Consequently, in many cases the hospital stay is an excellent time to begin simple nutritional teaching. A registered dietician can provide detailed information on the client's specific nutritional needs. The nurse can follow up to reinforce the specifics and provide the following general information on decreasing cholesterol levels and increasing calcium intake.

The six-point program of the cholesterol-lowering diet is presented below.[13]

1. Increase dietary fiber. Cholesterol levels can be lowered by increasing intake of vegetable, fruit, and some plant fibers.
2. Add fish oils to the diet. Ongoing research seems to confirm the fact that eicosapentaenoic acid (EPA) and docosasehexaenoicacid (DHA) do in fact lower cardiovascular disease rates. Studies indicate that regular consumption of fish oils may play a significant role in lowering blood lipid levels.
3. Include lecithin in the diet. Lecithin is the biologically active form of choline. Dietary supplementation with 2 to 10 grams of soy-derived lecithin has been found to reduce serum total cholesterol.
4. Increase intake of Vitamin C. People who have a low intake of vitamin C often have elevated cholesterol levels. Vitamin C is necessary for the conversion of cholesterol to bile needed for the digestion of fats. Doses of 1 to 3 grams daily may lower cholesterol.
5. Add alfalfa to the diet. Both animal and human studies have demonstrated a reduction in blood cholesterol and atherosclerotic plaques in the coronary arteries with the intake of alfalfa. In humans given 10 teaspoons of alfalfa powdered seed per day, declines of as much as 20 percent in blood cholesterol levels were seen.
6. Increase intake of garlic. The beneficial effects of this plant are probably due to the sulfur compound, allicin. Allicin inhibits cholesterol synthesis, thereby reducing serum cholesterol levels. Clinical studies have indicated that approximately 10 grams of garlic per day significantly reduce blood cholesterol and triglyceride levels and improve the HDL/LDH ratio.

For optimal health a high-calcium diet needs to be followed from early childhood, as about 85 percent of the bone mass is formed by the age of 18 and the remainder by age 35.[14] A high-calcium diet during the growing years increases the bone mass as the skeleton matures and may reduce the risk of fractures later in life.

Several factors influence how calcium is used. A diet high in phosphorus inhibits calcium utilization. High quantities of phosphorus are found in red meats, some fibers, and carbonated soft drinks. The optimum diet should include twice as much calcium as phosphorus. High sodium intake forces the kidneys to excrete more sodium, and in the process more calcium is also excreted, contributing to osteoporosis. Cigarette smoking and excessive alcohol intake are also associated with low bone mass and may increase calcium loss. The best natural sources of calcium are oysters, clams, sardines, salmon, dairy products, leafy green vegetables, and legumes. Children and young adults should consume 1,000 to 1,200 mg daily, pregnant or breastfeeding women should have an additional 500 mg, and postmenopausal women need 1,500 mg daily.

It is not within the scope of this chapter to review the numerous possible interventions for healthy eating. If nurses wish to explore this area in depth, read the recent publication, *Nutritional Guidelines,*[15] of the American Holistic Medical Association. This small book provides all the latest information about healthy eating. An excellent video cassette, *Supermarket Savvy,* is an aisle-by-aisle shopping tour in a supermarket that shows how to choose healthier foods and read labels. See the resource list at the end of the chapter.

Exercise

To reduce risks associated with exercise, it is necessary to know not only how often and how long to exercise but also how vigorously to work out. Although the target pulse range allows for a heart rate within 60 to 80 percent of maximal capacity, the American Heart Association guidelines state that positive cardiovascular fitness appears to result from regular exercise of moderate capacity, or from 50 to 75 percent of maximal capacity.

Maintaining the target pulse rate during physical exercise for 15 to 30 minutes three to five times per week reduces the risk of overexertion, enhances enjoyment, and results in cardiovascular fitness. However, uncontrolled exercising may result in injury, in order to avoid injury follow these guidelines:

- Always warmup for a minimum of 10 to 20 minutes.
- If you are tired, stop.
- If something hurts, stop.
- If you feel dizzy or nauseated, stop.
- Take your pulse at regular intervals.
- Cool down after exercising.

To ease your heart rate into the training range, begin with 10 minutes of low-intensity warmup exercise. To cool down, do 10 minutes of the same slow activity.

Movement

There are four components of creative movement: centering, warm-up, exploration of surrounding space, and stretching.[16]

1. *Centering* is the inward focusing on one's own physical reality. The duration of this process varies, but it usually lasts 3 to 10 minutes.
2. The stretching, breathing *warm-up* exercises follow the centering exercise and are designed to "wake up" the muscles while maintaining the harmonious integration of psyche and soma that was begun through centering.

- Musical accompaniment—When movement is synchronized to music there is a positive effect on one's ability to perform. Music seems to bypass the psychologic feedback of the sensations of exertion and fatigue and instead produces feelings of exuberance and strength.
- Exercises—These are done in order to synchronize breathing and symbolic imagery slowly and rhythmically. The individual uses images in concert with motion.
- Social involvement during warmup—This adds another dimension to creative movement. Initially people may be shy with one another, but this is overcome and enjoyment increases as the movement accelerates.
- Additional warmup techniques—Some people choose to delve deeper into their own personal inward life before proceeding further into group activities.

3. *Exploration of surrounding space* occurs as movement proceeds and there is an awakened sense of self-awareness. With this discovery of new physical capacities comes increased kinetic and spatial awareness. During this time there may be swinging, swaying, and laughter.
4. *Stretching* concludes a dance movement, allowing for relaxation as it brings the individual to a resting state. At the conclusion one should savor the feeling of energetic relaxation.

Case Study

Setting:	A nurse-based Wellness Center
Client:	B.V. a 40-year-old married female who seeks counseling for weight loss.
Nursing Diagnoses:	1. Alterations in nutrition 2. Potential activity intolerance related to a lack of exercise program 3. Alterations in self-esteem related to obesity 4. Ineffective reversal/prevention of CAD risk factors (hypertension, hypercholesterolemia, obesity) related to stress and low self-esteem

B.V. has just had a physical examination by a physician and been told for the sixth straight year that she needs to lose weight. Her total cholesterol is 340 mg. %, B/P 180/100, height 5' 7'', and weight 220 pounds. She is a nurse and seeks help from a nurse colleague at the wellness center because her elevated cholesterol level has finally motivated her to lose weight. Her husband has been encouraging this for years, but she just cannot seem to make it happen.

During the initial session, the nurse takes a eating and diet history. Like most self-referrals for weight loss, B.V. is very knowledgeable about various diet programs and has tried different plans for several years. She has a pattern of losing and then regaining up to 50 pounds on each attempt. At this point she is discouraged, but willing to try anything. During the interview the nurse discovers that B.V. has been on numerous antihypertensive drugs for 10 years without attaining consistent control. The assessment shows that, in general, B.V. is out of shape physically and is depressed and discouraged emotionally. She is a fellow health professional who has reached burnout.

During the first session, 6-week and 6-month goals are established, and weekly sessions with the nurse are scheduled. B.V. is given a standard form of a weekly diet, exercise, and emotion and attitude recording sheet. She is instructed to write down everything she eats, as well as the feeling she has before, during, and after the eating periods during the next week.

In her second session the eating/feeling diary is reviewed and where significant relationships between feelings and eating are observed they are discussed. During this and subsequent sessions it is important to examine and try to understand the client's feelings for they are closely tied to the eating behavior. In addition the physical parameters of weight and body fat calibration measurements are recorded.

During each session several small obtainable goals are set for the following week. It is important that both exercise and eating patterns be gradually improved. Goals that are too difficult to achieve can discourage the client altogether.

B.V. meets with the nurse on a regular basis for 6 months. During that time she reduces her weight to 160 pounds, works out in a regular aerobic exercise program four times a week, and has increased her knowledge and interest in healthful food consumption. At the end of this period B.V. and the nurse agree to move to monthly visits for the next three sessions and plan for termination of the appointments at that time.

Evaluation

In each nutrition, exercise, or movement counseling session, the outcomes must be measured as successful or not. At each session, the nurse evaluates with the client the goals that were planned for the session.

Nurses should chart the information they imparted to the client, as well as the evaluation of the session. When the nurse works in an inpatient facility, other staff need to be appraised of the program and the progress.

Nurses who work in wellness centers, independent practice, or other areas in which counseling sessions are done as the primary care modality should keep records on their clients that state the nursing diagnosis, type of counseling employed, and the effectiveness of each session.

SUMMARY

This chapter has focused on nutrition, exercise, and movement from the perspective of the general improvement of health, as well as a way to decrease the risk factors of major diseases. The nurse should be a role model of healthy nutrition, exercise, and movement behaviors.

DIRECTIONS FOR FUTURE RESEARCH

1. Investigate the hypothesis that those who exercise and eat a nutritionally balanced diet feel better and live longer.
2. Continue the investigations into how the lifestyle behaviors of nutrition, exercise, and movement affect a general sense of well-being.
3. Study the relationship between vitamin and mineral supplementation and disease prevention and high-level wellness.
4. Investigate the determinants that allow or cause exercise in unstructured or spontaneous situations.
5. Study what specific factors are important in tailoring exercise programs to ethnic and cultural groups.

NURSE HEALER REFLECTIONS

After reading this chapter, the nurse healer will be able to answer or begin a process of answering the following questions:

- What *sensations* accompany my physical well-being because of my improved nutritional, exercise, and movement status?
- How should I *feel* when I am physically fit?
- What comprises *healthy* eating both for myself and for my clients?
- What exercise and movement regimens can I *incorporate* to improve my flexibility and aerobic capacity now?
- How can I *model* healthy nutrition, exercise, and movement?

NOTES

1. Moshe Feldenkrais, *Awareness through Movement* (New York: Harper & Row, 1977), p. 32.
2. U.S. Senate Select Committee On Nutrition and Human Needs, *Dietary Goals for the United States* (Washington, DC: U.S. Government Printing Office, 1977), p. 1ff.
3. Frank Gaev, "Optimal Heart Health For Your Clients," *The Nutrition and Dietary Consultant,* April 1986, p. 5.
4. Ibid., p. 5.
5. Gale Maleskey, "Food Factors That Stop Cancer: Best News, Best Bets," *Prevention* 39, no. 10 (October 1987): pp. 88–109.
6. "The Gallup Poll: Six of 10 Adults Daily," *Los Angeles Times,* May 1984.
7. T. Stephens, D.R. Jacobs, and C.C. White, "A Description of Leisure Time Physical Activity," *Public Health Reports* 100 (1985): 147–157.
8. R.S. Paffenbarger and W.E. Hale, "Work Activity and Coronary Heart Disease Mortality," *New England Journal of Medicine* 292 (1975): 545–550.
9. W.L Haskett, "Overview: Health Benefits of Exercise," in *Behavioral Health: A Handbook of Health Enhancement and Disease Prevention,* ed. J.D. Matarazzo, et al. (New York: John Wiley & Sons, 1984).

10. Karen Whyte, *Sprouting* (San Francisco: Troubador Press, 1973), pp. 4–5.
11. Suzanne Boots and Catherine Hogan, "Creative Movement and Health," *Topics in Clinical Nursing* 3, no 2 (1981): 23–31.
12. R. Lange, *The Nature of Dance* (London: MacDonald and Evans, Ltd., 1975), p. 1ff.
13. Frank Gaev, "Optimal Heart Health For Your Clients," p. 5.
14. E.J. Kozora, ed., *Nutritional Guidelines* (Seattle: American Holistic Medical Association, 1987), p. 1ff.
15. Ibid., p 1ff.
16. Susan Boots and Catherine Hogan, "Creative Movement and Health," pp. 21–31.

SUGGESTED READINGS

Brewster, L., and Jacobson M.F. *The Changing American Diet*. (Washington, D.C.: Center for Science in the Public Interest, 1983).

DeVore, Steven A.; Remington, Dennis W.; Fisher, A. Garth; and Parent, Edward A. *The Neuropsychology of Weight Control*. Newark, CA: SyberVision Systems, Inc., 1985.

Hagler, Louise. *Tofu Cookery*. Summertown, TN: The Book Publishing Co., 1982.

Nugent, Nancy. *Food and Nutrition*. Emmaus, PA: Rodale Press, 1983.

Shurtleff, William, and Aoyagi, Akiko. *The Book of Miso*. Kanagawa-ken, Japan: Autumn Press, Inc., 1976.

RESOURCES

Nutritional Guidelines, American Holistic Medical Association, 2727 Fairview Avenue East, Suite G, Seattle, Washington 98102, (206)322-6842

Supermarket Savvy (videocassette), Supermarket Savvy, P.O. Box 25, Addison, Texas 75001-0025, (214) 620-0415

chapter **10**

Environment: Protecting Our Personal and Planetary Home

Lynn Keegan

> The Age of Nations is past. The task before us now, if we would not perish is to build the earth.
>
> *Pierre Teilhard de Chardin*

This chapter guides the nurse in becoming increasingly sensitive to environmental issues and presents ways to best utilize the environment to maximize the healing effort. How individuals use their personal space affects not only the way they feel but also, in today's shrinking world, the space around one another on our planet. Each of us needs to be alert to the concerns expressed in this chapter and work together to find individual and community solutions to the serious environmental issues that face us as we race toward the 21st century.

NURSE HEALER OBJECTIVES

Theoretical

1. Learn the various definitions of environment.
2. Examine some of the theories and research about the environment.
3. Become increasingly aware of the new literature documenting environmental hazards and commit to doing your part to reduce these hazards.

Clinical

1. Train yourself to become sensitive to the environmental space in your institution, home health agency, or clinic.
2. Choose several different environmental skill approaches and utilize them in clinical practice.
3. Consider utilizing some specific interventions in your workplace.

Personal

1. Begin to make positive changes in your own environmental space.
2. Begin to experiment with color, scents, textures, sound, and lighting in your personal environment.
3. Begin to eliminate negative aspects of your personal environment, i.e., stale air, inadequate lighting, subliminal noises, etc.

DEFINITIONS

Ambience: an environment or its distinct atmosphere; the totality of feeling one experiences from a particular environment.

Environment: everything that surrounds an individual or group of people; may be physical, social, psychological, cultural, or spiritual; includes external and internal, animate and inanimate objects, seen and unseen vibrations and frequencies, climate, and not yet understood energy patterns.

Ecominnea: the concept of an ecologically sound society.

Ergonomics: the study of and realization of the importance of human factors in engineering.

Harmonic Environment: the effect of melodious music or sounds that gently fill the personal space of a person; a significant part of an overall environment.

Personal Space: the area around an individual that should be under the control of the person inhabiting it; this space includes air, light, temperature, sound, scent, and color.

Toxic Substance: a substance that can cause harmful effects to a person by either short-term or long-term exposure; can be transmitted by (1) inhalation; (2) ingestion into the body in the form of vapors, gases, fumes, dusts, solids, liquids, or mists, or (3) skin absorption.

THEORY AND RESEARCH

Attempts To Document the Modern Dilemma

One of the reasons why the study of the link between environmental conditions and illness or disease is so difficult is that there are so many intervening variables. Trying to pinpoint one cause is very difficult when so many hundreds of substances and lifestyle factors are involved. Although many toxic substances and environmental conditions do not appear to induce immediate untoward reactions, many toxins seem to cause disease later, perhaps years after the period of exposure. Breathing asbestos fibers, for example, seldom causes immediate symptoms, but it often results in serious chronic disease many years later.[1] Other environmental elements now known to be hazardous include lead, cigarette smoke, silica, benzene, mercury, chlorine, poor lighting, stress, and noise.

In the 1970s efforts began to clean up the nation's environment and ensure workers' safety.[2] Two national agencies—the Environmental Protection Agency (EPA) and the

Occupational Safety and Health Administration (OSHA)—were formed to monitor environmental concerns. In the 1980s several states enacted statutes called "Right To Know Laws." These state laws require employers to notify employees of health hazards, provide formal education regarding safe use of toxic substances, and keep medical records of those workers routinely exposed to specific toxic substances.

General Environmental Concerns

As we near the 21st century environmental concerns range from eating contaminated poultry, hormone-fed beef, and irradiated fruits and vegetables to living near high-voltage power lines, the Antarctic atmospheric ozone hole, and other new high technology hazards that we are only now recognizing (Figure 10-1). Noise, lighting, air quality, space allocation, and workplace toxins have gained increasing recognition as chronic stressors. It is now time for the nurse to give environmental concerns full attention and serve as a fully present client advocate.

Noise

Noise pollution may be the most common modern health hazard, and its danger is still for the most part unrecognized. Studies have repeatedly demonstrated that a high noise level is the single most important factor in diminishing office productivity.[3] Yet, more than 20 million workers are exposed to hazardous levels of noise every year, and the majority of them are in the white collar work environment. Other studies here and in Europe have shown that high noise levels constrict blood vessels; increase blood pressure, pulse, and respiratory rates; and release extra fats into the bloodstream.[4]

The danger posed by noise pollution is a function of the volume of sound heard over a period of time. Sound and its intensity are measured in decibels, abbreviated dB. The scale is logarithmic, rather than linear. This means that each increase in 10 dB is equivalent to multiplying the intensity by 10. The arbitrary zero is the weakest sound that a young sensitive human ear can hear. Humans begin to perceive irritability around 50 to 90 dB, and actually feel pain around 120 dB. At levels above 70 dB, the autonomic nervous system can become aroused, often without the person even being aware of it. When exposed for 8 hours to noise at 70 dB, which is the sound level of many typing pools or cafeterias, people may become irritable or distracted or show signs of hypertension.[5] With prolonged exposure to noise levels over 75 dB, gradual hearing loss can occur as seen in Table 10-1.

People not only are disturbed by loud sound but also by dissonant or inharmonic sound.[6] Random, unstructured noises, even those below the threshold of awareness, can promote an irritating tension. In most hospitals and health care settings the quiet areas are actually flooded with random noises and subtle tension-promoting sounds. The irritability that dissonant sounds produce interferes with restfulness.

One study tested the hypothesis that healthy subjects who are confined to bed in a varied harmonic environment will perceive themselves to be more rested than those subjects confined in a quiet ambient environment.[7] Indeed, varied patterns of auditory input are more restful than quiet ambience. This finding supports the concept that the

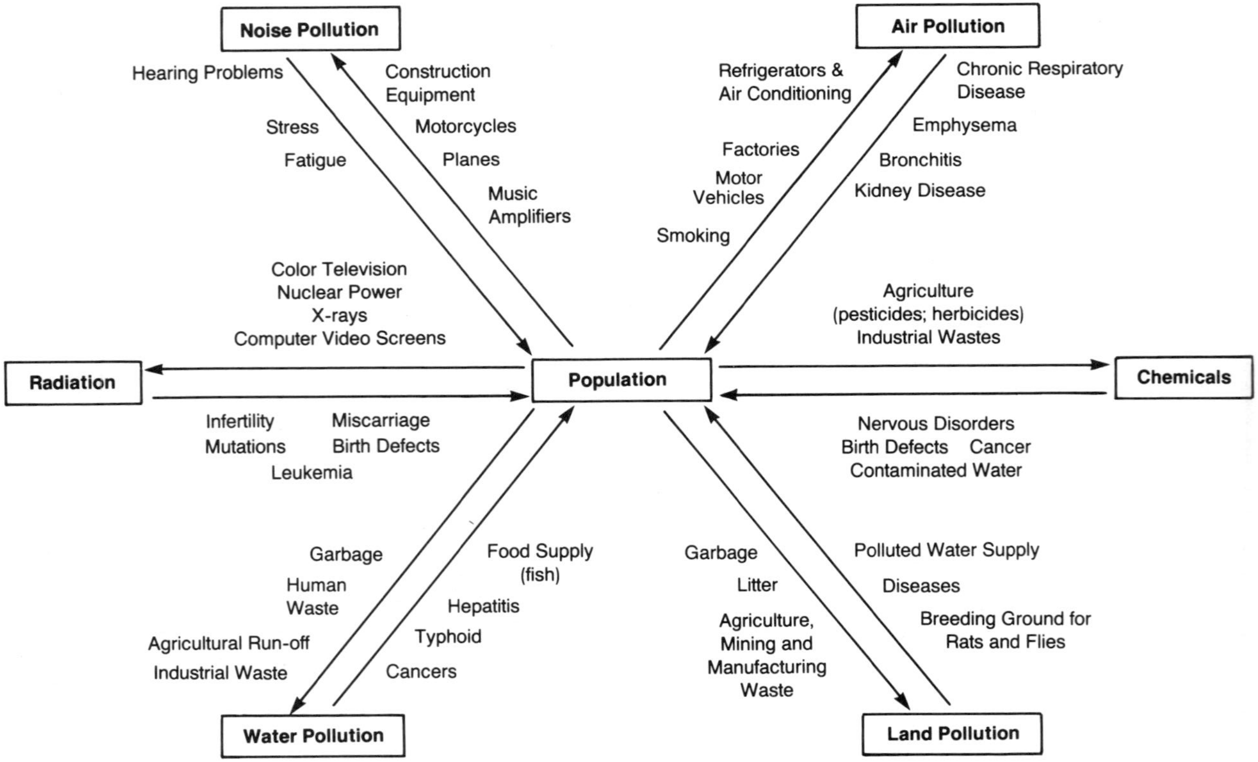

Figure 10-1 Current Environmental Concerns. *Source:* Reprinted with permission from *Health Education*, August/September 1986, pp. 26–27. *Health Education* is a publication of the American Alliance for Health, Physical Education, Recreation and Dance, 1900 Association Drive, Reston, VA 22091.

Table 10-1 Decibels and Hearing

Decibel Level (dB)	*Generating Sound*
120–140	Jet engine at take-off
	Amplified rock band at close range
100–110	Power lawn mower
	Oncoming subway train
	Chainsaw
	Jackhammer
80–100	Alarm clock
	Screaming child
	Truck traffic at close range
	Cocktail party
60–80	Electric kitchen aids
	Washing machine
40–60	Normal conversation
	Refrigerator hum
20–40	A cat's purr
0–10	Threshold of hearing

human environmental field is strengthened when the auditory input for those confined to bed is patterned.

To study the effect of noise exposure on vasoconstriction, plasma concentrations of the vasoconstrictor Angiotensin II (AII) were measured in subjects before and after either rest or exposure to 100 dB white noise.[8] Plasma AII concentrations decreased for subjects in the no-noise condition, but remained high in the noise condition. The results support the hypothesis that noise may stimulate AII production. The author suggests that elevated AII may be partially responsible for the reported vasoconstriction and blood pressure increases that appear to accompany noise exposure.

Food Irradiation

The stated purpose of food irradiation is to kill larval infestation, thereby (1) increasing the shelf-life of foods; (2) eliminating insects, bacteria, and other organisms; and (3) preventing sprouting. Even though the Food and Drug Administration (FDA) has pronounced it safe, this new technique has stirred controversial debate from the time of its first use.

Irradiation is a problem for three reasons. First, it partially depletes nutrients from the food, with vitamins C, A, B complex, and E being the most sensitive. In several studies, Temple oranges lost up to 28 percent of their ascorbic acid, corn lost 29 percent of its ascorbic acid and 44 percent of its carotene, and whole milk lost up to 61 percent of its vitamin E.[9] The transportation of highly radioactive materials (cobalt 60 and cesium 137) through communities to use in irradiation plants has also raised concern. Finally the process creates radioactive products in the form of trace chemicals in the irradiated food product. A study by the U.S. Army found that irradiated beef contained 65 volatile trace chemicals that had not been present before irradiation.[10] Some nuclear chemists contend that the radiolytic particles and substances have the possibility of being carcinogenic.

Although the safety of irradiation is still under investigation, nurses need to be aware of the controversy and both sides and stay abreast of the issues.

Meat and Poultry Supplementation

For a number of years cows, pigs, and chickens have been treated with both hormones and antibiotics. The purposes of these treatments are to increase the size and weight of the animal and to prevent Salmonella contamination. This supplementation, like irradiation, has raised safety concerns because a new element of pharmacological intervention has been introduced into a population that was previously free of disease. Its long-range effects are yet to be known.

Concerns about Passive Smoking

We are all aware of the health hazards related to smoking tobacco products. During this decade a new at-risk population has been identified. Nonsmokers exposed to tobacco smoke produced by others, referred to as passive smoking, are also at risk for the same illnesses as their smoking counterparts.[11] New studies reveal that sidestream smoke contains higher concentrations of carcinogens and other toxic substances than does mainstream smoke.[12] Nonsmokers who are chronically exposed to the pollutants in tobacco smoke scored lower on tests of small airway function than nonsmokers who were not exposed.[13] Nonsmoking women exposed to their husband's smoking are now showing a 2:1 increase in mortality from lung cancer as compared to control groups.[14] Such data should alert nurses and other health care professionals to the continual unfolding of new hazards to public environmental health and safety.

GENERAL EXPLANATIONS: ENVIRONMENT

Bodymind Connections: Environment

As we develop the optimal worksites and living areas to foster self-actualizing conditions and maximize bodymind responses, we must be aware of the impact of all aspects of the environment on human health. To increase your sensitivity to the environment and its impact, do the exercise in Exhibit 10-1.

It is the accumulation of noises that adds up in dB and adds up to stress. By becoming increasingly sensitive to all potential environmental stressors the nurse will become more attuned to making specific interventions when the opportunities arise.

Violence, Dehumanization, and the Technological Age

Life in the modern age has built-in inherent environmental dangers. For many, the very act of getting to and from the workplace is an encounter with smog, noise, congestion, stench, and debris. In addition, most Americans spend numerous hours a week in front of television screens vicariously engaging in violence and corruption.

Exhibit 10-1 Environmental Awareness Exercise

> At different times during the day, close your eyes, and take a few moments to listen carefully to all the sounds in your environment.
>
> - Jot down the many different sounds you hear, noting which are pleasant and which are distracting or disturbing noises.
> - Become aware of all the sounds that you ordinarily hear, such as the air conditioner, radios and televisions, the hum of fluorescent lights, the beeping and buzzing of hospital machinery, or the incessant MUSAK that some institutions play over the speaker system.
> - Notice new smells, feelings of temperature, etc. There will be many sounds, smells, and sensations of which you may not have previously been aware.

In the past, people and their environments were harmoniously intertwined. In contrast, in today's technological era we have for the most part changed the nature of the environmental relationship to one of *use of,* rather than an *exchange with* the elements of the environment. In the past when people worked, they walked from their dwelling to their field, toiled with the elements, and directly reaped the benefits of their labors. Today we have become increasingly alienated from the natural world. The artificial environment of the technological society has replaced nature as the all-encompassing environment. The technological society unconsciously evokes from us the emotions of fascination and dread that nature once did.[15] Searching for security, fulfillment, and meaning from our technological civilization, we unconsciously surrender our freedom and autonomy and replace it with efficiency. For many the result is dehumanization, demoralization, and victimization. For others who are knowledgeable and able to participate in effective choice making, the technological age can heighten the positive effects of the environment and thereby enhance the overall quality of life. In either case, there are specific interventions that the individual nurse can do.

NURSING PROCESS

Assessment

In preparing to utilize environmental control with clients, assess the following parameters:

- the client's personal space for comfort, lighting, noise, ventilation, and privacy
- if there are people or objects in the client's environment that induce anxiety
- if individual coping skills are affected by environmental concerns
- if family coping skills are affected by environmental concerns
- if objects or other environmental factors in the physical space surrounding the client induce comfort or discomfort
- if there are alterations in the family systems related to environmental concerns

- if situations in the environment are causing fear in the client such as a feeling of claustrophobia from being confined to a hospital intensive care bed or intravenous lines, or fear of death because the patient in the next bed just died
- the relationship of environmental factors to client grieving—Is the client in the same home atmosphere in which the spouse just died? Are others around the client sad and depressed? Are the colors in the environment dark and heavy?
- the relationship between the client's environment and personal health maintenance—Can the client easily reach self-care hygiene items, are throw rugs anchored, are sunglasses worn outside to prevent glare?
- what factors in the environment are related to alterations in the client's ability to maintain and manage his or her own home
- factors in the environment that have potential for injury to the client
- environmental factors that led to activity deficits in a client
- the client's home environment for its potential impact on effective parenting
- environmental factors that may contribute to client noncompliance
- environmental factors that contribute to impairment in physical activity for the client
- environmental factors that may relate to an impairment in respiratory function, such as feather pillows, polluted or stale air, cigarette smoking, known or suspected allergens, or overexertion with chronic respiratory conditions
- causative agents in the environment that relate to the client's sleep deficit, such as lighting, noise, overstimulation, overcrowding, or allergenic pillows
- alterations in thought processes that may be influenced by environmental factors, such as sensory bombardment with noise, lack of sleep, and transient living patterns

Nursing Diagnoses

Nursing diagnoses compatible with the environmental interventions described in this chapter and that are related to the nine human response patterns of unitary person are as follows:

- *Exchanging:* (Environmental issues can be used with all diagnoses in this category)
- *Choosing:* Potential for ineffective choices
- *Moving:* Alterations in selfcare; Alterations in growth and development
- *Perceiving:* Potential for sensory/perceptual alteration
- *Knowing:* Potential for knowledge deficit
- *Feeling:* Alterations in comfort

Client Outcomes

Table 10-2 guides the nurse in client outcomes, outcome criteria, and evaluation for the use of the environment as a nursing intervention.

Table 10-2 Nursing Interventions: Environment

Client Outcomes	*Outcome Criteria*	*Evaluation*
The client will demonstrate awareness of environmental issues.	1. The client will participate in shaping his or her own personal space environment. 2. The client will participate in contributing to a positive safe environment for those who share his or her personal space and community space.	1. The client will have personalized his or her own personal space environment. 2. The client: A. Monitors and controls the noise he or she contributes to the surrounding environment B. Regards the rights of others by not polluting air, water, and public places with wastes C. Does not violate the personal space of others with tobacco smoke
	3. The client will demonstrate concern for the concept of a healthy global environment.	3. The client participates in discussions, committees, or programs to work for a safe global environment.
The client will avoid contact and exposure to toxic substances and/or hazardous materials.	1. The client will participate in agency safety education programs. 2. The client will not handle unnecessary toxic substances.	1. The client participates in agency offerings of environmental safety programs. 2. The client does not handle unnecessary toxic substances and educates self about dangers of hazardous materials.

Plan and Interventions

What can the nurse do about all these wide-ranging environmental issues? Obviously changing society is much too large a task for any single individual. However, as each nurse becomes aware of personal thoughts, behaviors, and actions, each can begin to change his or her personal internal and external environment. Any work on big causes generally begins with oneself, and improving the environment is no different. It is the person who is most aware of the issues who makes the best committee member, chairperson, or agent for larger group activity.

In the health care setting, it is nurses who are accountable for the details of the environment. Because of this responsibility the nurse should be the one who takes the lead to initiate specific interventions in the health care agency setting and for the clients who seek care in those settings. Nurses can offer to serve on their agency's environmental control committee, or, if their agency does not have one, volunteer to form one. When forming or serving on this committee, it is important to consider ways to humanize the environment, as well as to protect it from hazards. Urge the committee to discuss the topics of sound (noise, music, machinery, etc.), air (quality, smell, circulation, etc.), and aesthetics (art, color, design, and texture), as well as other topics specific to the overall environment in the agency.

Clients in the acute care setting will appreciate the sensitive nurse who makes an effort to control the noise level. In addition to instituting simple noise control, the nurse is also in the position to educate hospitalized clients about the deleterious effects of too much noise. For example in a semiprivate room, the nurse can ask the patient with a loud television to turn it down to spare the patient and the roommate the ill effects of noise exposure. A superior choice for both hospitalized patients is to limit the time spent watching television, and to encourage them instead to listen to their own personal, hospital-dispensed cassette players with headphones. In this way, not only is the noise level vastly reduced but also opportunities for healing, relaxation, and imagery tapes and specially selected soothing music can replace much of the meaningless chatter of the television. The challenge for nurses is to create mechanisms whereby music, imagery, relaxation, color, aromas, and the like can be introduced into the hospital setting.

The sensitive nurse will also function as a role model. Simple voice control is a primary way in which the nurse can exemplify her understanding of noise control. When one person speaks softly, often others will do so also. This is particularly true when speaking with clients in crisis. In addition, nurses should restrict their laughter at change of shift report, carefully glide bedrails up and down, and, when appropriate, whisper.

Table 10-3 describes practical ways to cope with hazards in the environment.

Case Study

Setting:	Outpatient department, clinic, or private visit.
Client:	A.B., a 55-year-old married man
Nursing Diagnosis:	1. Alteration in comfort related to recurrent headaches
	2. Ineffective individual coping related to environmental stress

A.B. came to the occupational health nurse with the chief complaint of recurrent headaches and chronic fatigue. A physical examination and laboratory tests indicated no

Table 10-3 Coping with Workplace Hazards

Problem	*Solution*
Too much noise	1. Turn off radios and televisions. 2. Lower your voice. 3. Ask your colleagues to quiet down. 4. Ask to serve on the agency's environmental control committee. 5. Do not flush toilets in rooms unnecessarily.
Inadequate lighting	1. Add more lights. 2. Use incandescent bulbs instead of fluorescent tubes whenever possible. 3. Open curtains and blinds whenever possible. 4. Go outdoors for full spectrum light breaks, rather than taking cafeteria coffee breaks.
Stale air	1. Make sure agency ventilation systems work. 2. When doing home health visits, open the doors and windows and get fresh air in the home when appropriate. 3. Request that broad leaf green plants be stationed in the workplace. They are aesthetically pleasing and give off oxygen. 4. Wear masks or protective gear if there is any risk of toxic inhalants.
Long periods at computer video display terminal	1. Use a shield that cuts down glare and radiation and grounds the field of electrostatic charge. 2. Learn some relaxation exercises to do at your desk. 3. Ask your institution or agency to have minimassage available on the premises. 4. Take frequent eye and movement breaks away from the screen. 5. Use properly designed chairs.
Space allocation	1. Try to find some personal space in the workplace. 2. Respect other's personal space. Ask before entering the client's rooms, closet, or dresser. 3. Make the space you are allocated as pleasant as possible. Decorate with colorful objects, soothing scents, and aesthetic objects.

pathology or disease. However, his history warranted a closer examination of his environment. The nurse followed up his subjective declaration of feeling stress in the workplace by exploring his workplace environment with him in detail.

A detailed history of his work hours, commuting travel, and work setting yielded evidence of environmental imbalance. A.B. began his day with a 45-minute automobile commute through a suburban area to the inner city; he finished the day the same way. He had done this commute for years, but lately the traffic had increased and road repairs frequently slowed his pace. When he arrived at work he went to his office, an interior room with no windows and fluorescent ceiling lights. Instead of a secretary outside his office, he now had his own computer inside his office. During the company's modernization process, middle managers were taught computer skills and many secretarial positions were eliminated. Each manager was now responsible for developing reports and interacting with others via personal computer terminals. A.B.'s walls were the standard institutional beige color; he had done nothing to decorate or personalize his office. His work routine had little variation. It consisted of meetings, telephone work, and online computer time.

This information supported the nurse's diagnosis of environmental-related stress, and she worked with A.B. to develop a five-step plan of action:

1. Vary A.B.'s commuting time. Begin the commute 15 minutes earlier with the purpose of decreasing the rushed feeling of getting to work on time. Join a health club in the city, and stay after work to exercise. The traffic would be considerably less one hour later, and the commute time would then only be 30 minutes. Total morning and evening commute time would remain the same as before, but more would have been accomplished with less environmental stress.
2. Implement and practice computer protection skills as detailed in Table 10-3.
3. Mount a shoulder rest on the telephone to prevent neck strain after long periods on the telephone.
4. Personalize the office with soft soothing colors. Add a wall picture of a mountain valley and stream that had special significance for him.
5. Put an incandescent lamp on his desk and use that rather than the overhead fluorescent lights for deskwork.

A copy of this plan was posted in a prominent space in A.B.'s home. This environmental control plan was instituted, along with a plan for weight management and exercise as described in Chapter 9 and the development of relaxation and imagery skills as detailed in Chapters 11 and 12. All three plans were incorporated with the knowledge and understanding of A.B.'s need for motivation, lifestyle change, and values clarification as described in Chapter 7.

When A.B. returned for his followup visit 2 months later, his headaches had abated, and he had made some progress toward his weight loss. He and his wife had redecorated his office, and on his own he had added a small cassette player to play his favorite classical music to complete his personalization of his office.

Six months later, A.B. was free of headaches. He had spearheaded a no-smoking policy for his workplace and asked the company director to install full spectrum lights on all ceiling overhead panels. He felt he had regained some sense of control over his environment and was working on improvement in the other two action plans that he and the nurse had developed.

Evaluation

Each environmental intervention should be measured as successful or not. The nurse can evaluate with the client outcomes that should be established before implementing interventions (see Table 10-2). Charting and record keeping are effective ways to log the results of environmental changes for institutional or outpatient clients and home health visits. However, much of how we relate to and what we do about environmental issues is based on the development of our personal philosophy. We continue to become increasingly aware as this philosophy develops. Therefore, we should be aware that each of the small things that we do for or against the environment have short- and long-term ramifications.

SUMMARY

Nurses have always been sensitive to environmental issues. Historically, nurses were the health care providers primarily concerned with health promotion, sanitation, and improvement in the quality of life for all people. Our technological society has brought with it new issues and concerns. Nurses must now be cognizant of a new range of environmental issues, with increasingly toxic substances at one end of the spectrum, and high technology machinery at the other.

Last year's methods of handling laboratory specimens and chemotherapy preparations, for example, may be outdated next year. New concerns may be issues in the immediate future. Nurses must keep abreast of the changing face of the environment and equip themselves with the newest strategies to counteract hazards. Future nurses would be well advised to remember and recall some of the basic nursing tenets of yesteryear that are still most relevant today. These interventions include fresh air, control for a comfortable climate, cheerful colors and sights, and noise reduction.

Nurses should be alert for ways to contribute to positive environmental changes for their own life, their client's lives, and the overall health of the planet. Environmental concerns are important to all of us, and one person's actions can have a ripple effect on many other lives. Nurses can be key agents in ensuring that the environment is held sacred, supported, and tended as it in turn supports and gives life to all of earth's people.

DIRECTIONS FOR FUTURE RESEARCH

1. Study the perception of quality of rest by subjects with different types of auditory stimulation.
2. Study the relationships between environmental hazards, such as artificial lighting, working on video display terminals, unventilated air, shift work, high noise levels, and other environmental factors, to the rise in infertility rates, conditions affecting unborn fetuses, and neonate abnormalities.
3. Investigate the use of tactile, auditory, and/or olfactory stimuli on wound healing, rate of recovery, etc.
4. Study the effect of the environment on the reduction of stress and/or anxiety in ambulatory clients.

NURSE HEALER REFLECTIONS

After reading this chapter, the nurse healer will be able to answer the following questions:

- How does the environment *affect* my job satisfaction?
- What are the environmental *stressors* at work and at home?
- What *strategies* can I incorporate in my environment to be healthier?
- What things can I do to *improve* my own personal and workplace environment?
- How can I be *involved* with environmental issues at work and in my community?

NOTES

1. Bill Thomson, "Health Hazards in the Workplace," *East West* 17, no. 8 (August 1987): 35.
2. Kay Doxsey, "Toxic Substances in the Hospital Environment," *Journal of Nursing Staff Development* 3 (Winter 1987): 41–42.
3. Kenneth Pelletier, "The Hidden Hazards of the Modern Office," *Holistic Medicine Newsletter,* July/August 1987, pp. 1, 13.
4. Bill Thomson, "Health Hazards in the Workplace," *East West* p. 35.
5. Kenneth Pelletier, "The Hidden Hazards of the Modern Office," *Holistic Medicine Newsletter* p. 13.
6. Steven Halpern and Louis Savary, *Sound Health* (San Francisco: Harper and Row, 1985), pp. 3–9.
7. Mary Smith, "Human-Environment Process: a Test of Rogers' Principle of Integrality," *Advances in Nursing Science* 9, no. 1 (October 1986): 21–28.
8. John Dengerlink, et al., "Changes in Plasma Angiotensin II with Noise Exposure and their Relationship to TTS," *Journal of the Acoustical Society of America* 72, (July 1982): 276–278.
9. Geri Harrington, "The Nuclear Pantry," *New Age Journal,* November/December 1987, pp. 25–30
10. Ibid., p. 30.
11. Nancy Schlapman, "Concerns About Passive Smoking," *Nursing Success Today* 3, no. 6 (June 1986): 26–28.
12. T. Hirayama, "Passive Smoking and Lung Cancer: Consistency of Association," *The Lancet* 2 (1983): 1425–1426.
13. J.R. White and H.F. Froeb, "Small Airways Dysfunction in Nonsmokers Chronically Exposed to Tobacco Smoke," *The New England Journal of Medicine* 13 (1980): 720–723.
14. P. Correa, L. Pickle, E. Fontham, Y. Lin, and W. Haenszel, "Passive Smoking and Lung Cancer," *The Lancet* 2 (1983): 595–596.
15. Jacques Ellul, *The Technological Society* (New York: Knopf, 1964) p. ix.

SUGGESTED READINGS

Anderson, Robert A. *Wellness Medicine.* Lynnwood, WA: American Health Press, 1987.

Hilton, Ann. "The Hospital Racket: How Noisy Is Your Unit? " *American Journal of Nursing,* January 1987, pp. 59–61.

McCloskey, Lon. "Some Biological Effects of Electric and Magnetic Fields." *Holistic Medicine Newsletter,* November/December 1987, pp. 1, 12.

Wise, Pat. "Environmental Management: Creating a Learning Ambiance," *Journal of Continuing Education in Nursing* 18: 29–30.

chapter **11**

Relaxation: Opening the Door to Change

Leslie Gooding Kolkmeier

> Change may still be possible: It's just a matter first of finding the door through which beneficial improvement can enter, and then simply learning how to open it.[1]
>
> *Herbert Benson, M.D.*
> *Director of Behavioral Medicine*
> *New England Deaconess Hospital*

This chapter explores the many avenues by which we as nurses can learn to experience and teach the steps in relaxation. As we achieve and maintain a relaxed state, we connect all bodymind systems. Relaxation is a learned skill that can become a familiar, integrated part of the spectrum of interventions we offer to ourselves and others.

Watching a healthy infant or toddler sleeping is to observe one of the earliest and deepest forms of relaxation. Unfortunately, as we grow up, we receive many verbal and nonverbal messages that relaxation is *not* to be one of our goals in life. We receive no positive reinforcement for releasing our muscle tension, taking our time, or watching the floating clouds. Our early ability to let go of physical and emotional tension and sink peacefully into a deeply relaxed state becomes lost. Relaxation is not a new skill for nurses and clients; however it is one that must be relearned and practiced in order to use it successfully to increase wellness.

There are many definitions and descriptions of relaxation. This chapter focuses primarily on specific relaxation exercises and interventions that can be taught in the clinical setting and can be learned by the client and used independently. Such interventions as imagery, music, massage, play, and exercise also may be used to help induce a relaxed, healing state. These are addressed in separate chapters in the text.

NURSE HEALER OBJECTIVES

Theoretical

1. Learn the definition of relaxation and self-regulation.
2. Compare and contrast different relaxation exercises.

Clinical

1. Describe three different types of relaxation exercises and their appropriate clinical application.
2. Identify a commonly used piece of equipment in your practice and describe how it could be used as a biofeedback device.

Personal

1. Pick one or a combination of breathing techniques and apply them to the stressful moments in your day.
2. Identify through focused awareness and body scanning the places where you accumulate muscle tension most often.
3. Identify three personally meaningful relaxation cues and use them as reminders to perform a body scan and relax.

DEFINITIONS

Autogenic Training: self-generated therapy; includes repetition of phrases about the desired state of the body, e.g. "heaviness and warmth."

Biofeedback: the use of instrumentation to mirror psychophysiologic processes of which the individual is not normally aware and which may be brought under voluntary control; feedback allows the person to be an active participant in health maintenance.[2]

Body Scanning: the focus of conscious awareness on various parts of the body for the purpose of detecting early levels of accumulating tension.

Hypnosis: an altered state of consciousness that may be induced in an individual by a facilitator for the purpose of changing perception, memory, or sensations.

Mantra: a word or short phrase that is repeated silently or aloud as a focusing device during the practice of meditation.

Meditation: a means of focusing and concentrating one's attention while maintaining a passive attitude; a discipline that requires concentrated practice.

Open Focus: an intervention to establish permissive conditions for a state of attention that is nonexclusive, tension-diffusing, nonjudgmental, and self-integrating.[3]

Pain: *(Nursing definition):* whatever the experiencing person says it is, existing whenever he or she says it does, including both verbal and nonverbal behavior. *(Medical* *definition):* localized sensation of hurt or an unpleasant sensory and emotional experience associated with actual or potential tissue damage, or described in terms of such damage.[4]

Progressive Muscle Relaxation: the process of alternately tensing and relaxing muscle groups in order to become aware of subtle degrees of tension.

Relaxation: a psychophysiologic state characterized by parasympathetic dominance involving multiple visceral and somatic systems; the absence of physical, mental, and emotional tension; the opposite of Cannon's "fight or flight" response.[5]

Relaxation Response: an alert, hypometabolic state of decreased sympathetic nervous system arousal that may be achieved in a number of ways, including breathing exercises, relaxation and imagery exercises, biofeedback, and prayer. A degree of discipline is required to evoke this response, which results in an increase in mental and physical well-being.

Self-Hypnosis: an altered state of consciousness voluntarily produced by an individual for the purpose of changing perception, memory, or sensations.

Self-Regulation: conscious control of various functions of the sympathetic nervous system.

Stress: the felt effect of overactivity of the sympathetic nervous system.

Transpersonal: the experience that transcends or goes beyond personal, individual identity and meaning; includes purpose, meaning, values, and identification with universal principles; synonymous with spiritual.

THEORY AND RESEARCH

All the approaches to relaxation described in this chapter enable one to learn to quiet the bodymind and focus inward. One learns to retreat mentally from one's surroundings, still thoughts, relax muscles, and maintain the state of relaxation for a sufficient amount of time to reap the benefits of decreased tension, anxiety, and pain. Regardless of the approach preferred by each person, the end result is a movement of the person toward balance and healing.

This activity of retreating from one's surroundings is seen in the use of sweat lodges; vision quests; spiritual withdrawal to deserts, monasteries, or caves; or the mental equivalent attained through prayer or concentrative/restrictive meditation. Retreats, either physically to a different location or psychophysiologically through music, repetitive exercise such as jogging, daydreaming, naps, deep concentration, hypnosis, and other practices, are necessary to our health and not merely escapism. This ability to separate oneself from one's surroundings, or sensory deprivation, has been called "an effective way of turning *toward* reality, of *increasing* our sensitivity to and awareness of the world as it is."[6]

Relaxation interventions can be used with people in all stages of health and illness—with intubated intensive care unit (ICU) patients, the critically ill (Fig. 11-1), expectant mothers attending childbirth preparation classes, or bus drivers learning to regulate blood pressure while weaving through city traffic. Even in the acute phase of recovery from a myocardial infarction, patients can be taught basic breathing and muscle relaxation exercises by the nurse. This self-care strategy can be reinforced by nurses on all shifts, allowing patients to be actively involved in the healing process. Remember that

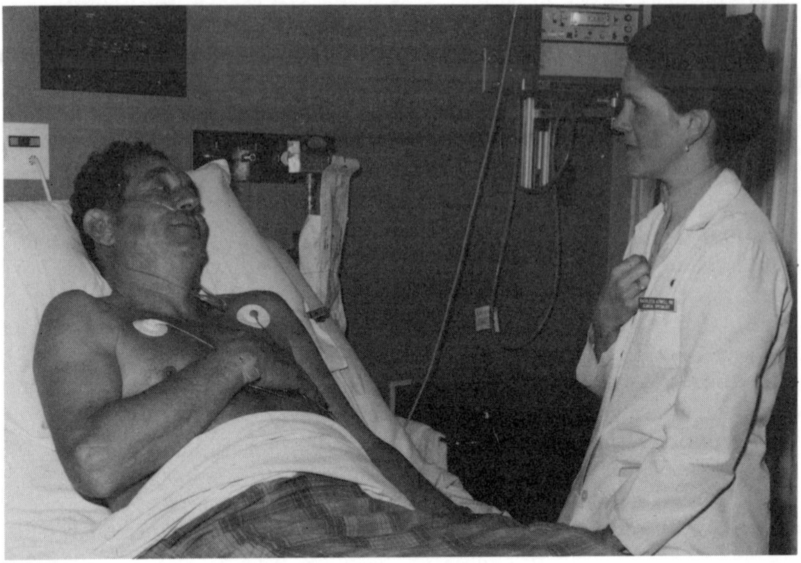

Figure 11-1 Relaxation Intervention during the Acute Phase of Recovery from a Myocardial Infarction. *Source:* Reproduced by permission from *Cardiovascular Nursing: Bodymind Tapestry* by C. Guzzetta and B. Dossey, The C.V. Mosby Company, St. Louis, © 1984.

you can also intervene in the tension/anxiety cycle being experienced by family members and friends of the patient, particularly those keeping vigil in emergency rooms, surgery waiting rooms, and ICU family areas.

Relaxation training has the following benefits[7]:

- decrease the anxiety associated with painful situations, such as debridement or dressing changes
- ease the muscle tension pain of skeletal muscle contractions
- decrease fatigue by interrupting the fight or flight response
- provide a period of rest as beneficial as a nap
- help the client fall asleep quickly
- increase the effect of pain medications
- help the client dissociate from pain

Meditation

Meditation practices have been recorded for many centuries. Meditation includes a variety of forms and is either religious or practical. Practical meditation is "essentially nonstriving and relatively goal-less."[8] The four major routes to the meditative state are: (1) the path through the intellect, (2) the path through the emotions, (3) the path through the body, and (4) the path through action.[9]

Meditation does not necessarily imply total body relaxation. Several meditative practices require the maintenance of a particular body posture over a period of time which can become uncomfortable. Other forms of active meditation, such as Sufi dancing, require a great deal of physical energy and activity. If relaxation of the body is sought, care must be taken to assure a relaxed body position, perhaps documenting the relaxation with the use of biofeedback.

In one study, when presented with a choice of 40 different words to use for mantra meditation, over 15 percent of the respondents chose the word "love." Next in order of choice were: OM, SHIRIM (Sanscrit mantras), LUM (a nonsense word), FLY, and RELAX. Forty percent chose words ending in M or N, apparently for the resonance created in the mind and body when those consonants are spoken.[10]

Progressive Muscle Relaxation (PMR)

In 1929, Jacobson published his book, *Progressive Relaxation,* which detailed a strategy leading to deep muscle relaxation. Research by Jacobson and others has demonstrated that the body responds to anxious thoughts and stressful events with increased muscle tension. This physiologic tension further provokes the subjective sensations of anxiety. By deliberately tensing muscle groups, focusing on the sensations of tightness and discomfort, and then slowly releasing that tension, the client becomes aware of an ability to control levels of muscle tension in order to remain comfortable.

Several studies report using PMR with asthmatic clients, reducing subjective feelings of anxiety and increasing peak expiratory flow rates. Progressive relaxation has also been used successfully with hypertensive patients and those undergoing invasive diagnostic tests. Significant positive results have been documented through use of the State Trait Anxiety Inventory and Internal-External Locus of Control.[11] It is felt that PMR is most effective with moderate to high panic-fear levels.[12]

Autogenics

Schultz in 1932 developed a series of brief phrases designed to focus the attention on various parts of the body and induce change in those parts. Similar to self-hypnosis, the phrases are called *autogenic* because of their ability to assist a person to change from within, a rather new approach to health care in the 1930s. Autogenic strategies are a means of gaining access to the natural homeostatic recuperative mechanisms of the brain and are effective with disorders in which cognitive involvement is prominent.[13]

Hypnosis and Self-Hypnosis

Hypnosis, the process of quieting the muscles in order to to enable one to attend mentally to positive statements, has been used with varying degrees of success for centuries. In the late 1950s the American Medical Association endorsed it as a part of medical education.[14] Since that time it has been integrated into medical and dental practices and is now becoming a part of holistic nursing practices. Nurses wishing to use hypnosis with clients should receive formal training and be aware of the position on hypnosis taken by their state nursing practice act.

Although hypnosis is used for general relaxation, it is used more frequently in a more active role: to assist a patient to gain relief from pain, as with childbirth and surgery; to enhance patient cooperation; to alter physiologic processes; to promote healing; or to assist in changing behaviors, such as smoking or eating behaviors.[15-17]

Both hypnosis and self-hypnosis enhance the ability of the client to form images because of the purposeful use of suggestion and guiding the client within an altered state of consciousness. Hypnosis is most successful when it is:

> tailored to client's individual modes of processing information (visual, auditory, and kinesthetic). Holistic hypnosis is a tool utilized within a therapeutic process that understands as much as possible about the person. As a psychophysiological interactive and interpersonal process, holistic hypnosis seeks to integrate mental and physiological processes.[18]

Self-hypnosis is a valuable tool for nurses as well as clients. Nurses working on an oncology unit who were taught to use self-hypnosis reported an increase in their ability to cope with both external and internal stressors.[19] Being able to employ self-hypnosis skills lends one credibility and enables one to teach such skills effectively to patients and clients.

Biofeedback

Without feedback, nothing can be learned.[20] With feedback, many skills can be learned much more easily and quickly. We are accustomed to employing conscious feedback, the type used when we learn through trial and error to play darts or drive a car. Through training and technology we are also capable of gaining access to many previously unconscious feedback loops, such as heart rate control, peripheral skin temperature, blood pressure, and muscle tension.

Elmer and Alyce Green are pioneers in the field of biofeedback. Arriving at the Menninger Clinic in 1964, they began to explore the realm of self-regulation as demonstrated by autogenic training. Their research, encouragement, and interest over the years led to the development of devices and strategies enabling clients to learn increasingly sophisticated control over autonomic events previously thought to be beyond the reach of the conscious mind. As Green states, "Biofeedback isn't the panacea—*it is the power within the human being* to self-regulate, self-heal, re-balance. Biofeedback does nothing *to* the person; it is a tool for releasing that potential."[21]

Biofeedback research and clinical application have centered on treatment of vascular and tension headaches, cardiovascular control (cardiac rate, rhythm, and hypertension), temporomandibular joint disorders and bruxism, disorders of motor function, gastrointestinal disorders, the management of chronic pain, and Raynaud's syndrome.[22]

Biofeedback has been used to teach relaxation skills to type A individuals.[23] Such individuals' type A characteristics, when combined with feedback of physiologic information, assisted them in learning relaxation skills. The implication is that coronary-prone individuals can be challenged by their own character traits to modify their symptoms.

Open Focus

Open Focus was developed by Lester Fehmi in the early 1970s as an adjunct to biofeedback training, particularly EEG biofeedback. Through use of the phrases that are felt to expand awareness to include all perceptible events simultaneously, the client learns to increase production of large amplitude and synchronous alpha waves, which signify deep levels of relaxation.[24] The intervention is particularly suited to those who approach the biofeedback task with a striving, goal-oriented attitude. It is particularly effective in treating pain and anxiety. According to Fehmi:

> As the positive effects of Open Focus become manifest, the imagery of space pervading and permeating all sensory, perceptual, emotional, and mental experience can be maintained and deepened. As a result, many negative sensations or experiences which have intruded into and doggedly persisted in consciousness begin to diffuse. For example, various types of pain can and often have quickly diffused and disappeared to the considerable surprise of long-suffering bearers of pain.[25]

The Relaxation Response

Benson's work with a nonreligious form of meditation, which is similar to Transcendental Meditation, has found applications in health care settings and been validated in a variety of studies.[26,27] Benson's strategy consists of 20 minutes a day of focused, passive concentration on a neutral word, such as "ONE." Slow repetition of the word, repeated with each exhalation, has been shown to bring about the same psychophysiologic responses as other deep relaxation processes.

GENERAL EXPLANATIONS

Bodymind Connections: Relaxation

We are all familiar with the intense internal reaction we experience when we are faced with an emergency: A truck pulls in front of us on the highway, we hear a "code 99" paged, a child runs into the street. What some researchers refer to as an "adrenalin rush," the felt sense of a cascade of internal changes, is actually a complex series of psychophysiologic processes that prepare us to deal with the real or *perceived* emergency. It is important to note that people respond in an identical manner to an imagined threat as to an actual threat to their well-being.

The changes that occur when an individual reaches a deep level of relaxation are exactly opposite to those of the familiar "fight or flight" response. Changes occur in the autonomic, endocrine, immune and neuropeptide systems as outlined in Exhibit 11-1.

Exhibit 11-1 Relaxation Response

Increases in:	peripheral blood flow
	electrical resistance of the skin
	production of slow alpha waves
	activity of natural killer cells
Decreases in:	oxygen consumption
	carbon dioxide elimination
	blood lactate levels
	respiratory rate and volume
	heart rate
	skeletal muscle tension
	epinephrine level
	gastric acidity and motility
	sweat gland activity
	blood pressure, especially in the hypertensive individual

Source: The Relaxation Response by H. Benson, William Morrow & Company Inc., © 1975.

Relaxation: Commonalities

Mindfulness

To succeed in using any of the interventions, one must cultivate the ability to focus only on one thing, that which one is presently doing. This activity may be meditation, dancing, breathing, or any other single, focused activity. Mindfulness is an attitude of remaining present, watchful, and aware of what is happening without becoming involved or captured by the images or feelings. Being truly present implies the absence of either anticipating or ruminating.[28]

Time

All of the interventions take time to learn. Many may be used in emergency situations or where there is a limited amount of time, but to be most effective they must be practiced regularly to become almost automatic. The discipline and self-responsibility involved in learning a relaxation intervention must be communicated to the client early in the intervention.

Timelessness

One goal of all the interventions is a decrease in muscle tension and its accomplice, anxiety. A sense of timelessness accompanies this achievement of relaxation. It is in these "timeless" moments that one is able to eliminate anxiety, manipulate pain, and gain voluntary regulation of physiologic change. This state of timelessness is the condition through which one goes even more deeply into the transpersonal and transcendent levels of creative insights and deeply meditative states, as explored in Chapters 2 and 3.

Mental Aikido: Passive Volition

One element that all the interventions share is passive attention or passive volition. This state is the opposite of *trying* or *making* a change happen. Similar to the skills learned in the Japanese martial art of *Aikido,* one learns to allow the energy of the thought or image of relaxation to carry one with it to the state of calmness. This is in contrast to the most familiar way of problem solving or learning a new skill, which is to try harder if one is not succeeding.

When learning relaxation skills this strategy of trying harder is no longer effective, a point beautifully illustrated with biofeedback. When attempting to lower muscle tension, clients may find that they are not succeeding. They immediately begin to *try harder,* which results in a further increase in tension and the realization that their old coping skill is no longer valid. In order to be successful, they must step aside mentally, adopt an expectant but nonstriving attitude, and *allow* the bodymind to let go of tension.

Compassionate Guide

A major factor in the success of any intervention is the building of rapport, openness, and trust between guide and patient. Nurses come into the profession with a large measure of compassion and empathy, but may need to re-evaluate their motives, particularly when dealing with "difficult" patients or clients. The nurse must be open to possibilities, be accepting of the other person's responses, and be able to adjust to that person's needs, likes, and dislikes as they appear during a relaxation teaching session. The client and the teaching of the relaxation skill must be approached with an attitude of loving acceptance.

Relaxation: Caveats

Control

Some people may resist the idea of passively "letting go," feeling that to do so would somehow cause them to lose control of themselves, their thoughts, environment, or actions. This resistance is seen in clients who have endured much pain or many surgical procedures and have a need to be in complete control of their schedules, medications, dressing changes, and so forth. These clients must be reassured that they will remain in control throughout the exercise and that they may test this control at any time by opening their eyes or moving a hand at will. Knowing that the interventions will indeed give them increased control over such previously overwhelming concerns as pain or insomnia will encourage and comfort them.

Other clients fear losing their competitive edge, going so far as to describe themselves as "adrenalin addicts." They must be reassured that relaxation will allow them to regulate their tension levels more appropriately and therefore more finely tune their "edge."

Belief

Clients may resist the idea of practicing relaxation on the grounds that it seems lazy or a waste of time. Relaxation must be presented to these clients as an active, creative, and dynamic process. It is far from "doing nothing," as it involves intention and practice and influences all other coping skills. Relaxation is not the same process as sleeping. Biofeedback studies have shown that some people actually increase their muscle tension levels when they sleep, a direct contrast to conscious relaxation.

Time

A common protest of clients is, "I can't find the time to do this." Assurances that the time invested in relaxation will be returned many-fold in the form of increased energy, efficiency, and comfort will help clients be creative in the ways they incorporate these skills into their daily activities. Clients can find time in their busy lives for relaxation exercises by trading household responsibilities with a housemate or spouse, taking public transportation and relaxing on the way to and from work, taking a few extra moments in the bathroom, relaxing while young children nap or in the evening after children are in bed, getting up 15 minutes early, or learning to let repetitive tasks, such as washing dishes, pulling weeds, or painting walls, become moving meditations. Clients may need guidance in order to avoid the trap of relaxation exercises becoming an additional stressor. Chapter 17 describes the use of diaries and other means of increasing compliance and documenting change achieved through relaxation training.

Choices

There is no formula to determine which relaxation intervention should be used with which client. The approach must be tailored to the individual based on his or her condition, personal preferences, and time available.

A few clients may resist the idea of relaxation in spite of your best efforts to present it in a positive manner. If this situation occurs, do not force the issue for the client may accept the intervention at a later time. However, acceptance of the intervention may be facilitated by the use of relaxation tapes that present relaxation instructions in a nonthreatening, gentle manner, often accompanied by soothing music. Exhibit 11-2 gives guidelines for the introduction and use of relaxation tapes.

Medications

As clients become more adept at the relaxation process, their need for certain medications may be reduced. Close monitoring and modification of dosages of antihypertensives, insulin, tranquilizers, antidepressants, and sleeping pills are essential. If,

---

Exhibit 11-2 Guidelines for the Use of Relaxation Tapes

1. Listen to an exercise at least once a day and preferably twice a day.
2. Never listen to a tape when you are driving or doing any other activity.
3. Arrange to have uninterrupted privacy while you listen to your tape.
4. Listen with headphones to help block out distracting noises from the environment.
5. Listen to your tape in a relaxing position, one in which you will not have to support your body.

however, the client chooses to discontinue the relaxation practice and return to old habits, the medications may be needed again.

Checking with the Body: Scans and Cuing

It is estimated that we spend 40 minutes a day, or at least 2 years of our lives, waiting.[29] We can choose to spend this time simply waiting (and probably growing impatient, thus adding to our tension burden) or we can use it to scan our bodies for muscle tension. Body scanning is taking a moment to mentally inventory all parts of one's body noticing where one is holding tension. By then allowing relaxation to replace tension, one has spent a great deal of time perfecting relaxation skills.

One of the main causes of increasing levels of tension in the body is a lack of *awareness*. We live in our heads—thinking, seeing, hearing, and talking our way through our daily activities. We become oblivious to the signals that the body sends concerning tension, tight muscles, maladaptive body positions, restricted breathing, and other clues to our state of well-being.

To remember to perform a body scan, one may link that activity with another frequently performed activity. Using these *cues,* one can monitor muscle tension levels and modify them before they have progressed to painfully tight muscles, headaches, or other stress-accentuated problems. Some cues around which to build a body-scan habit are a telephone ringing, amber or red light, when put on "hold" on the telephone, bathroom breaks, getting a drink of water, seeing a colored dot or gold star placed strategically in one's environment, entering a client's room, or between each client visit.

Supplying the client with a small counting device, similar to those used to keep track of golf scores, provides both an incentive and a means of record keeping. Each time the client takes a moment to recognize a personal cue and perform a body scan, that activity is recorded on the counter. Doing 20-30 scans a day can provide insight into tension-producing events, as well as several minutes of relaxation time. This practice may be increased with the use of contracts as described in Chapter 17.

NURSING PROCESS

Assessment

In preparing to use relaxation interventions with clients assess the following parameters:

- the client's perception of personal tension levels and need to relax
- the client's readiness and motivation to learn relaxation strategies; because relaxation is a very subjective and personal endeavor, the client must be ready and willing to participate
- the client's past experience with the process of relaxation, hypnosis, or meditation; elicit the client's definition of what it means personally to be relaxed
- the ability of the client to remain comfortably in one position for 15-30 minutes

- the acuity of the client's hearing so that you can speak at an appropriate level while guiding the client in relaxation exercises
- the religious beliefs of the client so that you can present the relaxation process in a way that will meld comfortably with the client's belief system
- the client's level of pain or discomfort, anxiety, fear, or boredom
- the client's perception of reality, history of depersonalization states, and locus of control; psychotic and prepsychotic individuals may experience an exacerbation of symptoms with deep relaxation
- the client's medication intake, focusing on medications that may alter response to relaxation, or which may need to be altered as relaxation progresses; be particularly alert for needed modifications in dosage for insulin, antihypertensive medications, sleeping pills, tranquilizers, and antidepressants

A questionnaire may be used to complete the assessment. The information gathered in the questionnaire serves as starting points for discussion and further exploration.

Nursing Diagnoses

Nursing diagnoses compatible with the interventions described in this chapter and that are related to the nine human response patterns of the Unitary Person Framework are as follows:

• Relating:	Social isolation
• Choosing:	Coping, ineffective individual and family
• Moving:	Activity intolerance: actual or potential Diversional activity, deficit
• Perceiving:	Powerlessness Self-concept, disturbance in: self-esteem, role performance, personal identity Sensory-perceptual alteration: visual, auditory, kinesthetic, gustatory, tactile, olfactory
• Knowing:	Thought processes, alteration in
• Feeling:	Anxiety Comfort, alteration in: pain Fear Violence, potential for: self-directed or directed at others

Client Outcomes

Table 11-1 guides the nurse in client outcomes, outcome criteria, and evaluation for the use of relaxation as a nursing intervention.

Table 11-1 Client Outcomes

Outcome	*Outcome Criteria*	*Evaluation*
1. The client will demonstrate a decrease in anxiety, tension, and other manifestations of the stress response as a result of the relaxation intervention.	1. The client will exhibit decreased anxiety, tension, and other manifestations of the stress response as evidenced by: a. heart rate within normal limits b. decreased respiratory rate c. increased tidal volume d. return of BP toward normal e. resolution of anxious behaviors, such as anxious facial expressions and mannerisms, repetitious talking or behavior, inability to sleep, restlessness, or expressed anxiety.	1. The client exhibited decreased anxiety, tension and other manifestations of the stress response as evidenced by normal vital signs, a slow, deep breathing pattern, and decreased anxious behaviors.
2. The client will demonstrate a stabilization or decrease in pain as a result of the relaxation intervention.	2. The client will demonstrate a decrease in pain as evidenced by: a. reduction or elimination of pain control medication b. an increase in activities and/or mobility.	2. Client intake of pain medication stabilized and then decreased over a 6-week period of relaxation skills practice. Client began to participate in activities previously limited by pain.
3. The client will link breathing awareness to a commonly occurring cue and use this combination to reduce bodymind tension.	3. The client will become aware of breathing patterns and habitually link relaxing breathing to a cue in the environment.	3. Client uses the ringing of a telephone as a cue to take slow, deep breath and relax jaw muscles.

Plan and Interventions

Before the Session

- Become personally familiar with the experience of the intervention before approaching the client.
- If the client has previous positive experience with a particular relaxation intervention, encourage further practice and use of that intervention.
- Review with the client or gather information from the chart, diaries, and/or verbal self-report concerning pain, anxiety, and activity levels since last session.

- Arrange medical and nursing care to allow for 15 to 45 minutes of uninterrupted time.
- Shut the door or otherwise decrease extraneous noise and distraction. Place a note on the door indicating a need for privacy until a designated time.
- Unplug the telephone or ask the family member or roommate to answer the phone should it ring during the relaxation training session.
- Reduce the lighting to a low level.
- Use incandescent lighting if possible; fluorescent lighting interferes with biofeedback equipment.
- Have the client empty his or her bladder before starting the intervention.
- Assist the client to find a comfortable sitting or reclining position with hands resting by the sides or on thighs.
- Assure comfort of client with a blanket or by adjusting thermostat to a comfortably warm setting.
- Arrange training session to be held before meals or more than 2 hours since the last meal. A full stomach coupled with relaxation may lead to sleep.
- Have available music tapes, tape recorder, and any other materials to add to the client's physical comfort, such as a small blanket and small, soft pillows for positioning.
- If the session is to be followed by drawing, have paper, crayons, or markers available.
- Tell the client that during the session simple "yes" or "no" questions may be asked to check the comfort level of music or his or her understanding of the verbal instructions. The client may answer these questions by raising a finger or nodding the head. Tell the client that if there is no response, the question will be repeated, such as "If you can hear my voice, raise a finger" or "If the music is at a comfortable volume, nod your head."

Beginning the Session

- Explain or review briefly the potential benefits of the experience with the client and enlist the client's cooperation.
- Explain to the client that relaxation may be easier if practiced with the eyes closed. However, rather than causing the client to drift off to sleep, this position will allow the client to focus attention inward while remaining wide awake.
- Explain that you will guide the client in breathing and relaxation exercises. The purpose of these exercises is to experience inward relaxation and become aware of the bodymind connections associated with relaxation.
- Make sure the client understands that you are merely a guide and that any results obtained from the session are because of the client's involvement, interest, and practice.
- Arrive at mutually agreeable goals for the session: reduction of pain, decreased time to sleep onset, reduction of anxiety, etc.

- Have client quantify the level of parameter to be changed, i.e. "My pain or anxiety level right now is a 7 on a 1 (no pain) to 10 (extreme pain) scale." Record the level.
- Record baseline vital signs, and if using biofeedback equipment, record baseline physiologic parameters.
- Assure the client that sensations of heaviness, warmth, floating, or spinning are naturally occurring indications of deep relaxation. If such sensations become uncomfortable, opening one's eyes will reorient a person, decrease or eliminate the sensations, and enable the exercise to continue.
- Begin soft background music. See Chapter 13 for suggestions for music selections.
- Guide the client through a basic breathing relaxation exercise. Examples of such exercises are found in Exhibit 11-3.
- Start the sessions with short breathing or relaxation exercises; lengthen the exercises as the client becomes better able to relax and attend to inner thoughts and feelings.

During the Session

- Phrase all suggestions and self-statements in a positive form, i.e., "I am aware of warmth moving into my fingertips each time I exhale, leaving my head cool and calm," rather than "My head doesn't hurt." These suggestions enhance the imagery process, and the unconscious mind may not hear the "not."
- Speaking in a relaxed manner, ask the client for feedback concerning appropriateness of the imagery and his or her ability to hear background music and instructions. Have the client respond with a finger movement or nod of the head and make adjustments as necessary.
- Pace your instructions according to visual feedback from client. Exhibit 11-4 describes visual cues indicating relaxation.

Exhibit 11-3 Breathing Exercises

Each of the following exercises may be repeated slowly for several minutes as an introduction to deeper relaxation.

- simply attending to the breath, counting ONE on each exhalation
- counting the breaths sequentially up to four and starting over
- imagining the body as hollow and allowing each breath to fill the hollow body slowly with relaxation
- in the mind's eye, seeing the breath as a soft relaxing color and breathing that color into all parts of the body
- breathing the relaxation up one side of the body and down the other, breathing the relaxation up the front of the body and down the back, breathing the relaxation up through the soles of the feet and relaxing the inside of the body, breathing the relaxation down from the top of the head, over the skin, and back into the feet

Exhibit 11-4 Visual Cues to Relaxation

- a change in breathing pattern: slower, deeper breaths progressing to slow, somewhat shallower breathing as relaxation deepens
- more audible breathing
- fluttering of eyelids
- blanching of the skin around the nose and mouth
- easing of jaw tightness, sometimes to the extent that the lips part and jaw drops slightly
- if client is supine, toes point outward, rather than straight up
- complete lack of muscle holding—ask client's permission to lift arm gently by the wrist; you should feel no resistance and arm should move as easily as any other object of similar weight.

- Modify your instructions and strategies to fit the situation. An intubated and ventilated patient who cannot control respiratory rate or volume can be encouraged to drop the jaw and allow the rhythm of the ventilator to soothe tight muscles, and so on.
- Intersperse your instructions with short phrases of encouragement that the client can use after the session as triggers to recapture a part of the relaxation experience. Examples of such phrases are:
- *Let go* of your tension.
- Feel the tightness *melting away*.
- *Loosen* and *soften* around your muscles.
- *Smooth out* your muscle tightness.
- Allow the tension to *drift away*.
- Gather up your tension and *throw it away*.
- As clients relax, they may experience a release of emotional life issues, which then surface in the conscious mind. Be alert for signs of emotional discomfort or letting go, such as tears, vomiting, or a change in breathing to deeper, faster breaths. If these occur, allow time for the client to express these feelings and deal with the material before continuing with or concluding the session. Often clients gain insight into resolution of problems or which directions to take in their lives when in a deeply relaxed state.

Closing the Session

- Bring the client back gradually into a wakeful state by suggesting deep, re-energizing breaths, beginning to move hands and feet, and stretching.
- Have client re-evaluate, on the same scale of 1-10, the level of severity of the previously determined parameter to be changed. Record the level.
- Allow time for discussion of the experience; what seemed to work especially well, what distractions were apparent, physical and emotional sensations associated with the experience, etc.

- Arrange for follow-up sessions.
- Ensure that medication changes, if indicated, are appropriately monitored.
- Engage client's cooperation in continuing practice on an individually assigned basis until the next session. See Chapter 17 for ideas to increase compliance with a practice regimen.
- Discuss homework assignments found in all Unit IV chapters under the sections on interventions.
- Help the client choose cues with which to associate practicing the relaxation skill, i.e., each time the telephone rings, whenever a commercial appears on television, whenever a particular person enters the room, or when the client opens a door, etc.
- Review log or journal to record symptoms, medications, practice time and results. See Chapter 17 for examples.
- Summarize by asking, "What did you learn that was helpful to you? . . . that was *not* helpful."

Specific Interventions: Relaxation

The following interventions should not be used to remove symptoms without knowing the cause of the symptoms. They are not meant to replace diagnosis and treatment, but to enhance healing and well-being. Each intervention is marked *basic* or *advanced* as appropriate.

Tension Awareness: Progressive Muscle Relaxation (Basic)

Purpose: To help the client identify subtle levels of mental tension and anxiety and the accompanying physical tension.

Time: 10-30 minutes. (See addendum for specific instructions on gross and threshold tension levels.)

Script: "First take a few moments to focus on your breathing. This will help you to focus better on internal cues of muscle tension and then relaxation. I will guide you as we begin to move through the muscles in your body. Become aware of how you can gain control over the tension found in those muscles. This process involves alternately tightening and relaxing muscle groups. Let yourself tighten each muscle group, hold the tension for 5 to 10 seconds or until mild fatigue is felt in the area, and then release the tension. . . . Begin with the muscles in your feet and calves; tighten that area as much as you can. Pull your toes up toward your head, and become aware that as the muscles tighten and as you continue to hold that tightness, they will perhaps tremble or shake a bit as they fatigue. . . . Now, let the tension slowly dissolve and feel the difference in your lower legs and feet. . . . Let your attention move up to your knees and thighs; tense those muscles by pressing your legs into the surface of the bed (couch, floor, or chair). . . . When you are aware of how they feel, then allow the tension to drift away as you exhale."

Proceed to the following areas: hips and buttocks, abdomen and lower back, chest and upper back, shoulders and biceps, forearms and hands, neck and shoulders, jaw and tongue, and finally facial muscles.

Addendum: If the client is experiencing pain or difficulty with a particular part of the body, begin the exercise as far away from the involved area as possible. Conclude the exercise with the primary area of difficulty.

When the client is aware of the *internal difference* induced by this process, he or she can move to *threshold* levels of tension, holding just enough tightness in the muscle group to be aware of beginning tension and then relaxing the group. By moving from strong contractions to very subtle ones, the client becomes aware of the ability to *fine tune* the relaxation process.

Clients should be coached to *breathe* throughout the session, thereby avoiding the temptation to hold the breath as they tighten up. Tension in muscles should be held short of true discomfort.

Progressive Muscle Relaxation is particularly effective for clients who are feeling physically tense, anxious, and perhaps agitated. Because it is an active intervention it may be preferred over other passive exercises, especially early in client training. However, it should be used with caution with hypertensive and backpain patients.

Return to Balance: Autogenic Training (Basic)

Purpose: To help consciously rebalance the internal homeostatic mechanisms of the cardiovascular and respiratory systems, which simultaneously affect the autonomic, endocrine, immune, and neuropeptide systems.

Time: 10-20 minutes

Script: ''Slowly and silently repeat the following phrases to yourself as I say them out loud to you: (repeat each phrase two to four times, pausing a few seconds between each repetition) 'I am beginning to feel quite quiet. . . . I am beginning to feel relaxed. . . . My feet, knees and hips feel heavy. . . . Heaviness and warmth are flowing through my feet and legs. . . . My hands, arms, and shoulders feel heavy. . . . Warmth and heaviness are flowing through my hands and arms. . . . My neck, jaw, tongue, and forehead feel relaxed and smooth. . . . My whole body feels quiet, heavy, and comfortable. . . . I am comfortably relaxed. . . . Warmth and heaviness flow into my arms, hands, and fingertips. . . . My breathing is slow and regular. . . . I am aware of my calm, regular heartbeat. . . . My mind is becoming quieter as I focus inward. . . . I feel still. . . . Deep in my mind I experience myself as relaxed, comfortable and still. . . . I am alert in a quiet, inward way.' As I finish my relaxation, I take in several deep, re-energizing breaths, bringing light and energy into every cell of my body.''

Addendum: Autogenic training should begin in a warm (75-80° Fahrenheit) room. Clients can then progress to cooler environments to generalize their training. Use of the phrases with a relaxed, receptive mind allows the peripheral circulation to increase and cardiac and respiratory rates and rhythms to slow and stabilize. It may take several weeks for the client to feel sensations of heaviness and warmth, although heart rate and respiratory control will usually be achieved much sooner.

The Golden Moment: Quieting Response (Basic)

Purpose: To become aware, on a frequent basis, of external stressors and one's internal responses to them. To let go of the internal responses and continue with daily activities.

Time: 6-10 seconds. (This is an abbreviated version that can be done frequently during the day.)

Script: "Check your breathing. Notice what is bothering you at this moment. Smile at yourself and say to yourself, 'What a silly thing to do to my body.' Take a slow deep breath to a count of 1-2-3-4 and breathe out slowly to a count of 1-2-3-4. Again, slowly breathe in and as you breathe out, let your body go as limp as possible, particularly your lips and jaw. Imagine warmth and heaviness flowing down your body to your toes. Allow your eyes to dance and inwardly smile. Go on with your activities, alert and relaxed."

Addendum: Developed by Stroebel, this intervention is an eclectic combination of stressor identification skills, breathing techniques, progressive relaxation, changing self-talk, and autogenics. The strategy has been modified into a program called "QR for Kids" to help children identify their bodily responses to stressors and replace them with relaxation.[30] Children learn to identify what is bothering them, let their eyes sparkle, breathe in through imaginary holes in their feet, and allow their bodies to become warm and relaxed as they exhale. This intervention is reinforced with a large variety of imagery exercises.[31]

Expanding Awareness: Open Focus (Advanced)

Purpose: To diffuse one's attention, rather than focus it narrowly on one point.

Time: 10-45 minutes. (The following contains excerpts from the complete script.)

Script: Begin each phrase with: "Is it possible for you to imagine . . ." or "Can you imagine . . ."

- the space between your eyes
- the space between your ears
- the space inside your throat
- that the space inside your throat expands to fill your whole neck as you inhale
- that your feet and toes are filled with space
- that the region between your arches and your ankles is filled with space
- that your buttocks and the region between your hips and your legs and feet and toes are simultaneously filled with space
- the space inside your lungs as you inhale and exhale
- that the boundaries between the space inside and the space outside are dissolving and that the space inside and the space outside become one continuous and unified space

Addendum: The entire series of exercises consists of 95 statements that expand and open the attention and awareness of the client, leading to a deeply relaxed state. The Open Focus exercise asks the client a series of questions relating to his or her imagination of something other than a concrete object or experience. Distance, no-thing-ness, and spaces between points and objects form the basis of the script. After repeated practice, clients can often return to the state of Open Focus simply by repeating a cue word or phrase to themselves.

Quiet Heart: The Relaxation Response, (Basic)

Purpose: To achieve a relaxed, alert, hypometabolic state.
Time: 15-20 minutes.
Script: "As you exhale, mentally repeat the word *ONE* with each breath out. As thoughts interfere with the single focus of breathing out to the count of *ONE,* let the thoughts go and come back to the activity of breathing and counting. Focus on your breathing and the word *ONE.*"

After 20 minutes, ask the client to stretch, take a deep breath, and continue with normal activities.

Addendum: As the length of hospital stays in acute care have been reduced, the Relaxation Response is an increasingly valuable intervention because it can be taught in a short time period. Clients involved in an outpatient wellness practice, long-term care, or a hospice situation are able to learn the more involved disciplines of meditation.

Quiet Heart: Meditation (Basic to Advanced)

Purpose: To gain access to more of our human potential, to increase our ability to function in reality more effectively
Time: 10 to 15 minutes.
Script: (Make sure client is comfortable with water image before beginning script) "Picture yourself sitting comfortably on the floor of a beautiful clear lake. Each time you experience a thought, feeling, or perception, picture it as a bubble rising slowly to the surface of the lake. Take 5-8 seconds to observe each thought, feeling, or perception rising until it passes from your sight. Do not explore or associate with any of the bubbles; simply notice them with a background of 'oh, that's what I'm thinking (or feeling, or sensing) now. How interesting.' As each bubble disappears, wait calmly for the next one.[32]

Addendum: This is a single example of a meditation strategy. Become aware of the many variations and of their specific purposes through community college courses, teachers in your town, books, but most importantly through *practice*.

As with all relaxation interventions, no one is any better than another; each provides different means to the same end: a voluntarily achieved, relaxed, hypometabolic state, accompanied by a quiet bodymind. Most teachers suggest staying with a particular meditation path for a minimum of 1 month before contemplating a change. One should follow what intuitively feels right. "Be" with the feelings experienced after a period of meditation and know that, if you feel better and less fragmented than you did before, you are on the right path.[33]

Quiet Heart: Prayer (Basic to Advanced)

Purpose: To provide the client with a tie to religious/spiritual roots.
Time: Seconds to minutes.
Script: Client's choice.
Addendum: Prayer is a way of eliciting the relaxation response in the context of deeply held personal religious or philosophical beliefs. Benson refers to this as incorporating the "Faith Factor" into relaxation. Many clients are comfortable with prayer as a meditative strategy. Strive to accommodate their needs, either by calling on your

background and resources or enlisting the help of appropriate family, clergy, or chaplaincy staff.

Utilizing Inner Awareness: Biofeedback (Advanced)

Biofeedback uses specialized instrumentation to reflect changes in physiologic function to clients in such a way as to allow them to intervene and change their own internal activity. A very simple biofeedback device is the common bathroom scale. One steps on the scale, sees one's weight, and according to that information, chooses whether or not to make a change in one's eating habits. A thermometer and mirror are other good examples to explain that biofeedback devices do not *do* anything to the client; they simply record information *about* the client.

Clinical biofeedback devices are electronically sophisticated, sometimes portable instruments that present information in a variety of engaging fashions. Through skin electrodes or thermistors they monitor subtle changes in temperature, muscle activity, brain waves, sweat gland activity, blood pressure, and cardiac rate and rhythm. This information, combined with other relaxation interventions covered in this chapter, allows the client to make internal adjustments toward a relaxed state and receive immediate rewards for having done so. The equipment externally validates the presence of internal change, thus greatly speeding up the learning and reinforcement of those changes.

Biofeedback is most frequently used to help clients learn to relax overactivity of the sympathetic nervous system. Biofeedback is also used for neuromuscular retraining in the context of *increasing* muscle activity after stroke or spinal cord injury. The reader is referred to local or national workshops, training courses, and seminars and resources at the end of this chapter for further information on biofeedback training and certification.

Door to the Inner Mind: Hypnosis (Advanced)

As the bodymind becomes alert but relaxed, self-talk decreases and one is able to communicate with the subconscious. Hypnosis has the features of motivation, relaxation, and concentration in common with the other interventions discussed, but in addition it adds the feature of *directing* by a person trained in hypnosis. The altered state of consciousness achieved through hypnosis is similar to, and at times indistinguishable from, guided imagery. One may use the hypnotic trance to rehearse new coping skills, open new possibilities, and gain self-regulatory mastery over various aspects of the sympathetic nervous system.

Hypnosis and particularly the hypnotic trance may have negative connotations to some clients and should be presented in a positive framework. To frame the hypnotic state in familiar circumstances, clients can be reminded of times that they have become completely engrossed in a movie or a book. Assurances that they will *always* remain in control and can only enter a hypnotic state voluntarily will help ease clients' misgivings.

There are four basic stages of hypnosis[34]:

1. *Induction:* achieved through gazing at a point, staring upward, or fixating on a monotonous action, such as a clock pendulum or waves on a beach

2. *Deepening:* increasing the depth of the trance through spiral images, moving down a staircase or elevator, counting breaths, etc.
3. *Plateau:* that stage of the trance in which one embeds suggestions for positive change or reinforces previously decided, mutually agreed-on behaviors or goals
4. *Reversing:* a return through the process followed in deepening to a state of relaxed alertness

Door to the Inner Mind: Self-Hypnosis (Basic)

Hypnotic strategies can give clients and patients a powerful tool in dealing with anxieties, behavior patterns, or pain. In addition to the immediate benefits, there is a long-term increase in self-esteem as the methods are applied successfully to a variety of situations.

> Self-hypnosis instruction will be most helpful, and safest, when it is coordinated with the client's physician and other health care providers. The client's willingness to understand the cause of his symptoms, to change his programming, his mental attitudes and his lifestyle, are essential to letting go of his symptoms.[35]

The reader is referred to Chapter 1 for affirmations and Chapter 12 for self-talk and imagery strategies to incorporate into the self-hypnosis experience.

Yoga (Basic to Advanced)

Yoga is a philosophy of living that attempts to unite physical, mental, and spiritual health. When practiced for the purpose of relaxation, it consists of breathing and stretching exercises and postures called "asanas."

Because the exercises vary greatly in difficulty, starting with very gentle stretches and breathing techniques, yoga is ideally suited for clients with stiff muscles and decreased activity levels who are attempting to begin an active relaxation and exercise program. Readers and clients are encouraged to pursue an interest in yoga through books, videotapes and classes, basing their activity level on their ability.

Evaluation

The nurse must evaluate with the client whether the outcomes established before the session were met. Because the accomplishment of these interventions may take place over a period of days or weeks, they must be reviewed and re-evaluated periodically. Continuing support and encouragement are necessary.

Case Studies

Case Study 1

Setting: Pediatric Pulmonary Care Unit; biofeedback-mediated relaxation

Client: A.B., an 11-year-old boy with end-stage cystic fibrosis
Nursing Diagnoses:
1. Alteration in oxygenation, impaired gas exchange, ineffective breathing pattern, ineffective airway clearance
2. Social isolation
3. Ineffective individual coping
4. Activity intolerance
5. Disturbance in body image
6. Powerlessness
7. Pain
8. Anxiety
9. Fear, all related to diagnosis of cystic fibrosis.

A.B. had been diagnosed with cystic fibrosis at the age of 7 months. Since that time he had spent much of his life in the hospital. He had seen most of his older friends die. His parents had divorced when he was 5 years old, and when not hospitalized he lived with his mother and 13-year-old sister.

His pediatrician felt that A.B.'s present admission would likely be his last. His pulmonary infections were not responding to intravenous antibiotics; he was losing weight and requiring continuous oxygen by cannula. In order to decrease A.B.'s fear and anxiety, which was interfering with his ability to sleep and further compromising his pulmonary status, the pediatrician asked that the biofeedback nurse therapist work with the patient.

With the aid of relaxation exercises, imagery, and electromyographic biofeedback devices, A.B. learned, over the space of five daily sessions, to decrease the activity of his accessory breathing muscles and increase the excursion of his diaphragm. He began to use his relaxation skills to help him sleep. He also discovered that he was better able to clear accumulated pulmonary secretions after a biofeedback session, further increasing his oxygenation and comfort level.

Knowing that the physical and emotional states achieved with relaxation are often difficult to communicate, the nurse asked A.B. to draw how he felt before a relaxation-biofeedback session. In Figure 11-2A the difficulty A.B. was having breathing is graphically illustrated by the heavy bands around his neck and chest. His self-concept is communicated through the unhappy face, stunted size, and only three fingers on each hand.

Figure 11-2A Drawing Done before Relaxation-Biofeedback Session.

After 20 minutes of biofeedback-mediated deep relaxation he drew the picture shown in Figure 11-2B. A.B. now depicts himself as well-proportioned, having a happy face, and five fingers on each hand, with powerful muscles in his arms, and breathing freely. When asked to comment on the lines coming out from the surface of his body, he explained, "Those are the warm, tingly feelings I get when I relax."

A.B. died 2 weeks later, sleeping quietly in his mother's arms. He practiced his new skills up until his last hours.

Case Study 2

Setting:	preoperative visit to physician's office; using cues to anchor relaxation
Client:	C.D., a 38-year-old female secretary
Nursing Diagnoses:	1. Alteration in physical regulation (rheumatoid, autoimmune disorder) 2. Alteration in physical mobility (right wrist, degeneration/dysfunction both knees) 3. Anxiety 4. Coping, ineffective individual

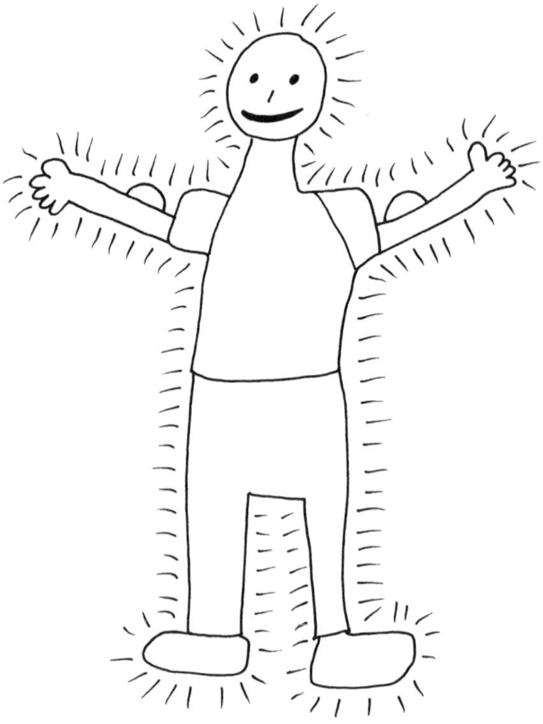

Figure 11-2B Drawing Done after 20 Minutes of Relaxation.

5. Fear
6. Powerlessness: all related to diagnosis of rheumatoid arthritis

Four years before, C.D. was diagnosed with rheumatoid arthritis. The present problem is scheduled surgery to remove three displaced bones from her right wrist that are causing radial nerve impairment. In addition to the long-term concern of whether she would be able to continue working at her present position, C.D. confided to her nurse her fear associated with the time period just before entering the operating room. She had undergone arthroscopic knee surgery several years before and still had vivid, unpleasant memories of lying in a preoperative area and hearing the voices of the nurses on the other side of the curtain. She felt abandoned and frightened and had wondered if anyone even knew she was there. Postoperatively she had experienced several hours of nausea and vomiting.

In addition to providing C.D. with the usual preoperative information, the nurse also taught her relaxation and imagery exercises. She was asked to relax for a few moments in a comfortable position so she could begin to rehearse in her imagination the following week's procedure. After guiding C.D. through a few moments of breathing relaxation (refer to Exhibit 11-3), the nurse asked C.D. to close her eyes and begin to imagine waking up on the day of her surgery. The nurse took her step-by-step through the morning routine of getting dressed, being driven through the early morning sunrise to the hospital, going through the outpatient admission process, going to her room, putting on a hospital gown, getting a preoperative injection, and waiting calmly while holding her husband's hand until the orderly came to take her to the surgery waiting area.

At this point in the relaxation imagery, the nurse directed C.D. to imagine being wheeled down the long corridor to the surgery doors, watching the ceiling lights passing above her. Each time she saw a light in the ceiling she was to use that as a cue to take a deep breath and release all the tension from her bodymind. C.D. was instructed to practice this rehearsal three times a day until the day of surgery. The nurse recorded this voice instruction so C.D. had her own *personalized* tape for healing before, during, and after surgery. (Even if the nurse only has a short time for teaching before surgery, there is time to teach rhythmic breathing exercises.)

At her first postoperative visit C.D. enthusiastically reported the positive results of her mental rehearsal and relaxation. She vividly remembered her mental relaxation and imagery as she had rehearsed, her confidence increasing as she was wheeled under each light. The surgery waiting area seemed calm and safe to her this time, and she had no postoperative nausea. At this first postoperative visit the nurse taught her imagery of healing and increasing mobility in the same format as her visit before surgery. Her success with using cues to help her remember to relax encouraged C.D. to use the intervention whenever she was faced with an unpleasant or frightening experience.

SUMMARY

Relaxation exercises can be taught to clients under almost any circumstances. They not only reduce the fear and anxiety associated with many medical and nursing interventions but, once learned, may also be used in all aspects of the client's life. They increase the overall movement toward wholeness and balance for both client and nurse and facilitate other interventions by allowing the client to move toward learning and participating in his or her health.

DIRECTIONS FOR FUTURE RESEARCH

1. Correlate the changes in psychophysiology with the specific interventions used in order to determine the most effective interventions and their presentation.
2. Conduct tightly structured studies that use control groups to validate changes brought about by relaxation exercises.
3. Monitor and validate the effect of the "compassionate guide" in the relaxation process.

NURSE HEALER REFLECTIONS

After reading this chapter the nurse healer will be able to answer or begin a process of answering the following questions:

- How does my *inner experience* of tension or anxiety shift when I release my muscle tightness?
- How do I *model* relaxation to my family, friends, colleagues, and clients?
- What is my *kinesthetic experience* of letting go of tension, concerns, and physical and emotional stresses?
- What cues about my *inner states* of tension or relaxation do I receive from my breathing pattern?
- What *peace of mind* do I experience as I move through my potentially stressful job activities?
- Am I *aware* that my attitudes toward my tasks are contagious to my clients?

NOTES

1. Hebert Benson, "Your Maximum Mind," *New Age Journal,* November/December 1987, p. 23.
2. George Fuller, *Biofeedback: Methods and Procedures in Clinical Practice* (San Francisco: The Biofeedback Institute of San Francisco, 1977), p. 1.
3. Lester G. Fehmi. Paper presented at the Council Grove Conference on Voluntary Control of Internal States, 1975.
4. Noreen T. Meinhart and Margo McCaffery, *Pain: A Nursing Approach to Assessment and Analysis* (East Norwalk, CT: Appleton-Century-Crofts, 1983), p. 377.
5. K.C. Phillips, "Biofeedback as an Aid to Autogenic Training," in *Mind and Cancer Prognosis,* ed. B.A. Stoll (New York: John Wiley and Sons, 1979), p. 153.
6. Michael Hutchison, *The Book of Floating* (New York: William Morrow and Company, Inc., 1984), p. 25.
7. Margo McCaffery, "Relieving Pain with Noninvasive Techniques," *Nursing 80,* 10, no. 12 (December 1980): 57.

8. Doris Sutterly and Gloria Donnelly, *Coping with Stress: A Nursing Perspective,* (Rockville, MD: Aspen Systems Corporation, 1982), p. 190.
9. Lawrence LeShan, *How to Meditate* (New York: Bantam Books, 1975), p. 32.
10. Donald Roy Morse and M. Lawrence Furst, *Women Under Stress* (New York: Van Nostrand Reinhold Co., 1982), p. 381.
11. Nola J. Pender, "Effects of Progressive Muscle Relaxation Training on Anxiety and Health Locus of Control among Hypertensive Adults," *Research in Nursing and Health* 8 (1985): 67–72.
12. Pauline D. Freedberg, Leslie A. Hoffman, Wilma C. Light, and Mary Kreps, "Effect of Progressive Muscle Relaxation on the Objective Symptoms and Subjective Responses Associated with Asthma," *Heart and Lung* 16, no. 1 (January 1987): 24–30.
13. Johann Stoyva, "Wolfgang Luthe: In Memoriam," *Biofeedback and Self-Regulation* 11, no. 2 (1986): 91.
14. Vicki Moss, "Beating the Stress Connection," *Association of Operating Room Nurses* 41, no. 4 (April 1985): 720.
15. William Kroger and William Fezler, *Hypnosis and Behavior Modification* (Philadelphia: J.B. Lippincott Co., 1976), pp. 179–221.
16. Harold Crasilneck and James Hall, *Clinical Hypnosis* (New York: Grune and Stratton, 1985), pp. 147–176.
17. Rothlyn P. Zahourek, "Clinical Hypnosis in Holistic Nursing," *Holistic Nursing Practice* 2, no. 1 (November, 1987): 22.
18. Ibid., p. 17.
19. Gil Boyne, ed., *Hypnosis: New Tool in Nursing Practice* (Glendale CA: Westwood Publishing Co., 1982), p. 8.
20. Elmer Green and Alyce Green, *Beyond Biofeedback* (New York: Delta Books, 1977), p. 24.
21. Ibid., p. 116.
22. John P. Hatch, Johnnie G. Fisher, John D. Rugh, eds., *Biofeedback: Studies in Clinical Efficacy* (New York: Plenum Press, 1987), p. 1ff.
23. Connie K. Moreno, "Concepts of Stress Management in Cardiac Rehabilitation," *Focus on Critical Care* 14, no. 5 (October 1987): 17.
24. Lester G. Fehmi, p. 2.
25. Ibid., p. 9.
26. Herbert Benson, S. Alexander, and C.L. Feldman, "Decreased Premature Ventricular Contraction Through Use of the Relaxation Response in Patients with Stable Ischemic Heart Disease," *Lancet* 2, no. 7931 (1975): 380.
27. Marilyn Frenn, Richard Fehring, and Susan Kartes, "Reducing the Stress of Cardiac Catherization by Teaching Relaxation," *Dimensions of Critical Care Nursing* 5, no. 2 (March-April 1986): 108–116.
28. Erik Peper and Elizabeth Ann Williams, *From the Inside Out* (New York: Plenum Press, 1981), p. 76.
29. Edward A. Charlesworth and Ronald G. Nathan, *Stress Management* (New York: Antheneum, 1984), p. 75.
30. Elizabeth Strobel, "Kiddie QR" (Wethesfield, CT: QR Publications, 1987), audiotape and workbooks.
31. Ibid., audiotape and workbooks.
32. Lawrence LeShan, *How to Meditate,* p. 60.
33. Ibid., p. 33.
34. Vicki Moss, "Beating the Stress Connection," pp. 720–722.
35. Gil Boyne, *Hypnosis: New Tool in Nursing Practice*, p. 10.

SUGGESTED READING

Benson, Herbert, with Proctor, William. *Your Maximum Mind*. New York: Random House, Inc., 1987.

Harmon, Willis, and Reinhold, Howard. *Higher Creativity*. Los Angeles: Jeremy P. Tarcher, Inc., 1984.

Horowitz, Barbara F.; Fitzpatrick, Joyce J.; and Flaherty, Geraldine G. "Relaxation Techniques for Pain Relief after Open Heart Surgery." *Dimensions of Critical Care Nursing* 3, no. 6 (November/December 1984): pp. TK

Shellenberger, Robert, and Green, Judith. *From the Ghost in the Box to Successful Biofeedback Training*. Greeley, CO: Health Psychology Publications, 1986.

Zahorek, Rothlyn P., ed. *Clinical Hypnosis and Therapeutic Suggestion in Nursing*. Orlando, FL: Grune and Stratton, Inc., 1985.

RESOURCES

Applied Psychophysiology and Biofeedback, 102001 West 44th Ave., #304, Wheat Ridge, CO 80033.

Hypnosis Workshops, American Society of Clinical Hypnosis, 2250 East Devon Ave., Suite 336, Des Plaines, IL 60018.

Open Focus Workshops, Lester Fehmi, 317 Mount Lucas Rd., Princeton, NJ 08540.

chapter 12

Imagery: Awakening the Inner Healer

Barbara Montgomery Dossey

> The human mind is a slide projector with an infinite retrieval system, and an endlessly cross-referenced subject catalogue. The inner images we show ourselves form our lives, whether as memories, fantasies, dreams, or visions. We can direct the mind's eye to our inner world to bring about the creative forces of spirituality and healing in our daily life.[1]
>
> *Mike Samuels, MD*
> *Nancy Samuels*

This chapter guides the nurse in use of imagery as a nursing intervention. Imagery, a nonverbal modality and a rich resource about all life processes, is a tool for connecting with the unlimited capabilities of bodymind. Using imagery, the nurse can help the client make changes in perception and behavioral attitudes that can promote healing. The end result for the client is more self-awareness, self-acceptance, self-love, and self-worth. Nurses and clients come to know themselves in a new way as they create and communicate in a *symbolic* language.

Why should nurses develop an awareness of imagery skills as a nursing intervention? This answer is simple: Imagery interventions are powerful, noninvasive, cost effective, and can be done alone by the client or with guidance.

NURSE HEALER OBJECTIVES

Theoretical

1. Learn the definitions and categories of imagery.
2. Compare the different theories of imagery.
3. Contrast and compare different imagery interventions.

Clinical

1. Choose several imagery interventions and use them in clinical practice.
2. Learn techniques to empower the spoken word to gain more skill at facilitating the imagery process.
3. Train your voice to have the qualities of calmness, softness, steadiness, reassurance, openness, and trust.
4. Use imagery and relaxation interventions for yourself at work everyday.

Personal

1. Choose a special image to focus on throughout the day.
2. Learn to trust your images and how to interpret their meaning.
3. Experience the internal change of "lightening your personal load" by using the imagery process.
4. Keep a journal/diary of your progress, questions, and self-reflections with your imagery process.

DEFINITIONS

General Definition

Imagery: internal experiences of memories, dreams, fantasies, and visions; may involve one, several, or all of the senses; serves as the bridge for connecting body, mind, and spirit; synonymous with visualization.

Basic Categories of Imagery[2]

Abstract: imagery that emerges spontaneously while in relaxed states.
Concrete: imagery developed for the purpose of problem solving, goal setting, and changing behavior.
End-Result: imagery that consists of the desired result as already having taken place.
General: imagery that is not directed toward a specific goal, but toward an overall response, such as a general relaxation response.
Induced: imagery that one creates with conscious or preconscious attention.
Process: imagery that is fantasized or an actual mechanism by which a desired effect can be achieved.
Spontaneous: imagery that arises in one's consciousness without effort.

Specific Types of Imagery

After-Image: images obtained when closing the eyes after looking at a bright object on a dark background or a dark object on a light background.

Daydreams/Fantasy: daydreams are usually spontaneous and fantasy has an induced quality; both may be concrete or abstract; they are usually fleeting but do give a person inner information.

Dreams: imagery that primarily involves the visual mode; they are spontaneous, may be concrete or abstract, and provide the person with inner phenomena that can be therapeutic.

Eidectic Imagery: photographic memory that is most prevalent in children and decreases as one gets older; images can be concrete or abstract; differ from memory images in that they have more detail and are less easily changed at will.

Guided Imagery: imagery of any of the specific categories that is suggested in part or whole to a person by a guide.

Hypnagogic: imagery that occurs just before falling asleep; images are spontaneous and may be concrete or abstract; are usually short lived because one moves on into sleep.

Hypnopompic: imagery that occurs immediately upon awakening; these images are spontaneous and may be concrete or abstract; they are usually short lived because the person becomes wide awake and starts logical processing of information.

Hallucinations: real-appearing imagery that can occur in any of the five senses; can occur with psychosis, in nonpsychotic states, with various drug states, sensory deprivation, and hypnosis.

Imagination imagery: imagery that differs in qualitative or quantitative ways from images originally perceived; can be symbolic (the representation of things by symbols) or abstract and usually contains all other types of specific imagery; commonly used in therapy in order to achieve end-result imagery. Example: symbolic figures attacking disease.

Memory imagery: imagery of past events brought back into awareness for therapeutic discovery.*

THEORY AND RESEARCH

Imagery is a complex phenomenon of mind modulation. It is a normal process that evokes change at the cellular level via activity of the right and left hemispheric brain function, and the autonomic, endocrine, immune, and neuropeptide systems as described in Chapter 5. People can be taught how to direct their imagery process to produce positive healing results.

In order to help the nurse understand the basics of the use of imagery as a nursing intervention, this theory and research section has two parts: (1) theories of how imagery affects physiology and learning (what imagery does), and (2) theories of how it is elicited (what imagery is).

Affects of Imagery on Physiology and Learning

The Senses and Physiology

With imagery all sensory modalities are involved: visual, olfactory, tactile, gustatory, auditory, and kinesthetic.[3] Each of the known senses has many different, extremely

---

**Source:* Adapted from *Visualization: The Uses of Imagery in the Health Professions* by E. Korn and K. Johnson, pp. 65–68, with permission of Dow Jones-Irwin, © 1983.

complex levels that perform distinct functions that are separate and parallel to each of the other senses.

In fact, as many as many as 17 senses have been identified.[4]

Some of the newly identified senses are:

- the *vomeronasal* system, which is capable of detecting pheromones, the chemicals that are given off to indicate intraspecific messages such as sexual receptivity, fear, and identification
- nociception, which is a separate sensory organ for pain that is distinct from touch and temperature sensing
- a parallel but separate sensory system for experiencing *thermal* and *tactile* sensations
- parallel but separate systems for detecting the visual *contour/contrast* form of an object and its colors
- a functional pineal gland, which is able to respond to light and synchronize internal body rhythms of night and day

Research findings on imagery and physiology are summarized as follows[5]:

- Images relate to physiologic states.
- Images may either precede or follow physiologic changes, indicating they have both a causative and reactive role.
- Images can be induced by conscious, deliberate behaviors, as well as by subconscious acts (electrical stimulation of the brain, reverie, dreaming, etc).
- Images can be considered as the hypothetical bridge between conscious processing of information and physiologic change.
- Images can exert influence over the voluntary (peripheral) nervous system, as well as the involuntary (autonomic) nervous system.

State Dependent Learning

All types of counseling and psychotherapy facilitate mind-body healing with imagery processes. There are now over 300 different forms of psychotherapy.[6] Regardless of the complexities of the therapies, all follow the same three-step routine for problem solving:

1. Therapist and client initiate a communication process together.
2. They engage in some sort of therapeutic work.
3. They develop some criteria for problem resolution so they know when to discontinue the interaction.

Memory is *state-dependent* learning that brings about mind-body healing. Because memory is dependent upon and limited to the state in which it was acquired, it is referred to as *state-bound information*.[7] Therefore, what is learned and remembered is dependent on one's psychologic state at the time it is experienced. The dramatic psychophysiologic changes that occur in hypnosis and imagery result from gaining access to state-dependent memory, learning, and behavior systems and making their encoded information available for problem solving. Every *access* of information can be seen as is a *reframe*. When one gains access to state-dependent memory, it then can be reassociated, reorganized, or reframed in a manner that resolves the negative memory. This theory is the basis for all interventions discussed in this chapter.

How To Elicit Imagery

Lexical and Enactive Modes of Imagery

Imagery is (1) encoded, (2) retrieved, and (3) expressed.[8] It flows among patterns of images, thoughts, physical responses, and a person's world view. Images form, express, and evoke emotions that directly affect physiologic response. Information enters the central nervous system, is encoded into images, and is stored in two modes: lexical and enactive. The *lexical mode* is that type of logical and analytical thinking that occurs in the left hemisphere. The *enactive mode* of thinking occurs in the right hemisphere where emotions and kinesthetic experiences evolve.

Eidetic Psychotherapy

Ahsen's eidetic psychotherapy has three unitary, interactive modes of awareness—(1) image-I, (2) somatic response-S, and (3) meaning-M—that comprise an *eidetic* (ISM).[9] The "I" (image) is the aroused sensation. It is the response to external reality and the objects around a person. *Simultaneously* there is an "as if" image that represents an internal reality that is real in its own way. The "S" (somatic response) occurs because as a person sees an image, a somatic or neurophysiologic response is produced. Images create "M" (meaning) in different ways for each person. Some meaning may be superficial whereas other images create meaning that is incomplete or unclear. The behavior in some images may be seen as defensive and self-limiting. A person can have a fixed, frozen image of past events that disrupts thought processes from taking on new meaning to evoke more effective behaviors in the present experience . The opposite is also true in that a person can have very vivid images that provide profound insight about life processes.

A person has the ability to learn a new solution or develop a new sensory-rich eidetic to different memories in one's life. If taught to suspend negative images, a person then has a basis for a new experience. Using this approach, a client confronts memory-images that are having a negative consequence on health and well-being in order to associate more healthy, adaptive imagery with new meaning and a new somatic responses.

Psychosynthesis

Assagioli's psychosynthesis model has three parts: (1) the lower unconscious, (2) the middle unconscious, and (3) the superconscious. The lower unconscious represents our past in the form of forgotten memories and repressed events.[10] The middle unconscious is the day-to-day processing of logical and intuitive information and daily functioning. The superconscious is the region where we touch the higher possibilities for living, such as inspiration, intuition, philosophy, and contemplation. This level is where the greatest challenge for living resides.

Psychosynthesis training focuses on three elements.[11] The "P" represents the patterns of thought, feelings, or attitudes of a person. These may be conscious or unconscious. The "L" represents these patterns as they are manifested in a person's daily life through behaviors, values, beliefs, and how a person relates to people and events. The "I" reflects the imagery that continually occurs in life. When a person is in pain or is suffering with illness, something in life, "L," is out of balance. Often, such situations evoke negative imagery, "I." The client can be taught to bring about healing imagery to decrease worry, fear, and stress. The rich symbolism of knowledge of a person's unconscious realm can be brought into full awareness. The information that comes forward in this way is enormously powerful in providing insight into changing unwanted behavior.

GENERAL EXPLANATIONS

Bodymind Connections

Messages—feelings, attitudes, beliefs, emotions, purpose, and meaning—in the form of images have to be translated by the right hemisphere into nonverbal terminology before they can be understood by the involuntary or autonomic nervous system.[12] The images so intimately connected with physiology, health, and disease, are preverbal, or without a language base, except through physiologic connection with the left hemisphere. If connections between the right and left hemispheres were severed, untranslated images would continue to affect emotions and alter physiology, but without intellectual interpretation.

Imagery and Wellness

The goal of the imagery process is for a person to create an *end-result* image of reaching one's potential that directly evokes positive psychophysiologic responses. End-result imagery helps one achieve a state where both hemispheres are involved in the imagery experience.[13] One literally steps aside and participates in pure experience. One is suspended in the present moment. There is no "ego" or "observer." There is only the present reality of pure experience. Imagery elicits increased self-awareness that leads to self-discovery. With practice one is able to get to this space more frequently in order to increase high-level wellness.

Imagery with Disease/Illness

Much emphasis is placed on treating disease and not illness. *Disease* is the pathologic changes in organic form either observed or validated by laboratory tests. *Illness* is the personal experience of the problem or one's general state of being. The nurse using guided imagery can help clients positively change their perceptions about their disease, treatment, and healing ability and thus work to reverse stress, tension, and anxiety that can lead to a devastating spiral of hopelessness.[14,15]

When a client has a medical diagnosis or known illness, there is some degree of imagery of the body functioning in an abnormal manner. A person's imagery process also occurs with undiagnosed symptoms, and often a person creates in the imagination all types of problems that may not exist. This may be conscious or preverbal and is noticed in a person's body as a *felt sense/shift*. Refer to focusing in Chapter 15 for further details about this process.

Guided imagery implies that a guide leads a person in gaining access to the imagination. Nurses must learn imagery and self-regulation skills in order to be effective guides.

Since it is possible to have only one conscious thought processing at any one time, one can be taught to image healing of the condition or stabilization of the disease or disability or an emotional feeling such as fear or anxiety. Clients should also be taught to mentally rehearse their procedures, treatments, surgery or other events related to hospitalization with relaxation and successful outcomes. The imagery process can help one develop healthy ways to function with a known disease or how to decrease episodes of illness along with increasing self-esteem, independence, and new self-control for healthy living.

Imagery education with specific diseases is fascinating and necessary. Often the education about the disease begins the cure. The psychophysiological arousal that has lead to the person's stress is decreased and one then begins to understand that symptoms and behavior are connected, and that what one thinks affects the course of the process. Use of diagrams and pictures from books, drug advertisements, magazines, or anatomy coloring books are very helpful. The nurse can guide in revamping weak or erroneous imagery by moving people toward health outcomes and strengthening the body's own defense mechanisms and normal processes. For example, images should focus on weak, confused cancer cells and strong immune system instead of the opposite of cancer cells stronger than the immune system.

To individualize the imagery process for a particular client, the nurse must (1) have a fundamental knowledge of the physiology involved in the disease or disability; (2) know the interaction of all treatments such as medication, tests, and surgery, that affect the client's psychophysiologic state; and (3) have an understanding of the client's belief systems.[16]

Preparatory Sensory Information

The best nursing research into the imagery domain has been conducted over the past 15 years in the area of *preparatory sensory information*. Preparatory sensory information is both the client's subjective and objective experience of diagnosis, hospitalization, and health care events.[17] The work to date shows that clients who receive preparatory sensory instruction recover quicker and are able to use more effective coping strategies than those who do not. When the nurse conveys a clear picture of the experience and what sensations the client may anticipate from a particular procedure, more effective coping naturally follows.[18] Table 12-1 describes sensations evoked by selected procedures as documented in the literature.

When providing preparatory sensory information, do the following:

- Identify the sensory features of the procedure to be used.
- Obtain the client's specific perception of the procedure/treatment/test to be experienced.

Table 12-1 Sensations Documented in the Literature for Selected Procedures

Threatening Event	*Sensation*
Gastroendoscopic examination	Intravenous medication: needle stick, drowsiness As air is pumped into stomach: feeling of fullness as if after a large meal Physician's finger in mouth to guide tube insertion
Nasogastric tube insertion	Feeling passage of tube Tearing Gagging Discomfort in nose, throat, and mouth Limited mobility
Cast removal	Hearing buzz of saw Feeling of vibration or tingling Seeing chalky dust Feeling of warmth on arm or leg as saw cuts cast; will not hurt or burn Skin under padding will be scaly and look dirty Arm or leg may be a little stiff when first trying to move it Arm or leg may seem light because cast was heavy
Barium enema	Lying on hard table Feeling of fullness, pressure, and bloating Uncomfortable Feeling as if might have a bowel movement
Abdominal surgery	Preoperative medications: sleepy, lightheaded, relaxed, free from worry, not bothered by most things, dryness of mouth Incision: tenderness, sensitivity, pressure, smarting, burning, aching, sore Sensations might become sharp and seem to travel along incision when moving Arm with intravenous tube will seem awkward and restricted, but will feel no discomfort or pain Tiredness after physical effort Bloating of abdomen Cramping due to gas pains Pulling and pinching when stitches are removed

Source: Adapted from *Nursing Interventions: Treatments for Nursing Diagnoses* by G. Bulechek and J. McCloskey, p. 273, with permission of W.B. Saunders Company, © 1985.

- Choose words that will have meaning for the client.
- Use synonyms that have less emotional impact, such as "discomfort" instead of "pain."
- Select typical experiences when giving examples because atypical experiences are only confusing.

Interpreting Imagery

Each individual is the best interpreter of the experienced imagery process. Symbolic material that surfaces in the imagination is rich with personal meaning. Frequently we close ourselves to our rich imagination. Recording these images in a diary or journal for further exploration is encouraged because symbolic imagery is easily lost in conscious thought during a busy day (see Chapter 17).

When we learn to own our images and interpret their meaning, then our lives become more balanced.[19] Once we ask for answers from within and allow the answers merely to appear through our images, we let go of judging and of old thought patterns. Trust that the answers will come in many forms, such as abstract ideas and symbols. Receive imagery information without criticism as appropriate for you as its appears.

Empowering the Spoken Word*

For more effective delivery of the spoken word in different imagery scripts, consider the following techniques.[20] The reader can refer to this section when reading case studies no. 2 and 3, because examples of these techniques are given in the case study scripts. When used correctly these techniques satisfy both brain hemispheres:

- truism
- embedded commands
- linkage
- reframing
- metaphor
- therapeutic double-bind
- synesthesia
- interspersal technique.

A **truism** is a statement that the client *believes* or *accepts* to be *true*. It may precede a suggestion and be connected to another truism. When this occurs the analytical left hemisphere is satisfied that a fact is logical. It does not analyze or negate, and it leaves the right hemisphere free to accept the suggestion.

Consider this example for use with a person learning relaxation and imagery for hypertension:

> As you take your next breath in, become aware of the fact that you are breathing air into your lungs (truism) and the oxygen from that breath moves from your lungs into your blood stream (truism), ... you can let yourself imagine that your blood vessels are very relaxed at this time as you continue into this deep state of relaxation.

The suggestion "to let yourself imagine" is preceded by two truisms: (1) that you are breathing air into your lungs and (2) that the breath moves from your lungs into your bloodstream. The truisms are followed by suggestions of hoped-for physiologic changes

---

*Source: Adapted from *Pregnancy As Healing: A Holistic Philosophy for Prenatal Care* by G. Peterson and L. Mehl, pp. 214–222, with permission of Mindbody Communications, © 1984.

of relaxed blood vessels while the person is in a deep state of relaxation. The left hemisphere is occupied with the truism and leaves the right hemisphere free to go with the suggestions of deep relaxation and to feel what is present when the blood vessels relax.

Embedded commands are separate messages for the right hemisphere. They are usually in *short phrases* that *stand out* because of pauses. The guide also uses a *change in intonation,* such as pitch, volume, speed, and textural quality of the voice, and a change in normal grammatical structure. This confuses the left hemisphere and causes the embedded command to stand out. When a person's name is also used, the right hemisphere may comprehend the short message much easier.

An example would be: "You don't have to . . . Susan, cry, . . . if you don't want to." When using (1) changes in the quality of the voice, (2) pauses, and (3) calling the person by name, the right hemisphere will hear the suggestion, "Susan, cry," in one or all three of the ways listed.

Linkages are *conditional statements* that *connect behaviors* or *actions* with a *suggestion*. Linkages are best used with a truism as a distraction to satisfy the left hemisphere.

A linkage could be used with a client lying flat on a stretcher who is about to undergo a procedure. The nurse would say, "Let yourself relax into the surface under your body. As you are moving down the hall, you will see overhead lights on the ceiling. Each time you pass under a light, let it remind you to take a deep breath and relax more deeply."

Reframing is a technique to help a person contact the part of a behavior that is keeping him or her stuck or that is preventing a certain behavior from occurring. Reframing suspends a person from the old or current belief systems. It *allows* the opportunity to *reassociate* and *reorganize* a *problem* or *experience* in a manner that *resolves* it toward a healthier state.

A **metaphor** is a figure of speech containing an implied comparison, in which a word or phrase ordinarily and primarily used for one thing is applied to another. Metaphor is used in imagery scripts for healing and teaching purposes. Metaphor works because the right brain can *deepen* the *experience* to the *spoken word*. For example, "Imagine the relaxation flowing down through your body *like* a gentle warm waterfall." Such words as warming, cooling, releasing, and sinking can be expanded upon to enhance right-brain activity.

The **therapeutic double-bind** is effective because the left hemisphere is occupied and involved in making several different choices that lead to participation in the given suggestion. For example, "As you are stretched out in the chair, you might find that you could change your position even more to go deeper into relaxation, and get more comfortable until you find just the right position."

Synesthesia is the technique of *cross-sensing* several of the senses simultaneously so that the client becomes more aware of the different sense modalities that are present. For example, "Can you *hear* the *color* of the wind," or " Can you *see* the *sounds around you?*"

Interspersal is a technique of making specific *words* or *phrases* within a script *stand out* as a separate suggestion. This is accomplished by changing the volume or tone of the voice more dramatically than with embedded commands. An example might be, "Allow yourself to . . . relax into the pain with the next breath . . . feel . . . as you . . . breathe into that pain now.'' The words that you would change with tonal inflection would be ''relax into the pain'' and ''feel, breathe into that pain now.''

NURSING PROCESS

Assessment

In preparing to use imagery as nursing interventions with clients, assess the following parameters:

- if clients have organic brain syndrome or are psychotic or prepsychotic; if so, general relaxation techniques instead of imagery techniques should be used
- the client's anxiety/tension levels before starting to determine which types of relaxation inductions will be most effective
- any homework assignments or tasks that were to be completed before the session if the client is returning for a session
- with the client what is to be gained from the experience, why help has been sought, and what he or she wishes to change
- which imagery to be used in scripts relates to the wants, needs, desires, or recurrent/dominant themes in the client's life; the nurse decides on script content following this assessment, or clients who know the process may say what they want in imagery scripts
- if the client understands that it is not necessary to hear, see, feel, touch, and taste literally when working with guided imagery; one merely has to experience what the image *might* be like to become involved in the process
- the client's primary sensory modalities
- if the client understands that imagery is basically a way in which we talk to ourselves and to make *friends* with our body systems. Imagery is a safe, normal phenomenon. What differs from one person to the next is the content. During the guiding phase, instruct that any time that the client wishes to stop or change an image he or she should modify or replace it with another image regardless of what the guide says.
- if a client has experience with the imagery process. If the client is a beginner, it is best to start with basic images. Begin slowly, remembering to build on a solid foundation. Be creative with cues to help the client release and tap into internal information that is not accessible in ordinary states of consciousness.
- if the client can work with eyes closed. This will help establish states of internal awareness and achieve profound imagery faster. If clients are reluctant or resistant to close their eyes, have them gaze at a fixed point about 3 or 4 feet in front of them. Their peripheral vision will blur and the eyelids usually will get heavy. They then have no trouble closing their eyes, and they begin to trust their relaxation process because they are experiencing a natural phenomenon.

- knowledge and presence of relaxation skills. If the client is not skilled in relaxation, explain what the normal sensations will be. Allow time for the person to shift to the "letting go" state. Once clients learn physiologic control with the phrases used in relaxation induction, they usually let go of the specific words to gain the relaxed state. This occurs because the left hemisphere has been satisfied in the learning process, and the client can trust the right hemisphere to dominate with symbolic ideas.
- if the client repeatedly falls asleep in the session. Is a sleep debt present? Has the client shifted to a deeply relaxed state and as yet has not learned how to stay awake with the process? Imagery is like any other skill. Practice is required to learn how to stay awake in deep states of relaxation and imagery.

Nursing Diagnoses

Nursing diagnoses compatible with imagery interventions described in this chapter and that are related to the nine human response patterns of Unitary Person are as follows:

- Exchanging: (Imagery can be used with all diagnoses in this category)
- Relating: Social isolation
- Choosing: Potential for ineffective coping
- Moving: Sleep pattern disturbance
- Perceiving: Alteration in self-concept
  Disturbance in body image
  Disturbance in self-image
  Potential hopelessness
  Potential powerlessness
- Feeling: Alteration in comfort
  Anxiety
  Fear
  Acute situational crisis

Client Outcomes

Table 12-2 guides the nurse in client outcomes, outcome criteria, and evaluation for the use of imagery as a nursing intervention.

Plan and Interventions

Before the Session

- Serve as a guide. Being a guide implies that one is present to help/assist another in a new experience. There is absolutely no way to predict what will surface in one's imagination, for every experience is different, even when the same script is used.

Table 12-2 Nursing Interventions: Imagery

Client Outcome	*Outcome Criteria*	*Evaluation*
The client will demonstrate skills in imagery.	1. The client will participate in imagery to learn basic skills.	1. The client practiced imagery and reported learning basic skills.
	2. Following the imagery experience the client will: a. Exhibit decreased anxiety and fear b. Demonstrate increased effective individual coping c. Demonstrate increased personal power over daily events d. Image strengths that move toward an effective life style e. Change image of self-defeating life style habits f. Recognize images that are created by self-talk g. Create end-result images of desired health, habits, feelings, wants, and needs in daily living	2. The client: a. Reported a decrease in anxiety and fear b. Demonstrated increased effective individual coping with life events c. Demonstrated increased personal power over daily events d. Imaged strengths that moved toward an effective lifestyle e. Changed image of self-defeating lifestyle behavior f. Recognized images that were created by self-talk g. Created end-result images of desired habits, feelings, wants, and needs for daily living.
	3. The client will participate in drawing of symptoms and free drawing as appropriate.	3. The client participated in drawing of symptoms and free drawing as appropriate.
	4. The client will: a. Demonstrate understanding of drawing as a form of communication with self and symptoms b. Choose colors that have personal meaning c. Express imagery drawing that has special meaning d. Allow drawing to be done in a nonjudgmental manner	4. The client: a. Demonstrated understanding of drawing as a form of communicating with self and symptoms b. Chose colors that had personal meaning c. Expressed images that had special meaning d. Allowed drawing to be done in a nonjudgmental manner.

- Become calm and centered. Let your bodymind release tension and tightness. Relax your vocal cords and prepare to guide the client with relaxation and imagery scripts.
- Focus on baseline feelings/emotions of the client obtained during the assessment.
- Prepare the room to ensure quietness and the client's comfort.
- Have the client tend to basic comfort needs such as urinating before the session begins because it is impossible to be relaxed with a full bladder.

- If possible, place a sign on the door stating that the session is in progress to avoid interruptions.
- Have the client lie down or sit, depending on client preference and clinical situation.
- If you are a novice with imagery and guiding, learn a few basic relaxation and imagery scripts and use them repeatedly while gaining experience and confidence with the intervention.
- Memorize several scripts. Once you trust and understand the value of the process, many different scripts can be used. For scripts not frequently used, keep a notebook or reference books that can be referred to while guiding clients. Once you gain confidence, you will be able to glance simultaneously at key script phrases, reassess, and guide. Refer to scripts under specific interventions.
- Learn a variety of scripts that pertain to common problems in your clinical practice, such as preoperative anxiety, successful recovery from surgery, postoperative coughing, effective wound healing, fear, anxiety, pain, and relationship problems. Refer to case studies 2 and 3 for examples of integrating these concepts.
- Have a selection of music tapes available from which the client can choose. Refer to Chapter 13 for music selections.
- Have a light blanket available if the client should feel cool.
- Have blank paper, crayons, and colored markers available if the client wishes to draw before or after the session.

Beginning the Session

- Give client a general definition of imagery: ''Imagery is a fast way to connect body-mind-spirit by quieting the busy mind and body in order to focus on particular events.''
- Establish with the client that the process is fascinating and a delightful way to make friends with our wise self and that this process is a key to our creative process.
- Give the following specific statements about the imagery process:
- Use positive imagery. Positive imagery that is directed toward a successful outcome is most helpful because it reinforces what you want to happen.
- Develop a positive expectation of what you want to occur.
- Choose imagery that has special meaning for you.
- Be aware that your imagery represents the expectation of an outcome.
- Reinforcing good imagery provides a focus and organizes energy to facilitate healing.
- Be aware of the present moment for the best imagery process to occur.
- Let spontaneous images emerge from the inner self without analyzing them. If you find that you begin to analyze the images, imagine that the images are just floating on and do not begin a logical process of working the images through to resolving conflicts, establishing goals, etc. These steps will come in the images, but not in a logical manner.

- Understand that, following guided relaxation and imagery scripts, different images will appear. If images appear that are uncomfortable and that you are not ready to deal with, the inner self (ego) will block this creative process and you may simply go with the next image process that appears.
- Changing imagery begins to change your expectatations.
- Let yourself begin to become deeply relaxed. **Let your eyes close to be fully awake.** Allow the images to emerge from this relaxed state. (Begin to guide the client in a general relaxation exercise).

During the Session

- With your guidance, let clients create their own images.
- Reassess states of relaxation throughout the session. Notice decreased tension in the face, chest, torso, and legs. The changes can be subtle or dramatic. Respirations become deeper with more space between the breaths. Eyelids may flicker, and the lips and face may change to a more pale color.
- Assess if the client is following the imagery process. An instruction can be given to the client, such as ''If you are following the imagery, raise a finger to indicate yes.'' This same process can be used to ask the client if the imagery is satisfactory, if the pace needs to be slower, or if he or she would like to get more comfortable, etc.
- Reassess if the client is following the guided imagery. Clients who are used to working with inner imagery states can usually clear their minds of distracting thoughts more easily. If the client cannot clear the mind, increase the length of the relaxation induction. Suggest to the client that, if the mind is wandering too much, focus once again on the image or on the breathing pattern.
- Determine the length of the session based on the client, the client's body responses, and session goals. The sessions can last from 10-15 minutes to 1 hour or longer.
- Listen to your personal intuition while guiding. What do you know moment by moment? *Trust your intuition* (see Chapters 6 and 17), which allows you to pick up on subtle cues from the client that something special is present in the imagery process. These clues are a shift in respirations, body language, and facial expressions showing pleasant feelings or sadness or tears.
- Watch the clues to the client's experience of shifts in emotions during the imagery process. This experience is the process of gaining access to inner wisdom. These clues help you know which techniques to use to empower the spoken word. These techniques help the client stay with the imagery process, and strengthen the imagery experience whereby the person shifts to profound levels of inner wisdom.
- It is not necessary to know the client's imagery during the session. Imagery interpretation and discussion follow the session.

Closing the Session

- Bring the client to an alert state gradually by allowing time for silence before discussion. Observe and take cues from the client as to when to begin talking. The moments following a session can be a time for deep personal insight; this opportunity may be lost if talking begins too soon. Both the client and guide need to be immersed in the healing of silence even for only 20-30 seconds.

- Have the client finish the session with drawing or recording thoughts if appropriate.
- Discuss imagery with client and let the client interpret the imagery. The nurse can facilitate the interpretation. Weave imagery questions into conversational interaction by asking open-ended questions that guide the client in further contemplation.

Specific Interventions: Imagery

Guidelines for Scripts

The following guidelines will help the nurse be successful in using these scripts as nursing interventions.

- Do not talk to the client during the process unless the client has a question that must be answered at the time. During the imagery process, the client is guided in releasing images and feelings from the imagery realm. Talking as a logical process, disrupts the free flow of images.
- Precede these scripts with a *general relaxation script*. Close the session with a general relaxation script (see Chapter 11).
- To lengthen the scripts, pick up cues from the client's behavior, and insert key words, such as good, relax even more.
- Repeat key words that increase the client's relaxation response.
- Speak slowly and pace the script as you watch the client's breathing patterns and other body responses.
- Use phrases to enhance the power of the spoken word as previously discussed.
- As you guide the client, relax, which increases your being very present in the moment with the client.
- Provide lots of encouragement. These positive statements are heard by the client and can guide him or her in positive self-talk following the session.
- Each time there are a series of statements, such as, ". . . this means to pause . . ." increase the length of the pauses or add more depending on the observed cues that you pick up from the client.

Guided Imagery Scripts (Basic)

1. Special/Safe Place

Purpose: To identify a place that is a special and safe retreat.

Time: 10-20 minutes

Script: ''Let your imagination choose a place that is safe and comfortable . . . a place where you can retreat at any time. This is a healthy technique for you to learn . . . this place will help you survive your daily stressors.'' (If the client is in the hospital include, 'This safe and special place is very important, particularly while you are in the hospital . . . any time that there are interruptions, just let yourself go to this place in your mind.').

Some suggestions for guiding the client in choosing a special place are:

- ''Form a clear image of a pleasant outdoor scene, using all of your senses. Smell . . . smell the fragrance of flowers or the breeze. Feel . . . feel the texture of the surface under your feet. Hear . . . hear all the sounds in nature, birds singing, wind blowing. See . . . see all the different sights around as you let yourself turn in a slow circle to get a full view of this special place.'' (Include taste if appropriate).
- ''Let a beam of light, such as the rays of the sun, shine on you for comfort and healing. Allow yourself to experience the warmth and relaxation.''
- ''Form an image of a meadow. Imagine that you are in the meadow. . . . The meadow is full of beautiful grass and flowers. In the meadow, see yourself sitting by a stream . . . watching the water . . . flowing by . . . slowly and gently.''
- ''Imagine a mountain scene. See yourself walking on a path toward the mountain. You hear the sound of your shoes on the path . . . smell the pine trees and feel the cool breeze as you approach your campsite. You have now reached the foothills of the mountain. You are now higher up the mountain . . . resting in your campsite. Look around at the beauty of this place.''
- ''Imagine yourself in a bamboo forest. . . . You are walking in a large bamboo forest. The bamboo is very tall. . . . You lean against a strong cluster of bamboo . . . hear the swaying . . . and hear the rustling of the bamboo leaves, gently moving in the wind.''
- ''Look into the sky of your mind . . . see the fluffy clouds. A cloud gently comes your way. . . . and the cloud surrounds your body. You climb up on the cloud and lie down. Feel yourself begin to float off gently in a gentle breeze.''

Addendum: The nurse should feel free to invent and create new scripts based both on the special information gathered before the session as well and the insight that comes from intuition during the session.

2. Red Ball of Pain

Purpose: Psychophysiologic pain control.

Time: 10-20 minutes.

Script: Scan your body . . . gather any pains, aches, or other symptoms up into a ball. Begin to change its size . . . allow it to get bigger . . . just imagine how big you can make it. Now make it smaller . . . See how small you can make it. . . . Is it possible to make it the size of a grain of sand? (Change the size several times in both directions). Now allow it to move slowly out of your body, moving further away each time you exhale. . . . Notice the experience with each exhale . . . as the pain moves away.''

Addendum: Watching the person's body cues will direct you in how many times to go in each of the opposite directions.

3. Pain Assessment

Purpose: Psychophysiologic pain control.

Time: 2-5 minutes (if not preceded by relaxation induction); 15-20 minutes (if relaxation induction is included).

Script: ''Close your eyes and let yourself relax. Begin to describe the pain in silence to yourself. Be present with the pain. . . . Know that the pain may be either physical sensations . . . or worries and fears. Let your pain take on a shape . . . any shape that comes to your mind. Become aware of the dimensions of the pain. . . . What is the height of your pain . . . the width of the pain . . . and the depth of the pain. Where in the body is it located. . . . Give it color . . . a shape . . . feel the texture. Does it make any sound?

And now with your eyes still closed . . . let your hands come together with palms turned upward as if forming a cup. Put your pain object in your hands. (Once again ask the above questions about the pain, preceding each question with this phrase, 'How would you change the size, etc.?')

And now, let yourself decide what you would like to do with the pain. There is no right way to finish the experience . . . just accept what feels right to you. You can throw the pain away . . . or place it back where you found it . . . or move it somewhere else. Let yourself become aware . . . of how pain can be changed. . . . By focusing with intention the pain changes."

Addendum: It is not unusual for the pain to go completely away or at least lessen. The client also becomes aware of how the pain can be manipulated and not be the controlling factor of his or her life. The exercise is also effective with severe pain. Give pain medication and have the person relax while the pain medicine is working during the imagery process.

4. White Light of Healing Energy

Purpose: Focusing energy awareness within the body toward health and balance.

Time: 10-20 minutes

Script: "Begin to imagine that there is a sphere of white light of healing energy about 4 inches above your head. The white light is now touching the top of your head. Begin to feel this light as it flows from the top of your head and allow it to flow down through the entire inside of the body.

The healing light has filled the inside of your head . . . and it now flows down your shoulders, back, down your arms, and into your fingertips. The white light is now flowing into your chest . . . around your sides . . . into your middle and lower back . . . below your waist . . . around your sides flowing into your abdomen . . . into your buttocks . . . and into your pelvis. The light now flows down your thighs . . . to your lower legs . . . and to your feet.

The white light has completely filled the inside of your body. There is now a wonderful abundance of this healing light . . . and it begins to bubble up and flow back out through the top of your head . . . down the outside of your body . . . coating the entire outside of your body. The more you allow it to flow throughout your body . . . the more abundant it is."

Addendum: Tell the client that the color of the light can be any color that he or she wishes. Check out with the client the color preference. This can be done by having the client tell you, or if the wish is to use white, ask the client to raise a finger.

Send the healing white light to specific areas that need extra attention, such as places of discomfort or disease. Give specific details to the client about the major problem areas. Refer to case studies 2 and 3 for information about physiology, treatments, procedures, and medication that can be used along with this and all other scripts.

5. Protective Shield/Space

Purpose: To create an imaginary personal space where the client is protected from outside influences. This exercise is particularly helpful when the client is hospitalized.

Time: 10-20 minutes

Script: "In your imagination let yourself begin to create a protective shield/space or protective bubble around yourself. This will serve as a filter to accept what you want to receive and protect you from those things that you wish to keep out. The shield is invisible, and only you know where it is around your body and how close it is to you.

Let yourself begin to move this shield. Experience it now as you move the shield close to your body. . . . Now let yourself move it out away from the skin. Imagine that you wish to protect yourself from an event or person. In whatever way that feels right for you, become aware of your protective shield. Place your shield where you wish now . . . close to your skin or further out from your body. This is your special way of receiving what you wish for yourself and a way of staying relaxed and calm."

6. Worry and Fear

Purpose: To help the client change the internal experience of worry/fear by creating helpful images that change that experience. Have client set aside 10-20 minutes a day to worry, preferable in the morning. Doing so satisfies the subconscious that it has worried, and one then has greater success at stopping habitual worry during the rest of the day.

Time: 10-15 minutes.

Script: "In your relaxed state, let a picture of your worries and fears flow forward in a moving stream. Let them come one by one . . . just watching as one replaces the other. As you do this for a short period of time, feel the experience that occurs with each of those worries and fears. Notice how just having a worry or fear changes your state right now.

Stop the images. Focus on your breathing . . . in . . . and out. . . . Allow yourself to have three complete cycles of breathing before continuing. In your relaxed state, become aware of these feelings of relaxed bodymind.

This time, take your relaxed state with you into your imagination. Let one worry come to your mind right now. See and feel it . . . see yourself in that situation relaxed and at ease.

Right now, just say to yourself, 'I can stop this worry.' Imagine yourself functioning without that worry or fear. See yourself waving goodbye to that worry and fear.

See yourself completely free of that worry and fear. Look at the decisions that you can make for your life that will lead you in new directions. Feel your energy as you breathe in. As you exhale, let go of all of the worry, fear, tension, and tightness.

Experience your comfortable bodymind. Know that you can work with many of your worries and fears that surface daily. Whenever they come, let the dominant worry surface . . . then feel what it is like as you gradually give up portions of the worry . . . till it is completely gone.

If that seems impossible right now, decide which part of that worry and fear that you need to keep and which part you can let go. And now, see yourself waving goodbye to the part that you can let go.

Now, feel what it is like in your mind with part of that worry or fear gone. Experience that and feel the changes within the body.

Assess the part of the worry or fear that remains. Again, allow a portion of that worry or fear to move away. See yourself waving goodbye. Feel the change inside as more is released.

Let yourself now be in a place where the worry and fear are diminished. Assess what part remains and see if you can now begin to give up the rest that remains. Pay attention to the experiences inside your body as you do this.''

Addendum: The basic script can be individualized by putting into words what the client revealed before the session. This script has many variations, i.e., write your worries/fears on a seashell; the shell is picked up by a seagull and carried away and dropped in the sea; feel the release as the worries/fears are dropped. Another version would be while running along a road, you drop your worries/fears by the road; the wind picks them up and blows them away.

7. Inner Guide

Purpose: A means of creating purposeful self-dialogue that gains access to inner wisdom and personal truth that resides in each person.

Time: 10-20 minutes. This exercise could be used as a basic technique of gaining awareness of inner wisdom. It is best to introduce this exercise after a client has done several imagery sessions.

Script: ''As you begin to feel even more relaxed now . . . going to a greater depth of inner being . . . more relaxed . . . more secure and safe . . . let yourself become aware of the presence of not being alone. With you right now is a guide . . . who is wise and concerned with your well-being. Let yourself begin to see this wise being with whom you can share your fears and excitement. You have a trust in this wise guide.

If you do not see anyone, let yourself be aware of hearing or feeling this wise being, noticing the presence of care and concern.

In whichever way seems best for you . . . proceed to make contact with this wise inner guide. Let yourself establish contact with your guide now . . . in any way that you wish. In what form does your guide appear to you . . . a person, an animal, or inner presence?

Notice the love and wisdom with which you are surrounded. This wisdom and love are present for you now. . . . Let yourself ask for advice . . . about anything that is important for you just now. Be receptive to what emerges . . . let yourself receive it. This inner guide may have a special messsage to share with you. . . . Listen with openness and pure intention to receive.

Allow yourself to look at any issue in your life. It may be a symptom, a choice, or decision. . . . Tell your wise guide anything that you wish. . . . Listen to the answers that emerge.

Imagine yourself acting on the answers and directions that you received. . . . Imagine yourself calling upon the wisdom and love of this wise guide to help you in the days to come.

Now in whatever way is best for you . . . bring closure to the visit with this inner guide. You can come back here any time that you wish. All you have to do is take the time.''

Addendum: This script is primarily visual. If a person is more of a auditory or kinesthetic learner, suggest that he or she ''hears'' or ''feels'' the inner guide. Seeking an inner guide can be done over many sessions. Let the client know that many different guides (can also be referred to as advisors or spirits) will surface over time. There are many versions to this script, so add, invent and explore. Much detail can be added to this imagery script to lengthen the session. When given extended time, a wealth of insight can emerge for the client. Pause frequently, and let a few seconds to a full minute pass in silence during the guiding. Listen to your own intuition as when to allow for more silence.

Eye Positions and Anchoring (Basic to Advanced)

Imagery interventions can be further enhanced with two techniques from neurolinguistic programming (NLP), a discipline that increases the understanding of communication and human behavior. The two techniques are eye positions and anchoring.[21]

When people are communicating, their *eye positions* indicate the dominant sense being accessed:

- eyes looking up or defocusing ahead: visual mode
- eyes moving from side to side: hearing mode; may be remembering the sounds or words
- eyes downward to dominant hand: feelings are intensified
- eyes downward to nondominant hand: self-talk taking place

Another process that occurs with communication is that of *anchoring* which is our basis for learning. Think of what occurs when you imagine touching a hot stove. The word "ouch," plus a sympathethic pain response is elicited. This pairing of associative events with the senses is an example of anchoring; this process occurs many times during the day. An anchor is a feeling, object, thought, or remembered scene that triggers the next associated thought. We can learn new anchors to elicit more helpful behavior patterns.

Anchors can involve all of the senses, and we normally choose our dominant mode for gaining information. Anchors can be used to enhance positive feelings that will then replace negative feelings:

- Touch is the easiest mode to gain access to an anchor. It is also inconspicuous. Examples of touching are (1) press the thumb and index finger together, (2) thumb touches a specific knuckle, or (3) hand touches chin.
- To evoke a complete feeling of a special memory, it is important to put pressure on a very specific spot. Whatever feeling you choose to evoke, make sure it is an uncontaminated feeling that is not mixed with a negative event. For example, a very special holiday that was magic for the first 5 days, but then was spoiled by credit cards and money being stolen, would evoke a contaminated feeling.
- To anchor right now, remember a feeling that you want to associate with frequently. Decide how you will touch yourself, and do so, holding that chosen anchor for a few moments while your brain locks in a associative pleasurable memory with the associated kinesthetic pressure.
- To decrease the stress of risk taking and new situations, practice pressing positive anchors that include reassurance, self-confidence, assertiveness, and relaxation.

In order for a positive anchor to integrate and eliminate a negative anchor, (1) the positive feeling must be fully experienced by as many senses as possible and not be contaminated by any negative feelings; (2) the intensity of the positive anchor must be much greater than the negative anchor; and (3) the negative anchor needs to be only mildly accessed to integrate anchors—that is, to change a negative to a positive feeling—choose places on your body that you can touch easily at the same time.

- Gain access to your positive feeling and press your positive anchor.
- Stay in the experience of the positive anchor continuing to hold that anchor; press the negative anchor position being aware of the negative feeling, but stay with the positive feeling.
- Continue to hold the positive anchor, releasing the negative anchor and fully re-experiencing the positive anchor with all the details of as many senses as you can. To determine the degree that the negative anchor is integrated into the positive anchor, press only the negative anchor. If the positive feeling comes, you have been successful. If the negative feeling is still present, repeat the steps.
- If the negative anchor is not transformed, add more positive detail to the positive anchor until you can associate with the positive experience when you touch only the negative anchor.
- Once you have transformed the negative anchor, now *future-pace*. Imagine you are in a situation where you want to reach the positive feelings without the negative emotions that you had feared. If the future-pacing is not completely successful, practice the same repetition pressing the positive anchor that is yours forever.

Drawing: General Guidelines (Basic to Advanced)

In the imagery process paper and crayons are important tools that can be used on an individual basis or in groups. Drawing externalizes previously internal mental images and emotions. The emphasis in this intervention is *not* on how well someone can draw, but on one's ability to use drawing to get in touch with feelings and healing potential. Drawing is another way to open up communication with the self and others.

When clients are overwhelmed with emotions, drawing the feelings in the form of images can be therapeutic. Then the client can have a dialogue with the elements expressed. Within the intensity of the emotionally charged event resides many answers that can move us toward healing. Drawing is helpful with children who are not verbally sophisticated. Tremendous insight can be gained in this process with children who are going through painful procedures, as well as experiencing certain concerns, fears, or problems in daily life.[22] This intervention becomes advanced when in-depth psychological explanations of the drawing are explored.

When using drawing as an intervention the nurse can suggest the following general ideas:

- Allow yourself to express yourself with paper and crayons. There is no one best way to draw. Drawings can be realistic or symbolic. The most important thing is that you express yourself in a nonlogical way. This can bring insight into your life.
- Do not judge your drawing. Allow your body, mind, and spirit to connect as you begin to simply be with the paper and crayons in the present moment.

- Notice the energy flow from you. Let your body energy resonate with your imagery/spirit energy. If one gets ahead of the other, just notice and let the energies slowly begin to resonate together. Do not try to control it. This cannot be stated clearer than this, because this inner quality comes from the experience of being immersed in the imagery and drawing process.
- The drawing process often breaks down the resistance that we have around a certain life event. Giving ourself the space and time to explore within allows the emergence of insights toward new outcomes.
- On the blank piece of paper, allow an image to begin to form that represents your feelings and thoughts in this moment. Choose colors that speak to you. If you start working with a color and you wish to change, feel free to do so.
- After you have drawn, you might want to write out the details of your images because more of your experience you heard or felt during the imagery drawing may surface into conscious awareness that can provide much insight. This is very important, because some people may be expressive with another sense as previously discussed.
- During the drawing period, there is always constant inner talk. You might like to write a poem, key phrases, or journal entry during or following a session (see Chapter 17).

Frequently, after the client has been guided through an imagery exercise or is listening to an imagery tape or music alone, drawing can bring tremendous insight, creativity, and an "Ah-HA!" experience that cannot be achieved when he or she shifts to a logical mode and starts to explain in words the felt experience. Drawing also works very well when the client is crying and is unable to talk easily, but wants to express what is being experienced.

1. Symptom/Disease Drawing (Basic)

The reader is referred to the excellent Image-Ca tool developed by Achterberg and Lawlis that gives a numerical rating to the client's drawing and dialogue to predict the course of the disease.[23] To attain the best end-result imagery, the guide should identify the following elements:

- *Disease or disability:* the vividness of the client's views of the disease, illness, or disability and, if the process is ongoing, its strength or ability to overcome health or focus on the reverse—the ability of the client to stop the process.
- *Treatment:* the vividness of the treatment description and the effectiveness of some positive mechanism of action.
- *Healing ability:* the vividness of how the client perceives the healing ability and effectiveness of this ability/action to combat the disease.

Symptoms or disease can keep a person from attaining a quality life or moving toward accomplishment of life goals. Drawing is a very helpful intervention with people who are at high risk for burnout. The drawings of people at high risk for burnout often exhibit symptoms throughout the body, split of self, disconnection from feelings, and very small images without detail that represent the self. Lack of color or empty space on the paper usually is indicative of high stress. Members of low-burnout groups frequently draw different stressors at work or with colleagues, but their drawings usually show some evidence of solutions to the current stressors. Using drawing often helps one establish the problem, the solutions, and effective versus ineffective coping. This work has been validated by using psychological inventories along with drawing.[24]

When working with a client's specific disease/symptoms, encourage the client to become more aware of the normal body process; the disease/symptoms and its medication, treatments and procedures; and his or her belief systems. Then encourage the client to draw the disease/symptoms in the way that has self-meaning. That drawing often reveals how a client may sabotage recovery, has a constricted view of possibilities, or has a misunderstanding of the disease/symptoms.

Helping the client understand the disease and his or her ability to participate in the healing process is part of the nursing process, as well the recovery process. The client learns that disease does not have to control his or her life. He or she learns how to join the disease process and let go of the inner struggle and resistance in order to move to positive outcome. Case studies 1, 2, and 3 integrate these concepts.

The challenge for nurses is to develop innovative teaching worksheets, booklets, and verbal descriptions of bodymind healing. Two examples of bodymind healing education have been used with burns and bone healing as seen in case studies 2 and 3.[25,26]

2. Family and Group Drawing (Basic to Advanced)

Drawing can play an important role in family therapy sessions.[27] The intervention becomes advanced when the nurse facilitates in-depth interpretation of drawings and uses family therapy interventions. A helpful process is to have the family members at the same time but on separate sheets of paper, draw what their main concern or problem is, what they see as a solution, and how they see the steps from problem to solution. Each family member may draw a variation of the same problem or perhaps identify something that has never been shared with the other members. The dynamics of the family unit come out in ways that words may not express, and insight is provided on how individual members view the same problem. During the interpretation of the drawings, family members can be asked to list positive and negative events in the family and then to discuss the importance of the events listed. The light and shadow of each situation is usually revealing to the individual as well as the family.

With groups, a nurse can use 4-foot long paper on a large roll and stretch it out on the floor or a table. There are many variations to this exercise. One technique is to ask all people to draw simultaneously (in a realistic or symbolic way) all the things that they are thankful for or excited about in living. Then each person takes a turn and shares with the group what his or her drawing represents. When everyone has had a turn, the first person who started the sharing, draws a line to an object or several objects drawn by one or more persons that has personal meaning and places a circle around one or more objects. By the time everyone has had a chance to share, the paper and symbols are connected by many lines, showing the group members' interconnectedness. This exercise establishes that other people can remind us of many important perceptions and events in our own lives. When people share their joy or sadness, it often evokes deep feelings in others of forgotten memories or current life events. This exercise is very effective in rehabilitation groups, such as cardiac, cancer, and diabetic classes. The focus can shift to drawing or listing worries, fears, or problems as related to health problems.

Another way to approach group work is to ask everyone to contribute to a mural on clear plexiglass. Let half of the group be on one side and the other half on the opposite side. Another exercise is to let half the group lie down on a large piece of paper. Let a partner trace the other person's body outline curled up or stretched out depending on the emotions being expressed.

Symbolism, Colors, and Associations (Basic to Advanced)

Another process that allows a deep inner understanding of the human condition is the drawing of mandalas that is discussed below. People should be encouraged to experiment with free drawings which elicit a multitude of images. Exhibits 12-1, 12-2, and 12-3 give general explanations to common symbols, colors, associations and feelings that people either draw or choose to focus on in their imagery process from paintings of other artists or recognized universal symbols.

Mandalas (Basic to Advanced)

The purpose of drawing mandalas is to actively listen to inner widsom and to experience enhanced free associations and symbolism as described in Exhibits 12-1, 12-2, and 12-3. It is a creative experience that facilitates self-reflection. This drawing experience allows an enormous capacity of inner wisdom and resources to be revealed into conscious awareness. Process and patterns of living are seen in a new way by the client. Mandalas are best drawn while listening to music. It can take from 10 minutes to one hour and can be successfully used in individual or group sessions.

General Mandala Information: A client is first introduced to the general information and process of drawing a mandala.

Exhibit 12-1 Shapes: Symbolism and Associations

Circle	Heaven, ether, intellect, thought, sun, the number ten, unity, perfection, eternity, oneness, the masculine-active principle, celestial realm, hearing, sound
Triangle	Communication, between heaven and earth, fire, the number three, trinity, aspiration, movement upward, return to origins, gas, sight, light
Square	Pluralism, earth, feminine-receptive principle, firmness, stability, construction, material, solidity, the number four
Rectangle	Most rational, most secure, used in grounding objects such as houses and desks
Spiral	Evolution of the universe, orbit, growth, deepening, cosmic motion, relationship between unity and multiplicity, macroscom, breath, spirit, water

Source: From *Seeing with the Mind's Eye* by Mike Samuels and Nancy Samuels. Copyright © 1975 by Mike Samuels and Nancy Samuels. Reprinted by permission of Random House, Inc.

Exhibit 12-2 Color Symbolism, Association, and Effects

Red	Sunrise, birth, blood, fire, emotion, wounds, death, passion, sentiment, mother, the planet Mars, the Note "C," anger, chakra #1, excitement, heat, physical stimulation and strengthening the blood, iron, alcohol, oxygen, treatment of paralysis and exhaustion
Orange	Fire, pride, ambition, egoism, the planet Venus, the Note "D," chakra #2, stimulation of the nervous system, treatment as emetic and laxative
Yellow	Sun, light, intuition, illumination, air, intellect, royalty, the planet Mercury, the note "E," luminosity
Green	Earth, fertility, sensation, vegetation, death, water, nature, sympathy, adaptability, growth, the planets Jupiter and Venus, the note "G"
Blue	Clear sky, thinking, the day, the sea, height, depth, heaven, religious feeling, devotion, innocence, truth, psychic ability, spirituality, the planet Jupiter, the note "F," the chakra #5, physical soothing and cooling, treatment as a sedative, anti-inflammatory, cure for headache
Violet	Water, nostalgia, memory, advanced spirituality, the planet Neptune, the note "B," a treatment for madness

Source: From *Seeing with the Mind's Eye* by Mike Samuels and Nancy Samuels. Copyright © 1975 by Mike Samuels and Nancy Samuels. Reprinted by permission of Random House, Inc.

- A mandala is an ancient symbol of wholeness and has been recorded throughout time. Mandalas can be found in all religions. However, they are not confined to religion or therapeutic uses, but serve as a vehicle for self-expression.[28]
- Mandalas have nothing to do with how well someone can draw. They have to do with reflecting on our inner life in order to move to a higher level of awareness.
- Each person has many different levels of the self. There are different voices or personalities within each of us. We can think of these voices as advisors. Listen to the constant self talk that goes on during drawing.
- Reflect on mandalas from art, museums, or books. They are usually drawn as round circles.

Supplies

The supplies needed are a variety of different colors of crayons, felt tip markers, or oil pastel crayons. White newspaper quality paper in a variety of sizes such as 9x12 and 14x17 inches is suggested. A paper dinner plate measuring 10½ inches should be available to lightly trace the outline of the plate onto the blank sheet. This size and shape is recommended because it is roughly the size of the human head and serves as a mirroring device for contemplation.[29]

Beginning to Draw Mandalas: Have several different selections of music for the client. Before drawing, it is helpful to instruct clients to sit in silence, invite the music in to conscious awareness, and watch the thoughts as they flow through one's mind. Another way is to reflect on the emptiness within the circle while listening to the music (refer to Chapter 13 for music selections). If it feels right, the guide may leave the room after all the materials are set up and the client is comfortable. Frequently this allows the client more space and time for self-reflection. People can work at a desk or draw on the floor.

Exhibit 12-3 Common Symbols

Air	Activity, male principle, primary element, creativity, breath, light, freedom, liberty, movement
Fire	Ability to transform, love, life, health, control, spiritual energy, regeneration, sun, God, passion
Water	Passive, feminine, abysmal, liquid
Earth	Passive, feminine, receptive, solid
Ascent	Height, transcendence, inward journey, increasing intensity
Descent	Unconscious, potentialities of being, animal nature
Duality	Opposites, complements, pairing, away from unity, male-female, life-death, positive-negative, is-is not
Unity	Spirit, oneness, wholeness, centering, transcendence, the source, harmony, revelation, active principle, a point, a dot, supreme power, completeness in itself, light, the divinity
Center	Thought, unity, timelessness, spacelessness, paradise, creator, infinity, neutralizing opposites
Cross	Tree of life, axis of the world, ladder, struggle, martyrdom, orientation in space
Dark	Matter, germ, before existence, chaos
Light	Spirit, morality, All, creative force, the direction East, spiritual thought
Mountain	Height, mass, loftiness, center of the world, ambition, goals
Lake	Mystery, depth, unconscious
Moon	Master of women, vegetation, fecundity
Eye	Understanding, intelligence, sacred fire, creative
Image	Highest form of knowing, thought as a form
Sun	Hero, son of heaven, knowledge, the Divine eye, fire, life force, creative-guiding force, brightness, splendor, active principle, awakening, healing, resurrection, ultimate wholeness

Source: From *Seeing with the Mind's Eye* by Mike Samuels and Nancy Samuels. Copyright © 1975 by Mike Samuels and Nancy Samuels. Reprinted by permission of Random House, Inc.

The nurse can instruct the client to:

- Start in the center of the circle and work outward. One can draw within or outside of the circle. The circle is merely a starting place. Reflect on the first mark and the color/s chosen and continue to draw.
- The space within the mandala can be thought of as sacred space. It is waiting for a part of the unexpressed self to be revealed. A certain idea may have been taken into the drawing process, but if one lets inner wisdom flow, the mandala may begin to take on a life all of its own. It is as if one awaits wisdom to reveal itself to the conscious mind to say, "Pick up purple and draw circles in a clockwise manner."
- The content of the mandala is reflective of one's personal journey at the moment. During the session, many emotions can come forward such as laughter, tears, excitement, or anger. If you feel stuck in the process, just be present in the moment and invite the music in to conscious awareness. It will help release the block.
- The drawing can take the form of designs that are abstract or familiar, or literally contain specific objects that are important to you, such as a pet or prized possessions.
- Encourage clients to place a date on the mandala and to keep it. A series of mandalas are very helpful and can be revealing to a person about life patterns and processes.

Closure to Exercise: The nurse can express some general closure remarks as follows:

- Each of us is a living mandala that changes moment by moment. When we are alive with ideas, the mandalas seem to flow freely.
- During periods of illness or extreme emotional turmoil, we forget to use our creative self. We often use only conscious awareness and forget about the wisdom in the subconscious. Mandalas can facilitate the release of creativity. We acknowledge the enormous reservoirs of wisdom and strengths in the subconscious.
- The patterns and processes that a person produces in a mandala can lead to important insight that can be blocked by ordinary states of consciousness.

Addendum: The nurse must draw mandalas in order to understand the process. Mandalas from healthy, well-functioning people should be studied, which will serve as a basis for contrasting the work of clients with chronic illness or who are in depressed states. Clients who are on heavy doses of medications can block their creative process. When a healthy person is drawing mandalas, they always change depending on the person's state. However, mandalas of chronically ill people are usually repetitive. This is an excellent group exercise. If done in a group, encourage participants to share their mandalas with others present.

Interpretation of Mandalas: The following discussion will focus on the process for basic self-discovery and give some general guidelines in order to begin to understand the process. Refer to Exhibits 12-1, 12-2, and 12-3 for interpretation of symbolism, colors, and associations. Mandalas can be used for psychological evaluation and treatment. The reader is referred to art therapy journals for a detailed discussion of mandalas that show pathology and treatment. Mandalas can become very complex. Some are symmetrical and others have shape and color that are different in each quarter of the mandala that represent conscious and unconscious material that surfaces over time.

Mandalas should be interpreted first by the person that produced the mandala because the results reflect that person's consciousness. It can be thought of as a mirror reflection that reveals unique properties. There may be times when an individual does not like the drawing or does not want to describe the process and that is okay. Mandalas are not static and change over time. It is like a flower that moves from a tight bud into a full blossom.

Evaluation

After each session, the outcomes that were established before the imagery session (Table 12-2) must be measured as successful or not.

Develop client teaching sheets that cover anatomy and explanations of ways to change the physiology by bodymind communication. Short teaching sheets that are one to two pages are best because clients tend to take the time to read short exercise material. For example, when teaching clients to warm hands, include the following content on an imagery teaching sheet: (1) a drawing of how blood flows to the hands via radial and ulnar arteries that branch into intricate blood vessel networks; (2) normal physiology; and (3) images that create hand warming. These sheets can be handed to the client to refresh the learning that took place and to convey what additional information can be learned. This approach to client education teaches both hemispheres simultaneously.

In order to speed the imagery learning process following the session evaluation, give the client this additional information:

- Notice your relaxation at different times during the day.
- Recognize your imagery patterns each day.
- Notice your constant self-talk and focus on creating positive end-result images that are healthy.
- Trust images that come forth in inner awareness. What is their reason for surfacing? Keep journals/diaries of images.
- **Practice** is the key to developing the deep levels of insight that can be gained from this process.
- Create a scheduled time to practice imagery. Just as one takes medication on a schedule, routine scheduled imagery practice increases one's skills.
- Alternate between short and long sessions.
- Chart your daily, weekly, and monthly progress.
- Experiment with different exercises.

Case Studies

Case Study No. 1

Setting:	Biofeedback department with a biofeedback nurse therapist
Client:	L.C., a 42-year-old woman with severe temporomandibular joint (TMJ) dysfunction and tension headaches.
Nursing Diagnoses:	1. Alteration in comfort related to TMJ dysfunctions and tension headaches
	2. Ineffective individual coping related to enabling behavior of client with family members

L.C. was referred for biofeedback training due to continuing clenching following disk implants for severe TMJ dysfunction. With sobbing tears, she told the nurse that she could not remember a time with freedom from headaches or jaws hurting over the last 20 years. The nurse asked L.C. what her pain level was on a scale of 1 (no pain) and 10 (incapacitating pain). Her response was a 20.

Intuitively feeling that the drawing experience could facilitate a breakthrough in perception, the nurse handed L.C. crayons and paper and asked her to draw her pain as seen in Figure 12-1. The client cried during the entire drawing period, which lasted 30 minutes. The nurse sat at her side as she was drawing, encouraging L.C. to stay with what she was feeling and to continue her silent inner self-talk. At times L.C.'s crying would stop, and then she would burst into tears again and continue to draw her pain by retracing areas of greater pain. Classical music was playing softly in the background to help facilitate the process. The nurse asked for no explanations, but sat silently and on occasion would encourage L.C. to feel the release of pain with the tears. When L.C. was crying intensely, the nurse would reach out and touch her arm. When the client put down the crayons and said, "This is my pain," then the nurse asked with focused intention for the client to share the meaning of the drawing.

As can be seen in Figure 12-1 there is no face and only details of pain. The new disk implants are drawn in bright red. The client said that "they feel like they are on fire." The lines on the left (also red) indicate the postsurgical numbness that she felt from the jaw through the half of her tongue. The pain even flowed down to her throat and chest (bright pink) where she had frequent pain due to continuous tension and anxiety. The line (bright yellow) on the right showed bone degeneration that has occurred due to her TMJ problem. The zig-zag line (bright blue) across the top is the constant headache that had been present for 20 years.

Following the detailed description of the pain, the client was asked to imagine herself without the pain; this drawing is shown in Figure 12-2. She says that she can imagine a smiling face, free of pain and headache. Her disks are now described as blue fluffy clouds, and she has frosted her hair and has a new permanent. She even laughed as she did this drawing which took only a few minutes. She was astounded that she could actually allow a spontaneous image of happiness. This exercise helped her become more aware that she did not allow herself to focus on being without pain. Before the end of the first session, the client was guided with the pain assessment script. She immediately felt dramatic pain relief. She was instructed to recognize negative images and to focus on a new image of being pain-free. She was encouraged to practice basic rhythmic breathing and frequently during the day to do a pain body scan and breathe relaxation into the pain

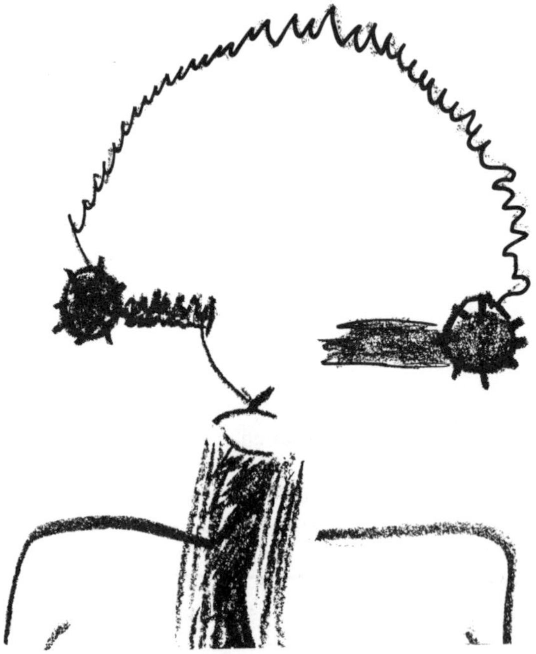

Figure 12-1 Drawing of a Client with Severe Temporomandibular Joint (TMJ) Dysfunction following Disk Implants.

Figure 12-2 Drawing of Client with Freedom from TMJ Pain

on the inhale and release the pain on the exhale. At the end of this talking session, L.C. reported her pain level as being a 6 on the pain scale.

The second session focused on the client's ineffective coping related to family members. L.C. referred to herself as helpless without any means of changing. She was introduced to the concept of enabling behavior and she gained understanding about her role in the ineffective family structure. The nurse asked L.C. to draw her family and special people in her life (Figure 12-3). She was asked to write her name in the center of the paper and then place names of family members around her name. She was to draw arrows to the members who ask her for help and then to draw arrows from those members who helped her. (This is another version of a mind map or clustering technique described in Chapter 17.) All of the arrows went out to other family members with no arrows returning to her name, indicating that she gave but did not receive help from the others. God was also a significant force in her life. She said that during her prayers God gave her answers, but she rarely followed through on the wisdom that she gained through prayer.

The husband (Bob) was unemployed due to a back injury. The three sons (John, Ron, and Don), ages 17, 19, and 21 who were living at home, were always fighting, and in and out of work. The oldest two were again using drugs following participation in a drug

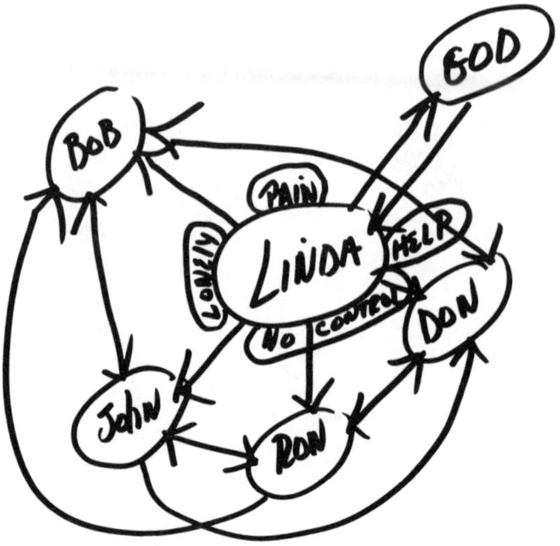

Figure 12-3 Mind Map of a Dysfunctional Family

rehabilitation program. Her reason for allowing the adult sons to be living at home was that they had no money, and if they were on the streets they might be worse off. L.C. did all the cooking, cleaning, and errands for them.

This woman was in therapy for 14 sessions. During this period she made significant strides in learning biofeedback skills, stress management skills, goal setting, asking for help from the family, and establishing house rules. As she became stronger, she came to understand her victim role and the enabling behavior in which she had been participating. As she grew healthier, she insisted that the two older sons move out because they were not keeping basic house rules. She was encouraged by the nurse to join a women's support group, which she did.

One year after therapy, she divorced and started college. Before the divorce her husband had always told her she was "smart enough and didn't need book learning." If she went to college, he would leave her. She decided that she was receiving nothing from her marriage and she left him. At the 1-year follow-up visit L.C. felt freedom and strengths that she had known before her marriage. Her pain was minimal, and her headaches were infrequent.

Case Study No. 2

Setting: Orthopedic floor in a community hospital
Client: R.M., 36-year-old male posttraumatic motorcycle accident
Nursing Diagnoses:
1. Alteration in comfort related to compound fracture, right femur
2. Impaired physical mobility related to traction, right leg
3. Alteration in bowel elimination related to immobility and pain medications

R.M. was taught relaxation and imagery exercises to promote comfort and to increase the bone healing process. This was begun on the third day postsurgery because that is when the nurse first established a readiness to learn. He was given a teaching sheet that illustrated the four stages of the normal bone healing process (Figure 12-4): (A) *Cellular proliferation*. Within the hematoma surrounding the fracture, cells and tissues proliferate and are arranged in a random structure. (B) *Callus formation:* At 10–14 days after the fracture, the cells within the hematoma become organized in a fibrous lattice. With sufficient organization the callus becomes clinically stable. The callus obliterates the medullary canal and surrounds the two ends of bone by irregularly surrounding the fracture defect. (C) *New bone formation:* At about 25 to 40 days after the fracture, calcium is laid down within bone that has spicules perpendicular to the cortical surface. Fiber bone is gradually replaced and remodeled by osteonal bone. (D) *Healed bone:* The fracture has been bridged over by new bone. Conversion and remodeling continue up to 3 years following an acute fracture.

The teaching sheet also included information about the role of bodymind connections—between physiology, stress management, relaxation, imagery, and music. R.M. was given an audio cassette tape made by the nurse on which an introductory relaxation exercise was followed by guided imagery of bone healing. He was encouraged to listen to the audio tape three times a day, as well as to use the relaxation and imagery suggestions throughout the day. He said to the nurse who made the tape, "I am glad that I have learned these relaxation and imagery exercises. I feel like I am helping myself get well faster." The bone healing script follows, with the physiologic terms and examples of ways to empower the spoken word in italics and parentheses.

Script (Bone healing):[30] "In your relaxed state, allow yourself to imagine a natural process that is occuring within your body. . . . New cells are gathering very fast at the site of your fracture *(Cellular proliferation)*. This is an important process as it lays the foundation for your bone healing. With your next breath in . . . become aware of the fact

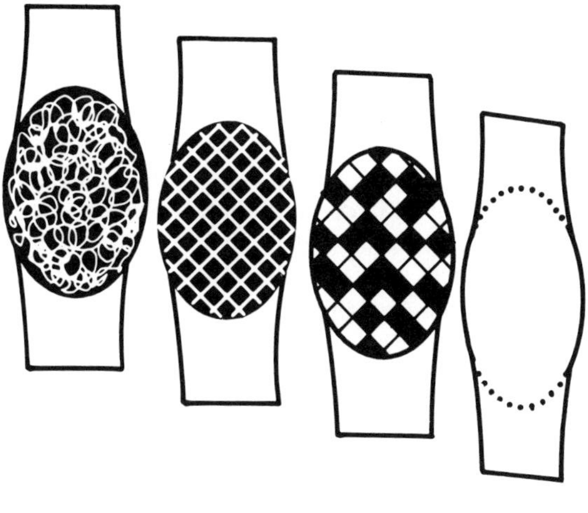

Figure 12-4 Teaching Sheet for Bone Healing and Guided Imagery. *Source:* Reprinted from *Critical Care Nursing: Body-Mind-Spirit*, 3rd ed., by Barbara Montgomery Dossey, Cathie E. Guzzetta, and Cornelia Vanderstaay Kenner, with permission of J.B. Lippincott, copyright © 1992 by Barbara Montgomery Dossey, Cathie E. Guzzetta, and Cornelia Vanderstaay Kenner.

. . . that right now your body is allowing those new cells to multiply rapidly (truism). Your blood cells . . . at the site of your fracture, are arranging themselves in a special healing pattern *(Within the hematoma surface rounding the fracture, cells and tissues proliferate and are arranged in a random structure)*. You can relax . . . R . . . even more . . . if you want to . . . as you continue with this very natural healing process *(embedded command)*.

In a few days . . . your wise body will begin to create a strong lattice network of new bone *(Callus formation: At about 10 to 14 days after the fracture, the cells within the hematoma become organized in a fibrous lattice)*. This will allow your bone to become stable, bridging the new bone that is forming *(Wth sufficient organization, the callus becomes clinically stable. The callus obliterates the medullary canal and surrounds the two ends of bone by irregularly surrounding the fracture defect)*. As you focus in a relaxed way . . . you help in your healing . . . for relaxation increases this natural process *(linkage)*. Imagine your relaxation to be like a gentle breeze of wind that flows over and throughout your body *(metaphor)*.

In a few more weeks, your new bone will be formed . . . natural deposits of calcium from your body will be taken into the place of healing *(New bone formation at about 25 to 40 days after the fracture: Calcium is laid down within the fibrous lattice. The early bone of the callus is fiber bone that has spicules perpendicular to the cortical surface. Fiber bone is gradually replaced and remodeled by osteonal bone)*.

Allow an image to come to your mind now of beautiful, healed bone. In about 6 weeks you will have a beautiful bridge where the calcium has formed new bone *(Healed bone: The fracture has been bridged over by new bone. Conversion and remodeling continue up to 3 years following an acute fracture)*. Can you imagine the hearing colors that are within you right now, and seeing sounds *(synesthesia)?* Just for a few minutes more . . . allow yourself . . . to relax into the healing process . . . feel . . . as you breathe into this healing movement *(interspersal)*.

Case Study No. 3

Setting:	Burn unit in a county hospital
Client:	W.C., a 57 year-old-male with second- and third-degree burns of chest, right arm, and right shoulder
Nursing Diagnoses:	1. Alteration in comfort related to anxiety and pain
	2. Inadequate tissue perfusion related to peripheral burn wound edema
	3. Alteration in nutrition related to metabolic response following burn injury
	4. Potential for bleeding related to stress ulceration and to local gastrointestinal changes and system hormonal alterations
	5. Potential for sepsis related to tissue destruction
	6. Ineffective individual coping related to fear and anxiety
	7. Impaired skin integrity related to burn trauma
	8. Impaired physical mobility related to burn wound, edema, and pain

W. C. was instructed in the natural healing process of his burn grafts according to the teaching sheet in Figure 12-5. The purpose of this guided imagery intervention was to

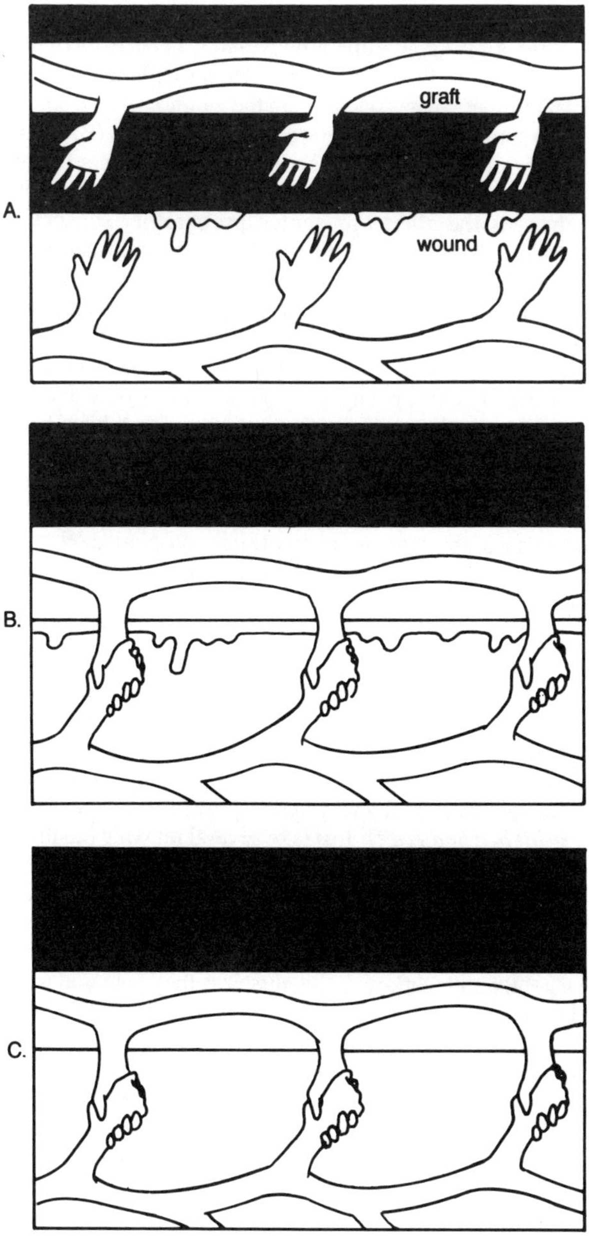

Figure 12-5 Teaching Sheet for Burn Graft Healing. *Source:* Reprinted from *Critical Care Nursing: Body-Mind-Spirit*, 3rd ed., by Barbara Montgomery Dossey, Cathie E. Guzzetta, and Cornelia Vanderstaay Kenner, with permission of J.B. Lippincott, copyright © 1992 by Barbara Montgomery Dossey, Cathie E. Guzzetta, and Cornelia Vanderstaay Kenner.

facilitate wound healing and to give the patient something on which to concentrate in the days immediately after grafting. Preoperatively, W.C. learned to visualize the daily progression of wound healing. Postoperatively, after completing a relaxation exercise, he formed a mental picture of what is occuring in the wound: (A) the adhesion of surfaces and the bridging of the space between the graft bed and the graft, (B) the vessels from the patient grow into the graft, and (C) the vessels establish vascular continuity.

This guided imagery was combined with relaxation and music therapy interventions. Before dressing changes the nurses presented preparatory sensory information to decrease fear and anxiety. Specific relaxation and imagery information was recorded on an audiotape for W.C. to listen to several times during the day. In the script below, normal physiologic events of effective burn graft and wound healing and techniques to empower the spoken word are in italics and parentheses.

Script (Burn Graft):[31] "In your relaxed state now, let's begin on a journey into your body. . . . Begin to identify the capacity that you have to work with the healing process with your new graft. In your mind, go to the area where you have been burned. I am going to describe the healing process . . . that is taking place with your new graft. In your mind . . . go to the area of your body where you have received your new graft. If you begin to feel any tension . . . just take a deep breath, and know that you can let yourself relax and release any tension at this time . . . Notice W . . . how you can deepen your state of relaxation *(embedded command)* . . . release the tension as you breathe out *(truism)*. Your relaxation is like a still mountain lake. Imagine that the gentle wind has formed ripples on the surface of the lake . . . and as the ripples spread out, they are the ripples of relaxation that move into your body and mind (metaphor). Before your graft, the area where you were burned was cleaned very, very well. In this clean area, the graft was gently placed and covered with a thick layer of dressings.

In your mind, begin to imagine the healing process. On Day One, imagine that your own skin secretes a kind of glue. This glue is very important, because it will allow your new graft to stick and hold in a healthy way *(Adhesion of surfaces and the bridging of the space between the graft bed and graft)*. Just take several relaxing breaths now . . . in and out . . . feeling the pause between each of those breaths. As you increase your relaxation . . . allow yourself . . . to relax . . . *(interspersal)* into the natural healing process that will occur . . . your skin secreting a glue, and your new graft sticking to it and becoming part of your body and part of the healing *(linkage)*. During this first day, you will also remember to move gently and work with the nurses as they help you with your comfort, your healing, and your recovery.

Now begin to move to Day Two. On this day, after receiving your graft, your body continues the healing process. Your own body now . . . sends nutrients to the graft, and small blood vessels begin to sprout out . . . just like little 'hands' moving out, sending nutrients to every cell in this area for healthy survival *(Vessels fron the patient grow into the graft and establish vascularity continuity)*. Remember to stay as still as possible and let the nurses help you move. This is important . . . for it also helps those tiny blood vessels grow in a very healthy manner. During this time, you will continue to increase your relaxation to that particular area where your grafts will take hold. And as you exhale, let go of any tension and tightness.

Now move to Day Three of your recovery process. By Day Three, the blood vessels from your own body . . . and the blood vessels from your graft actually grow together

(Vascular continuity). You might even imagine this as those blood vessels joining hands *(metaphor)*. As you feel this experience of your blood vessels joining hands, just imagine now that this graft is part of your body just like all the other tissues of your body *(linkage and truism)*. Imagine that happening . . . the graft is now a part of your body.

Again, let us go over these three important areas that will occur after your graft. On Day One, your skin secretes a glue, and the glue sticks to your own skin. On Day Two, blood vessels from your own skin and the blood vessels from the graft begin to grow together. By Day Three, those blood vessels have joined together, and this graft is now a part of your body.

Addendum: *Include this information if the grafts are from the patient. "Spend some time now focusing on that area where the graft from on your body came from. The natural healing ability is also occurring there, with new skin now being formed (normal wound healing)."* Repeat information in the above script on wound healing but substitute the words "new skin" for "graft."

SUMMARY

This chapter has focused on imagery as a nursing intervention. Research and theory provide evidence that imagery evokes bodymind communication. Specific interventions, such as imagery scripts, drawing techniques with health and illness, and guidelines with group work, can be used.

DIRECTIONS FOR FUTURE RESEARCH

1. Evaluate the structural and functional properties of imagery.[32]
2. Formulate studies that examine the clinical efficacy of imagery in an interdisciplinary model, such as that reviewed under theory.
3. Develop valid and reliable tools that measure imagery.
4. Determine the relationship of script, physiologic response, and healing in different clinical settings.
5. Determine if subjects can be trained through manipulation of both imagery scripts and their verbal reports to eliminate or modify negative psychophysiologic responses.
6. Determine the effectiveness of a client's specific images and if these images simultaneously alter the client's condition toward increased psychophysiologic healing.

NURSE HEALER REFLECTIONS

After reading this chapter, the nurse healer will be able to answer or begin a process of answering the following questions:

- How do I *feel* about my imagination?
- When I work with imagery what *inner resources* can I use in understanding my life processes?
- How am I able to *remove* the barriers to my imagery process?
- In what way do I *recognize* the *nonrational* part of myself?
- Am I *able* to image with my clients?
- Can I *allow* my clients to *interpret* their *own imagery* in order to *facilitate* their *own healing?*

NOTES

1. Mike Samuels and Nancy Samuels, *Seeing With the Mind's Eye* (New York: Random House, 1975), p. 66.
2. Errol Korn and Karen Johnson, *Visualization: The Uses of Imagery in the Health Professions* (Homewood, IL: Dow Jones-Irwin, 1983), pp. 64–68.
3. Jeanne Achterberg and G. Frank Lawlis, *Bridges of the Bodymind: Behavioral Approaches to Health Care* (Champaign, IL: Institute for Personality and Behavior Testing), pp. 28–30.
4. Robert Rivlin and Karen Gravelle, *Deciphering the Senses: The Expanding World of Human Perception* (New York: Simon and Schuster Inc., 1984), pp. 16–18.
5. Jeanne Achterberg, *Imagery in Healing* (Boston: Shambhala Publications, Inc., 1985), pp. 115–116.
6. Ernest Lawrence Rossi, *The Psychobiology of Mind-Body Healing: New Concepts of Therapeutic Hypnosis* (New York: W.W. Norton, 1986), p. 70.
7. Ibid., p. 38.
8. Mardi Horowitz, *Image Formation and Cognition* (New York: Meredith Corp., 1970), pp. 73–79.
9. A. Ahsen, "Imagery, Dreams and Transformation," *Journal of Mental Imagery* 8 (1984): 53–78.
10. Roberto Assagioli, *Psychosynthesis: A Manual of Principles and Techniques* (New York: Hobbs, Doorman and Co., (1965), pp. 17–18.
11. Marty Rossman, "Imagery In Medical Self-Care" in *Imagination and Healing,* ed. Anees A. Sheikh (Farmingdale, NY: Baywood Publishing Co, 1984), pp. 231–258.
12. Jeanne Achterberg, *Imagery in Healing*, p. 123
13. Ibid.
14. Piero Ferrucci, *What We May Be: Techniques for Psychological Growth* (Los Angeles: J.P. Tarcher Inc., 1982), pp. 47–58.
15. Ibid., pp. 49–50.
16. Jeanne Achterberg and Frank Lawlis, *Bridges of the Bodymind: Behavioral Approaches to Health Care,* p. 63.
17. Norman J. Christman and Karin T. Kirkoff, "Preparatory Sensory Information," in *Nursing Interventions: Treatments for Nursing Diagnoses,* ed. Gloria M. Bulechek and Joanne C. McCloskey (Philadelphia: W.B. Saunders Co., 1985), pp. 259–276.
18. Ibid, p. 64.
19. Peggy Barrett, "Self-Hypnosis: A Self-Empowering Tool," in *Hypnosis: New Tool in Nursing Practice,* ed. Gil Boyne (Glendale, CA: Westwood Publishing Co., 1982), pp. 1–18.
20. Gayle Peterson and Lewis Mehl, *Pregnancy as Healing: A Holistic Philosophy for Prenatal Care* (Berkeley, CA: Mindbody Press, 1984), pp. 213–243.

21. Ruth Knowles, *A Guide to Self-Management Strategies for Nurses* (New York: Springer Publishing Co., 1984), pp. 127–136.

22. Patricia A. McGrath and Leveret L. Deveber, ''Helping Children Cope With Painful Procedures,'' *American Journal of Nursing* 86, no. 11 (November 1986): 1278–1279.

23. Jeanne Achterberg and G. Frank Lawlis, *Imagery and Disease: A Diagnostic Tool for Behavioral Medicine* (Champaign, IL: Institute for Personality and Ability Testing, 1984), pp. 23–24.

24. Mary Haack and John Jones, ''Diagnosing Burnout: Using Projective Drawings,'' *Journal of Psychosocial Nursing and Mental Health Services* 21, no. 7 (July 1983): pp. 9–16.

25. Barbara Dossey, ''Psychophysiologic Self-Regulation,'' in *Critical Care Nursing: Body-Mind-Spirit*, 3rd ed., Barbara M. Dossey, Cathie E. Guzzetta, and Cornelia Kenner (Philadelphia: J.B. Lippincott, 1992), pp. 37–38.

26. Barbara Dossey, ''Psychophysiologic Self-Regulation,'' in *Critical Care Nursing: Body-Mind-Spirit*, 3rd ed., Barbara M. Dossey, Cathie E. Guzzetta, and Cornelia Kenner (Philadelphia: J.B. Lippincott, 1992), pp. 36–37.

27. Anees A. Sheikh, P. Richardson, and L.M. Moleski, ''Psychosomatics and Mental Imagery: A Brief Review,'' in *The Potential of Fantasy and Imagination*, ed. Anees A. Sheikh and J.T. Shaffer (New York: Brandon House, 1979), pp. 105–118.

28. Joan Kellogg, Margaret MacRae, Helen Bonny, and Francesco Di Leo, ''The Use of the Mandala in Psychological Evaluation and Treatment,'' *American Journal of Art Therapy*, 16 (July 1977): 123–134.

29. Ibid., p. 124.

30. Jeanne Achterberg and Frank Lawlis, *Bridges of the Bodymind*, pp. 45–46.

31. Ibid., pp. 61–63.

32. Deborah E. Mast, ''Effects of Imagery,'' *Image: Journal of Nursing Scholarship* 18, no. 3 (Fall 1986): 118–120.

SUGGESTED READINGS

Charlesworth, E.A., and Nathan, R.G. *Stress Management*. New York: Atheneum, 1984.

Crasilneck, H.B., and Hall, J.A. *Clinical Hypnosis: Principles and Application*. New York: Grune and Stratton, 1986.

Gawain, S. *Creative Visualization*. Mill Valley, CA: 1978.

Kroger W.S., and Fezler, W.D. *Hypnosis and Behavior Modification: Imagery Conditioning*. Philadelphia: J.B. Lippincott Co., 1976.

Sheikh, A.A., *Anthology of Imagery Techniques*. Milwaukee, WI: American Imagery Institute, 1987.

chapter 13

Music Therapy: Hearing the Melody of the Soul

Cathie E. Guzzetta

> Grown-ups love figures. When you tell them that you have made a new friend, they never ask you any questions about essential matters. They never say to you, "What does his voice sound like? What game does he love best? Does he collect butterflies?"
>
> Instead they demand: "How old is he? How many brothers has he? How much does he weigh? How much money does his father make?" Only from figures do they think they have learned anything about him.
>
> *The Little Prince*
> St. Exupéry[1]

> And we must learn
> that to know a man is not to know his name
> but to know his melody
>
> *Unknown Oriental Philosopher*

The theory and research related to music therapy and the systematic application of music as a nursing intervention to bring about desired changes in emotional and physical health are described in this chapter. Because of its broad appeal, music therapy enjoys widespread acceptance. The critical implementation issue is to discover the best way to apply music therapy to achieve maintenance, restoration, and improvement of psychophysiologic states.

Music and medicine have been linked throughout history. According to Greek mythology, Orpheus was given a lyre by the god Apollo and was instructed in its use by the muses; hence the word "music." Apollo was the god of music, and his son Asclepius was the god of healing and medicine. The Greeks believed music had the power to help heal the body and soul. The shaman and medicine men provided patients with healing chants along with medicine.

Likewise, music has been a vital part of all societies and cultures, no matter how primitive or advanced. It is used in spiritual ceremonies and in celebrations. Armies march to battle with music, and mothers lull their infants to sleep with song. Music is played during rites of initiation, during funeral ceremonies, and on harvest and feast days. There is something about the power of music that cannot be expressed in verbal language. It is of no surprise then that music is currently being applied as a therapeutic self-regulation modality.

NURSE HEALER OBJECTIVES

Theoretical

1. Discuss the definitions of terms associated with music therapy.
2. Discuss the principles of sound.
3. Discuss the psychophysiologic theories that explain why music therapy works as a self-regulation modality.

Clinical

1. List the factors involved in choosing music selections that are relaxing for clients.
2. Develop a music library for use with clients.
3. Choose several different music therapy techniques and use them in clinical practice.
4. Discuss with clients their internal responses when listening to music in a relaxed state.

Personal

1. Participate in "experimental listening."
2. Record your responses to various types of music in a music notebook.
3. In a music log, record your most intimate memories associated with music.
4. Participate in a music bath each day.
5. Participate in a toning and groaning exercise before listening to music.
6. Practice focused and conscious hearing each day to recognize subtle differences in sound.
7. Experience your internal responses when listening to music in a relaxed state.

DEFINITIONS

Cymatics: study of patterns of shape evoked by sound.

Frequencies: the number of vibrations or cycles per unit of time.

Music Therapy: systematic application of music to produce relaxation and desired changes in emotions, behavior, and physiology.

Oscillation: fluctuation or variation between minimum and maximum values.

Resonance: a structure that vibrates at a frequency that is natural to it and most easily sustained by it.

Resonant: increasing the intensity of sounds by sympathetic vibration.

Sonic: of or having to do with sound.

Sound: that which is produced when some object is vibrating in a random or periodic repeated motion.

Sympathetic Resonance: the reinforced vibration of an object exposed to the vibration at about the same frequency as another object.

THEORY AND RESEARCH

Origin of Sound

Sounds are used to create music. Sounds produce changes in our bodymind and are involved in modulating simultaneous changes in the autonomic, immune, endocrine, and neuropeptide systems. It is necessary to appreciate the principles and theories of sound to understand fully its tremendous capacity to achieve therapeutic psychophysiologic outcomes.

Sound is that which is produced when some object is vibrating in a random or periodic repeated motion. Sound can be heard by the human ear when it vibrates between 20 and 20,000 cycles per second. We also hear and perceive sound by skin and bone conduction. Our other senses, such as sight, smell, and touch, allow us to perceive an even wider range of vibrations than those sensed by hearing. We are sensitive to sounds in ways that most people do not even consider.

The interrelationship between wave forms and matter can be understood by rendering vibrations into physical forms. When scattered liquids, powders, metal filings, or sand are placed on a disk with a vibrating crystal, thereby causing the disk to vibrate, repeatable patterns form on the disk. As the pitch is changed, the harmonic pattern formed on the disk also changes. Thus, matter assumes certain shapes or patterns based on the vibrations or frequency of the sound to which it is exposed. The study of patterns of shapes evoked by sound is called *cymatics*.[2] The forms of snowflakes and faces of flowers may take on their shape because they are responding to some sounds in nature.[3] Likewise, it is possible that crystals, plants, and human beings may be, in some way, music that has taken on visible form.

The human body also vibrates. The ejection of blood from the left ventricle during systole causes the aorta to become distended with blood. The pressure produced by aortic distension causes a pressure wave to travel down the aorta to the arterial branches. The pressure wave travels faster than the flow of blood and creates a palpable pulse called the *pressure pulse wave*.[4]

Waves are a series of advancing impulses set up by a vibration or impulse. The pressure pulse wave is composed of a series of waves that have differing frequencies (number of vibrations per unit of time) and amplitude. In the arterial branches, there is one fundamental frequency and a number of harmonics that usually have a smaller amplitude than the fundamental frequency. The arterial vessels resonate at certain frequencies (fundamental frequency), thereby intensifying some waves while other waves are damped and disappear. This phenomenon is called *resonance*.[5]

The human body vibrates, from its large structures, such as the aorta and arterial system, down to the genetically preprogrammed vibrations coded into our molecular cells. Our atoms and molecules, cells, glands, and organs all have a characteristic vibrational frequency that absorbs and emits sound. Thus, the human body is a system of vibrating atomic particles, acting as a vibratory transformer that gives off and takes in sound.

Because our bodies absorb sound, this concept of the body as transformer is worthy of exploration. Sympathetic vibration or *sympathetic resonance* refers to the reinforced vibration of an object exposed to the vibration at about the same frequency as another object.[6] For example, consider two tuning forks that are designed to vibrate at approximately the same pitch. When one of the tuning forks is struck, it produces a sound that spontaneously causes the second tuning fork to vibrate and produce the same sound *as if* the second fork was physically struck. The sound wave from the first fork actually does physically strike the second fork, causing the second to resonate responsively to the tune of the first. This sympathetic resonance occurs because both forks contain similar vibratory characteristics, which allows energy transfer from one to the other. When two objects have similar vibratory characteristics that allow them to resonate at the same frequency, they form a resonant system.

The atomic structure of our molecular system is also a resonant system. Nuclei vibrate, and the electrons in their orbit vibrate in resonance with their nucleus. Moreover, as long as the atom, cell, or organ contains an appropriate vibrational pattern, it can be ''played'' by *outside* stimuli in harmony with its vibrational make-up.[7] The phenomenon of sympathetic vibration depends on pitch. Thus, environmental sounds, such as those emitted from a dishwasher or television, may be capable of stimulating or producing sympathetic vibrations in the molecules and cells of our body. Our entire body vibrates at a fundamental inaudible frequency of approximately 8 cycles per second when it is in a relaxed state. During relaxed meditation, the frequency of brain waves produced is also about 8 cycles per second. Moreover, the earth vibrates at this same fundamental frequency of 8 cycles per second. This phenomenon is called Schumann's Resonance and is a function of electromagnetic radiation and the earth's circumference. Thus, there is a sympathetic resonance between the electrically charged layers of the earth's atmosphere and the human body. Therefore, ''being in harmony with oneself and the universe'' may be more than a poetic concept.[8]

Music Therapy: What Is It?

Music therapy is defined as a behavioral science that is concerned with the use of specific kinds of music and its ability to affect changes in behavior, emotions, and physiology.[9] It complements traditional therapy, providing clients with integrated bodymind experiences and encouraging them to become active participants in their health care and recovery.

It is important to distinguish between *two* principal *schools* of *music therapy*. One school seeks to achieve a therapeutic effect by involving the client in communicative music-making; the other seeks to achieve its effects by listening to vibrational sound.[10] This chapter is primarily concerned with the latter school of music therapy and its application to nursing.

Goal of Music Therapy

Music therapy should not be confused with listening to music for entertainment, nor should it be confused with music education, which pursues the art of music. In Western society, we hear music for general entertainment purposes in department stores, restaurants, airports, and while waiting on the telephone. We turn on music in our homes, in our cars, and at work. The goal of music therapy, however, is not to provide entertainment.

Rather, the goal of music therapy, which is nonmusical in nature, is the reduction of psychophysiologic stress, pain, anxiety, and isolation. It helps clients achieve a state of deep relaxation, develop self-awareness and creativity, improve learning, clarify personal values, and cope with a variety of psychophysiologic dysfunctions.[11]

Appropriate music serves as an important vehicle in achieving the relaxation response by removing one's inner restlessness and quieting ceaseless thinking. It can be used as a healing ritual to stop the mind from running away and enable thinking to become still so that one can achieve inner quietness. The healing capabilities of music are intimately bound to the personal experience of inner relaxation.[12]

Shifting States of Consciousness

When appropriately applied, music can be a way of reaching nonordinary levels of human consciousness.[13] One is able to pass from ordinary states of consciousness to an altered state of consciousness to achieve the mind's fullest potential. With music therapy, individuals are able to shift their perception of time. Individuals perceive two types of time: virtual and experiential.[14] *Virtual time* is perceived in a left-brain mode and is characterized by hours, minutes, and seconds. In contrast, *experiential time* is perceived through the memory.

Experiential time exists because we experience both a state of tension and resolution.[15] Tensions and resolutions are perceived by our memory in a linear sequence that is called a *disturbance* or an *event*. An emotion or a sound, for example, is a disturbance that can produce tension (producing psychophysiologic effects), which is followed by a return to equilibrium or resolution. Perception of time is influenced by the rate of these linear sequences or events. For example, slow-moving music lengthens our perception of time because our memory has more time to experience the events (tensions and resolutions) and the spaces between the events. Thus, clock time becomes distorted, and clients can actually lose track of time for extended periods, enabling them to reduce anxiety, fear, and pain.

In a relaxed state, abstract thinking is slowed. Music can assist the individual in moving through six states of consciousness: normal waking state, expanded sensory threshold, daydreaming, trance, meditative states, and rapture.[16] During relaxation, music is first perceived in a normal wakeful state. As relaxation continues, sensory thresholds are lowered, and expanded awareness states predominate. The individual can then continue to move to daydreaming, trance, and meditative states and progress to rapture, depending on the level of involvement with the music and relaxation.

Psychophysiologic Responses

Music produces alterations in *physiology*. The goal of music therapy and the type of music played (i.e., soothing or stimulating) determine the direction of the physiologic changes. Soothing music can produce a hypometabolic response characteristic of relaxation in which autonomic, immune, endocrine, and neuropeptide systems are altered. Likewise, music therapy produces desired *psychologic* responses, such as reductions in anxiety and fear. Some of these responses have been linked to the effects of music on the *hemispheric functioning* of the brain and the *limbic system*.

Effects of Music Therapy on Hemispheric Functioning

Left-brain functioning involves the rational, analytical, and logical way of processing information. Right-brain functioning, in contrast, is concerned with the intuitive, creative, and imaging way of processing information. Music may activate the flow of stored memory material across the corpus collosum so that the right and left hemispheres work in harmony, rather than conflict.

The right hemisphere is employed differently in the musical process than the left. The right "metaphoric" hemisphere is responsible for the major aspects of musical perception and music behavior, i.e., the recognition of pitch, a gestalt sense of melody, rhythm, style, and musical memory. The commonalities between the components of speech and music are a basis for the perceptual processes of the right hemisphere, which influence language functions and behavior. The left hemisphere is predominantly involved with analytic thinking, especially in verbal and mathematical functions.[17] It has been suggested that, when we ignore or do not listen to our right brain because we are busy, rushed, and stressed, the right brain probably sends foggy messages to the left brain. Such messages of imbalance may conflict with the logic of the moment in our left brain to produce physical illness.[18]

It appears that, as one's musical knowledge grows, the brain's response to music shifts from a holistic to a more sequential and linear experience.[19] Music students and musicians tend to analyze the music to which they listen, classify the instruments, and critique the compositional techniques. Instead of integrating right and left brain functioning while listening to music in a relaxed state, such individuals tend to remain in or change to the left-brain mode. With practice, however, they can let go of these conditioned responses to achieve integration of both hemispheres.[20]

Because music is nonverbal in nature it appeals to the right hemisphere, whereas the traditional verbalization that the nurse uses in therapy with a client has its primary effect on the logical left brain. Music therapy therefore provides a means of communication between the right and left brain.[21] The more connections that can be made in the brain, the more integrated the experience is within memory.[22] (Figure 13-1).

Music, even more than the spoken word, "lends itself as a therapy because it meets with little or no intellectual resistance, and does not need to appeal to logic to initiate its action. . . is more subtle and primitive, and therefore its appeal is wider and greater."[23] In a relaxed state, individuals can let go of preconceived ideas about listening to music and its patterns, instruments, and rhythm and shift their thinking to the right side of the brain to alter their states of consciousness.[24]

Figure 13-1 Musical Beginnings. *Source*: Courtesy of Andrea Prendergast.

Effects of Music Therapy on the Limbic System

Music therapy evokes psychophysiologic responses because of its influence on the limbic system.[25] This system is influenced by musical pitch and rhythm, which in turn affect emotions and feelings. Our emotional reactions to music may occur because the limbic system is the seat of emotions, feelings, and sensations. The quieting and calming effect of music can also produce other desired autonomic, immunologic, endocrine, and neuropeptide changes (see Chapter 5). Thus, the immediate influence of music therapy is on the mind state, which in turn influences the body state, producing a hypometabolic response and a balance of body-mind-spirit.

GENERAL EXPLANATIONS

Bodymind Connections

Our entire body responds to sound, whether we consciously hear the sound or not. Even though we can consciously tune out the sounds of airplane or automobile traffic, our bodies cannot. There are many sounds that in fact assault our body because they are not in harmony with our fundamental vibratory pattern. On the other hand, it is possible that musical vibrations that are in tune with our fundamental vibratory pattern could have a profound healing effect on the entire human body and mind, affecting changes in emotions and in organs, enzymes, hormones, cells, and atoms. Musical vibrations theoretically could help restore regulatory function to a body out of tune (i.e., during times of stress and illness) and help maintain and enhance regulatory function to a body in tune. The therapeutic appeal of music may lie in its vibrational language and ability to help bring the body-mind-spirit in alignment with its own fundamental frequency without having to appeal to the left brain to work.[26]

Imagery, Emotions, and the Senses

Music elicits a variety of different experiences in individuals. During relaxation and music therapy, clients reaching an altered state of consciousness may visualize settings, peaceful scenes, images, or may experience various sensations or moods.[27] Music passages can evoke scenes from fantasy to real life. Melodic patterns can evoke love, joy, and deep peace.

During music therapy and relaxation, individuals can be guided in experiencing *synesthesia,* or a mingling of senses.[28] Musical tones can evoke color and movement, or tastes can evoke shapes. Many children spontaneously "see" sounds and "taste" textures.[29]

Music and color can be expressed in terms of vibrations. When color is translated into music vibrations, the harmonies of color are 40 octaves higher than the ear can hear. A piano spans about 7 octaves. If the piano keyboard could be expanded another 50 octaves higher, then the keys played at these higher octaves would produce color, rather than audible sound.[30]

One musical selection entitled "Spectrum Suite" (see Resources at the end of chapter) is designed to evoke colors. While listening to this selection, clients are guided in focusing on seven main energy centers known to exist in the body. In Eastern culture these centers are called *Chakras*. Each energy level is then associated with a specific musical tone and a specific color. For example, while focusing on the spine (the first energy center), the client is guided to hear and feel the keynote of C resonating in the spinal area and image the vibrations of red bathing this area of the body.[31]

Uses and Outcomes of Music Therapy

Music has been used as a vehicle to foster a variety of desired outcomes. One such outcome is enhanced creativity. Creativity involves the development of new ways of association. It is determined by how one approaches and considers things, rather than by one's education or professional qualifications.[32] Creativity incorporates the unexpected, the unknown, and the peculiar. It can be enhanced by relaxation wherein the busy mind settles into a more quiet and receptive state. Through visualization the mind can envision new ideas and ways of thinking. When appropriate music is played, alpha and theta brainwaves occur, which are known to stimulate creativity.[33]

Music and movement and/or tonal exercises have been used to help clients become aware of their bodies and the energies released in them. Such techniques are used to achieve body-mind balance and to release blocked energies. Therapists have used musical instruments as another form of music therapy, particularly with disabled individuals. Various instruments are played by clients during the therapy to develop the qualities of perseverance, perceptiveness, concentration, and initiative and to promote perceptual-motor coordination and group interaction.[34]

Music has been used as a vehicle to improve learning. When individuals demonstrate high psychophysiologic stress levels, learning is inhibited or blocked. When music and relaxation are combined, students become relaxed and learn better. Their learning can become more fun, and they are more fully involved in the experience and process.[35] Music has been used also as a catalyst during the process of accelerated learning. Some of the techniques that involve music-learning are Suggestology™, Super Learning™, Optimalearning™, and Accelerated Learning.™[36]

Music is used to correct and reprogram unhealthy unconscious thought patterns. Audiotapes are now available in the marketplace to repattern thought processes. Such tapes are enhanced by music. Their aim is to put the listener in a relaxed and balanced state. During relaxation, the reprogramming message is delivered to the deeper unconscious mind where the new thought pattern will ultimately reside. Such self-help tapes frequently include desired affirmations or suggestions combined with meditative music or white noise.[37]

Music can be used to facilitate reframing of past memories and experiences.[38] In achieving an altered state of consciousness, the unconscious mind can remember complete details of an individual's past experiences that the conscious mind may have forgotten. Past memories and experiences can be remembered and relived. When the conscious mind remembers such experiences, they can then be reframed or reorganized to produce a more healthy and positive experience.[39]

Music has also been combined with subliminal suggestions for self-help or enhanced learning. The subliminal technique delivers verbal messages to the individual at a volume so low or through a change in speed or frequency so fast that the conscious mind cannot perceive it. The conscious mind responds to the music while the unconscious mind absorbs and responds to the verbal suggestion.[40]

Music has been used to evoke imagery for a number of therapeutic ends (see Chapter 12). It is likely that clients who have difficulty imaging may be helped by the addition of relaxing background music. Appropriately selected music can activate right-hemispheric functioning and release a flow of images.[41]

Bonny has developed an innovative approach to listening to music combined with the use of imagery called *Guided Imagery and Music* (GIM).[42] GIM is the conscious use of imagery that is evoked by relaxation and music. It is a method of self-exploration, self-understanding, growth, healing, and transformation. In this approach, one listens to classical music in a relaxed state, allowing the imagination to come to conscious awareness and sharing these experiences with a guide. The guide helps integrate the experience into the listener's life.

Bonny and Savary describe their work in their book, *Music and Your Mind*.[43] They have also founded the Institute for Music and Imagery (formerly called the Institute for Consciousness and Music), a nonprofit educational institution dedicated to furthering the use of music and the arts as agents of healing, renewal, and change (See Resources at the end of the chapter). The Institute engages in research and writing to expand human consciousness through music. It provides workshops and training for therapists who are interested in incorporating GIM into their practice.

Music Therapy in Clinical Settings

Music can act as a catalyst to facilitate mental suggestion and enhance a client's own self-healing capacities. Thus, music has the potential to be useful in the treatment of many health problems, such as cardiovascular disease, hypertension, migraine headaches, gastrointestinal ulcers, Raynaud's disease, and cancer. As seen in Chapter 5, mind modulation exists in the autonomic, immune, endocrine, and neuropeptide systems. As a result, every tissue, end-organ, and cell is capable of responding to mental healing suggestions.

Several hospitals are using relaxation music to reduce stress and pain in hospitalized patients.[44] Music has been used in birthing, counseling, and massage rooms; during physical therapy; in helping stroke, burn, and cancer victims; with brain damaged and multiply handicapped children; and in psychiatric hospitals, addiction treatment centers, and prisons.

A recent study investigated the effects of music and relaxation on the psychophysiologic stress levels of patients admitted to the coronary care unit with the presumptive diagnosis of acute myocardial infarction.[45] There were statistically significant reductions in psychophysiologic stress in the music and relaxation group. The experimental group had lower heart rates, blood pressures, psychologic anxiety scores, higher peripheral temperatures, and fewer complications than the control group. Other outcomes related to music therapy can be found in the *Journal of Music Therapy*, which publishes research articles that explore the use of sound and music as they affect physiology, behavior, emotions, learning, and therapeutic outcomes.

Selecting Appropriate Music

Selecting the appropriate music for use in music therapy is an important and challenging task. There is no doubt that musical selections can influence the outcomes of music therapy. No one musical selection or any one type of music works best for all people in all situations. Musical selections that are relaxing and meditative to one client can be disruptive and annoying to another. Moreover, the music that some individuals identify as relaxing to them may, in fact, not be physiologically relaxing at all.[46] In addition, the music preference of the nurse, which changes as he or she matures, can influence the type of music selected.

Most music is not composed for the purposes of relaxation and healing. Thus, it is important to choose the appropriate music for the desired response. Individuals associate relaxing and displeasing events in their lives with certain kinds of music.[47] This conditioned learning response will influence their music preference and perception of whether the music selection is relaxing. Although music experts tend to agree that rock music does not evoke psychophysiologic relaxation (even if the individual thinks it does), many experts also agree that soothing classical, spiritual, or popular music also may not be relaxing for some clients.[48]

Musical selections (i.e., popular, classical, operatic, folk, jazz) should be judged for their soothing and relaxing qualities. A variety of selections should be available when working with clients because it is difficult to predict the client's music preference and the response to the particular selection. When musical selections with words are chosen, the analytic left brain tends to pay attention to the message. Clients may concentrate on the words, their messages, and their meaning, rather than allowing themselves to concentrate and flow with the music.[49] Thus, selections without words are recommended.

New Age Music

Most traditional musical selections are based on tension and release. Such music is designed to create a sense of anticipation followed by a sense of relief. The sense of anticipation is used most in popular and classical music. The tension-release music may be emotionally exciting and helpful in eliciting imagery, but it is not designed to relax most individuals.[50]

A new type of music has evolved for the purposes of "orchestrating human instruments." The goal of this music is to allow the bodymind to choose whatever response mode that it needs to operate at a higher level of efficiency. This new kind of music has been called *nontraditional, meditative,* or *New Age* music. Nontraditional meditative music potentially has a wide appeal because it is designed to transcend personal taste. There is no recognizable melody and no harmonic progressions to which we have been conditioned to respond. Frequently, there is no central rhythm or natural beat. Nontraditional music requires neither intellectual analysis nor emotional involvement. It is a vibrational language that helps the bodymind attune itself with its own pattern or resonance. The music tends to flow endlessly and serves as a vehicle for relaxation, self-absorption, and contemplation.[51] A word of caution is necessary, however. Not all music labeled as "New Age" can be judged as relaxing and meditative. Evaluate New Age musical selections to determine their soothing and meditative qualities.

Hospital Music

Relaxing music selections have been developed by a variety of companies and individuals (see Resources at the end of the chapter). Some have been developed specifically for use in the clinical setting. For example, Halpern has created several nontraditional long-playing music selections that contain up to 8 hours of continuous relaxing music. These tapes are designed for patient use in hospitals during surgery, childbirth, and postoperative recovery.

Helen Bonny, has also developed a set of music tapes called *Music Rx*™ for use in various hospital settings. Music Rx was tested at two hospitals in a study using intensive care and surgical patients. Patients participating in the *Music Rx* had reduced heart rates, greater relief from pain, and positive psychologic ratings.[52] The Music Rx tapes use classical selections and are designed to reduce stress, provide a pleasant diversion, and quiet mood states. Music Rx is recommended for patients in the critical care units and operating and recovery rooms, as well as other inpatient and outpatient settings.

It has been suggested that, as we learn more about how vibratory frequencies and patterns affect our bodymind, healing compositions will be composed to strengthen our altered vibratory patterns and bring them back to balance.[53]

Individual Preference

Individuals should evaluate their response to various types of music. Many people already intuitively know how they respond. Although different musical selections can produce various effects, the fullest effect occurs when the listener is appropriately prepared to experience the sounds. The therapeutic effect of music is lessened when individuals are angry, distracted, critical, analytic, or resistant. With a relaxed and receptive bodymind, music has the potential to enter the body and play through it, rather than around it. Thus, some form of relaxation exercise is recommended before the music experience.

Depending on the individual's psychophysiology, mind state, and mood, music can produce different feelings at different times. An important rule to follow when listening to music is the *iso-principle*.[54] The iso-principle matches the individual's mood to the appropriate music to obtain the best results from the experience. Music that matches the individual's mood helps achieve an altered state of consciousness because it is as if the mind and feelings are vibrating at a certain frequency and are satisfied when the music is in resonance with that frequency. For example, if you are feeling carefree and gay, it is not advisable to play solemn music.

Create your own tapes that match your moods and your musical preference. If your mood is tense or angry, you might start out with a short selection (3 minutes or less) of music that resonates with your mood, and then add selections that increasingly move you to a relaxed state. Before creating your own tape, spend some time experimenting with music.

When selecting your own nourishing music, you should experience a variety of musical selections. Pay attention and become aware of what is happening to you when listening to specific selections. No one can direct you in what music will work best for you. You must discover that for yourself. It is important to identify your preference, your moods, and your specific psychophysiologic state at the moment.

Try "experimental listening."[55] Listen to various types of music at different times of the day and week. Spend 20 minutes listening to each type of music and then systematically evaluate your response to the selection. Exhibit 13-1 outlines the psychophysiologic parameters to assess when evaluating your response to specific types of music. Based on your response, create your own relaxation music tape of 20-30 minutes in length. The more regularly you use the tape, the more effective it will become.

Experiencing music can be a holistic experience. As more individuals come to realize that music can be a principal source of healing and stress reduction, they will take great care to select their music. Music therapy might be incorporated into daily living activities, such as taking a "music bath" after a morning shower as a means of balancing the bodymind for the events of the day (see p. 280).[56]

Exhibit 13-1 Evaluating Your Response to Music

1. Set aside 20 minutes of relaxation time.
2. Find a comfortable position.
3. Find a quiet uninterrupted place.
4. Check your pulse rate.
5. Observe your breathing pattern (fast, slow, normal).
6. Assess your muscular tension (pain, muscle tightness, shoulder stiffness, jaw and neck tension). Are you loose, limp, sleepy?
7. Evaluate your mood state (angry, happy, sad).
8. Listen to the music for 20 minutes. Let your body respond to the music as it wishes: loosen muscles, lie down, dance, clap, hum.
9. Following the session, assess your breathing pattern.
10. Assess your muscular tension (more relaxed? more stimulated? tighter? tenser? calmer?).
11. Evaluate your mood state.
12. Record the name of the music selection and your before-and-after responses in a music notebook for use when developing your own therapeutic tapes.
13. On a separate page in your notebook, recall and write down the many ways that music has empowered your life psychologically, physically, and spiritually. Include your most dramatic, intimate, and emotional memories associated with music. You will begin to realize the importance of sound in your life and recognize its healing potential.

NURSING PROCESS

Assessment

In preparing to use music therapy interventions with clients, assess the following parameters. Assessment parameters outlined in Chapter 11 (Relaxation) and Chapter 12 (Imagery) should also be included because music, imagery, and relaxation cannot be separated.

- the client's music history and the types of music that the client prefers, e.g., classical, popular, country, folk, hymns, jazz, rock, blues, other
- the types of music that the client identifies as making him or her happy, excited, sad, or relaxed
- the types of music that the client identifies as being distasteful and making him or her tense
- the importance of music in the client's life: Is music played at home? In the car? At work? For relaxation? For excitement? For enjoyment? During times of stress? As a means of coping with stress?
- how often (per day or per week) the client listens to music
- whether the client primarily listens to radio, phonograph, or cassette recordings
- whether the client sings (hums) during the day; determine how much and under what circumstances
- whether the client has ever participated in relaxation/imagery techniques combined with music: How long? How regularly?

- if the client uses some type of music for relaxation purposes; if so, ask the client to describe what bodymind responses are evoked by the music
- the client's insight into the use of music to produce psychophysiologic alterations
- the client's mood (iso-principle) that will determine the type of music to choose and the goals of the session

Nursing Diagnoses

Nursing diagnoses compatible with music therapy interventions described in this chapter and that are related to the nine human response patterns of Unitary Person are as follows:

• Exchanging:	(Music therapy can be used to enhance coping and recovery with all diagnoses in this category)
• Relating:	Social isolation
• Valuing:	Spiritual distress
• Choosing:	Ineffective individual coping Noncompliance
• Moving:	Sleep pattern disturbance
• Perceiving:	Alterations in self-concept Disturbance in body-image Disturbance in self-esteem Hopelessness Powerlessness
• Feeling:	Alterations in comfort: pain Anxiety Fear

Client Outcomes

Table 13-1 guides the nurse in client outcomes, outcome criteria, and evaluation for the use of music therapy as a nursing intervention.

Plan and Intervention

Before the Session

- Establish the goals for the session with the client.
- Discuss how music therapy relaxes the bodymind and facilitates relaxation and self-healing.
- Discuss the length of the session, which is usually 20-30 minutes.
- Ask the client to urinate, if necessary.
- Dim the lights.

Table 13-1 Nursing Interventions: Music Therapy

Client Outcome	*Outcome Criteria*	*Evaluation*
1. The client will demonstrate positive physical and psychologic effects in response to music therapy.	1. The client will participate with music therapy in the healing process.	1. The client utilized music one to two times a day to facilitate healing.
	2. The client will select music of choice for listening.	2. The client chose music of choice for listening.
	3. The client will demonstrate positive physical and psychologic effects.	3. The client demonstrated positive physical and psychologic effects.
	Physical effects a. Decreased respiratory rate b. Decreased heart rate c. Decreased blood pressure d. Decreased muscle tension e. Decreased fatigue	Physical effects a. Decreased respiratory rate from 28 to 18 per minute b. Decreased heart rate from 120 to 90 beats per minute c. Decreased blood pressure from 160/100 to 130/70 d. Decreased muscle tension e. Decreased fatigue
	Psychologic Effects a. Positive emotions b. Decreased restlessness and agitation c. Decreased anxiety/ depression d. Increased motivation e. Increased nonverbal expression of feelings f. Increased positive imagery g. Decreased isolation	Psychologic Effects a. Positive emotions b. Decreased restlessness and agitation c. Decreased anxiety and depression d. Increased motivation e. Increased nonverbal expression of feelings f. Increased positive imagery g. Decreased isolation

- Close the drapes.
- Ask the client to remove eyeglasses or contact lenses.
- Ask the client to lie in a supine or semi-Fowler's position. It is sometimes helpful to place a small pillow under the knees to relieve lower back strain. Have a light blanket available for warmth, if needed.
- Spend a few moments centering yourself to be fully present with the client.

Beginning the Session: Script

- The purpose of the session is to relax in a wakeful state and have a quiet experience listening to music.

- First I will guide you in a few exercises to relax.
- Then I will guide you in how to listen to music (of your choice).
- Then you will try to relax for 20 minutes as you listen to the music.
- Now close your eyes if you wish.
- Find a comfortable position with hands at the side of your chest or on your body—whatever is most comfortable.
- At any time, you may change positions, scratch, or swallow.
- There may be noises around, but these will not be important if you concentrate on my voice.
- Guide the client in general relaxation or imagery scripts. Refer to Chapters 11 and 12.

During the Session: Script

- Now, as you continue to relax, I will turn on the music.
- Listen to the music.
- Tell yourself that you would like to go wherever the music takes you.
- Allow yourself to follow the music.
- Let the music suggest to you what to think and what to feel.
- Do not try to analyze the music.
- Allow the music to relax you even more than you are now.
- The music will play for 20 minutes, and I will leave the room.
- I will quietly come back into the room before the music is over.

Closing the Session

- Tell the client, "When the music is over, I will guide you in counting from 5 to 1. You will come back into the room easily and quietly. You will feel very relaxed, calm, and peaceful. Now continue to relax your body and your mind; let the music help you. You will remember the pathways that led you to this new experience and you will be able to find them quickly whenever you wish to return."
- When clients have experience with music, instruct them to finish the session whenever they wish. Suggest that the client will come back to an alert state slowly and quietly.
- While the client is in a self-reflective state, lead him or her in further guided imagery exercises, or journal entries, if desired.

Developing an Audio Cassette Library

Nurses should develop an audio cassette library on each clinical unit or in each practice area. Relaxation, imagery, and music therapy are recommended for use in all clinical settings from the birthing process to the dying process. Tapes can be developed and collected that are of specific benefit to a particular client/patient population. Follow these suggestions to build a successful tape library:

Tapes and Recorders

- Have several tape recorders with comfortable headsets per unit.
- Place all equipment in a safe and convenient location.
- Have a variety of music tapes available. Commercial tapes are relatively inexpensive and readily available. A complete tape library will include music, relaxation, imagery, stress management tapes, and specific tapes for smoking cessation, pre- and postsurgery, weight reduction, pain management, insomnia, self-esteem, subliminal learning, etc. Consider different types of music such as easy listening, light and heavy classical, popular, jazz, hymns, choral, and nontraditional selections.
- Ask staff members to donate one favorite tape to the library.
- Write the different tape companies listed in the Resource list, and request their tape selections and descriptions.
- Encourage nurses to develop tapes for specific client/patient problems that can help with procedures, tests, and treatments. The tapes may or may not have soothing background music.
- Have brochures and catalogues of recording companies available upon request from the patient.
- Encourage use of different tapes for further relaxation, imagery, and stress management training.

Tape/Recorder/Headset Check-Out Procedure

- If tapes are checked out on an outpatient basis, have the client make a deposit for the tape. It is suggested that the deposit cover the cost of the tape in case it is not returned.
- Establish who will have authority to check out the tapes and recorder. If in the hospital, a volunteer could assist in checking out the equipment for the patient after the nurse has assessed the patient's needs and selected the appropriate tape.
- Prepare a sign-out log that records the patient's name, room, date, and check-out time.
- Instruct the patient in the use of the recorder and specific tapes if required.
- Allow 20-30 minutes of listening without interruption twice a day. Place a sign on the client's door stating, "Session in Progress—Do Not Disturb."
- Following the listening session, evaluate the patient's response to the tape and answer any questions.
- Chart the patient's specific response to tape/s. For example, were the desired outcomes achieved, e.g., lowered respiratory rate, decreased heart rate and blood pressure, decreased muscle tension and anxiety? Identify the client's subjective evaluation, e.g., found the experience relaxing, helped with sleep, assisted in coping with pain, assisted with painful procedure, etc.
- Return the tape/recorder/headset to the library and record the check-in information in the log.

Specific Interventions: Music Therapy

Music Bath (Basic)

Purpose: To prepare for a balanced day, prevent stress, and reduce stress.
Time: 20 minutes.
Script: (Prepare the client with a general relaxation script before proceeding with this script. Turn on the music and begin reading the script slowly, pacing the words with the client's increased relaxation). "As the music begins, you will begin a music bath. Allow the sound to wash over you, letting the music touch every surface of your body. Permit the sound to rinse off any tension, unpleasant emotions, and any sound pollution to prepare for the day. . . .

Allow yourself to be immersed in the musical sounds as if you were in a warm, relaxing tub of water or standing under the warm water in a shower. Imagine the water filled with soothing, relaxing sounds. The sounds are cleansing your body and calming your emotions. . . .

As you allow your entire body to become immersed in the sounds, notice how the music resonates in different parts of your body. As you become more relaxed, notice how much more you are enjoying the music (pause).

As the music rinses away your tension, permit yourself to feel refreshed. The music bath has reached every part of your body. You have renewed and refreshed energy (pause).

Allow any remaining tension to be washed away, permitting you to feel balanced, calm, and refreshed.

Continue listening to the music now for 20 minutes. As the music ends, gradually come back into a wakeful, relaxed, and refreshed state."

Expanding the Senses (Basic)

Purpose: To expand awareness, to open up the senses, and to participate in the mingling of the senses.
Time: 10-20 minutes.
Script: (Prepare the client with a general relaxation script before proceeding with this script). "Let the music take you to a soothing peaceful place that is filled with various textures, sights, colors, and sounds. . . .

Take a moment to find this place (pause). You feel comfortable and relaxed in this peaceful place. Slowly begin to explore the surface and texture of your surroundings. Permit the music to help you experience softness, smoothness, and gentleness (pause).

As you continue to explore, discover the colors associated with the shape, texture, and feelings of things. Let the music suggest the sound of the colors and textures.

Touch the things in your environment. Let your fingers, tongue, and cheeks experience the textures. Take time to enjoy each feeling. Do not feel rushed as you explore (pause).

As you touch each thing in your surroundings, take time to investigate its source. Where did it come from? Why does it feel as it does? And why is it here?

With each surface, explore its color, its sound. The deeper you travel into the essence of your surroundings, the richer the experience will be. . . .

Continue this experience for another 10-20 minutes. Gradually come back into the room awake, alert, and ready to continue the day.''

Merging the Bodymind with Music (Basic)

Purpose: To have a quiet listening experience, to mingle the senses, and to produce the relaxation response. (Suggest nontraditional music, with nonmetered beat and periods of silence between sounds. See nontraditional selections in Resources).

Time: 20 minutes.

Script: (Prepare the client with a general relaxation script and then proceed with this script). ''Image your ears. Explore your ears. Feel your ears expanding and becoming larger. Permit your ears to become channels in the sides of your head that open and lengthen throughout your body and into your feet. Allow these channels to hear all parts of your body.

Think of the sounds you are hearing as something more than a pleasant hearing sensation. The sounds are nourishment and energy for your body—your mind-your spirit. . . . Let the sound of the music move in you, around you, above you, below you. The sound is everywhere and you can hear it throughout your body. . . .

See the sound, taste it, feel it, smell it, hear it. Turn the sound into light and color and see it. Concentrate your attention on the sounds and the silence between (pause).

Open your ears. You have beautiful big ears—channels throughout your body. Let the sounds pass through these channels to totally experience the event. Merge with the music. There will no longer be music and a listener, rather a state of total experiencing of the sound. Total concentration of the sound—moment-by-moment and on the silence between (pause). You can go beyond. . . . You will experience the soundless sound, the state where sound becomes silence, silence becomes sound, and they merge together. . . .

Continue the experience for another 10-20 minutes. Gradually come back into the room awake, alert, and ready to continue the day.''

Toning and Groaning (Basic)

Purpose: To release intense emotions, to prepare for meditation, or to induce an altered state of consciousness for music listening.

Time: 10-20 minutes.

Script: ''Lie comfortably on your back. Begin with an audible groan such as ''Ohhh'' or ''Ahhh.'' Let the groan be as deep as possible without forcing it. Let it give you a feeling of release, of emptying out any tension. Feel your skin and bones vibrate with the sound.

Many people spontaneously groan when they have taken off a tight belt or tight shoes. Your groaning should be a comparable release of and freedom from constraint. Let it be loud and natural without forcing the sound (pause). You might even feel a bit silly about groaning. You might giggle or laugh. That's okay. Just let it out. . . .

Stretch your arms and legs now. Then let your body relax and groan again. Notice the sound becoming effortless, relaxing, and deeper. . . . Be sure to let the groan come from deep down in your feet. Notice the vibrations starting up your body. As you continue to groan, feel a weight being lifted from you. Heaviness is being lifted while a sense of lightness sets in (pause). Groaning is a healing process. Allow it to happen. Enjoy the feeling of release. . . .

You will notice a tendency for your voice to rise as your tensions are allowed to leave. Let your voice do what it wants as you continue to groan. It will find its natural place. When your body reaches its tune, it will be satisfied and you will sigh a deep satisfying sigh.

At this point you are toning. You have found your tone. You are sounding your tone. You are resonating with your body. This is your own music. (End session or prepare for imagery scripts, meditation, or music listening).

Training for Skillful Listening (Basic)

Purpose: To become more aware that the art of listening is multifaceted, to improve the art of listening, and to train oneself consciously to hear sounds clearly.

Time: 15 minutes.

Script: ''Concentrate on the sounds around you. Let your ears hear every possible sound. Explore the subtle sounds, breathing, distant cars, wind blowing, hum of the lights. . . .

Limit your sensations. Keep your eyes closed. Avoid touching. Heighten and isolate your perception of sound. Listen to the parts of sound. Listen to a sound. Imagine the sound makes a line. Bend the line that the sound makes. Does it go up? Does it go down? Does it curve or have humps? The word *bend* itself has a bend. Notice the height of the bend. Image the top and bottom of the bend. . . .

Image the grain of the sound. Is it rough or smooth? Rough like sandpaper or smooth like silk or something in between? What is the volume? High/low? What is the intensity? Loud or soft? What color do you associate with the sound? What emotions do you notice as you listen to this sound?

Now use your voice to imitate sound. Imitate the sound of a jet flying high through the air. . . . Now imitate the sound of a helicopter flying through the air. . . . Imitate the sound of a soft wind. . . . Imitate the sound of an autumn leaf falling. The point of this exercise is not to become an expert jet imitator, but to realize there is more to the art of listening and hearing than we think. When you practice focused and conscious hearing, you will recognize subtle differences in sound. You will expand your skills in the art of listening.''

Evaluation

With the client, evaluate whether the outcomes of music therapy (Table 13-1) were successfully achieved. To evaluate the session further, explore the effects of the experience with the client based on the evaluation questions in Exhibit 13-2.

It is important to ask clients to share their experience. The sharing helps evaluate the experience and clarify any misconceptions they may have. Clients may worry if they cannot image, see colors, or feel relaxed. You can reassure them that there is no right response and that all people do not experience the same type of sensations, feelings, sights, or sounds in the same way. Practice with the technique, however, will result in progressively more rewarding experiences. Some people may share that they had a

Exhibit 13-2 Evaluating the Client's Subjective Experience with Music Therapy

1. Was this a new kind of music listening experience for you? Can you describe it?
2. Did you have any visual experiences? Of people, places, or objects? Can you describe them?
3. Did you see any colors while listening? Did the colors change as the music changed?
4. Were you less aware of your surroundings? Were you able to concentrate on the music?
5. Did you like the music?
6. Did the music produce any feelings or emotions?
7. Did you notice any textures, smells, movements, or taste while experiencing the music?
8. Was the experience pleasant?
9. Did you feel relaxed and refreshed after the experience?
10. Would you like to try this again?
11. What would be helpful to make this a better experience for you?

totally different experience than anything else they had felt before. They may discover mind spaces that they never knew existed.

Many clients do not perceive any beneficial effects of the therapy after the first or second sessions. Many express concern that they "cannot do it," that it is "not working," or they have "failed." It is important to allow clients to express these feelings, to explain that there is no right way or failure, and to encourage them to continue to practice the technique a few more times before drawing any conclusions regarding its effectiveness. The desired outcomes of music therapy are relaxation or a hypometabolic response and a psychophysiologic quieting of body-mind-spirit. Clients should understand that relaxation is an acquired skill that requires practice and that the effectiveness of such therapy is usually a function of practice. Because the therapies require skill, the more that clients practice relaxation skills, the better they become in producing changes in their psychophysiology.

Likewise, some people may feel that they need two or three or more sessions with the nurse before they have acquired the skills to practice the technique themselves. In reality, no guide can force or "teach" the client the skills of relaxation. Any changes that occur happen because of the individual's motivation, involvement, and skill and not because a guide is present. As soon as clients realize they can make similar suggestions to themselves to induce relaxation, they are ready to continue the technique alone. Some people may wish to make an audio cassette of the guide's voice during the session or record their own script. The audio cassettes then serves as the guide.

Case Study

Case Study No. 1

Setting:	Coronary care unit in a large teaching military hospital.
Client:	W.R., a 62-year-old male admitted to the coronary care unit with the presumptive diagnosis of acute myocardial infarction
Nursing Diagnosis:	1. Alteration in comfort: Chest pain related to acute myocardial infarction

2. Anxiety related to cardiovascular stressors and acute hospitalization

W.R. was admitted to the coronary care unit (CCU) at 3:00 A.M. because of severe substernal chest pain that radiated to the left shoulder, arm, and hand and was associated with nausea, vomiting, and shortness of breath.

W.R. was the chief of military police at a local military base. He stated that he worked 10-12 hours a day and was a hard-driving individual. He had been in excellent health before this episode and denied any previous hospitalization.

W.R. was attached to a cardiac monitor, was receiving nasal oxygen, had an intravenous nitroglycerin drip infusing, and was on bedrest. He had no current chest pain, and his vital signs and cardiac rhythm were stable. W.R. was assessed to be highly anxious, with clenched fists and jaw, obvious muscle tension, startle reactions to minor noise, and flight of ideas with constant talking.

When asked by the nurse if he wanted to participate in a relaxation exercise that would help him better deal with his admission to the CCU and his illness, W.R., although reluctant, agreed because he said he did not have much else to do.

A music history was elicited from the client, and a soothing classical music tape was selected by the client from the CCU's audio cassette library. The client was supplied with a tape recorder and comfortable headsets. The music was checked for the appropriate volume and then turned off, and the headset was placed at the side of the client's pillow.

A small finger thermistor was taped to the client's left index finger, and his apical heart rate was taken. The nurse guided the client with a head-to-toe relaxation script and continued with the "Merging the Bodymind with Music" script. The headsets were then placed on the client, and he continued the relaxation exercise while listening to music for 20 minutes.

Following the first session, the client stated that he was sure he was not doing it "right" and that he did not wish to try it again. The nurse explained that it was okay if he did not want to participate again. She also explained that there is no "right" way to experience relaxation and that everyone experiences it a little differently. She explained that relaxation is a skill to be learned, like riding a bike, and that, the more people practice the technique, the better they get at doing it. She encouraged the client to try one more session by explaining that the more individuals practice the skills, the better and richer is their response. The client agreed to "try one more" session that afternoon. The nurse also noted that there had been no change in W.R.'s finger temperature or heart rate following the session.

Following the second session, W.R. was noticeably quiet. When the nurse inquired how he perceived the session, W.R. said, "Okay—see you tomorrow." Following the third session, the nurse identified an 8-degree increase in finger temperature and a 10 beat/minute decline in heart rate from presession readings. W.R. had a small grin on his face and stated, "I can't believe what just happened to me. This stuff really works. I felt really relaxed. You know, I have a tough job. I work 10 hours a day. For me, relaxing means having a beer after work or going on a vacation 1 week a year. I have been walking around for 62 years with a stiff neck, and I never knew it. No one ever told me how to really relax. After this [session], I know now that when I thought I was relaxing, I really wasn't. I have never felt like this in 62 years."

The client was transferred out of the CCU to the telemetry unit that afternoon. He stated that he planned to continue his music therapy sessions twice a day during the remainder of his hospitalization and after his return home. The client was given catalogues on relaxation music tapes and informed that such tapes could also be purchased from the hospital's gift shop.

SUMMARY

This chapter has focused on music therapy as a self- regulation intervention. Theory and research validate that music therapy evokes bodymind communications. Specific methods can be used to improve listening, encourage mingling of the senses, and develop a music therapy library. Interventions include the use of various music therapy scripts combined with relaxation.

DIRECTIONS FOR FUTURE RESEARCH

1. Pretest and posttest various types of "relaxing" music to validate that such music is perceived by clients as relaxing.
2. Create a sound-and-color healing room within a hospital setting and evaluate its effects on client recovery.
3. Evaluate several music scripts to determine whether one script is more effective than another in achieving specified outcomes.
4. Evaluate the effects of music therapy versus other forms of self-regulation techniques with various client groups to determine which technique is the most effective for which type of clients.
5. Develop valid and reliable evaluation tools that assess a client's subjective response to music therapy.
6. Evaluate the effects of a music audio cassette library on hospitalized clients' length of stay, recovery, and complications.
7. Evaluate the attitudes and stress level of nurses who routinely use music as a nursing intervention as compared to nurses who do not use music.

NURSE HEALER REFLECTIONS

After reading this chapter, the nurse healer will be able to answer or will begin a process of answering the following questions:

- How do I *feel* about music as a healing ritual?
- How and when do I *sense* my own rhythm?
- What is my *melody?*
- When do I hear my *harmony?*
- How does music help me *remove* the barriers to my inward journey?

- When I listen to music, how do I *allow* myself to let go into the music?
- Am I able to use music with my clients to *facilitate* the healing process?

NOTES

1. Antoine de Saint Exupery, *The Little Prince* (New York: Harcourt, Brace, & World, Inc., 1971), p. 16.
2. Hans Jenny, *The Structure and Dynamics of Waves and Vibrations* (Basel, Switzerland: Basilius Press, 1967), p. 1ff.
3. Steven Halpern and Louis Savary, *Sound Health: The Music and Sounds that Make Us Whole* (San Francisco: Harper & Row, 1985), p. 33.
4. Elaine Daily, ''Hemodynamic Monitoring,'' in *Cardiovascular Nursing: Holistic Practice*, ed. Cathie E. Guzzetta and Barbara M. Dossey (St. Louis: Mosby Year Book, 1992), pp. 182–183.
5. Ibid., pp. 115–116.
6. Steven Halpern and Louis Savary, *Sound Health,* pp. 33–37.
7. Ibid., p. 37.
8. Ibid., p. 39.
9. Cecilia Schulbert, *The Music Therapy Sourcebook* (New York: Human Sciences Press, 1981), p. 13.
10. Peter Michael Hamel, *Through Music to the Self* (Boulder, CO: Shambhala Press, 1979), p. 166.
11. Helen Bonny and Louis Savary, *Music and Your Mind* (New York: Harper & Row, 1973), p. 15.
12. Peter Michael Hamel, *Through Music to the Self,* p. 174.
13. Helen Bonny and Louis Savary, *Music and Your Mind,* p. 14.
14. R. McClellan, ''Music and Altered States of Consciousness,'' *Dromenon* 2 (Winter 1979): 3–5.
15. Ibid., pp. 3–5.
16. S. Krippner, *The Highest State of Consciousness* (New York: Doubleday & Co., 1972), pp. 1-5.
17. Don G. Campbell, *Introduction to the Musical Brain* (St. Louis: MMB Music, Inc., 1984), pp. 14–65.
18. Ibid., p. 54.
19. Ibid., p. 45.
20. Helen Bonny and Louis Savary, *Music and Your Mind,* p. 90.
21. R. Beebe, ''Synesthesia with Music,'' *Dromenon* 2 (Winter 1979): 7.
22. Don G. Campbell, *Introduction to the Musical Brain,* p. 14.
23. I. Altshuler, ''A Psychiatrist's Experience with Music as a Therapeutic Agent,'' in *Music as Medicine,* ed. D. Schullian and M. Schoen (New York: Henry Schuman, 1948), p. 267.
24. R. McClellan, ''Music and Altered States of Consciousness,'' p. 4.
25. Don Campbell, *Introduction to the Musical Brain,* pp. 20–22.
26. Steven Halpern and Louis Savary, *Sound Health,* pp. 39–43.
27. Helen Bonny and Louis Savary, *Music and Your Mind,* p. 30.
28. Jake Page, ''Roses are Red, E-Flat is Too,'' *Hippocrates,* September-October 1987, pp. 63–66.
29. Jean Houston, *The Possible Human* (Los Angeles: J.P. Tarcher, 1982), pp. 47–48.
30. Steven Halpern and Louis Savary, *Sound Health,* p. 183.
31. Ibid., p. 185.
32. Steven Halpern and Louis Savary, *Sound Health,* p. 115.
33. Don Campbell, *Introduction to the Musical Brain,* pp. 62–63.
34. Cecilia Schulbert, *The Music Therapy Sourcebook,* p. 104.
35. Steven Halpern and Louis Savary, *Sound Health,* p. 116.
36. Ibid., p. 119.
37. Ibid., p. 136.

38. Ibid., p. 129.
39. Helen Bonny and Louis Savary, *Music and Your Mind,* p. 31.
40. Steven Halpern and Louis Savary, *Sound Health,* p. 137.
41. Helen Bonny and Louis Savary, *Music and Your Mind,* pp. 96–97.
42. "Guided Imagery and Music Brochure" (Port Townsend, WA: Institute for Music and Imagery, 1986), p. 1ff.
43. Helen Bonny and Louis Savary, *Music and Your Mind,* pp. 13–41.
44. Steven Halpern and Louis Savary, *Sound Health,* p. 58.
45. Cathie E. Guzzetta, *Effects of Relaxation and Music Therapy on Coronary Care Patients Admitted with Presumptive Acute Myocardial Infarction,* Department of Health and Human Services Division of Nursing Grant NU-00824, August, 1987.
46. Steven Halpern and Louis Savary, *Sound Health,* p. 46.
47. Peter Michael Hamel, *Through Music to the Self,* p. 169.
48. Ibid., p. 169.
49. Steven Halpern and Louis Savary, *Sound Health,* p. 98.
50. Ibid., p. 142.
51. Peter Michael Hamel, *Through Music to the Self,* p. 142.
52. Helen Bonny, "Sound Spaces: Music Rx is Proven in the ICU," *ICM West Newsletter* 2, no. 4, (December 1982): 2.
53. Steven Halpern and Louis Savary, *Sound Health,* p. 104.
54. Helen Bonny and Louis Savary, *Music and Your Mind,* p. 43.
55. Bibi Wein, "Body and Soul Music," *American Health,* April, 1987, pp. 67–74.
56. Steven Halpern and Louis Savary, *Sound Health,* p. 150.

SUGGESTED READINGS

Clynes, M. *Music, Mind and Brain*. New York: Plenum Press, 1982.

Drury, N. *Music for Inner Space*. San Leandro, CA: Prism Press, 1985.

Johnston, W. *Silent Music*. London: Collins Press, 1974.

Priestley, M. *Music Therapy in Action*. London: Constable, 1975.

Rudyar, D. *The Magic of Tone and the Art of Music*. Boulder, CO: Shambhala Press, 1982.

RESOURCES

Relaxation, Imagery, and Music Tapes

Bodymind Systems, 910 Dakota Drive, Temple, TX 76504

Halpern Sounds, 1775 Old County Road, #9, Belmont, CA 94002

Mystical Rose Books and Tapes, P.O. Box 38, Malibu, CA 90265

Narada Distributing, 1804 E. North Ave., Milwaukee, WI 53202

Sound of Light, Box 835704, Richardson, TX 75083

Source Distributing and New Age Co-op, P.O. Box 1207, Carmel Valley, CA 93924

Sources Cassette, Dept 99, P.O. Box W, Stanford, CA 94305

Inner Guidance System, GWYNEDD, Plaza 2, Suite 301, Springhouse, PA 19477

Fortuna Records, 11 Kavon Ct., Navato, CA 94947

Aura Communications, P.O. Box 5256, San Diego, CA 92105

Valley of the Sun Publishing, P.O. Box 38, Malibu, CA 90265

Hummingbird Records, P.O. Box 30714, Seattle, WA 98104

Windham Hill Records, P.O. Box 9388, Stanford, CA 94305

Helen Bonny and Louis Savary, *Music and Your Mind* (New York: Harper & Row, 1973). Appendix C: listing of recordings found successful for altering states of consciousness; include classical, inspirational, popular, jazz, rock, Eastern music

Ann McClure and Marilyn Spafford, Institute for Consciousness and Music. A Children's Imagery Cassette.

Music Therapy Tapes Designed for Hospital Use

Music Rx, P.O. Box 173, Port Townsend, WA 98368, 202/385-6160, 202/385-3743

Steven Halpern, Hospital Suite: (long-playing cassettes) See address for Halpern Sounds.

Additional Resources

Institute for Music and Imagery, formerly the Institute for Consciousness and Music (ICM), Historic Savage Mill, 8600 Foundry Street, Savage, MD 20763

National Association for Music Therapy, 1133 15th Street, N.W., Washington, DC 20005, 202/429-9440 (publishes *Journal for Music Therapy*)

chapter **14**

Play and Laughter: Moving Toward Harmony

Leslie Gooding Kolkmeier

> We don't stop playing because we grow old, we grow old because we stop playing.
>
> *Unknown*

> When we laugh, our perception shifts. We let go of feelings of judgment, blame and self-pity to embrace a more extended knowing of ourselves and others. Deliberately taking the time to amuse and be amused allows us to sustain a great deal of change that would otherwise be overwhelming.[1]

Play is part of the richness of life; it enables us to live and grow and become more than we would be without it. As infants and children, we play to learn. As adults, we play to relax, to enjoy interaction with others, to grow, and to gain a different perspective on our lives. Our play can be a variety of activities, from the simple experience of skipping or dancing for the kinesthetic joy of movement, to the excitement of "playing to win" in a tournament or game.

Most animals play for at least some portion of their lives.

> Animals that play are the ones that can benefit from experience, that can learn—both step-by-step and on occasion by leaps of the imagination. The ones that play are those that must learn by discovery and practice, acquiring through trial and error the skills they need to survive.[2]

The form of play that is the focus of this chapter is the noncompetitive, health-promoting, experience of having fun. The chapter also explores the role of humor and laughter in health and the life process.

NURSE HEALER OBJECTIVES

Theoretical

1. Read and understand the definitions and types of play and humor.
2. Understand the differences and advantages of both physical and mental play.
3. List the psychophysiologic responses to play and laughter.

Clinical

1. Integrate preparatory play in your clinical practice.
2. Document the psychophysiologic changes that occur in clients when they allow themselves to be playful.
3. Begin to build a library of humorous stories, jokes, games, cartoons, comedy videotapes or audio cassettes suitable for use in your area of nursing practice.

Personal

1. Identify times during the day when you are playing freely and without guilt, rather than competing.
2. Learn to use playfulness and humor to reduce your tension and anxiety and to reduce fatigue in the middle of difficult days at work and home.
3. Heighten your awareness of your psychophysiologic shifts that come with play, such as increased energy and alertness, decreased heart rate after play, and a change in perception of pain or discomfort.
4. Learn to laugh out loud, practicing alone until you are comfortable with a deep, clear, "belly laugh."

DEFINITIONS

Humor: the quality that appeals to a sense of the comical or the absurdly incongruous[3]; the mental faculty of discovering, expressing, or appreciating wit or comedy; can be kindly and gentle, or sarcastic and bitter; can be intellectual and witty, or broad, slapstick, and visual; the acknowledgement of humor leads to laughter.

Laughter: as defined by Houston:

> the coordinated contraction of 15 facial muscles in a stereotyped pattern and accompanied by altered breathing. Laughter is the loaded latency given us by nature as part of our native equipment to break up the stalemates of our lives and urge us on to deeper and more complex forms of knowing.[4]

Play: a pleasurable, enjoyable activity undertaken spontaneously and without specific goals for productivity; may be physical, as in skipping or dancing, or mental, as in solving word puzzles or lying in the grass and identifying figures in the clouds.

Preparatory Play: play specifically structured to prepare clients for procedures and interventions; designed to allow them to come into imaginary contact with specific people and equipment in a playful, nonthreatening manner before the event; includes playing with models, actual pieces of equipment and instruments, and imitating the anticipated procedure on dolls, stuffed animals, or other figures that simulate the procedure.

THEORY AND RESEARCH

Laughter has been one of our major survival skills since earliest times and follows as a natural extension of the activity of *playing* or being *playful*. The "ability to laugh is one of the most characteristic and deep-seated features of man. Many psychologists and philosophers have even argued that man is the only creature who laughs or has a sense of humor."[5]

Play in Ancient Cultures

Playing is as old as humankind, as evidenced by the remains of toys found in ancient ruins of Egypt, Babylonia, China, and Aztec civilizations.[6] Toys have been buried with the remains of both children and adults, indicating the ancient belief in the need for play not only in this world but the next.

The ancient Greeks wrote of the value of play and toys for the development of children. Plato, in *The Laws,* wrote of the need for play opportunities for children. He felt that children would invent games and playthings naturally, especially when left to play among themselves.[7] According to Erik Erikson:

> Plato saw the model of true playfulness in the need of all young creatures, animal and human, to leap. To truly leap, you must learn how to use the ground as a springboard, and how to land resiliently and safely. It means to test the leeway allowed by given limits; to outdo and yet not escape gravity. Thus, wherever playfulness prevails, there is always a surprising element, surpassing mere repetition or habituation, and at its best suggesting some virgin chance conquered, some divine leeway shared.[8]

Classic Studies in Play

In 1837 Friedrich Wilhelm August Froebel opened the first kindergarten for the education of young children. Believing that children learn best through play, he developed many playthings for the children to help them learn the concepts of color and shape, coordination and cooperation through playing.

Spencer in the 1870s theorized that humans accumulate energy, which must be discharged. Children discharge their surplus energy in the form of play.[9] Adults are more likely to discharge their surplus energy in work activities or more organized and ritualized games.

Groos, around the beginning of the 20th century, postulated that play for children was an imitation of adult activity and preparation for adult performance.[10] He also saw play as a safety valve for the release of children's negative and destructive feelings.[11]

The value of play began to be formally recognized in this country in the late 1800s. The city of Boston opened "sand gardens" for children, which gradually developed into the playground systems we see today in every schoolyard, as well as in small towns and city park areas.

In the 1930s Sigmund Freud and his psychoanalyst daughter Anna described play as a re-enactment of conflicts and unpleasant events in order to master them. Play and its attendant fantasies were also felt to be a projection of wishes.[12] Bettelheim agreed, "Children use play to work through and master quite complex psychological difficulties of the past and present."[13] On this concept is based the vast field of play therapy.

Piaget considered play to be an aspect of intellectual development, a way of learning about the world and solving problems.[14] He divided children's mental development into three periods: (1) the sensorimotor period, lasting until the age of 2; (2) the period of concrete operations, lasting from about 2-7; and (3) the period of formal operations, lasting from about 11-15.[15] Activities that stimulate play and laughter shift as the child develops through these stages. Laughter can be elicited by tickling in the infant and younger child and by more elaborate and subtle jokes and games in older children.

Spitz, in a landmark study done in the 1950s, showed that one of the significant factors that determined the physical and developmental health of institutionalized infants and toddlers was the opportunity and encouragement to play. Children who played alone and with others developed at a normal rate, had an expected amount of resistance to disease, and gained social and motor skills appropriate for their age. Children raised in an environment that prevented interaction with others, and was devoid of playthings and visual and tactile stimuli actually decreased in "developmental quotient" points (a scale similar to intelligence quotient) and failed to learn motor and communication skills. They succumbed to disease at a greater rate than their counterparts who were allowed to play.[16]

Play in Today's Society

Child labor laws, a shorter work week, summer vacations from school, increased leisure time, and higher average family incomes have all led to increased participation in play and recreational activities. As play has become more accepted for both children and adults, teams and competitive sports have replaced simpler forms of play. A high value is placed on winning, rather than on the joys of physical and mental activity. We have become a nation of spectators, rather than a nation of participators.

Nurses and clients are encouraged to consider the benefits of approaching daily life without regard for winning or losing, just for the joy of having fun. We must relearn the skill and excitement of participating, whether in quiet, solitary play or in cooperative active games.

Play is universally felt to be a vital part of a well-rounded lifestyle. The value that play and laughter impart to our lives along the wellness-illness continuum cannot be underestimated.

GENERAL EXPLANATIONS

Bodymind Connections

Play and its natural outcome, laughter, produce a number of psychophysiologic effects. They exercise major body systems, including the cardiovascular system. They are thought to stimulate the release of endorphins, which alter mood and help reduce pain perception.[17] Hearty laughter decreases muscle tonus, thus reducing the anxiety that leads to muscle tightness and tension.[18] The psychophysiologic basis of the smile is thought to be a process of tension relaxation.[19]

In one study subjects were administered either the stimulant epinephrine, normal saline, or the tranquilizer chlorpromazine. They were then shown a humorous film and asked to rate how funny the film was. Those who were physiologically aroused by the injection of epinephrine rated the movie as very funny, those with the saline rated it as moderately funny, and those who received the tranquilizer did not see any humor in the film. "The most intriguing implication of these findings is that even humor, something we generally regard as being so clearly psychological and emotional in basis, has a profound connection with physiological states of the body."[20]

Norman Cousins, in his best-selling book, *Anatomy of an Illness As Perceived by the Patient,* describes in detail the effects of full laughter on the pain of his severe ankylosing spondylitis. Ten minutes of belly laughs induced by watching films of *Candid Camera* and old Marx Brothers movies frequently gave him respite from pain and 2 hours of sound sleep.[21]

Having seen the role played by the neuropeptide-immune-hormone network in Chapter 5 one can easily understand the beneficial effects on the bodymind of the positive emotions generated by play and laughter. When we play and laugh we not only feel better emotionally, we have positively influenced the basis of our physical well-being.

Play in Language

The role of play in our lives is evident in the way it pervades our language; we "toy with ideas" and "play with the possibilities." Even in school and work environments, we learn to "play by the rules" in order to advance. In the language the play concept has even eroded into conscious or unconscious attempts at manipulation, as in "the games people play."

Laughter and Humor As Coping Responses

Laughter eases tensions and may facilitate discussion of more serious matters. The humorist Victor Borge has said, "Laughter is the shortest distance between two people.'' Many difficult discussions are eased into smoothly by a gentle joke or funny comment. The ability to laugh at oneself gives one permission to forgive oneself for imperfections, mistakes, and failures. This then removes the incredible burden of striving to be perfect. Striving to be perfect demands a high degree of self-involvement that stifles the ability to be amused. Timing and appropriateness are vital in these situations and must be carefully assessed before being verbalized.

Clients who are disfigured or otherwise handicapped in a visible manner may adapt to their situation by using a sense of humor to put others at ease and overcome awkward moments. Having a repertoire of one-liners to introduce themselves or help extricate others from embarrassing situations helps these clients cope with their disability in a healthy manner.[22]

Playing versus Winning

''Pure play'' is entirely *different* from the concept of ''winning.'' When we play to win, we are competing, not simply having fun. When we count points scored or try to beat our best time when running, the activity has slipped from the play category into the category of competition. Bettelheim feels that children recognize early on that play is an opportunity for pure enjoyment, whereas games may involve considerable stress. He wrote of one 4-year-old, who when confronted with an unfamiliar play situation, asked, ''Is this a fun game or a winning game?'' It was clear that his attitude toward the activity depended on the answer he was given.[23]

When we truly play, we seek to impress no one, we produce no product, we just enjoy being in the moment. These are not attributes for which we receive external rewards, and therefore nurses and clients may have allowed the skill to atrophy, retreat to a back corner of their beings, and in some cases die.

As we grow older, our ability to ''take the leap,'' as described by Plato, both actually and figuratively, becomes constrained and reserved. Our willingness to laugh and play is frequently replaced by a serious attention to the business at hand and a subsequent reduction in health behaviors.

Playing, much like relaxation, is a skill that in most adults must therefore be relearned. Play and playfulness are often only faint memories for nurses and adult clients. Playing is sometimes difficult to incorporate into our lives again because it does not always fit our image of what is necessary and proper for an adult human. Erikson notes that:

> What seems to become of play as we grow older depends very much on our changing conceptions of the relationship of childhood to adulthood and, of course, of play to work. Adults through the ages have been inclined to judge play to be neither serious nor useful, and thus unrelated to the center of human tasks and motives, from which the adult, in fact, seeks ''recreation'' when he plays. Such a division makes life simpler and permits adults to avoid the often awesome suggestion that playfulness—and, thus, indeterminate chance—may occur in the vital center of adult concerns, as it does in the center of those of children.[24]

We have the opportunity to help clients re-create the joyfulness and play of childhood both through instruction and role modeling. Help patients and clients identify the self-talk that inhibits play. Such self-statements as "act your age," "don't be foolish," or "grow up" stand in the way of health-promoting play and laughter.

Play behaviors need to be reinforced in the face of lifestyle changes, such as are brought about by retirement, recuperation from an illness, or hospitalization. Clients who are able to be playful at times during their adaptation to new circumstances have the best prognosis for surviving change. There is a psychophysiologic basis for this effect:

> When we laugh we dramatically alter our existence on the grid of space and time. At the height of laughter the universe is flung into a kaleidoscope of new possibilities. High comedy, and the laughter that ensues, is an evolutionary event. Together they evoke a biological response that drives the organism to higher levels of organization and integration.[25]

Playfulness in the Work Environment

> It's not the activity you choose that determines whether you're working or playing; it's your attitude toward it that counts. Sustained effort toward a goal, no matter how gratifying, runs you down after a while if it isn't balanced by freedom, spontaneous feeling, and laughter. Work drains your battery; play charges it up.[26]

Nurses turn to humor to defuse the stress of life-and-death situations they face on a daily basis. This form of humor can relieve tension and stabilize high-stress situations, but must be used with caution. Some of this humor is dangerous and destructive if used carelessly. Always presume that a client can hear your comments, even if he or she appears to be comatose. Hearing is the sense that is maintained longest.

The Game of Games

Leonard, a New Games enthusiast, reminds us of what it is like to become a player in the game of living instead of a spectator[27]:

> An athlete in the Game of Games is one who plays life intensely, with heightened awareness of this endeavor. An Athlete is one who can perceive discord and harmony both, who can accept contradiction as the very stuff of play while not losing sight of the ultimate harmony. An athlete in this Game plays voluntarily and wholeheartedly, even while realizing that this Game is not all that is; knows the rules and limitations of play, and sees beauty in the order thus imposed; seeks to expand any frontier available and yet is not unmindful of ethical imperatives and the needs of others. This athlete contends in a game for a prize, and the prize is play itself, a life fully experienced and examined.

The athlete in the Game of Games may be a musician or a carpenter, a householder or a yogi, an Olympic runner or a farmer. No one can be excluded merely because of occupational specialty, and differences between the purely physical and nonphysical begin to fade. It is only through a heresy in Western thought that we could consider any aspect of life as "nonphysical." The body is always involved, even in what we call the most cerebral pursuit. Einstein tells us that the Special or Restricted Theory of Relativity came from a feeling in his muscles. Surely he was a great athlete of the Game of Games, in which we are all embodied. Embodiment is indeed the primary condition of play. When Western philosophy and theology attempted to cut away the body from the Higher Life, the Life of the Mind, the attempt failed. The body, unacknowledged, remained a part of every formulation. To the precise extent that it has been ignored, Western thought has become fragmentary and misleading.

Spirit in flesh, flesh in spirit. Abstractions in the muscles, visions in the bones. We can no longer deny the conditions of embodiment—nor can we ever entirely explain them. However far we pursue the mystery, it finally eludes us. The "answer" lies in the unsayable statement, the unprovable proposition that prevents paradox and foreclosure. There are no closed systems. The body opens us to wonders in this and other worlds. Its movements through space and time can launch us on a timeless voyage to a place beyond place.

NURSING PROCESS

Assessment

In preparing to use play and laughter interventions with clients, assess the following parameters:

- the client's ability and willingness to smile and laugh
- the appropriateness of the client's sense of humor and laughter
- the client's attitude toward the ideas of play and laughter
- the kinds of humor that the client has enjoyed in the past
- the client's ability to read or watch videotapes
- the client's physical limitations that would influence his or her ability to engage in play activities
- the client's previous experience with play
- how long it has been since the client has engaged in playful activities

Nursing Diagnoses

Nursing diagnoses compatible with the interventions described in this chapter and that are related to the nine human response patterns of Unitary Person are as follows:

• Relating:	Parenting, alteration in: actual or potential Social isolation
• Choosing:	Coping, ineffective individual and family
• Moving:	Activity intolerance: actual or potential Diversional activity, deficit Mobility, impaired physical
• Perceiving:	Powerlessness Self-concept, disturbance in: self-esteem, role performance, personal identity Sensory-perceptual alteration: visual, auditory, kinesthetic, gustatory, tactile, olfactory
• Knowing:	Thought processes, alteration in
• Feeling:	Anxiety Comfort, alteration in: pain Fear Violence, potential for: self-directed or directed at others

Client Outcomes

Table 14-1 guides the nurse in client outcomes, outcome criteria, and evaluation for the use of play as a nursing intervention.

Plan and Interventions

Before the Session

- Practice smiling and laughing out loud in front of a mirror or on a videotape until you are comfortable with your ability to do so.
- Gain experience with the techniques you intend to employ in order to know which to use and how best to use it.
- Center yourself before making contact with the client.
- Sense your own needs and evaluate your own stress load.
- Review the client's chart or consult with others to become familiar with any changes in the situation since you last met.
- Have supplies, such as tape recorder, books, drawings, cartoons, or videotapes, on hand in working condition.

Beginning the Session

- Assess the client according to the assessment parameters.
- Record vital signs and have client verbally assess pain, anxiety, or tension level on a numerical scale, i.e., "My pain level right now is a 6 on a 1 (no pain) to 10 (extreme pain) scale."

Table 14-1 Client Outcomes

Outcomes	*Outcome Criteria*	*Evaluation*
1. Client will engage in playful activities.	1. Client will engage in playful activities as demonstrated by: a. increased occurrence of smiling b. volunteering of puns, jokes, stories, riddles, or other forms of humor c. participation in active or passive games, alone or with other players	1. Client was observed playing cards with a family member during evening visiting hours. Client requested two comedy films from the unit library in 1 week. Client greeted afternoon shift nurse with corny "knock-knock" joke.
2. Client will exhibit appropriate spontaneous laughter.	2. Client will smile or laugh appropriately when presented with humorous greeting cards, comedy films, audiotapes, jokes, stories, etc.	2. Client was heard laughing in response to a comedy audio cassette loaned from the unit library. Client laughed when describing learning to eat soup with her nondominant, uninjured hand.
3. Client will have a decrease in subjective severity of target symptom as a result of the play/laughter intervention.	3. Client will grade severity of symptom on a 1 to 10 scale before and after the intervention, grading it at a lesser level after the intervention.	3. Client graded pain level at 6 before playing the video game and graded pain level at 3 (on 1 to 10 scale) after playing the game.

- Describe to the client the benefits and psychophysiologic changes that may be expected from the intervention.
- Provide the client with appropriate materials and instruction.

During the Session

- Use all interventions with empathy and sensitivity to the client.
- Provide support for the client in terms of your physical presence, encouragement, or time alone if the client desires to read or watch a videotape of humorous material. Remember that humor is contagious and social. The intervention may be most effective if used with a group, rather than individually.
- Remember that humor and play are spontaneous and therefore are most successful when not precisely planned.
- Continue to evaluate the mood and response of the client and flow with the perceived needs.

Closing the Session

- Record vital signs and have client re-evaluate pain or discomfort level on a 1 to 10 scale.

- Discuss the intervention with the client and obtain feedback for future sessions.
- Answer any questions that the client may have.
- Encourage further work on an individual basis.
- Arrange for follow-up sessions.

Specific Interventions: Play

Cultivating Spontaneous Silliness (Basic)

Some nurses and clients may have difficulty employing and participating in what they perceive as being ''silly'' behavior. Begin simply by doing a familiar activity in a different way:

- Part hair on the opposite side.
- Eat with the nondominant hand.
- Put socks on last.
- Go to therapy by a different route.
- Pretend you are someone else.

Help clients remember youthful tricks, such as pretending to be asleep, moving food around on a plate to give the impression of it having been eaten, or identifying images in cloud formations. Ask your patients how old they would be if they did not know their age.

Encourage visualization with humor: picture a disagreeable teacher as an animal or the forbidding authority figure dressed only in underwear. Helping a client deal with difficult people in humorous ways gives the client a sense of control and perspective.

Playing Games (Basic to Advanced)

Games are a form of play upon which we have imposed rules and rituals. Games usually imply an element of competition and can therefore easily lose some of the spontaneity of pure play. However, because games may require less physical activity than some other forms of play, they may be appropriate for the client who may be confined to bed or coping with decreased physical abilities.

Cards, board games, puzzles, and word games are appropriate for clients with decreased mobility and may encourage socializing and decrease isolation. They can be played in a particular area of an inpatient facility, outdoors, or in a client's room. Nurses or hospital volunteers may maintain and distribute game materials to clients from a central location, or each nursing area may have a game drawer or shelf with supplies.

For clients who are more physically active, the nurse is encouraged to learn about New Games. According to its founders:

> New Games is an attitude that encourages people to play together. To learn only the form and not the essence would be to miss the lifeline that gives rise to

> that attitude. Solely for the purpose of having fun, we can be free and foolish in the arena of New Games and let the spirit carry us.[28]

Various New Games are appropriate for two to several dozen players. They combine physical activity with spontaneity (if you do not like the rules you are encouraged to change them), develop physical and social skills, and provide very little chance of incurring injury.

Cartoon Collections (Basic)

The value of humor in coping with the tension of hospitalization and illness is obvious in the selection of funny greeting cards one finds displayed in client's rooms. Keeping a scrapbook of cartoons or jokes related to hospital life can help pass time for both clients and families. Encouraging staff members, as well as clients and families, to add to the collection helps develop a sense of camaraderie. Some clients may choose to draw their own cartoons based on their hospital experiences.

As with all play and laughter interventions, great care and sensitivity must be used when dealing with clients and families. This is particularly important during an acute event when there may be great uncertainty and concern for the client's outcome. Evaluate the emotional status of the client or family member carefully before suggesting any playful intervention.

Humorous Books, Audio, and Videotapes (Basic to Advanced)

The health-promoting effects of laughter evoked by humorous material have been well publicized by the works of Cousins, Simonton, and others. Because humor is a very individual experience, it is appropriate to have a large choice of materials to offer to the client who chooses to take part in this type of intervention. With the advent of videotape players and tiny personal audiotape players, the use of these materials is within the reach of almost all health care facilities.

Audio and videotapes especially lend themselves to use with groups, increasing opportunity for clients to interact with one another and build upon a framework of common appreciation and experiences. Cassette tapes are available that contain nothing but 20 minutes of laughter. Listening to them can be a delightful way to help a group relearn the joy of being silly.

Evaluation

The nurse must evaluate with the client whether the outcomes established before the session (Table 13-1) were met. Some of the interventions described in this chapter may take place over days or weeks and must therefore be periodically reviewed and re-evaluated. The process of developing playfulness and a sense of humor in a client takes time, and continued support and feedback are necessary.

Case Studies

Case Study No. 1:

Setting: Outpatient clinic using bubble blowing for a breathing exercise
Client: J.B., 45-year-old woman with adult-onset intrinsic asthma
Nursing Diagnoses:
1. Activity intolerance
2. Anxiety
3. Breathing pattern: ineffective
4. Fear
5. Powerlessness, all related to the diagnosis of asthma

J.B. had been seen in the clinic for treatment of her asthma over a period of several months. Her bronchodilator medications had been adjusted, she was using a cool mist to thin secretions, her activity level had increased, and she had returned to full-time employment.

In the process of teaching J.B. breathing techniques it was determined that she had difficulty maintaining prolonged exhalation. She was able to lengthen her expiratory time between attacks, but would forget the intervention when under the stress of wheezing and shortness of breath.

She arrived at the clinic in mild distress after using an inhaler to open her airways with only partial success. After sitting J.B. in a straight chair, the nurse began coaching her breathing pattern while applying gentle pressure on her shoulders with each exhalation. As her breathing became easier the nurse opened a bottle of bubble solution and invited J.B. to blow bubbles. J.B. felt this was a rather nontraditional approach to her condition, but agreed to participate.

In order to blow bubbles successfully one must exhale slowly and for a long period of time. J.B. quickly remembered this from her childhood and from playing with her own children. She was soon blowing long streams of fragile bubbles, her wheezing disappearing as she did so. As the attack eased, the nurse coached J.B. to visualize the bubbles as containing her tension triggers and watching them float away. J.B. expressed delight with her new application of an old skill. Her tension decreased, and she returned to work confident in her ability to apply her skill during stressful situations. Linking the skill with an unusual and playful activity made the breathing strategy stand out in her memory and easier to recall under stress.

Case Study No. 2

Setting: Pediatric oncology unit; using preparatory play to prepare for chemotherapy
Client: F.W., a 7-year-old boy
Nursing Diagnoses:
1. Anxiety
2. Coping, ineffective individual
3. Diversional activity, deficit
4. Fear
5. Powerlessness
6. Social isolation: all related to diagnosis of acute lymphocytic leukemia

F.W. had been diagnosed with leukemia only a few days before his first contact with the play group organized for pediatric patients on the oncology service. His diagnostic workup had been prolonged and frightening for him, and he had become more withdrawn, tearful, and frightened as the days went by. Knowing that a course of chemotherapy was to begin shortly and aware of F.W.'s terror response to needles and intravenous setups, the nurse invited F.W. and his mother to join her and several children in the playroom.

F.W. clung to his mother, but was able to sit on her lap at the periphery of the group as they began to play with stuffed dolls, intravenous bags of water, tape, and, under close supervision, intravenous needles. He listened and watched intently as the nurse helped the children start intravenous lines in the dolls' arms and hands, and he soon began to venture closer to the group. By the second day of watching the other children, F.W. began to take part in the activities. He played with the tubing and needles and talked encouragingly to his doll as he rehearsed the chemotherapy procedure as coached by the nurse and the other children.

During his first chemotherapy treatment F.W. took his rehearsal doll with him into the treatment room. He cried quietly, but sat still on his mother's lap and even corrected the nurse's technique when she began to tape the intravenous needle somewhat differently than how F.W. had rehearsed with his doll.

As his therapy progressed F.W. became more confident and began to participate actively in the playroom. He was still frightened of his chemotherapy sessions, but endured them without his original terror. Within a week of his first encounter with the preparatory play dolls and equipment, he was explaining the process to a new patient.

SUMMARY

Whether helping a client through a difficult procedure or strengthening our own ability to move smoothly through a shift assignment, humor and playfulness help keep us centered and whole. Humor can help us tap into the spiritual and evolutionary possibilities inherent in all events.

DIRECTIONS FOR FUTURE RESEARCH

1. Determine the physiologic changes that occur with the use of play and laughter.
2. Develop toys and games as interventions for specific nursing diagnoses.
3. Evaluate the degree of decrease in anxiety when preparatory play is used.

NURSE HEALER REFLECTIONS

After reading this chapter the nurse healer will be able to answer or begin a process of answering the following questions:

- Can I recall the *kinesthetic imagery* of weightlessness and timelessness at the top of a wonderful, tall swing?
- What is my *inner sense of joy* when I hear myself or another laugh out loud?
- Do I *nurture* my ability and the ability of my clients to be playful?
- Can I play *freely* and *without guilt,* even when my work is not yet finished?
- Do I play *without competing* or feeling that I must accomplish a particular goal?

NOTES

1. Jeanne Segal, *Feeling Great* (Van Nuys, CA: Newcastle Publishing Company, Inc., 1981), p. 68.
2. Maria W. Piers and Genevieve Millet Landau, *The Gift of Play* (New York: Walker and Co., 1980), p. 19.
3. *Webster's New Collegiate Dictionary* (Springfield, MA: G. and C. Merriam Co., 1951), p. 403.
4. Jean Houston, *The Possible Human* (Los Angeles: Jeremy P. Tarcher, Inc., 1982), p. 119.
5. Raymond A. Moody, *Laugh after Laugh: The Healing Power of Human,* (Jacksonville, FL: Headwaters Press, 1978), p. xiii.
6. Lillian Frankel, "Play," in *The World Book Encyclopedia,* (Chicago: Field Enterprises Educational Corp., 1975), p. 506.
7. Frank and Theresa Caplan, *The Power of Play* (New York: Anchor Press/Doubleday, 1973), p. 256.
8. Erik H. Erikson, *Toys and Reasons* (New York: W.W. Norton and Co., Inc., 1977), p. 17.
9. Catherine Garvey, *Play* (Cambridge, MA: Harvard University Press, 1977), p. 3.
10. Ibid., p. 3.
11. Frank and Theresa Caplan, *The Power of Play,* p. 267.
12. Susanna Millar, *The Psychology of Play* (New York: Jason Aronson, Inc., 1974), p. 30.
13. Bruno Bettelheim, "The Importance of Play," *Atlantic Monthly,* March 1987, p. 35.
14. Susanna Millar, *The Psychology of Play,* p. 58.
15. Robert G. Weyant, "Jean Piaget," in *World Book Encyclopedia* (Chicago: Field Enterprises Educational Corp., 1975), p. 397.
16. Piers and Landau, *The Gift of Play,* pp. 23–25.
17. Lyda Hill and Nancy Smith, *Self-Care Nursing* (Englewood Cliffs, NJ: Prentice-Hall, Inc., 1985), p. 228.
18. Raymond Moody, *Laugh after Laugh,* p. 5.
19. Catherine Garvey, *Play,* p. 20.
20. Raymond Moody, *Laugh after Laugh,* p. 8.
21. Norman Cousins, *Anatomy of an Illness as Perceived by the Patient* (New York: W.W. Norton and Co., 1979), pp. 39–40.
22. Raymond Moody, *Laugh after Laugh,* p. 26.
23. Bruno Bettelheim, "The Importance of Play," p. 37.
24. Erik Erikson, *Toys and Reasons,* p. 18.
25. Jean Houston, *The Possible Human,* p. 119.
26. Robert S. Eliot and Dennis L. Breo, *Is it Worth Dying For?* (New York: Bantam Books, 1984), p. 157.
27. Andrew Fleugleman, ed., *The New Games Book* (Garden City, NY: Dolphin Books/Doubleday and Co. Inc., 1976), p. 188.
28. Ibid., p. 20.

SUGGESTED READINGS

Carse, James P. *Finite and Infinite Games*. New York: The Free Press, 1986.

Pearce, Joseph Chilton. *Magical Child*. New York: E.P. Dutton, 1977.

Pearce, Joseph Chilton. *Magical Child Matures*. New York: E.P. Dutton, 1985.

Robinson, Vera. *Humor and the Health Professional*. Thorofare, NJ: Charles B. Slack, 1977.

chapter **15**

Relationships: Learning the Patterns and Processes

Barbara Montgomery Dossey

> One cannot truly accept others unless one also accepts oneself, and self-acceptance at any level is essential for satisfying relationships. In the absence of self-acceptance, relationships with an intimate other, with family, community, the world, nature, and the universe may be confined to fulfillment of social role expectations. If every encounter with another is viewed as an opportunity to heal and be healed and extend love, one may learn to heal and be healed in a relationship.[1]
>
> *Frances Vaughan*

This chapter explores the following aspects of relationships: systems theory, bodymind influences on wellness and illness, and strategies/interventions to strengthen and bring about healing in relationships.

All of our lives we search for answers to questions about living. Our relationships can provide us with many aspects of these answers, for they help us recognize blind spots within ourselves. A healing relationship is present if that relationship nurtures expression of feeling, needs, and desires and helps remove barriers to love.

Wholeness and healing can exist only when we have meaningful relationships. The major factor that determines the quality of our relationships is the extent to which we are willing to work on ourselves, that is to take responsibility for understanding ourselves. We cannot know who we are unless we are aware of our interconnectedness with other people. Qualities of healthy relationships exist when we exhibit mutual love, sharing, and the ability to forgive ourselves and others.

NURSE HEALER OBJECTIVES

Theoretical

1. Study the information on family systems.
2. Identify characteristics of open and closed systems.

Clinical

1. Identify core elements that need to be present in a nurse, counselor, therapist, or healer for a therapeutic relationship to be established.
2. Study the interventions and discuss them with a colleague.

Personal

1. Identify at least one person whom you are close to, and share some special feelings with that person about your relationship.
2. Use more "I" than "you" statements to enhance sharing of feelings.
3. Be aware of sharing love with your family and friends.
4. Choose specific times to be alone to reflect on your relationships.
5. Practice forgiveness with yourself and others on a daily basis.

DEFINITIONS

Aloneness: being by oneself for solitude and self-reflection.

Counseling: interactive therapeutic process between nurse and client/family characterized by the qualities of acceptance, authenticity, and empathy; use of a variety of interventions that focus on the feelings, needs, problems, and challenges of the client that interfere with the client's adaptive behavior.

Crisis: any sharp or decisive change for which old patterns of behavior are inadequate, leading to disorganization and degrees of dysfunction.

Forgiveness: canceling our expectations of perfection in ourselves and others.

Intimacy: involves trust and the ability to share deepest levels of the self, including hurts.

Loneliness: a melancholy state that exists due to the absence of significant relationships or our lack of ability to engage in them.

Love: the human quality of being open to feelings that allow understanding and awareness of caring, seeing goodness, and forgiveness of self, others, animals, and all living creatures.

Relationships(Healthy): finding one, two, or more nonjudgmental people with whom you can share your hurts, failures, successes, interests, and excitements; people who facilitate and accelerate your life potentials.

Resources: facts, basic options, means, and opportunities available to people whereby they can improve and help themselves and others.

Self-Validation: one's capacity to express that self-worth is present.

Spontaneity: flexibility and acting in accordance with a natural, unstaged feeling.

Stressor: (negative) a situation, event, or change for which a person has had little or no prior preparation, or cannot effectively cope; (positive) an event or change that motivates a person toward reaching life potentials.

THEORY AND RESEARCH

Patterns in Family Systems and Relationships

In order to view the client as a whole person, the client's family or significant relationships must be considered. No person can live in constant or perpetual isolation and be healthy. The involvement of a person with the environment, relationships, and one's total life experiences are so interrelated that if one part is separated, it is impossible for the person to reach his or her maximal potentials.

In counseling others toward greater harmony and health, the sequences, patterns, simultaneous events, and circular reactions that occur within families and relationships must be recognized. In family system theory the repetitive patterns and sequences seen in families are referred to as the " family system."[2] A change in behaviors on the part of any family member automatically interrupts the system in either a positive or negative direction. Continuous actions, reactions, and actions of people in response to actions produce a state referred to as a "reverberating feedback loop."[3] For example, a family in chaos fails to sit together to talk about the event that produced the chaos. Instead, there are a number of individual reactions, each of which makes known only a small portion of the event. If they would sit together to hear each others' perception of the event, then there would be more chance of working as a cohesive family unit rather than continuing in a state of chaos. Each member then is able to interpret the experience, as well as listen to the other family members' experience. Although this discussion focuses on family, the same patterns and sequences are seen in all close relationships.

Each family unit has a set of many behaviors. Take for example, a family where daughter Ann lives with her father and mother and brother. In order to form a complete picture of Ann as a family member, it is important to see how she experiences and behaves in all of the following individual, dyad, and triad situations:

- Ann alone
- Ann with her mother
- Ann with her father
- Ann with her brother
- Ann with her mother and father
- Ann with her mother and brother
- Ann with her father and brother
- Ann with her mother, father, and brother

As shown with this small family, one can view Ann in eight different relationships, as well as viewing each other family member in eight different relationships. It is easy to see how family scenarios can become so complex. Think how these dyads and triads are multiplied after a divorce when parents remarry and there are increased sets of siblings, step siblings, grandparents, step-grandparents, aunts, uncles, and cousins, and so on. Patterns and characteristics of family systems and personal relationships are extremely changeable and fluid.

Characteristics of Open and Closed Systems

In order to apply systems theory to the family and any other relationship, the nurse should recognize the following family or relationship system characteristics[4]:

- **Change:** a shifting of components or relationships within a system (first-order change) or new information entering the system from outside the systems boundaries (second-order change).
- **Viability:** an ability of the system to change and re-form, regulate itself, and adjust collectively to encountered stress.
- **Entropy:** increased randomness and increased disorder within the system.
- **Open System:** constant state of influx of new information within a system that allows new input and the constant succession of necessary adjustments to unending changing inputs.
- **Closed System:** a system that rearranges present structure without incorporating new information from outside the system; the only change within this system is first-order, but according to rigid, inflexible rules.
- **Boundaries:** a continuum of permeable to impermeable borders that acts as a filter to separate the people within the system from the elements of the environment outside. In open systems some boundaries are flexible and become blurred as they merge with another. In closed systems boundaries are totally closed off from one another and are described as rigid and inflexible.
- **Homeodynamic:** a mechanism whereby a system scans itself to bring about balance at all times.
- **Feedback:** information that a system receives about itself that is used to maintain or regain homeostasis.
- **Interconnectivity:** the interlocking network of a system whereby a structure is able to endure under stress because of the collective strength of the whole.
- **Enmeshment:** the interlocking network that allows for no new input, thereby becoming entangled and deeply involved in an unhealthy manner, adding to the confusion of the system.
- **Individuation:** the ability of a system to encourage an individual to develop unique style and characteristics and be accepted by the system.

An *open family system* is one that is able to change and re-form. A metaphor for an open family might be a bay that allows tidewaters to flow in and out to refresh itself. It can create new states while at the same maintaining boundaries that make it a system. An open system has great viability to integrate first- and second-order changes. There are stated and unstated rules that allow the system to maintain openness to new ideas and to adjust collectively to the changes that occur within the system. There is also flexibility within an open system. Family members are encouraged to pursue individuality, role versatility, and new roles. Open family systems also allow interconnection between and among members, and individual boundaries become blurred/blended without overinvolvement. In times of stress family members band together to strengthen the family unit.

A *closed family system* tends to isolate itself from the community. Members do not become involved in community or with each other and in fact there may be spoken or unspoken rules that forbid input and output of information. Rigidity, inflexibility, adherence to roles, and discouragement of individuality are characteristics of the closed family system. There tends to be an overinvolvement; an enmeshment leads to pathology. A closed family system responds to stress in a rigid way. If resources become unavailable, they do not look outside the system for new alternatives. Over time the family will either disintegrate, with a healthier member breaking away from the system or the system will be so destabilized that significant pathology begins to manifest. Often, enmeshed family members under stress form alliances and work against other family members, rather than bonding together for a more cohesive system.

GENERAL EXPLANATIONS: RELATIONSHIPS

Bodymind Connections: Relationships

A major thrust of current research in psychophysiology is the study of all the variables that influence verbal and nonverbal communication with the autonomic, immune, endocrine, and neuropeptide systems. Because our relationships evoke every conceivable emotion and communication pattern available to us, they have a significant impact on our physiologic state. Communication patterns and our openness to dealing with our emotions affect our health.

Research into the effect of stress indicates that we react to stress in direct correlation to the way we perceive it. When we do not perceive an event as being stressful, our bodymind will not be as negatively affected by the stress. Those who are exposed to high levels of stress and who have a poor social network are most susceptible to illness.[5] Strong social networks can act as *stress buffers* by decreasing the stress of being present to help a person through a crisis or cope more effectively with a new challenge, such as a job promotion or returning to school. There is no doubt that when people nurture relationships their social networks can have a significant health-maintaining influence across the life span.

Relationships: Counseling versus Psychotherapy

Nurses can be involved in both counseling and psychotherapy. A basic nursing education prepares a nurse to counsel clients, whereas psychotherapy requires advanced education and training. Counseling occurs in a setting in which a client exhibits normative behavior; its goals are focused on coping behaviors.[6] In contrast, psychotherapy is indicated when a client exhibits severe personality disorders or pathologic behaviors. However, one does not have to demonstrate pathologic behavior to begin psychotherapy. For example, a person who recognizes that he or she needs help with stopping smoking, weight reduction, or changing certain relationship patterns in a marriage might seek the expertise of a nurse trained in advanced psychologic skills. Major areas that nurses focus on in counseling clients and families are struggles and challenges of life roles, individual/family priorities, and intimacy.

A counselor involved in a therapeutic relationship must possess these qualities[7]: (1) acceptance of the client's intrinsic worth and dignity, (2) empathy that conveys to a client that feelings are valued, which facilitates the client's disclosure of personal information, and (3) genuineness and congruency, which conveys that counselor's honesty and personal caring to the client.

The counseling process has three overlapping stages[8]:

1. Initial phase—the establishment of a therapeutic relationship. Goals are established, and there is discussion about the length of sessions.
2. Working or maintenance phase—the focus is on the client's self-understanding and self-regulation, and learning alternative health behaviors using active and passive techniques. Refer to Table 15-1 which provides a summary of counseling techniques and strategies.
3. Closure and termination—The client is utilizing new behaviors in daily living. Termination is mutually agreed upon.

Defenses in Relationships

Defenses are learned at an early age and are a way of protecting our self-image. They are used so routinely and unconsciously that they hinder authenticity in our communication with the important people in our lives. The degree with which defenses are used determines the blocks within relationships. The major defenses used are:

- **Denial:** the refusal to acknowledge or see what one does not wish to see or does not wish to cope with; for example, a refusal to acknowledge that a friend or mate is drinking too much, thus producing enabling behavior.
- **Projection:** shifting blame onto others or shifting one's own feelings onto another; for example, calling work colleagues competitive and aggressive when, in fact, one's own behavior reflects these characteristics.
- **Rationalization:** the process whereby one explains and justifies feelings, thoughts, and actions that one has previously thought to be unacceptable; for example, one explains in great detail why an angry outburst was totally appropriate toward a mate when anger is typically avoided at all costs.
- **Reaction Formation:** the process whereby one becomes or exhibits that which one fears or wants to avoid; for example, a young girl prides herself on thinness and becomes adamant about obesity. She represses her fear of becoming obese and she starts hating all people who are the least bit overweight. (This pattern may lead to anorexia nervosa.)
- **Repression:** the process of selectively forgetting unpleasant memories or tasks to be done; for example, repressing uncomfortable events in one's past or present often prevents one from communicating authentically.
- **Regression:** the process of reverting to an earlier level of behavior or stage of development to avoid anxiety, fear, and responsibility; for example, a woman going through a divorce returns home to have her parents care for her and provide her with basic needs for an indefinite period of time. (If she returned only on a temporary basis, this action would not be considered a defense mechanism, but a supportive family relationship.)

Table 15-1 Common Counseling Strategies

Strategies	*Description*	*Uses*
Active listening	An attitude of total attentiveness focusing on the client's expression of both verbal and nonverbal behavior	Most effective tool to communicate counselor empathy with the client To provide cues to the client's inner experience To minimize the counselor's tendency to make premature judgment
Questioning	Inquiring or asking for more information in the form of a question	To clarify a matter which is open to discussion; to minimize doubt or uncertainty To facilitate client exploration of a problem or situation
Reflecting	Restating or rephrasing the content or feeling of a client's statement (one type of active listening)	To understand the meaning of what the client is trying to express in either behavior or speech
Clarifying or interpreting	Stating the client's message with additional feedback or explanation	To increase the clearness of communication between counselor and client
Providing information or feedback	Using professional expertise to transmit pertinent information into facts, data, responses	To add to current knowledge or relate new knowledge to prior understanding
Selecting or weighing alternatives	Assisting the client to list and prioritize all possible alternatives to a problem	To aid in expanding options and narrowing choices May facilitate the client's experimentation with unfamiliar options in a nonthreatening setting
Confrontation	Verbalizing the discrepancy between the client's feelings and behaviors (between real and ideal self)	To focus the client's awareness on actions that are incongruent with self-image and actual behavior
Tests and appraisal tools	Using psychological paper and pencil tests or other appraisal tools which the counselor can administer and interpret	To help increase client self-awareness To add to the counselor's data base about the client (Examples: self-inventory of cardiac risk factors or the Holmes and Rahe Social Readjustment Rating Scales)
Self-disclosure	Revealing selected aspects of one's own experiences or personality	To foster genuineness and trust in the counseling situation when used appropriately

Source: Reprinted from *Nursing Interventions: Treatments for Nursing Diagnoses* by G. Bulechek and J. McClosky, p. 106, with permission of W.B. Saunders Company, © 1985.

NURSING PROCESS

Assessment

In preparing to use relationship interventions with clients, assess the following parameters:

- the client's perception of the problem/situation with a person or specific relationships. Obtain part by part *who* is doing *what* (that presents a problem), to *whom,* and *how* does the behavior constitute a problem.
- how the problem is currently being handled
- the client's minimal goals in regard to the perceived problem and set priorities
- the client's position in the relationship/current problem
- the client's body and verbal language as the situation is being described
- how long the problem has existed and why the client seeks help at this time
- the client's perception of all the people involved in the situation. If appropriate meet the people involved
- what behaviors the client would like to possess or determine what the client would consider to be a more desirable situation

Nursing Diagnoses

Nursing diagnoses compatible with the interventions described in this chapter and that are related to the nine response patterns of Unitary Person include:

- Relating: Parenting, Alteration in
  Sexual dysfunction, Alteration in
- Valuing: Spiritual distress
- Choosing: Coping, Ineffective individual or family
  Family Process, Alteration in
- Moving: Self-care deficit
  Self-care dysfunction
- Feeling: Anxiety
  Grieving
  Violence
  Fear
  Rape-Trauma

Client Outcomes

Table 15-2 guides the nurse in client outcomes, outcome criteria, and evaluation for the use of relationships in nursing intervention.

Table 15-2 Nursing Interventions: Relationships

Client Outcome	*Outcome Criteria*	*Evaluation*
The client will recognize family and relationship systems patterns	1. The client will verbalize the dynamics that occur within the family and relationship system.	1. The client verbalized the dynamics that occurred within the family and relationships systems.
	2. The client will state the difference between open and closed relationships systems.	2. The client stated the difference between open and closed relationships systems.
	3. The client will recognize the stressors and resources in living.	3. The client recognized the stressors and resources in living.
	4. The client will become aware of the effects of relationships of health and illness.	4. The client became aware of the effects of relationships of health and illness.
	5. The client will be able to identify the human needs that are fulfilled by quality relationships.	5. The client was able to identify the human needs that are fulfilled by quality relationships.
	6. The client will recognize bodymind responses to stress and to human dialogue.	6. The client recognized bodymind responses to stress and to human dialogue.
	7. The client will identify personal, family, and relationship life priorities.	7. The client identified personal, family, and relationship life priorities.
	8. The client will engage in awareness exercises to increase intimacy.	8. The client engaged in awareness exercises to increase intimacy.
	9. The client will recognize defenses that can occur in relationships to block effective communication.	9. The client recognized defenses that occurred in relationships to block effective communication.
The client will demonstrate awareness of the effect of human dialogue on bodymind.	10. The client will learn skills to improve effective expression of emotions when communicating with others.	10. The client learned skills to improve effective expression of emotions when communicating with others.
The client will learn new strategies to improve the quality of relationships.	11. The client will learn interventions to improve relationships, such as: a. "I" statements b. intimacy exercises c. focusing d. storytelling e. stem phrase completion f. empty chair g. self-reflection exercises	11. The client learned interventions to improve relationships, such as: a. "I" statements b. intimacy exercises c. focusing d. storytelling e. stem phrase completion f. empty chair g. self-reflection exercises

Plan and Interventions

Before the Session

- Whether the session will last only a few minutes or an hour, or longer, control the environment as much as possible to create a space conducive to a therapeutic relationship. The environment must be safe, both emotionally and physically, for the client to work on feelings and issues.
- Center yourself in preparation to facilitate healing for the client. Clear your mind of other clients and personal issues in order to be present with the client and the perceived problem/situation.
- Spend a few moments centering self before counseling the client.

Beginning the Session

- Greet the client in a relaxed manner and assess the client's degree of tension or relaxation.
- Be aware of active listening to the client as the problem/story unfolds.
- See whether the client tells one or two sides to the problem.
- Help the client continue to share feelings and hurts that are involved in the situation.
- Following the assessment, decide which interventions are most appropriate for the client. Explain those interventions that you believe the client will benefit from and obtain his or her agreement to try the interventions during the session.

During the Session

- Help the client gain insight about the situation part by part and then help the client put the parts together.
- Help the client identify the strengths and the weaknesses within the situation.
- Help the client identify personal strengths for this is the ground for changing behavior.
- Have client describe options as you move through the situation.
- Be aware of timing and pacing of comments in accordance with the client's responses.
- Reassess how new insights are being received by client.
- Avoid using qualifying language if the client wants you to agree on how a particular person might act: for example, the client who says, "Don't you think my wife is being unfair?" A "yes" by the nurse validates the client's viewpoint. A "no" can set up an argument. A noncommittal response might be, "I have not met your wife, but from what I hear from you I might agree. Is it possible that your wife. . . ."
- Use qualifying language that can lead toward positive outcomes, such as: "I have a suggestion, how much, ability, use imagination, and . . . readiness to take a step."

- Continue to encourage the client to be specific about the emotions being shared as he or she talks about the situation and to recognize any body sensations that are felt as the emotions are discussed (refer to focusing intervention).

Closing the Session

- Formulate specific tactics to bring about change in the client.
- Have the client identify options.
- Have the client choose the most realistic and promising course of action.
- Once choices are identified, have the client affirm the choice to increase his or her awareness of energy and actions to resolve the situation.
- Make a concrete plan to proceed with change. This plan, however, is not carved in stone and can be changed following the above steps.
- Have the client rehearse in the imagination the course of action.
- Reassess if there has been a reframing of the situation as compared to the start of the session.
- Help the client formulate new goals.
- Evaluate the outcomes of the session.

Specific Interventions: Relationships

These techniques can be incorporated into all areas of nursing, although some of the advanced techniques lend themselves better to individual counseling. However, the nurse who is aware of the techniques can integrate various levels of the techniques in the acute care setting.

Improving Communication (Basic to Advanced)

Communication patterns have a direct impact on mind modulation of the autonomic, immune, endocrine, and neuropeptide systems. Nurses can help clients improve communication patterns by teaching an awareness of the psychophysiologic response that occurs with communication. With an increased awareness of how body and emotions are directly linked, the client can be taught how to recognize and increase healthy dialogue versus stressful dialogue. The outcomes are more awareness of sharing and owning of emotions, which lead to healthier relationships.

Communication involves state-dependent learning and the imagery process, so there are an enormous number of variables with communication interventions. These interventions are helpful for all nurses and clients because they facilitate the incorporation of relaxation skills and awareness of bodymind responses with all dialogue. Advanced communication interventions incorporate in-depth psychophysiologic therapy and biofeedback training.

Transactional Psychophysiologic Therapy (TP) has been developed by Lynch and Thomas over 20 years of working with clients with psychophysiologic symptoms and with patients in critical care.[9] Its basic premise is that people with stress-linked physical disorders have in common certain interpersonal struggles that lead to health or to illness.

During stressful dialogue it is difficult to control increased cardiovascular responses, such as increased blood pressure, heart rate, and respirations. However, a person can be taught to modulate the magnitude of these cardiovascular changes by slowing the rate of speech, doing deep breathing, releasing muscle tension, practicing nondefensive attending to others, and learning to use relaxation techniques. The purpose of the therapy is to (1) teach a variety of physical maneuvers and awareness to modulate the significant change in heart rate and blood pressure during stressful dialogue, (2) observe vascular reactions to one's interpersonal world, (3) link the cardiovascular system with human dialogue and an awareness of human feelings, (4) view *all* relationships as essential aspects of TP dialogue, and (5) learn to feel and modulate cardiovascular reactions when relating to others. The TP process follows six steps to increase healthy dialogue[10]:

1. Obtain a psychophysiologic assessment focusing on relationships and the client in dialogue.
2. Teach the client to observe vascular responses as a dynamic and not a static response. This means that the client learns to own his or her personal bodymind responses to dialogue and becomes more aware of how the cardiovascular system is very sensitive to interpersonal interactions. If such equipment as continuous blood pressure monitoring or biofeedback equipment is available, the learning of techniques is faster and dramatic. However, one can teach these techniques by instructing the client in increasing self-awareness and self-monitoring skills.
3. Teach the client awareness of how the cardiovascular system responds to human communication. The following aspects of communication are linked to changes in blood pressure and heart rate: fast talking; listening, talking, and human dialogue; breathing and relaxing while talking; emotional content of speech; language as a cry; and language as a communication. The client should be taught to watch his or her rate of speech and breathing patterns. Rapid rates significantly increase the cardiovascular response, producing an increase in heart rate, blood pressure, etc. While listening to others, the client can be using relaxed breathing to reduce the increased cardiovascular responses. The client is taught the difference between talking in an inarticulate manner—for example, as when a baby cries or when we hold back and do not share emotions—and expressing oneself in an articulate manner. If the client has known cardiovascular responses/symptoms, ask the client to estimate blood pressure and pulse before participating in a stressful or emotionally charged dialogue.
4. Teach the client to be aware of how human feelings are linked to the cardiovascular system. Instruct the client to notice body responses that occur with dialogue; for example, a change in heart rate, breathing patterns, or temperature of the face, torso, hands, and feet. Help the client recognize the changes and to correlate emotions with physiologic changes. Emphasize the importance of getting in touch with feelings, rather than controlling them, and that there is no such thing as good or bad response.
5. Teach clients that our bodymind responds to the presence of people. The cardiovascular responses are a rich source of *beingness* that must not be denied. All our emotions, thoughts, and feelings are translated into physiologic changes. It is our responsibility to *decode* what the interpersonal awareness means to each of us.

6. Teach the client to increase awareness of cardiovascular changes when alone and when relating to others. Encourage the practice of these skills in daily living, such as when talking on the phone, or when at work, when casually talking in nonstressful situations. The end result is that the client learns how to engage in dialogue, sharing more honest feelings by recognizing cardiovascular responses and even becoming more capable of stressful dialogue without such drastic changes in cardiovascular response.

"I" Statements (Basic)

A common habit of many people is to open dialogue with the use of the pronoun "you" instead of "I." This practice masks the expression of feelings. A helpful strategy is to make clients aware of the use of "I" statements that can increase the sharing of feelings and emotions (Exhibit 15-1).

This tool can be used in the session and as a homework assignment. The client should be encouraged to share these self-reflective statements with family, special friends, and work colleagues.

Intimacy Awareness (Basic)

Intimacy is a skill from which all can benefit. A simple tool that increases the skills and awareness of intimacy is seen in Exhibit 15-2. These questions can be used in counseling sessions as homework assignments. The client should be encouraged to focus on one or all aspects of increasing intimacy. These self-reflective questions also can be shared with family and special friends. Encourage the client to use these questions in expressing feelings with others and then to check out his or her inner response in the actual conversation.

Focusing (Basic to Advanced)

Focusing is an intervention that teaches a person to identify and change the way that personal problems actually exist in the body. It can be taught as a basic way to recognize subtle body changes that are related to stressful situations. It becomes an advanced technique when used in psychotherapy with complex life issues. Focusing can be integrated with all interventions presented in Unit IV.

Focusing is a good strategy to increase skills of intuition for it helps one learn awareness of listening to the body wisdom of the *felt sense*—the marked shift in sensations within the body as a result of the release of tension. Focusing helps guide a person in learning to be more aware of bodymind. It is at this level of connection that answers to many of our life questions and conflicts can be found.

In order for the nurse to use focusing successfully, the nurse must know the felt shift from personal experience. To learn the skill, record the focusing questions into a tape recorder, leaving space for the questions to be answered by you silently to yourself. Critique the tape that you make. Did you pace yourself? Did you leave enough time to answer the questions? In places where it moves too fast, record the tape again until you refine the technique to a point where you experience that body change, the *felt shift* inside. With practice, you literally feel body sensations. Once you experience it, then

Exhibit 15-1 ''I'' Statements

Name ______________________________

Date ______________________________

Homework Assignment

''I'' STATEMENTS

Some people have trouble starting sentences with the pronoun ''I''; instead, they most often use the pronoun ''you.'' Using the ''you'' pronoun can be very hurtful to marriages and to families. The purpose of this task is to give you practice in making ''I'' statements. Using sentences that begin with ''I'' can be especially helpful when trying to express feelings or deal with emotional issues in your relationship. The following sentence stems have been found helpful in making ''I'' statements. One blank has been provided under each heading so that you can make up a stem of your own. Write your completions for each of the sentence stems on the lines provided, and start thinking about other possible completions for these sentences. After completing all the responses, discuss your answers with your partner.

Self

I wish ______________________________
I should ______________________________
I need ______________________________
I feel ______________________________
I ______________________________

Marriage relationship with partner

It pleases me when ______________________________
I fear ______________________________
I love ______________________________
I hurt ______________________________
I ______________________________

Children

I remember ______________________________
I want ______________________________
It pleases me when ______________________________
It hurts me when ______________________________
I ______________________________

Parents/in-laws

I avoid ______________________________
I understand ______________________________
I must ______________________________
I won't ______________________________
I ______________________________

Siblings or relatives

I feel ______________________________
I ought ______________________________
I avoid ______________________________
I trust ______________________________
I ______________________________

Exhibit 15-1 continued

Work

I sometimes ______________________________
I enjoy ______________________________
I dread ______________________________
I'd like ______________________________
I ______________________________

Friends

I sense ______________________________
I fear ______________________________
I wonder ______________________________
I enjoy ______________________________
I ______________________________

Leisure time

I like ______________________________
If I could ______________________________
I enjoy ______________________________
I don't want ______________________________
I ______________________________

Now spend a few minutes discussing your responses with your partner.

Source: Reprinted from *Systematic Family Therapy* by L. L'Abate, p. 267, with permission of Brunner/Mazel, © 1986.

confidence is gained about how helpful the experience is for problem solving. The technique is best used after the client has learned basic relaxation and imagery exercises and trusts the benefit and power of these self-reflective techniques. Guide the client in a general relaxation or imagery script and then ask the focusing questions. (See Chapters 11 and 12 for general relaxation and imagery scripts.)

Script: "What I will ask you to do in a moment is to increase your relaxation. With your eyes closed, begin to focus on the silence and sensations within your body. Let yourself answer the questions silently to yourself. As you answer in silence to yourself, you are better able to focus and stay with the sensations that you feel within your body. After the exercise we will discuss your experience. There is no particular way to answer to yourself. Just trust any feelings or answers that come as right for now. Stay with the feelings and try to let go of any judging or analyzing. Do you have any questions?

So . . . let yourself begin to close your eyes . . . and relax. All right—inside you, I would like you to pay attention inwardly, in your body, somewhere within your body and. . . .

1. Clear a space

- How are you? What's between you and feeling fine?
- Don't answer; let what comes in your body do the answering.

Exhibit 15-2 Intimacy Awareness

Love-Caring
What is love?
What is caring?
What is showing caring?
How do you show caring (physically, mentally, emotionally)?
How do you care for yourself (physically, mentally, emotionally)?
How can you improve the way you care?

Seeing the Good
What does "seeing the good" mean to you?
What is "goodness" in you?
Why do you think it is hard to see your goodness?
Can you rate your ability to see the good in all the people in your family and your friends?

Love-Forgiveness
What does forgiveness mean to you?
Is it possible to love without forgiving self and others?
What are you aware of when you forgive?
Do you forgive yourself?
Who has been the most forgiving person in your life?
Who has been the least forgiving person in your life?
What are some ways that you can forgive to heal a special relationship?

Love-Intimacy
What does intimacy mean to you?
What does sharing mean to you?
Are you able to share your hurt with family and friends?
Do you have a sense of your self when you share your hurt with others?

Source: Adapted from *Systematic Family Therapy* by L. L'Abate, pp. 287–289, with permission of Brunner/Mazel, © 1986.

- Don't go into anything.
- Greet each concern that comes. Put each aside for a while, next to you.
- Except for that, are you fine?

2. Felt sense

- Pick one problem to focus on.
- Don't go into the problem. What do you sense in your body when you recall the whole of that problem? Sense all of that, the sense of the whole thing, the murky discomfort or the unclear body-sense of it.

3. Get a handle

- What is the quality of the felt sense?
- What one word, phrase, or image describes this felt sense?
- What quality or word would fit it best?

4. Resonate

- Go back and forth between the word (or image) and the felt sense. Is that right?
- If they match, feel the sensation of matching the word and felt sense several times.
- If the felt sense changes, follow it with your attention.
- When you get a perfect match, the words (images) being just right for this feeling, let yourself feel that for a minute.

5. Ask

- What is it, about the whole problem, that makes me so __________
- When stuck, ask questions
- What is the worst part of this feeling?
- What's really so bad about this?
- What does it need?
- What should happen?
- Don't answer; wait for the feeling to stir and give you an answer.
- What would it feel like if it was all OK? Let the body answer: What is in the way of that?

6. Receive

- Welcome what came. Be glad it spoke.
- It is only one step on this problem, not the last step.
- Now that you know where it is, you can leave it and come back to it later.
- Protect it from critical voices that interrupt.

Does your body want another round of focusing, or is this a good stopping place?[11]

At this point, the client will nod yes or no to another round of focusing. Finish the session with a brief relaxation script and gradually bring the client back into an alert state.

Storytelling (Basic to Advanced)

Storytelling is a healing ritual that is also an excellent nursing intervention. Stories reveal how we assign importance to our experiences in life and how we perceive our world. The anthropologist Bateson uses the metaphor that a story is a knot or complex of specific connectedness that we call relevance.[12] The storytelling technique becomes advanced when parables and metaphors are used. Parables and metaphors relate to imagery which acts as a type of double-exposure to the actual process being described (refer to section on empowering the spoken word in Chapter 12).

All stories may be a means of building double descriptions and enabling higher-order patterns to be perceived.[13] This occurs because we can take our stories from one situation to the next. As we do this, we create different contexts and structures for those stories. This creates the potential for opening new dialogue with the self, which can also contain new purpose and meaning. An additional way to enhance storytelling is to incorporate relaxation, imagery, music, life review, and self-reflective interventions.

Nurses are always listening to clients' stories. If they listen with focused attention, what they hear are stories about stories and so on. *These stories are the therapy; they are the basis for the healing event. We should see therapy as conversation, rather than always classifying it in medical terms.*[14] The following guidelines are suggested in order to enhance your ability to use stories as therapy.

- Listen for the themes that bridge one story to the next; listen for the threads of information that also weave through one story to the next.
- Train yourself to listen for how a client tells only one side of a story.
- Get the client to talk about what the two sides of any story might be because frequently clients perceive only one side of a story. It is viewing the other side that gives new meaning and context and enables one to create double descriptions of stories. For example, it is very easy to identify things and events that are wrong in one's life, but finding the strengths in the current situation and the underlying meaning or message of the present situation is more valuable.
- As a nurse listens to the client's stories he or she is also constructing a story that guides the therapy. Become aware of the importance of the stories that you construct from the client's stories. When the nurse's stories are told to the client, an exchange of stories results from which the client can see or hear new patterns and relationships. With this feedback, the client gains new information and can construct a new way of viewing life. All stories are a means of building double descriptions that facilitate change.

Stem Phrase Completion (Basic to Advanced)

Stem phrase completion is a therapeutic and diagnostic tool that is a form of active imagination. It is most helpful when clients are masking (hiding feelings) or are reluctant to share feelings.[15] Stem phrases that the client is asked to complete, are vague stimuli that facilitate one to search for answers from within. The nurse can invent sentences that seem appropriate for the situation at hand. This nursing intervention lends variety to the usual way of conducting an individual or group session and is a way to engage and promote increased client participation. It can be used when working with clients on a one-to-one basis, and also in client groups that are recovering from the same condition, such as grief, cancer, or cardiac dysfunction.

This intervention allows a client to share both conscious and unconscious perceptions about events, people, and environment. The answers from the client's realms of consciousness begin to form patterns and processes. Most clients are fascinated by their own answers. They begin to put the pieces of the puzzle together about their own life. Stem phrase completion elicits a novel approach to listening to one's self, as well as listening to another. It creates new stimuli that are beyond the client's habitual communication patterns.

This intervention is extremely effective when working in family or other group situations. When working with family members, introduce them to this technique as a way to increase healthy communication. Seat people so that they have direct eye contact with the nurse or each other. If this intervention is done in a group, people can work in pairs, taking turns asking each other stem phrases provided by the nurse facilitator. Either each member of the dyad can take the lead to ask all the questions or both members can respond to each stem phrase before moving to the next. Exhibit 15-3 lists some typical phrases for completion.

The nurse can precede the intervention with these introductory comments: "I am going to give you a series of open-ended phrases for which there are no right or wrong answers. Be spontaneous with your answers, allowing the first thought that surfaces to be spoken. I will take turns giving each of you a phrase. Let the person to whom I give the phrase respond. You may be tempted to respond to the phrase for the other person or you may want to correct the other person's response, but let their response be. When the phrase comes around again, you can change your response at that time. Do you have any questions?"

Use your intuition and listen carefully to the client's answer, as this can become the stem for the next question. For example, "I must learn to be more assertive" can be "An assertive person must. . . ." In addition, some answers are very profound, and encouraging the client to repeat them can provide valuable insight. See Case Study 1 for an example of this intervention.

The Empty Chair (Basic to Advanced)

The empty chair, popularized by Perls, is an intervention to help people get in touch with and own "parts" of the self that have not been integrated into the whole self.[16] The purpose of the exercise is to get a person to own feelings and beliefs that are projected or rationalized onto another person. This projection can create a distortion of reality within a family or group system.

This approach is helpful in individual or group sessions exploring issues of lack of assertiveness or not sharing of feelings. It is also helpful in guiding staff or students when there is conflict among group members. The technique becomes an advanced technique

---

Exhibit 15-3 Stem Phrase Completion

I can . . .
I will . . .
I must . . .
I am clear about . . .
I get angry . . .
I am most excited about . . .
I get angry when . . .
I wish I could . . .
I feel important when . . .
If I could change . . .
If you knew me, you would say . . .
The thing that I am most excited about now is . . .
The person I love most . . .
The person who is a guiding force in my life is . . .
If I had the wisdom to change, the thing I would change would . . .

when used in one-to-one intensive psychotherapy sessions where in-depth feelings and life issues are the focus.

To implement this intervention, position a client across from an empty chair. The client then places, in imagination, the person with whom they are in conflict on the empty chair. The client begins a dialogue with the empty chair, imagining that the person is physically in the chair. The client is instructed to say anything that he or she wishes to this person. Once that is said the client switches to the other chair and responds the way he or she thinks that the imagined person would respond.

An example of the use of the empty chair intervention in a counseling session with a mother who is in conflict with her son follows. The nurse might say to the mother during a session, "I want you to imagine that your son is sitting in this empty chair. Say whatever you want to tell him. As soon as you make statements to him, I will have you switch chairs and move to the other chair. From this chair you will speak as you think your son would respond. Speak for your son to yourself in the empty chair. You will alternate between the two chairs."

The nurse may interject statements or paraphrase what the client appears to be experiencing, such as "You mean you are very angry and you want to yell at him." Or the nurse may assume the role of the alter ego and succinctly express what the client seems to be experiencing. Case study 2 includes an example of this intervention.

Self-Reflective Experiential Exercises: Relationships (Basic to Advanced)

Habits, beliefs, assumptions, expectations, judgments, and misconceptions can be major blocks in relationships. They create conflicts and barriers that block effective communication and sharing of our perceptions. Use of relaxation, imagery, and music during counseling sessions is very effective in helping clients make significant shifts in their awareness of relationships. These strategies can be combined with self-reflective statements or guided imagery to enhance relationship awareness. The questions that follow could be presented over several sessions, as homework assignments, or as starting points for creating new goals in relationships. The interventions are basic if used in a reflective way. They become advanced when used in psychotherapy to elicit deeper, more complex life issues.

The following ten reflective questions are suggested to increase an awareness of patterns in relationships so that the process of healing can occur[17]:

1. Reflect on the important relationships in your life. Do they satisfy you? Are you getting your needs met? What do you bring to your relationships? What are the predominant qualities that you experience in your relationships? Do you feel competitive, manipulated, victimized, or rejected? Do you experience joy, vitality, synergy, love, and shared purpose? What qualities do you bring to your relationships?
2. What patterns of your relationship are you aware of? Do you consistently feel misunderstood or mistreated? Do you think you give more than you receive? Do you experience the universal Self as the source and context of relationships?
3. What beliefs and assumptions do you hold about relationships? Recognizing patterns can help uncover such assumptions as "Loving someone means always doing what the other person wants," or "I can't tell him or her how I feel,

because it will hurt him or her." After taking an inventory of beliefs, do you recognize any restricted patterns? Did you become aware of any areas that you are unwilling to address?
4. What do you identify with as your true self? Is it your physical, mental, emotional, or spiritual potential or are all of these areas combined? Do you practice being authentic in your relationships? Do you find that, when you are honest with yourself, your relationships are more satisfying?
5. What is the purpose of your important relationships? Remember that our values reflect our personal attitudes. For example, if you feel manipulated, chances are that you are manipulative or would like to be. Be honest in examining your motives in relationships.
6. What relationships in your life have had the most meaning?
7. Imagine that you are ready to die. Reflect on the qualities of relationships in your life. Do you have any regrets? Is there anything that you would have changed?
8. If you could change your relationships unilaterally, what qualities would you want to cultivate in your relationships?
9. Which of your relationships are in need of healing right now? What are you willing to do to bring about that healing?
10. Are you willing to forgive? What part of yourself do you have trouble forgiving?

Removing Obstacles in Relationships (Basic to Advanced)

The following exercise is very effective in healing a specific relationship. It is best done with a partner. If a partner is not available, the responses can be written down.[18]

1. Identify and describe a relationship that is troublesome to you.
2. List your grievances and resentments in this relationship.
3. Clarify your wants, demands, and expectations in this relationship.
4. Communicate your fears with respect to this relationship.
5. Communicate guilt feelings in this relationship.
6. Visualize this relationship as it would be if it were healed. What would it be like? What would you feel like?
7. Can you say what you must do to move in this direction?

Another way to do this same exercise is with receptive role playing.[19] It is called receptive because another uninvolved person merely listens as the troubled person talks out the troublesome relationship. The listener monitors his or her internal responses to the dialogue. As the person is talking out the trouble, often he or she attains new body awareness, (felt sense) emotions, and shifts in attitudes that have never before been present. It is important for the nurse to bring closure to these exercises and help the client integrate this new information.

Evaluation

In each counseling session, the outcome must be measured as successful or not. The nurse will evaluate with the client the outcomes that were established before the sessions as listed in Table 15-2.

Case Studies

Case Study No. 1

Setting: Cardiac Rehabilitation Unit

Client: W.B., a 59-year-old male, after triple bypass graft surgery, in second week of outpatient cardiac rehabilitation; his wife is present at this session

Nursing Diagnoses:
1. Anxiety related to fear of death
2. Potential noncompliance related to new health behaviors after open-heart surgery

This case study illustrates the use of the stem phrase intervention to enhance communication between two people. The cardiac rehabilitation nurse assessed that the couple was experiencing conflict over perceived meaning in recovery. The assessment showed that neither the husband nor the wife were listening to one another.

Rather than ignoring the problem, the nurse asked the two into her office. This session took 20 minutes. It was her second encounter with the couple. After hearing both sides of the conflict, with both people interrupting each other to correct each other's statements, the nurse said, "I see and hear two people who love each other very much who are not listening to each other. I value what each of you are concerned about, and I believe that if each of you really hears what the other is saying, that you can gain some new insight about the other." The stem phrase completion exercise was explained and they both agreed to participate.

The nurse gave the stem, and then each had a turn to complete the phrase. The couple was sitting face to face, smiling because the nurse had set the stage of ease without competition. The atmosphere conveyed that the nurse's caring about the couple was genuine.

Nurse to Husband: Why don't you start. Complete this phrase in what ever way seems right to you just now. IF I WEREN'T SO ANGRY . . .

Husband(H): IF I WEREN'T SO ANGRY I might listen to you.

Wife (W): IF I WEREN'T SO ANGRY I might quit nagging.

H: I AM ANGRY for not making faster progress after surgery.

W: I AM ANGRY because you are not doing what the doctors tell you to do.

H: I AM CLEAR ABOUT I am having a tough time with recovery (tears in his eyes).

W: I AM CLEAR ABOUT I feel frustrated because I don't know how to help you.

H: IF I COULD CHANGE I would learn how to relax.

W: IF I COULD CHANGE I would quit being so afraid. (As the nurse listens the best stem comes from the wife's last completion.)

H: THE THING THAT I AM MOST AFRAID OF is dying.

W: THE THING THAT I AM MOST AFRAID OF is your dying. (Again the best stem comes from the intuitive feeling that the nurse gained from the wife's last answer, which allowed the nurse to spontaneously generate this next stem.)

H: THE PERSON THAT I LOVE THE MOST is you.

W: THE PERSON THAT I LOVE THE MOST is you.

The nurse concluded the exercise at this point to lead into a discussion of death and spiritual concerns. The couple was given a teaching sheet with guidelines on integrating relaxation techniques, along with a relaxation tape to begin practicing the skills. This brief session concluded with the couple being deeply grateful for the special attention that they received from the nurse. Some tears were shed, and tension levels between the couple decreased.

Case Study No. 2

Setting:	Biofeedback department
Client:	A.C., divorced 42-year-old woman with severe migraine headaches, and anxiety, who was frustrated with 16-year-old son
Nursing Diagnoses:	1. Alteration in comfort related to incapacitating pain with recurrent weekly migraine headaches 2. Ineffective individual coping related to anxiety, stress of headaches and parenting, and frequent outbursts of aggression toward son

A.C. is having weekly migraines and feels "like I am in quicksand sinking very fast." She describes her son as exceptionally aggressive and belligerent. She experiences herself as "acting like things in her life are very much in order." At this particular session she had only a slight headache. The nurse guided her in a relaxation and guided imagery exercise to increase her skills in biofeedback training.

At this session, she had great success at achieving relaxation of specific muscle groups being monitored by biofeedback. She said, "I am so proud of myself. I wish my son was here right now so I could finish a conversation with him while I am free of my headache." The nurse took the cue and said, "That is a wonderful idea!" The client abruptly said, "What do you mean?"

Nurse: A., Could you please imagine your son in this empty chair? (A. nods "yes"). Would you tell him what you are feeling just now and how he makes you feel.

A.: Ron, you don't give a damn about me. It seems like you are always doing things to hurt me. I try to please you, but you are so disappointing; you are just walking trouble.

Nurse: Now, can you sit in this other chair and give Ron a voice. Let him speak to you in this chair (the chair A. has just left).

A.: (As Ron) That's right, I hate you! Did it ever occur to you that you always want me to do things that I don't want to do. I'm sick of hearing you say that this or that will be good for me.

Nurse: (As Ron's alter ego) And so I fight you even more because I want to decide, for myself, what is best. You never give me a chance to prove to you that I can do something that is right by your standards. I'm sick and tired of your nagging me. You never let up. Give me a break. Please go back to Mom's chair and speak to Ron.

A.: You make me have to constantly try to guide you because you are always doing the wrong thing.

Nurse: Go back to Ron's chair and speak for Ron.

A.: (As Ron) I can never do anything to please you. (A. says with tears to the nurse) "That's the way it was with my mother, I could never do anything to please her. It would make me so mad, I would want to do things out of spite, but I just worked harder to please her and it still didn't work."

Nurse: Is it that your mother was angry and aggressive toward you, and that you are always angry toward your son; then your son becomes angry with you and defies you instead of pleasing you as you did with your mother?

A.: It seems that way. I really had not realized that I was doing the same thing with my son that my mother did to me.
Nurse: Imagine that your mother is in that chair and speak to her. Tell her how angry you are with her.

The same approach is now used with the empty chair, but the person in it is now her mother. When a client deals with family issues, the issues and values in the family of origin concerning his or her own parents and upbringing frequently surface.

The nurse helped A. begin to integrate her past feelings of powerlessness with her mother. By integrating her own aggression she then can have more success dealing with the aggression of her son.

SUMMARY

This chapter has focused on the importance of relationships for increased health and wholeness. Family and relationship patterns can exhibit characteristics of either open or closed systems. Relationships have a direct impact on health and disease. The role of the nurse in counseling clients about relationships was discussed. Specific tools and interventions guide the nurse in facilitating change within the client in order to bring about an openness to increased health and healing within the context of relationships.

DIRECTIONS FOR FUTURE RESEARCH

1. Formulate studies that utilize a family systems approach to identifying relationship problems and challenges.
2. Develop valid and reliable tools that help nurses measure relationship stressors.
3. Evaluate tools that are most effective for the nurse to use in measuring functional and dysfunctional relationships.
4. Determine which are the best interventions for nurses to use when counseling clients about relationships in the acute care setting when time is limited.
5. Formulate studies to determine if teaching sheets that promote guidelines about enhancing relationships affect the quality of relationships.

NURSE HEALER REFLECTIONS

After reading this chapter the nurse healer will be able to answer or begin a process of answering the following questions:

- What are the *purposes* of relationships in my life?
- Do I *relate* to my family and friends in an open manner?
- Am I able to identify the *resources* within myself and my relationships?
- Am I able to identify the *stressors* in my relationships?
- Am I able to *express* love?

- What *defenses* surface in my relationships?
- What are my *inner feelings* when I share my love?
- Am I able to *see* the *good* in my family and friends?
- Am I able to *share* my personal *hurt* with myself and others?
- Can I *forgive* myself, my family, and friends?
- Am I aware of using *"I" statements* in order to share more of my feelings and emotions?
- What *choices* are available to me now to improve my relationships?

NOTES

1. Frances Vaughan, *The Inward Arc* (Boston: Shambhala Publications, Inc., 1985), p. 183.
2. Ellen Watchel and Paul Watchel, *Family Dynamics in Individual Psychotherapy: A Guide to Clinical Strategies* (New York: The Guilford Press, 1986), pp. 43–64.
3. Ibid., p. 43.
4. Evelyn Sieberg, *Family Communication: An Integrated System Approach* (New York: Gardner Press, Inc., 1985), pp. 32–55.
5. Brent Hafen and Kathryn Frandsen, *People Need People* (Evergreen, CO: Cordillera Press, 1987), p. 37.
6. Linda Banks, "Counseling" p. 104.
7. Ibid., p. 105.
8. Ibid., p. 105.
9. James Lynch, *The Language of the Heart: The Body's Response to Human Dialogue* (New York: Basic Books, 1985), p. 311.
10. Ibid., pp. 311–321.
11. Eugene Gendlin, *Focusing* (New York: Bantam Books, 1978), pp. 173–174.
12. Gregory Bateson, *Mind and Nature: A Necessary Unity* (New York: E.P. Dutton, 1979), p. 13.
13. Bradford Keeney, *Aesthetics of Change* (New York: The Guilford Press, 1983), p. 195.
14. Thomas Szasz, *The Myth of Psychotherapy* (New York: Bantam Books, 1978), p. 11.
15. Robert Sherman and Norman Fredman, *Handbook of Structured Techniques in Marriage and Family Therapy* (New York: Brunner and Mazel, 1986), pp. 36–38.
16. Fritz Perls, *Gestalt Therapy* (New York: Julian Press, 1951), pp. 1–21.
17. Frances Vaughn, *The Inward Arc: Healing and Wholeness in Psychotherapy and Spirituality* (Boston: Shambhala Publications, Inc. 1986), pp. 195–198.
18. Ibid., p. 198.
19. Ibid., p. 198.

SUGGESTED READINGS

Efron, Donald. *Journeys: Expansion of the Strategic-Systematic Therapies*. New York: Brunner/Mazel, 1986.

Fisch, Richard; Weakland, John; and Siegal, Lynn. *The Tactics of Change: Doing Therapy Briefly*. San Francisco: Jossey-Bass Publishers, 1982.

Haber, Judith. *Comprehensive Psychiatric Nursing*. 3rd ed. New York: McGraw-Hill, 1987.

Huffines, Launa. *Connecting With All the People in Your Life*. San Francisco: Harper and Row, 1986.

L'Abate, Luciano. *Systematic Homework Assignments and Follow-up Questionnaire*. New York: Brunner/Mazel, 1986.

L'Abate, Luciano, and Weinstein, Steven. *Structured Enrichment Programs for Couples and Families*. New York: Brunner/Mazel, 1987.

Minuchin, Salvador, and Fishman, H. *Family Therapy Techniques*. Cambridge, MA: Harvard University Press, 1981.

Satir, Virginia, and Brown, Michelle. *Step By Step: A Guide to Creating Change in Families*. Palo Alto, CA: Science and Behavior Books, Inc., 1983.

Stuart, Gail, and Sundeen, Sandra. *Principles and Practices of Psychiatric Nursing*. 3rd. ed. St. Louis: C.V. Mosby Co., 1987.

chapter **16**

Touch: Connecting with the Healing Power

Lynn Keegan

I tend the flow of your life
With my open hands
To heal, soothe,
Love and protect.[1]

Dorothea Hover-Kramer

This chapter guides nurses who choose to use touch as an intervention in their healing work. Nurses refer to the "hands on" phenomena as touch therapy, therapeutic massage, body work, or other labels. Despite the different names, the intent of all the approaches is the same: caring for another through some mode of touch. Although the techniques vary among practitioners, the objective of the nurse is to relax, soothe, or relieve physical, mental, emotional, and spiritual discomfort. Most nurses who use touch as a modality do so from a calm, centered place and believe that the transference of healing energy may be facilitated through focused intention.

Just as all nurses do not relate well to the technical nature of an intensive care unit or operating room, likewise not all nurses have the ability or desire to use the medium of touch. Generally people know after a few encounters if this approach works for them. If it does, then it can become a powerful healing modality with the skill that comes through practice and intent.

NURSE HEALER OBJECTIVES

Theoretical

1. Learn the definitions and various types of touch techniques.
2. Compare and contrast the various touch therapies.

3. Observe for subjective and objective changes in the client after the touch therapy session.
4. Compare and contrast your responses to touch therapy with the published descriptions of other healers.

Clinical

1. Develop your abilities to center and become calm before you use touch therapies in your practice.
2. Learn to calm, soften, and steady your voice as you use it as an adjunct to touch therapy.
3. Experiment with soothing music or guided imagery (spoken or from cassette tapes) as an adjunct to the touch session.
4. Create opportunities to practice the touch therapies in your clinical area.
5. Notice whether you have any changes in your emotions during or after you use touch therapy.
6. Notice any change in your sense of time when you use touch. Does it slow down or speed up?

Personal

1. Become aware of how you utilize touch in your everyday life.
2. Examine the significance of touch in your personal and professional relationships.

DEFINITIONS

Acupressure: the application of finger and/or thumb pressure to specific sites along the body's energy meridians for the purpose of relieving tension and re-establishing the flow of energy along the meridian lines.

Body Therapy and/or Touch Therapy: the broad range of techniques that a practitioner uses with the hands on or near the body to assist the recipient toward optimal function.

Caring Touch: touch done with a genuine interest in the other person; involves empathy and concern.

Centering: a sense of self-relatedness that can be thought of as a place of inner being, a place of quietude within oneself where one can feel truly integrated, unified, and focused.[2]

Energy Meridian: an energy circuit or line of force; Eastern theories describe meridian lines flowing vertically through the body with culminating points on the feet, hands, and ears.

Foot Reflexology: applying pressure to points on the feet that correspond to other parts of the body.

Intention: the motivation or reason for touching.

Procedural Touch: touch done to diagnose, monitor, or treat the illness itself; touch that focuses on the end result of curing the illness or preventing further complications.

Shiatzu: using thumb and/or heel of the hand for deep pressure work along the energy meridian lines.

Therapeutic Massage: using one's hands to apply pressure and motion on the skin and underlying muscle of the recipient for the purposes of physical and psychologic relaxation, improvement of circulation, relief of sore muscles, and other therapeutic effects.

Therapeutic Touch: a specific technique of centering intention used while the practitioner moves the hands through a recipient's energy field for the purpose of assessment and treatment of energy field imbalance.

THEORY AND RESEARCH

Touch in Ancient Times

Healing through touch is as old as civilization itself. This therapeutic mode was practiced extensively in all ancient cultures. Egyptians used bandages, poultices, touch, and manipulation. In this oldest form of treatment the innate response was to "rub it if it hurts."[3] The oldest written documentation of the use of body touch to enhance healing comes from the Orient. The *Huang Ti Nei Ching* is a classic work of internal medicine that was written 5,000 years ago. The *Nei Ching,* a 3,000- to 4,000-year-old Chinese book of health and medicine, records a system of touch based on the acupuncture points and energy circuits. The ancient Indian Vedas also described healing massage, as did the Polynesian Lomi and the native American Indians.

During the height of the Greek civilization Hippocrates wrote of the therapeutic effects of massage and manipulation and gave instructions of how they should be carried out. He wrote at the time of the great healing centers—the Aesclepions—at which many whole body therapies, including touch, were practiced during healing. Touch therapies were also employed to assist individuals who came to the healing centers because they wished to make the transition to a higher level of function. Massage was used as a mode of preparation for dream work, which was a significant part of therapy in the healing rites. In *The Odyssey* Homer describes how the heroes' bodies were rubbed and kneaded upon their return from battle. Following the Greek era, the Roman historian Plutarch writes of Julius Caesar being treated for epilepsy by being pinched over his entire body every day.

Touch was widely used by both shamans and traditional practitioners until the rise of Puritan culture during the 1600s and the shift from primitive healing practices to modern scientific medicine.[4,5] Puritan culture equated touch with sex, which was associated with original sin. As science evolved life expectancy rose significantly. During the late 19th and early 20th century the movement from anything associated with superstition and primitive healing and toward the new miracle maker—scientific medicine—began. Because touch had always been associated with primitive healing and because of the strong Puritan ethic, all unnecessary touch was discouraged. Consequently, touch as a therapeutic intervention in American health care remained undeveloped until the research into its benefits that began in the 1950s.

Cultural Variations

The fact that all cultures, both ancient and modern, have developed some form of touch tells us that rubbing, pressing, massaging, and holding have evolved as natural manifestations of the desire to heal and care for one another. Yet, touch varies from culture to culture.[6] One society may view touch as necessary, whereas another may view it as taboo. Diverse qualities of touch serve as symbols of communication. The nurse must be aware of personal and cultural views and reactions to touch.

Philosophical and cultural differences have influenced the development of touch in various areas of the world. The Oriental world view is founded on *energy,* whereas the Western world view is based on *reductionism of matter*. This basic cultural difference has resulted in the evolution of widely differing approaches to touch. Westerners believe that it is the physical effect of cellular changes that influences healing. Massage stimulates the cells to aid in waste discharge, stimulates the vascular system to dilate, and encourages lymphatic drainage. Swedish and therapeutic massage were developed to produce these physical changes.

The Oriental world view holds that "Qi," also described as chi, energy, or vital force, is the center of body function. A *meridian* is an energy circuit or line of force that runs vertically through the body.[7] Magnetic or bioelectrical patterns flow through the microcosm of our bodies in the same way that magnetic patterns flow through the planet and the universe. Meridian lines and zones are influenced by pressure placed on points along those lines. A blending of Eastern and Western techniques has resulted in an explosion of new and widely practiced modalities. Expert practitioners in acupuncture or Shiatzu purport to direct healing energy to the recipient via an energy flow through the body and out through their hands.[8]

From antiquity through the present day the healing arts using touch have remained. The modern-day renaissance of body therapies is probably a response to the fast-paced technological revolution that has swept our culture. This revolution has left little room for the practice of the art of touch.

Modern Concepts of Touch

Within this decade nursing research has finally emerged to document what healers have always intuitively known. Some of the first studies documenting the significance of touch were done by Harlow in the 1950s with baby monkeys and surrogate mothers.[9] Harlow investigated the role of touch in the rearing of "normal" offspring by studying two groups of monkeys. One group was placed in a cage with a monkey-shaped wire form, and the second group was caged with a soft cloth mother surrogate. When frightened, the monkeys housed with the wire form reacted by running and cowering in a corner. The other group reacted to the same stimuli by running and clinging to the soft cloth surrogate for protection. These baby monkeys even preferred to cling to an unheated cloth surrogate mother, rather than sit on a warm heating pad. Even though the cloth surrogate was unresponsive the offspring raised with it developed basically "normal" behavioral outcomes. This and other classical studies conclusively documented the significance of touch in normal animal growth and development.

Other studies of human development soon followed. One study of abandoned infants and infants whose mothers were in prison found that the babies whom the nurses held and cuddled thrived, but those who were left alone became ill and died.[10] Other studies examined the positive effect of touch on the immune system.[11]

These early studies in the 1950s and 1960s awakened scientific interest in the phenomena of healing touch. Grad, a biochemist at McGill University, was one of the first to investigate healing by the laying on of hands.[12] He conducted a series of double-blind experiments using the renowned healer, Oskar Estebany. These experiments divided wounded mice and damaged barley seeds into control and experimental groups. Estebany used healing touch in the "energy fields" of the experimental groups and demonstrated a significantly accelerated healing rate in comparison to the control groups.

In a subsequent study an enzymologist worked with Grad using the enzyme trypsin in double-blind studies.[13] After exposure to Estebany's "treatments" the activity of trypsin was significantly increased in the experimental groups.

Nursing Studies

Although touch therapy is as old as mankind, documentation of how, why, and where it works is relatively new in the nursing literature. Hand holding has been described as a positive means of communication and one that seems to break down barriers.[14] Through the mechanism of touch, a nurse can convey feelings of caring and understanding to the client.[15]

Acute Care

We are familiar with the high anxiety levels of myocardial infarction (MI) patients in coronary care units. The coronary care nurse is in a position to manipulate the client's environment to reduce or eliminate anxiety. Glick did a quasi-experimental study to determine the relationship between the type of touch and anxiety experienced by the MI patient in the intermediate cardiac care unit.[16] The results showed those receiving the greatest benefits from the caring touch of nurses were patients with pre-existing coronary artery disease and men under the age of 60 years. Those experiencing the least benefit were those touched both by significant others, as well as by the investigator, and they were all women.

McCorkle investigated the effects of touch as nonverbal communication on a group of seriously ill middle-aged adults and found that the nurses' touch increased the duration of verbal responses.[17] These findings support another study that concluded that the use of touch increased verbal interactions between nurses and patients.[18]

Elderly

Professionals must first examine their own feelings about the meaning of touch before using it as a therapeutic tool. In a study of student nurses' perceptions about touch and their feelings about infants and nursing home residents, students were asked to write five words to describe the tactile and affective sensations of touching.[19] The students described the infants as cuddly, small, warm, soft, and smooth, but the terms used to describe the elderly were wrinkled, loose, flabby, bony, and cold. The students were more comfortable touching newborns than the geriatric patients. A nurse who reacts adversely to the skin changes of old people may find it difficult to touch clients.[20] The nurse's reluctance might then communicate a negative message to the elderly person.

It is also important to note that not all clients may want to be touched. It has been reported that 2 percent of nursing home patients are uncomfortable with touching.[21] Two factors were associated with the discomfort: the sex of the nurse and the part of the body that was touched. Female patients were not comfortable being touched by older male nurses. Second, hand or arm holding did not evoke a negative reaction, but when the nurse placed an arm around the patients' shoulders, many patients reported feeling discomfort or pain. An older female nurse's touch to the face, however, was well accepted by almost all the patients.

Rozema cites reasons why the elderly need touch as much or more than any other age group.[22] First, they often have fewer family members or friends, and secondly, touch functions as an effective communication channel at a time in life when the effectiveness of other communication channels are reduced.

Our culture has been described as suffering from ''skin hunger,'' a form of malnutrition that has reached epidemic proportions in the United States.[23] Skin hunger or poverty of touch often is acute among the elderly. A study of the utilization of touch by health care personnel found that patients in the age range of 66-100 received the least amount of touch.[24] Clients in geriatric institutions show not only their hunger for affection but also the great value they place on the smallest gesture, the simplest touch.[25] A study that used an experimental design to examine the effects of anger and hostility among nursing home residents found that the less mobile patients responded more positively to touch and were less angry than their more mobile counterparts when touched.[26,27]

The art of touch can be a learned behavior, and students can and should be taught the importance of touch as therapy. Students need exposure and experience to overcome their cultural conditioning against touching adults, especially unfamiliar ones, to increase their ease in initiating this intervention.

Therapeutic Touch

Therapeutic touch (TT) is a movement of the practitioners' hands through the recipient's energy field without body contact. It was initially described, researched, and taught in the 1970s by Dolores Krieger at New York University. It is an intervention that has gained increasing attention during the past decade. A controlled study, which investigated the use of TT with 90 subjects in a cardiovascular unit of a large medical center, found that those patients who received TT showed a significant decrease in anxiety compared with those who received only casual touch or no touch at all.[28] Another study investigated the effects of TT on tension headache pain in comparison with a placebo simulation of TT.[29] It found that an average 70 percent pain reduction was sustained over the 4 hours after TT. This was twice the average pain reduction following placebo touch. Therefore, TT may have potential beyond a placebo effect in the treatment of tension headache pain. Krieger[30] and others[31] continue to document the importance of TT and encourage its investigation using controlled studies.

Although we know touch has been used consistently and effectively through the ages, it has only been in the past few years that we have developed some rudimentary tools to document how and why some of the techniques work. Even with this documentation, much of what we use to validate the effectiveness of touch stems not from our scientific linear minds, but rather our knowing intuition. Dallam eloquently describes this knowing intuition when caring for the institutionalized elderly who have lost most of their functions, yet continue to yearn for touch.[32] Much of their behavior is an attempt to reach out to touch and to be touched. In her work she calls for nurses to sensitize their minds and hearts to look for and see the needs of the elderly and not be afraid to respond for the sake of loving, living, and healing.

Research in the area of touch therapy has primarily focused on therapeutic touch. More validation would be valuable for the many new therapies that are evolving as East and West continue to blend and add to the therapies that are now in use.

GENERAL EXPLANATIONS

A variety of techniques are employed under the umbrella heading of body therapies. Except for therapeutic touch, all the body therapies involve actual physical contact. The contact usually consists of the practitioner touching, pushing, kneading, or rubbing the recipient's skin and underlying fascia tissue. However, each of the therapies has its own body of knowledge, history, and technique. Some of these more commonly used therapies are described in this chapter. The interested student will need to seek out additional reference material to learn about the more esoteric body therapies.

Bodymind Communication

Touch is perhaps one of our most highly used, yet least applauded of the five recognized senses. It is the first sense to develop in the human embryo and the one most vital to survival.

Touch has been described in the literal sense in myriad ways ranging from the subtle fleeting brush stroke to violent physical attacks. Touch evokes the full range of emotions from hatred to the most intimate love relationship. Figuratively, touch is used in poetry, literature, and even daily conversation to describe emotions. "That speech really *touched* me," or "this workshop will allow you to *touch* one another heart to heart." These are figurative expressions, but ones often used in our culture to signify the deep importance and value of touch.

As the largest and most ancient sense organ of the body, the skin enables the organism to experience and learn about its environment.[33] It is through the skin that the external world is perceived. The skin, and the face in particular, not only communicate to the brain the knowledge about the external world but also convey to others information about the state of an individual's body, mind, and spirit.

> A piece of skin the size of a quarter contains more than 3 million cells, 12 feet of nerves, 100 sweat glands, 50 nerve endings, and 3 feet of blood vessels. It is estimated that there are about 50 receptors per 100 square centimeters, a total of 900,000 sensory receptors.[34]

Viewed from this perspective, the skin is a giant communication system that, through the sense of touch, brings the messages from the external environment to the attention of the internal environment, the bodymind.

Because care is increasingly being delivered in very complicated technological settings, nurses are concerned with assuring that the human, spiritual, and social needs of patients are met and not ignored.[35] Yet, we must determine what the client thinks about touching before engaging in energetic efforts to provide touch therapy. Social contexts and cultural differences must be taken into account for each individual. Never assume that someone will be comforted by having his or her hand held. Remember, always ask before touching. If no response or a pained expression is evoked, try a tentative touch and observe the client's response carefully. In order for touch to be truly effective it must be authentically given by a warm, genuine, caring individual to another who is willing to receive it. It cannot and should not be packaged and dispensed. Phony touching may be more upsetting than none at all.

Hugging and touching, like any other nursing intervention, demand careful assessment. The nurse needs to recognize her own feelings, as well as consider the client's age, sex, and ethnic background.[36] A few key questions (e.g., would a back massage help you relax or would it help if I held your hand) can help the client clarify his or her own beliefs and values regarding different types, locations, and intensities of touch.

There are many variations and names for the touch therapies available for use as nursing interventions. Some are basic human contacts, such as hand holding and hugging. More detailed therapies can be learned in a school skills laboratory or by reading textbooks, and applying them to one's self, friends, or family first. After learning techniques and evaluating their outcomes, you can apply them in the clinical setting.

The following four touch therapies are used by holistic practitioners who often advocate and teach healthy lifestyle behavior patterns to their clients to augment well-being during the course of the touch therapy treatments. The relaxation response elicited during touch therapies may be heightened by the addition of guided imagery and/or music before and during treatment. The setting, be it acute care, long term, home care, rehabilitation, or a wellness center, will also affect the focus and length of the treatment.

Therapeutic Massage

Therapeutic massage as a nursing intervention has a two-fold purpose. First, clients who are on bedrest or immobilized in a wheelchair require the circulatory stimulation that massage brings. Second, it is a means of relaxation.

During this century nurses have used therapeutic massage primarily on the backs of their patients. Back care is not new; for decades it has been incorporated into the standard bathing and evening care routine of most hospitals. Because of time constraints and traditional neglect of the body therapies in institutions these patients receive only a portion of the complete range of touch therapies.

The basic massage techniques may be greatly augmented and expanded by learning full body massage. Most practitioners learn these techniques in continuing education classes. The techniques are also illustrated in books on massage.

Because no two clients will have the same needs either within or outside the institutional setting, the therapist must become skilled at adapting the therapy to the setting and the time permitted. Learning massage techniques that can be done quickly on the hands, feet, or neck and shoulders may have equally beneficial results in similar short time periods.

Acupressure and Shiatzu

These two modalities are based on the Oriental energy system of meridian lines and points. Finger and/or thumb pressure is applied to energy points along the meridians to release congestion and allow energy flow.

There are 657 designated points on the human body that can be stimulated or treated with acupuncture, acupressure, or shiatzu.[37] These points run along 12 pathways or meridians that connect the points on each half of the body. In addition to the 12 pairs of body meridians, there are two coordinating meridians that bisect the body. Acupressure is primarily concerned with the 12 organ meridians.

The word "shiatzu" comes from the Japanese "shi" (finger) and "atzu" (pressure).[38] It is a product of 4,000 years of Oriental medicine, therapy, and philosophy. Although this technique is widely known and practiced in Japan, it was virtually unknown in the West until acupuncture began receiving widespread public attention. Shiatzu is based on the same points that are used in acupuncture, but instead of inserting needles the practitioner applies pressure on the points with thumbs, fingers, and heels of hand. Another difference between acupuncture and shiatzu is that shiatzu's main function is to maintain health and well-being, rather than to treat illness.

Reflexology

Reflexology evolved from Zone Therapy, which was developed by Dr. William FitzGerald in the early 1900s.[39] FitzGerald, an ear, nose, and throat specialist, noted that pressure applied on certain points on the hands caused anesthesia of other parts of the body. Another physician, Dr. Edwin Bowers, learned of FitzGerald's work and joined him in the exploration and development of this field. Zone Therapy became more specific as it evolved into Reflexology which encompasses many more pressure points.

This therapy is based on the theory that there are ten equal, longitudinal zones running the length of the body from the top of the head to the tips of the toes.[40] This number corresponds to the number of fingers and toes. Each big toe corresponds to a line up the medial aspect of the body, through the center of the face, and culminating at the top of the head. The reflex points pass all the way through the body within the same zones. Congestion or tension in any part of a zone will affect the entire zone running laterally throughout the body.

Over 72,000 nerves in the body terminate in the feet.[41] When there is a problem or disease in the body, it often manifests itself by forming deposits of calcium and acids on the corresponding part of the foot.

The purpose of this therapy is two-fold.[42] First, relaxation alone is seen as an important goal. Good health is dependent on one's ability to return to homeostasis after injury, disease, or stress. From this perspective, reflexology is effective in aiding the bodymind to restore and maintain its natural state of health because of the deep relaxation that foot manipulation triggers. The second goal of this therapy is to release congestion or tension that runs along the longitudinal and lateral zones by pressure manipulation at the precise endpoint of the zones. This pressure stimulates the reflexes in the feet to cause a corresponding release. All skeletal, muscular, vascular, nervous and organ systems are believed to be affected. Manuals with specific diagrams are used to instruct the therapist.

At this time there is no documented scientific research to validate the effectiveness of this touch therapy. However, it affects the body at a local level causing muscle relaxation and causes a simultaneous bodymind connection that results in the relaxation response. This affects the autonomic response, which is tied into the endocrine, immune, and neuropeptide systems (see Chapter 5).

Therapeutic Touch

Therapeutic touch (TT) is a healing modality that involves touching with the conscious intent to help or heal. Its major effects are to decrease anxiety, relieve pain, and facilitate the healing process.[43] Much research has been conducted and many workshops have been held on the modality of therapeutic touch during the past decade. The (TT) process has four phases[44]:

1. centering oneself physically and psychologically; that is, finding within oneself an inner reference of stability
2. exercising the natural sensitivity of the hand to assess the energy field of the client for clues to differentiate the quality of energy flow
3. mobilizing areas in the client's energy field that the healer may perceive as being nonflowing; that is, sluggish, congested, or static
4. the conscious direction by the healer of his or her excess body energies to assist the client to repattern his or her own energies

Four factors ensure the safe and successful practice of TT: *intention, motivation, personal recognition,* and *acceptance* by the practitioner of the reason he or she chooses to act in the role of healer.[45] Krieger, the founder of TT, describes these four qualities:

> Intention connotes a clear formulation of a goal; it suggests that the TT practitioner should have a lucid concept of how to help/heal, as well as the mere desire to do so. The practitioner's motivation, of course, provides the psychodynamic thrust, the direction that this healing/helping act will take and, therefore, it colors the emotional tone of the dyadic relationship between healer and healee. Finally, it is important for the practitioner to understand his/

> her own drives in wanting to play the role of healer. It does not matter what these drives are; what is important is that the practitioner willingly recognizes the personal foundations for his/her involvement in this highly personalized interaction.[46]

TT touch is taught at beginning, intermediate, and advanced levels in continuing education programs, graduate nursing education, and summer intensive workshops.

NURSING PROCESS

Assessment

In preparing to utilize touch interventions with clients, assess the following parameters:

- the client's perception of his or her bodymind problem
- the possibility of overt pathophysiologic problems; if problems are detected, refer to a physician for evaluation
- the client or the client's chart for a history of psychiatric disorders. The nurse must modify the approach with clients with present or past psychiatric disorders. Touch itself may present a problem, and the deeply relaxed semihypnotic state that a balanced person finds enjoyable may actually frighten or alarm an imbalanced individual.
- the client's cultural beliefs and values about touch
- the client's past experience with body therapies. There is a wide variation in the knowledge level of clients. The approach will differ markedly depending on the client's previous experience. Assisting a client to transfer prior learning, such as from childbirth preparation classes, to a new situation is a valuable nursing intervention.

Nursing Diagnoses

Nursing diagnoses compatible with touch interventions described in this chapter and that are related to the nine human response patterns of Unitary Person are as follows:

- Exchanging: Alterations in circulation
Impairment in skin integrity
- Relating: Social isolation
- Valuing: Alterations in spiritual state
- Moving: Physical mobility, impaired
- Perceiving: Alterations in meaningfulness

- Feeling: Alterations in comfort
  Anxiety
  Grieving
  Fear

Client Outcomes

Table 16-1 guides the nurse in client outcomes, outcome criteria, and evaluation for the use of touch as a nursing intervention.

Plan and Interventions

Before the Session

- Wash your hands.
- Wear loose fitting, comfortable clothing. If you have on street clothes, cover them with a lab coat.
- Have client empty the bladder for comfort.
- Prepare the hospital bed, therapy table, or surface on which you will be working. If you will be using a therapy table, drape it with a cotton blanket and place a sheet over the top. Lay out a large towel for the client to cover when with he or she lies on the table. Adjust the height of the table/bed for optimal use of your body mechanics.
- Have small pillows or towel rolls available for supporting the head, back, or lower legs.
- Control the room environment to be warm, dimly lit, and quiet. If you are in a client's hospital room, the curtain should be drawn and television turned off. A radio or cassette tape player could be left on for soothing music.
- Use relaxation and breathing techniques, imagery, or music to elicit the relaxation response.
- After you have talked with the client, spend a few moments to quiet and center yourself, to focus on your healing intention, and then begin.

Beginning the Session

- Explain to the client the steps in the touch process to be used.
- As you progress through the intervention, explain what you are about to do before you actually begin.
- Position the head comfortably. If the client has long hair, pull it up and away from the neckline.
- If working on the client's entire physical body, the client is completely disrobed and is covered first with a towel from the chest to the thighs. The client lies on a padded therapy table or hospital bed that is covered with a cotton blanket and sheet. The sides of the sheet and blanket are then wrapped over the client so that he or she feels protected and warm. (This procedure is done for the physical touch therapies and is not needed with therapeutic touch.)

Table 16-1 Nursing Intervention: Touch

Client Outcome	*Outcome Criteria*	*Evaluation*
The client will be relaxed following a touch therapy session.	1. The client will receive the touch therapy in order to evoke the relaxation response. 2. Following the touch therapy session the client will: a. Exhibit decreased anxiety and fear b. Exhibit decreased pulse and respiratory rate c. Recognize a feeling of bodymind relaxation d. Exhibit a sense of general well-being e. Demonstrate increased effectiveness in individual coping skills f. Exhibit an increased sense of belonging and lessened loneliness g. feel less alone and will express that feeling	1. The client willingly accepted touch therapy. 2. The client: a. Exhibited decreased anxiety and fear b. Demonstrated a decrease in pulse and respiratory rate c. Reported muscle relaxation d. Exhibited satisfied facial expression and expressed inner calmness e. Reported greater satisfaction in individual coping patterns
The client will have improved circulation.	1. The client will have improved circulation and tissue perfusion.	1. Clients with white skin will have a reddened color in the area where the nurse has used effleurage and petrosage massage strokes. Skin in the massage area will be warmer than before the therapy.
The client will receive touch therapy to maintain and enhance health.	1. The client will ask for touch therapy. The client will seek out the nurse. The client will accept the touch when offered by the nurse.	1. The client asked for touch therapy.

- Unwrap only the body area that is being massaged or pressed as the therapy proceeds.
- Most total body therapy begins with the client lying on the back. When the medial aspect and limbs of the body are completed, the wraps are lifted and reapplied after the client turns over.
- Encourage the client to take slow, deep, releasing breaths. When he or she lets go of tension through breath, affirm in a soft tone, "Ah, feel the release of tension."

- During the turning process, the nurse slides the towel around the client's body, thereby assuring that the client will not be exposed. As the client lays prone, the therapy continues on the dorsal aspect of the body.

During the Session

- Be attuned to the client's responses to therapy. This will help the client build trust and achieve optimal relaxation.
- In initial sessions, continue to explain what the client can expect to happen so that he or she may feel comfortable with the continued direction of the touch sessions. After trust has been established and the relaxation response learned, the client will learn to relax more quickly and to move to deeper levels in subsequent sessions.
- On subsequent sessions, proceed the same as in the initial session, but you may choose to shorten the explanation of what you are going to do.
- Remember to use your voice in a soft soothing manner that enables the client to relax.
- Reassess the client's responses as you proceed.
- The length of the session may be from 15 to 60 minutes.
- The first session always takes the most time because of the needed explanations and adjustment.

Closing the Session

- When you have finished the touch therapy session, verbally let the client know that it is time to return gradually to the here and now, begin to move around slowly, and fully awaken.
- Anticipate that it takes a few minutes for the client to reorient to time and place due to deep states of relaxation.
- Allow for periods of silence for the client to appreciate fully the wisdom of his or her relaxed bodymind.
- Stay in the room while the client arouses and sits up. Give necessary assistance to assure a safe transfer to an ambulatory position.
- Allow time to receive the client's verbal feedback about the meaning of the session, if this need to talk surfaces. If this does not occur spontaneously, the nurse can ask for feedback. The insight gained provides guidelines for further sessions or specific ideas that the client can follow up with in daily life.
- When the touch therapy is used for relaxation or sleep induction for hospitalized patients, close the session by softly pulling the bed covers up over the patient's back, and quietly turning off the light as the patient proceeds to move into sleep.

Specific Interventions: Touch

Each of the therapies discussed in the text has basic, intermediate, or advanced levels. The complexity depends on the amount of time spent studying the multiple variations of the therapy and whether or not they are used in conjunction with other therapies, such as music and imagery. It is expected that anyone who begins with the basic level and likes this approach will study or take continuing education courses to learn the intermediate and advanced levels.

Therapeutic Massage

Although called by different names (massage, Swedish massage, massotherapy) these techniques are all essentially the same. They involve the use of effleurage, petrosauge, and tapotment: all the classical nursing back rub strokes.

These strokes are directed toward enhancing circulation of both blood and lymph. Therapeutic massage increases dispersion of nutrients to enhance removal of metabolic wastes by increasing both lymphatic and blood flow.

Acupressure and Shiatzu

There is a broad range and depth of technique involved with this therapy. Most practitioners receive continuing education in this area; some spend years perfecting these techniques.

Reflexology

The primary purpose of reflexology is to evoke bodymind relaxation. Some practitioners believe that the systems shown in Figure 16-1 are the nerve or meridian endings for the specific vital body parts. When these specific areas are worked, a corresponding energy release or relaxation occurs in the internal body system.

Nurses who have not studied reflexology can still use general massage on the client's feet to elicit relaxation. The primary caution in this, as well as other body areas, is to stop massage in any area that provokes pain.

Therapeutic Touch

Therapeutic Touch (TT) is generally taught by experienced practitioners in continuing education seminars. The courses include all or part of the following elements: assessment, hand scan, intuition, energy field reading, mapping—recording, pattern comparison, verbal information, stress levels, relaxation levels, meditation experience.

In a TT session, the practitioner may ask the client to visualize clearly the part of the body that is to be influenced with the intent of enhancing contact with that body part's energy field. The practitioner's goal is to ascertain the degree of blockage in the energy field of the muscles or viscera. In order for practitioners to come in contact with these energies they must develop an awareness of events that are normally unconscious to them or the client. The imagery and visualization process is one way of tuning into this unconscious process. Therapists can use the effect of one modality (imagery) to synergistically affect another (touch).

Figure 16-2 illustrates a 5-year-old child's use of imagery and drawing to describe her self-perception before and after use of TT to treat an asthmatic episode. When she has asthma, the child says she "feels bald headed and sad." In drawing A, disconnected arm is moving up to wipe away her tears. Note the size of the figure and the lack of sturdy legs

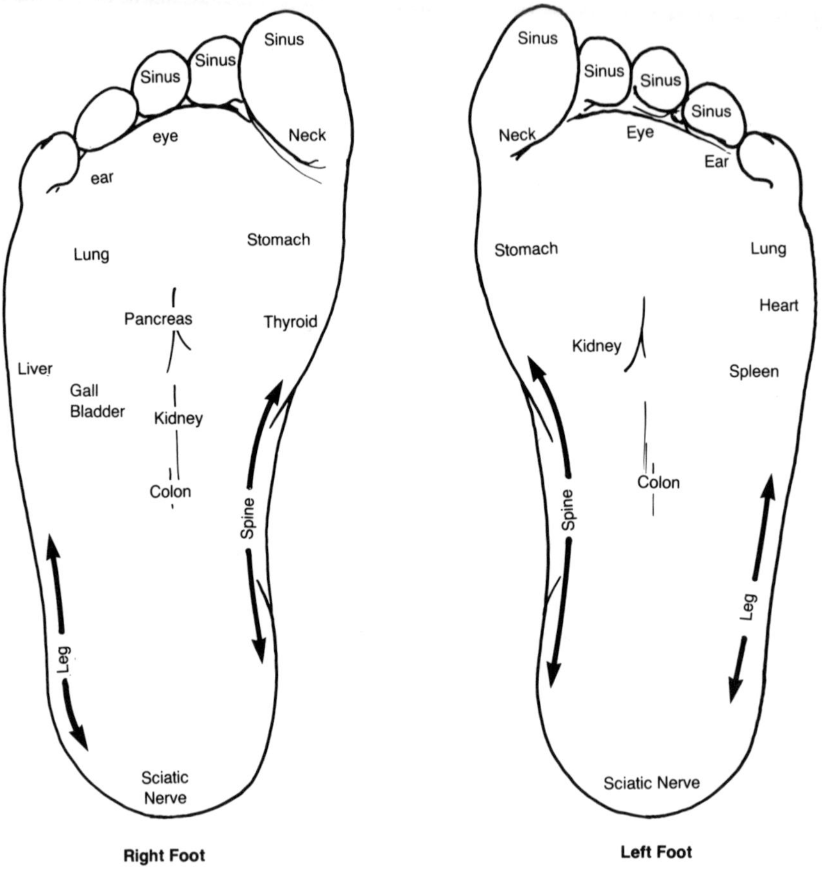

Figure 16-1 Foot Reflexology Chart.

---

support system. At the completion of the 15-minute TT session, the child feels well and happy and is free of respiratory distress. In drawing B, note the increase in figure size, strength of lines, and long hair that symbolizes strength to the child.

It is important to recognize when it is time to stop the TT process. One stops when there are no longer any clues of differences in body symmetry relative to density or temperature variation. Stop when the client's energy field is "full" and you are "pushed away" by the energy. Four commonly seen responses are: (1) flushed skin, (2) deep

A

B

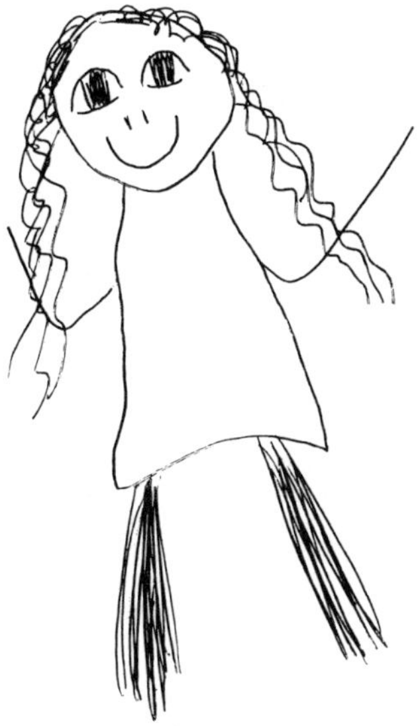

Figure 16-2 Drawing before (A) and after Therapeutic Touch Session. When she has asthma, the child says she ''feels bald headed and sad.'' In drawing A, disconnected arm is moving up to wipe away her tears. Note the size of the figure and the lack of sturdy legs support system. At the completion of the 15-minute TT session, the child feels well and happy and is free of respiratory distress. In drawing B, note the increase in figure size, strength of lines, and long hair that symbolizes strength to the child.

sighs, (3) physical relaxation, and (4) verbalized relaxation. A caution in TT is to limit the amount of time and/or energy sent to the very young, the old, and the ill infirmed.

Other touch therapies are discussed in Table 16-2.

Case Studies

Case Study No. 1

Setting:	Oncology Unit in general hospital
Client:	E.S., a 58-year-old, single, black, male
Nursing Diagnoses:	1. Anxiety
	2. Alterations in comfort related to terminal cancer
	3. Social isolation related to terminal stage of cancer

E.S. was a patient on the oncology unit of a general hospital. He knew he was in the terminal stage of cancer, yet was in basic good humor and was ambulatory. E.S. had grown up in the city in which he now found himself hospitalized. He had never married and had no remaining living family.

A nurse who was knowledgeable about touch therapy and felt comfortable using this modality worked evenings on the unit where E.S. was assigned. This nurse made the assessment of E.S.'s need for touch to increase comfort and to ally apprehension. Because the unit was continually short staffed and little time was available for lengthy one-on-one interventions with clients, this intervention had to become a priority item in E.S.' care. ''Evening back care'' was entered on his care plan, and despite sometimes hectic assignments back care was never omitted when this particular nurse was on duty.

Back care became so important to E.S. that he would eagerly greet the nurse when she came on shift, and he would be ready and waiting when she arrived at the appointed time. The touch he received from this nurse was the high point of his hospital stay. During the sessions he relaxed so deeply that his breathing rate became slowed; he stated that his perception of pain decreased and that he felt the pleasure of closeness to another caring human being. When the nurse was about to go off a 10 consecutive day shift, E.S. was profoundly saddened because he might have to go without this daily anticipated ritual. The nurse assured him that she had left specific orders for his back care to the oncoming nurse for the next evening. The next evening the regular nurse called in sick, a float nurse was assigned to the unit, and as you might expect, E.S. received no special attention. He unexpectedly died in his sleep during the night shift.

At this point in our development we do not have sophisticated tools to measure relationships between deaths such as the one described above and the omission of certain nursing interventions. Consequently, we cannot make any direct correlations. We can, however, begin to ask research questions and gather anecdotal data about whether the omission of a nursing intervention such as back care, can so grieve a client that physiological changes leading to death can occur.

Table 16-2 Descriptions of Various Touch Therapies

Therapy	*Originator*	*Primary Purpose and Function*
Applied Kinesology	George Goodheart	Focuses on the relationship of muscle strength and energy flow. The therory is that if muscles are strong, then circulation and other vital functions are also strong.
Chiropractic	D.D. Palmer	Based on alignment of spinal vertebrae. This therapy involves manipulations to restore natural alignment.
Feldenkrais	Moshe Feldenkrais	Purpose is to give the client gentle manipulations to heighten awareness of the body. As awareness increases clients can make more informed choices about how to move the body in daily situations.
Jin shin Jyutsy	Master Jiro Murai of Japan in early 1900s	A milder form of acupressure that involves pressure along eight extra energy meridians.
Kofutu Touch Healing	Frank Homan	System developed in the early 1970s when a series of symbols for use in touch came to the originator during meditation. It is called "Kofutu" for the symbols and "touch" healing because the auras of the healer and recipient must touch. This therapy uses higher consciousness energy symbols for the purpose of self-development and spiritual healing.
Lomi	R.K. Hall, R.K. Heckler	Directs attention to current muscle tension to aid learning of postural alignment to enhance free flow of the body's physical and emotional energies.
Polarity	Randolph Stone	Repattern energy flow in the individual by rebalancing positive and negative charges. The practitioner places finger or whole hand on parts of the client's body of opposite charge for the purpose of facilitating energy balancing where it is needed. Through these contacts, with the help of pressure and rocking movements, energy can reorganize and reorder itself.
MaríEL	Ethel Lombardi	A 1980s variation of Reiki.
Neuromuscular Release		Practitioner moves the limbs into and away from the body to assist the client in learning to "let go" for the purpose of enhanced circulation and emotional release.
Reiki	2,500-year-old Buddhist Practice Lost and Rediscovered in Late 1800's	Term means universal life energy. A touch technique in which the practitioner places hands in one of 12 positions on the recipient's body to direct healing energy to those sites.
Rolfing	Ida P. Rolf	Purpose is to help the client establish deep structural relationships within the body that manifest themselves via a symmetry and balanced function when the body is in an upright position. Technique involves deep muscle manipulation.
Trager	Milton Trager	Limbs and often the whole body are rocked rhythmically to aid relaxation of the muscles to promote an optimal flow of blood, lymph, nerve impulses, and energy.

Case Study No. 2

Setting:	Wellness center
Patient:	J.S., a 36-year-old white married woman
Nursing Diagnoses:	1. Anxiety related to personal and family stress
	2. Alteration in self-image related to obesity.

J.S. was referred by a psychologist to a nurse in a wellness center for weight management. In addition to the weekly counseling program this client elected to follow each counseling session with a therapeutic massage. She also continued to work with the psychologist for resolution of personality disorder problems. Both the psychologist and the nurse saw this client regularly for over a year until her move away from the area terminated the relationship.

The focus of her counseling sessions with the nurse was on her eating disorders, nutritional education, and discussion about how to institute lifestyle changes that would change the overweight pattern. These sessions were sometimes emotional, but for the most part were straightforward and unevocative of emotional, spiritual, or attitudinal change. In contrast, the elective sessions involving touch elicited a response that allowed this client to make connections with a deeper level of herself and finally gain the understanding of the true nature of her physical problems. While the nurse used touch, she also played relaxation music and/or guided the client in imagery. In addition the nurse did foot reflexology and concluded the sessions with therapeutic touch.

When the nurse first began work with this client, the client complained of a feeling of a knot in her stomach that had not abated for 15 years. The only time her stomach felt better was after eating. After a few sessions of therapeutic massage she stated that this stomach pain was relieved during the time she received the touch therapies.

As the client became more trusting of the nurse, she gradually began divulging more of her feelings while in the deeply relaxed state experienced during the session. She revealed that she was physically distant from her husband and her 14-year-old daughter. After receiving the massage for approximately 6 weeks she learned to immediately relax upon reclining on the table, which dissolved her stomach knot. By 8 weeks the pain stayed away for from 2 to 3 days after a session, and weight loss became possible. By the fourth month she began to hug and touch her daughter at home to dissolve the discomfort she had with their relationship.

The power of touch became so important to her that by the eighth month she brought her daughter to the nurse so that her daughter could experience first-hand what massage was all about. The daughter, of course, did not have the emotional response or release felt by the mother for she had not experienced the years of holding tension and withdrawal. The daughter was happy to see how massage was done as she and her mother planned to exchange massage sessions at home between visits to the nurse. The healing bond that occurred between mother and daughter was initiated by and through touch.

Case Study No. 3

Setting:	Wellness center
Client:	A.R. a 50-year-old white woman
Nursing Diagnoses:	1. Alteration in spiritual state related to death of husband
	2. Grieving, related to death of husband

A.R. came regularly to the wellness center three to four times a month over a period of 18 months before the unexpected death of her husband. A strong therapeutic relationship had been established between the nurse and the client. Her initial reason for coming to the center was for therapeutic massage. However, the nurse also used therapeutic touch, acupressure, reflexology, guided imagery, and music. The combination of all of these modalities enhanced the overall therapeutic value of the sessions, which A.R. found particularly effective in maintaining her own high level wellness.

The private individual sessions at the wellness center were her opportunity to relax, completely unwind, and say whatever she needed as she simultaneously allowed her physical body to receive healing touch. Initially she struggled with "letting go" and allowing the deep relaxation to come. After only three or four sessions, however, she became increasingly able to immediately move into the relaxation mode so that she was able to use her time most effectively. Over the months she had various muscle stresses and strains that were addressed with extra attention. The nurse recommended exercises to strengthen those areas. A.R. came to view these sessions as a safe place where she could be completely herself and trust the nurse. She received nurturance and empowerment to increase peak performance in her busy professional and social life. A.R. holds a demanding executive position and a prominent social position that require national travel and being in the public eye.

In addition to the weekly individual sessions A.R. attended two separate series of group classes that the nurse conducted at the center. One series was on stress management, and the other was on high-level wellness. She learned all she could from the classes and continued regular individual sessions whenever she was in town.

The unexpected sudden death of her husband was an emotional blow with which she was unprepared to cope. Because of her husband's prominence, she was overwhelmed with the condolences, the demands of decision making, and well-meaning friends' attempts to cheer her up. All of her friends' diversionary tactics and inability to allow her to grieve only served to deepen her sadness and mask her true feelings of despair.

Within a week of the funeral, as soon as the relatives had departed, she was back at the wellness center. Here she had already established the therapeutic relationship, and thus the healing could proceed. During these sessions touch and the therapeutic relationship were the channels that opened her release of grieving. Here in the safe environment of the wellness center the power of the music, the touch of the hand, and the guiding of the nurse's voice allowed her to let go completely. She no longer had any of the neck or shoulder pain that she often came in with because, as she said, "My body is limp."

At this point muscle release was no longer the primary goal, but rather the therapy that had achieved a physical release was now used for emotional release. She learned how to use her breath in conjunction with the effleurage massage strokes to release the sorrow and permit the tears. The sessions were always concluded with her lying prone and wrapped cocoon-like in a sheet and blanket as the nurse did therapeutic touch and guided imagery.

During the 3-month bereavement period she would occasionally come for sessions as often as twice a week. She symbolically and literally would leave her reality of worldly demands, shed the clothing of literal and figurative protection to allow release and healing. Through the modality of touch a therapeutic bond had been established that allowed a place and medium for not only bereavement but also the beginning of spiritual transformation. She sought spiritual answers and was able to begin a transformation process that will affect her and those she interacts with for years to come.

Case Study No. 4

Setting:	School nurse's office
Client:	7-year-old second-grade student
Nursing Diagnoses:	1. Alterations in respiration related to asthma
	2. Fear related to difficulty breathing

A seven-year-old second-grade student was brought to the nurse's office by a teacher's aide. The child was coughing and apprehensive. The school nurse listened for and heard bronchial wheezes. She had the child sit upright in a chair and spoke soothingly to her as she used therapeutic touch. The nurse spent approximately 7 minutes quietly talking and moving her hands over the child's chest area. The child stopped wheezing, her apprehension disappeared, her facial features relaxed, and her color returned to normal. The nurse then called her mother to explain what had happened. The mother was amazed at her daughter's quick recovery because on every previous occasion the child had to be taken to the hospital or doctor's office for intravenous medication and respiratory treatments. The mother asked the nurse to teach her the technique so she could use it at home when the asthma occurred there.

Evaluation

In each touch therapy session the outcomes must be measured as successful or not. The nurse should evaluate with the client the outcomes that were established before the touch session (Table 16-2).

Nurses who work in institutional settings should chart the use, type, location, and duration of the touch therapy and its subjective and objective effects on the patient. When sessions are effective they should be reported in writing, as well as orally at change of shift report. Other nurses need to be appraised of the effectiveness of this independent nursing intervention.

Nurses who work in wellness centers, independent practice, or other areas in which the touch therapies are done as the primary care modality should keep records on their clients stating the nursing diagnosis, touch therapy employed, and the effectiveness of each session.

SUMMARY

This chapter has focused on touch from several perspectives: historical, theory and research, general uses of touch, and how to use touch in the nursing process. Four case studies were presented to illustrate touch therapy in clinical practice areas. Nurses wishing to learn these specific touch therapies should enroll in continuing education courses and do further reading.

DIRECTIONS FOR FUTURE RESEARCH

1. Investigate the effects of therapeutic massage on relaxation, on pain relief, sleep induction, stress management, sensory deprivation, apprehension, and a host of other parameters.
2. Examine the effects of reflexology on pain relief, relaxation, and/or specific physiologic parameters.
3. Develop valid and reliable tools to measure the effects of touch.
4. Formulate studies to examine the relationship among guided imagery, music, smell, color, taste, and touch.
5. Determine if clients can be taught relaxation techniques by imaging the sensations and emotions evoked during the touch therapy session.
6. Conduct qualitative studies that investigate the meanings of nonprocedural touch throughout the life cycle.
7. Investigate if periodic touch therapy sessions increase work or performance productivity.
8. Examine the relationship between the touch therapies and healing.

NURSE HEALER REFLECTIONS

After reading this chapter, the nurse healer will be able to answer or begin a process of answering the following questions:

- How do I *feel* about using touch as an intervention?
- What do I experience with touch therapy when I touch a client from a place of *being centered?*
- When I touch with *intention,* what is my inner experience?
- When I use touch, what happens to my *sense of time?*
- How does my touch as a nurse *affect* the recipient?
- Whom do I *know* who can be my mentor for helping me increase skills with touch?
- What other *modalities* can be used concurrently to heighten the effectiveness of touch?

NOTES

1. Dorothea Hover-Kramer, "The Healer," *The Path to the Well-Spring*. (Farmingdale, NY: Coleman Publishing, 1983), p. 42.
2. Dolores Krieger, *The Therapeutic Touch,* (Englewood Cliffs, NJ: Prentice Hall, Inc., 1979), p. 36.
3. "Quest for Healing: Massage, Manipulation, Movement," *The Discovery Channel,* May 14, 1987.
4. Roger Jahnke, "The Body Therapies," *Journal of Holistic Nursing,* Spring 1985, pp. 7–14.
5. Linda Baldwin, "The Therapeutic Use of Touch with the Elderly," *Physical and Occupational Therapy in Geriatrics* 4 (Summer 1986): 45–50.

6. Cathie E. Guzzetta and Barbara M. Dossey, *Cardiovascular Nursing: Holistic Practice* (St. Louis: Mosby Year Book, 1992), pp. 586–587.
7. Roger Jahnke, ''Body Therapies,'' *Venture Inward,* March/April 1986, pp. 41–45.
8. Sophy Burnham, ''Healing Hands,'' *New Woman,* March 1986, pp. 72–77.
9. Harry Harlow, ''Love in Infant Monkeys,'' *Scientific American* 200 (1958): 68–74.
10. R. Spitz, *The First Year of Life*, (New York: International Universities Press, 1965).
11. L. L. Roth and J. S. Rosenblatt, ''Mammary Glands of Pregnant Rats: Development Stimulated by Tickling,'' *Science* 151 (1965): 1403–1404.
12. Bernard Grad, ''Some Biological Effects of the Laying-On of Hands: A Review of Experiments With Animals and Plants,'' *Journal of the American Society for Psychical Research* 59 (1965): 95–127
13. Sister M. J. Smith, ''Enzymes are Activated by the Laying On of Hands,'' *Human Dimensions,* February 1973, pp. 46–48.
14. J. Knable, ''Handholding: One Means of Transcending Barriers of Communication,'' *Heart Lung* 10 (1981): 1106.
15. C. Schmahl, ''Ritualism in Nursing Practice,'' *Nursing Forum* 11 (1964): 74.
16. Marilyn Glick, ''Caring Touch and Anxiety in Myocardial Infarction Patients in the Intermediate Cardiac Care Unit,'' *Intensive Care Nursing* February 1986, pp. 61–66.
17. Ruth McCorkle, ''Effects of Touch on Seriously Ill Patients,'' *Nursing Research,* 1974, pp. 125–132.
18. D.C. Aguilera, ''Relationship between Physical Contact and Verbal Interaction Between Nurses and Patients,'' *Journal of Psychiatric Nursing* 5 no. 1 (1967): 5–21.
19. S.J. Tobiason, ''Touching is for Everyone,'' *American Journal of Nursing* 4 (1981): 728–730.
20. Ann Yurick et al., *The Aged Person and the Nursing Process* (New York: Appleton-Century-Crofts, 1980), p. 298.
21. M. DeWever, ''Nursing Home Patients' Perceptions of Nurses' Affective Touching,'' *Journal of Psychology* 96 (1977): 163–171.
22. Hazel Rozema, ''Touch Needs of the Elderly,'' *Nursing Homes,* September/October 1986, pp. 42–43.
23. S. Simon, ''Please Touch! How to Combat Skin Hunger in Our Schools,'' *Scholastic Teacher,* October 1974, pp. 22–25.
24. K. Barnett, ''A Survey of the Current Utilization of Touch by Health Team Personnel with Hospitalized Patients,'' *International Journal of Nursing Studies* 9 (1972): 195–209.
25. I.M. Burnside, ''Touching is Talking,'' *American Journal of Nursing,* December 1973, pp. 2060–2066.
26. E. Duffy, ''An Exploratory Study: The Effects of Touch on the Elderly in a Nursing Home'' (Unpublished master's thesis, Rutgers State University, 1982).
27. E. Steuding, ''Selected Psychosocial Effects of Touch on Residents of a Nursing Home'' (Unpublished master's thesis, Rutgers State University, 1984).
28. Patricia Heidt, ''Effect of Therapeutic Touch in Anxiety Levels of Hospitalized Patients,'' *Nursing Research* 30 (1981): 32.
29. Elizabeth Keller and Virginia Bzdek, ''Effects of Therapeutic Touch on Tension Headache Pain,'' *Nursing Research* 35 (March/April 1986): 101–106.
30. Dolores Krieger, *The Therapeutic Touch,* p. 36.
31. Janet Quinn, ''One Nurse's Evolution as Healer,'' *American Journal of Nursing* 79 (1979): 662.
32. Linda Dallam, ''Touching You, Touching Me,'' *American Journal of Nursing,* January 1987, p. 140.
33. Ashley Montagu and Floyd Matson, *The Human Connection* (New York: McGraw-Hill 1979), p. 89.
34. Ibid. p. 90.
35. Shirley Smoyak, ''High Tech, High Touch,'' *Nursing Success Today* 3, no. 11 (November 1986): 9–16.
36. Sue Hartman, ''Hug a Patient, P.R.N.,'' *Nursing 86* 16, no. 8, (August 1986): 88.
37. Yukiko Irwin, *Shiatzu,* (Philadelphia: J.B. Lippincott Co., 1976): pp. 15–19.
38. Ibid. pp. 15–19.
39. Anika Bergson and Vladimir Tuchak, *Zone Therapy,* (New York: Pinnacle Books, 1974), p. 15.

40. Kevin and Barbara Kunz, *The Complete Guide to Foot Reflexology,* (Englewood Cliffs, NJ: Prentice Hall, Inc., 1980), pp. 2–6.

41. Dolores Krieger, *Foundations for Holistic Health Nursing Practices: The Renaissance Nurse,* (Philadelphia: J.B. Lippincott Co., 1981), p. 158.

42. Kevin and Barbara Kunz, *The Complete Guide to Foot Reflexology,* pp. 46.

43. M. Bogusalawski, "The Use of Therapeutic Touch in Nursing," *The Journal of Continuing Education in Nursing,* October 1979, p. 9–15.

44. Dolores Krieger, *Foundations for Holistic Health Nursing Practices: The Renaissance Nurse,* p. 158.

45. Marianne Borelli and Patricia Heidt, *Therapeutic Touch: A Book of Readings,* (New York: Springer Publishing Co.), p. v.

46. Ibid., p. v.

SUGGESTED READINGS

Homan, Frank and Kragnes, Verna. *Kofutu Touch Healing*. Philadelphia: Sunlight Publishing, 1986.

Kunz, Dora, ed. *Spiritual Aspects of the Healing Arts*. Wheaton, IL: The Theosophical Publishing House, 1985.

Kunz, Kevin, and Kunz, Barbara. *The Practitioner's Guide to Reflexology*. Englewood Cliffs, NJ: Prentice Hall, 1985.

Lidell, Lucinda. *The Book of Massage*. New York: Simon and Schuster, 1984.

chapter **17**

Self-Reflection: Consulting the Truth Within

Leslie Gooding Kolkmeier

> As the Gods created the universe they discussed where they should hide Truth so that human beings would not find it right away. They wanted to prolong the adventure of the search.
>
> "Let's put Truth on top of the highest mountain," said one of the gods. "Certainly it will be hard to find there."
>
> "Let's put it on the farthest star," said another.
>
> "Let's hide it in the darkest and deepest of abysses."
>
> "Let's conceal it on the secret side of the moon."
>
> At the end, the wisest and most ancient god said, "No, we will hide Truth inside the very heart of human beings. In this way they will look for it all over the Universe, without being aware of having it inside themselves all the time."[1]
>
> *Piero Ferrucci, PhD*
> *Psychosynthesis Institute*
> *Florence, Italy*

This chapter discusses the use of diaries, journals, logs, reviews, and records to enable us to keep track of and enhance the patterns of our lives. As adolescents we may have written in a diary, entering into it both the mundane and the deeply moving events of our days. With the transition into adulthood, these diary entries may well have been reduced to lists of things to do, appointments, chores, and dates. We find time only for jotting short notes on a calendar or in a blank book, making longer entries in a loose-leaf notebook, or perhaps putting into a box scraps of paper containing ideas, thoughts, bits of poetry, and plans for a golden tomorrow. Even these abbreviated records provide a skeletal reflection of our lives, which can be filled out and given form by memories.

As nurses we can refresh our own self-reflection techniques and perfect new ones to help us record and grow from our experiences, intuitions, and connections. We can learn to help ourselves and our clients tap into the spiritual and self-healing aspects of the complex and beautiful web of our existence.

NURSE HEALER OBJECTIVES

Theoretical

1. Read and define the types of self-reflection tools.
2. Discuss the theories of adult learning that describe the ability and readiness of the client to use and benefit from the tools.
3. Discuss how right-brain activity of intuiting information can be used and applied to left-brain analysis of clinical data.

Clinical

1. Implement one of the interventions with a client in whose care you are involved.
2. Keep an intuition log for 1 week, recording all instances of intuitive thought concerning your clients.
3. Make a list of opening questions or statements to help initiate the life review process with clients.

Personal

1. Use self-reflection in your life as a healing intervention in order to tap into intuitive knowledge.
2. Choose one intervention with which you are less familiar and spend 1 month increasing your expertise.
3. Practice interpreting your intuitions and dreams in order to become more adept and confident in your daily life decisions.

DEFINITIONS

Clustering: a visual representation of an information web; a cluster of ideas starting from a core word and branching outward.

Contract: a written or verbal formalization of an agreement between two people: a nurse and client, client and family member, or client and friend.

Diaries and Journals: records kept on a periodic or daily basis; contain factual material and subjective interpretation of events, thoughts, feelings, and plans.

Dreams: unself-conscious reflections of the psyche; may occur as hypnagogic or hypnopompic imagery (see Chapter 2) or during the rapid eye movement sleep period.

Letters: a simple way of talking to another in written words; may be to new or old friends, family, body parts, or acquaintances who are alive or deceased.

Life Review or **Reminiscence Therapy:** the remembering of significant past events.

THEORY AND RESEARCH

Self-reflection interventions are teaching tools, but they differ from most client education modules because the learning comes from inner knowledge and is primarily client-generated. The nurse is involved principally as a facilitator. In order to understand the successful application of these tools it is necessary to review some assumptions about adult education.

Adults, as opposed to children, are *voluntary* learners and must be engaged in satisfying learning experiences in order to succeed. Educators have identified four ways in which adults differ from children in the ways they learn[2]:

1. An adult's *self-concept* has shifted from that of a dependent person to one who is capable of self-direction.
2. An adult has a large data base of *life experience* to use as a resource for learning.
3. An adult's motivation for learning is oriented toward *problem solving,* rather than learning for the sake of learning.
4. An adult's time perspective has changed in that an adult desires *immediate applicability* of the knowledge gained.

Self-Concept

The adult self-concept is based on independence and self-sufficiency. Illness or injury threatens self-concept and necessitates a modification in teaching techniques. When judiciously presented, self-reflection tools bolster self-concept and self-esteem and help direct the client to former feelings of independence. Using such techniques as clustering of strengths and possibilities or writing journal entries of feelings surrounding an illness or injury can help the client reintegrate a shaken self-image and actually speed physical and emotional healing.

Experience

Adults base many of their coping skills on what has worked well for them in the past. Because serious illness or injury is not usually a part of becoming an adult, the ability to cope with it is not something the client can easily call up from past experience.

The more information that nurses can provide clients concerning the illness or injury, the more quickly the client can move toward healing. In the acute phase of an illness or injury such information will need to address short-term goals, such as anxiety reduction, environmental information, and details concerning nursing and medical procedures. As clients incorporate this knowledge into their experience base, they can move to somewhat longer-term teaching goals, such as behavior change. Using a diary and writing letters to family and friends help the client integrate the health care experience into the "whole story" and thus remove barriers to further learning and healing.

Problem Solving

Adults learn new information and life skills primarily through the identification of problems in daily life that need to be solved. Nurses can become discouraged if their teaching is focused on areas in which the client fails to see a problem. Using clustering or lists may help the client identify problems and areas related to those problems and become open to learning new ways to deal with them. Dream logs may also help point out areas of conflict that may be more unconscious in nature.

Applicability of Knowledge

Children are accustomed to learning material that appears to have little application to daily life but which experience has shown will have benefit for them at a later time. Adults need to be able to see a direct application of their learning to a perceived problem. In order to apply self-reflection techniques successfully, the nurse must be able to help the client make the connection between the technique and the alleviation of the identified problem.

GENERAL EXPLANATIONS

Bodymind Connections

Self-reflection interventions act as intermediaries between the various aspects and expressions of the bodymind. Each of the interventions becomes a tool for exploring thoughts, feelings, and emotions. As these are brought to consciousness, they stimulate shifts in the endocrine, neuropeptide, immune, and hormonal systems (see Chapter 5).

We are all familiar with how our body responds when we think of anxiety-laden events. Simply telling or writing about emotionally charged material or a time of physical pain triggers activity in the hypothalamus and pituitary: the heart and respiratory rate increases, palms sweat, and the entire General Adaptation Syndrome is activated. The bodymind connection is immediate and uncomfortable.

The connections are just as strong, although perhaps more subtle, when we process thoughts and memories of a less troubling nature. We are still participating in an electrical, chemical, and spiritual dance each time we examine our life process and patterns through the use of a self-reflection intervention.

The interventions that follow fit under the heading of what Ira Progoff calls transpsychologic. That is, they bring about therapeutic effects not by striving toward therapy but by providing active techniques that enable an individual to call up inner strengths and inherent resources for becoming a whole person.[3]

Reconnecting with Life Events

Self-reflection interventions help the client reconnect with events, to reinterpret the actions and emotions connected with those events, and reframe their physiologic and emotional implications. Whether the client is reminiscing about episodes that happened in childhood or listing the pros and cons of an anticipated lifestyle change, thinking, talking, or writing about such events elicits a psychophysiologic response. By calling up and examining events in a relaxed and open manner, the event can be reframed and modified in a safe and receptive environment. Previously frightening, upsetting, or threatening occurrences and their attendant internal responses are seen in a clearer, more realistic light.

Left- and Right-Hemispheric Learning

Self-reflection skills utilize the left-hemispheric abilities of logical, analytical organization of data in addition to the right-hemispheric skills of intuitive, feeling, nonlogical ways of knowing (see Chapters 2 and 5). By incorporating and blending these styles of gathering and organizing information the nurse and the client build levels of self-esteem, confidence, and feelings of connection within themselves and as members of a larger group.

Intuition

Self-reflection techniques enhance self-esteem and understanding and lead to increased confidence in and use of inner, intuitive knowledge and self-healing. They bring the client to higher levels of physical, mental, emotional, and spiritual wellness.

The word "intuition" comes from the Latin "in-tuire," which means looking inward or knowing from within. "Like sensation, feeling, and thinking, intuition is a way of knowing. When we know something intuitively, it invariably has the ring of truth; yet often we do not know how we know what we know."[4] Frequently we add elements of intuitive insight to our clinical decision making, but we seldom consciously acknowledge the existence of the rather "fuzzy" processes.

Rational and intuitive aspects of human beings are "complementary modes of knowing".[5] By developing and integrating these two, we move to a wholeness greater than the sum of the parts.

Nurses must learn to acknowledge the existence of their intuitive wisdom and add it to their rational, linear ways of caring for clients to increase the base upon which the nursing profession rests. Nurses also need to begin to process the intuitive leaps; that is, to explain and translate intuition into operational and functional knowledge.[6] By listening closely to inner voices, we can sharpen our ability to recognize subtle knowledge as valid and become confident employing this intuition with our clients.

It is not necessary to have all the answers to the questions that will surface with the use of self-reflection interventions. Posing reflective questions or asking for more information (e.g., "What do you think that means?," "Can you tell me more about that"?) are ways of keeping the lines of communication open without placing your own interpretation on the client's material. As you gain experience, you will be more comfortable offering your thoughts for the client's consideration, but remember that the client alone is the one living the event and is the one who will eventually recognize the personal meaning of that experience.

Diaries and Journals

With the dawn of the 20th century came the recognition of the subconscious and the importance of self-reflection. As we enter the 21st century, diary and journal keeping are becoming valid tools for growth. They are "personal book(s) in which creativity, play, and self-therapy interweave, foster, and complement each other."[7] They become safe places in which to explore thoughts, ideas, and feelings.

In the words of the great diarist, Anais Nin, the diary allows us to:

> discover a voice for reaching the deep sources of metaphysical and numinous qualities contained in human beings . . . the ultimate instrument for explorations of new forms of consciousness and ecstasy . . . a way of opening vision into experience, deepening understanding of others; as a way to touch and reach the depths of human beings; as nourishment; as a means of linking the content of the dream to our actions so that they become harmonious and interactive.[8]

Introducing his reasons and methods for maintaining a journal, Progoff states:

> Many persons have already had experiences in which they have sensed the presence of an underlying reality in life, a reality which they have recognized as a personal source of meaning and strength. It may have come to them in a brief, spontaneous moment of spiritual exaltation, or it may have come as a flash of awareness in the midst of darkness and pain. They came very close then to the deep, unifying contact, but it slipped away from them because they had no means of holding it and sustaining the relationship.[9]

When the nurse or the client feels the need for structure or a place to express immediate feelings and concerns freely—whether they are coming from a moment of exaltation or pain—diaries and journals provide an ideal means for this expression and growth.

Letters

A variation of journal keeping is letter writing. Writing to new and old friends and relatives during a time of hospitalization, illness, or approaching death is a way of maintaining and renewing relationships. Writing letters to yourself or to body parts may facilitate expression of emotions, thoughts, and feelings. This activity should be encouraged in both clients and their family members and friends. Receiving letters can also aid the healing process of wholeness.

Contracting

Contracting is a way to increase the quality of communication between the client and nurse. Contracting can also help a client become a more willing participant in self-care and responsibility. Successful completion of a contract deepens self-esteem and the client/nurse bond. Failure to comply with the terms of a contract opens the door to frank discussion of why compliance was a problem and how the situation could be adjusted to achieve a mutually acceptable goal.[10]

Dreams

Jung writes that "the general function of dreams is to try to restore our psychological balance by producing dream material that re-establishes, in a subtle way, the total psychic equilibrium."[11] Both daydreams and those experienced during the rapid eye movement stage of sleep are one of our richest sources of inner information. Dreams are "the imagistic formulations of what one knows intuitively."[12]

Most adults dream for approximately 100 minutes during an 8-hour night's sleep; they frequently remember only small disconnected portions of the dreams that occur in the later part of the sleep segment, although some people claim never to remember their dreams.[13]

In ancient Greece and Turkey, dream therapy that used dreams as diagnostic and healing tools reached a fine art. The time immediately before falling asleep, during which our altered state of consciousness experiences what we now call hypnagogic sleep, was used by the medical practitioners of the day to stimulate the inner healing of their clients.

The Christian churches, particularly those in England, have used the technique of incubation sleep or "divine sleep of the saints" for diagnosis and treatment from the second century A.D. to the present. Churches dedicated to Saints Cosmas and Damian, patron saints of Western healing, cared for the sick and employed healing imagery and dream states based on the techniques of the early Greeks.[14]

Dreams are used by people of various cultures to find information concerning life goals, the source and cure of illnesses, and as windows into the inner world. Vaughan describes the use of dreams by the Senoi people of Malaya:

> The Senoi people of Malaya, noted for the peaceful and cooperative nature of their society, use dreams on a daily basis for guidance in personal and social affairs. Children are taught to share their dreams at breakfast, and to control their dreams by lucid dreaming. One of their basic rules is to always confront and conquer danger or threatening figures in dreams instead of running away from them.[15]

Reminiscing and Life Review

On many occasions we think, write, or talk about our successes, disappointments, failures, sources of pride, plans, and goals. This is an especially important activity during times of illness or as death approaches. It is during these periods of reminiscence and life review that we organize our past experiences and imagine future outcomes in light of past and present circumstances. As these past events and future outcomes are reviewed, the accompanying emotions are also experienced and integrated.

Reminiscence has three components: memory, experiencing, and social interaction.[16] Memories, when recalled, are affected by the client's values, hope, and openness to the review process. More than a simple inner remembering, these memories take on new meaning when related to a concerned other, whether a family member, friend, nurse or therapist. Small gestures of social interaction, such as touch and a comment by the listener, do much to improve the quality and quantity of the memories.

Guiding clients through the life review process is a skill that can only be developed when one has integrated the disciplines of reflection and meditation into one's own life. The guide must be balanced and facilitate questions and comments from a place of compassion and intention. The guide's responses must be based on a felt sense of the direction that the process is taking. The guide may ask questions about significant people in the client's life or personal objects or pictures of friends or family in the client's room. Such comments as "This is a lovely picture of your wedding. Could you tell me something special you remember about that day?" may open new vistas of understanding for you and your client. If questions elicit memories of stressful events, the guide must help the client determine how stressful events have been worked through in the past.

Most investigators feel that guided and supported life review helps clients adapt to changes in lifestyle brought about by illness and aging. It can also increase the level of wellness as indicated by higher survival rates. Improved coping skills are also a frequent outcome of using the life review process.[17]

Life review or reminiscence should not be confined to the elderly, but may be used with preteens and adolescents who are experiencing life-threatening illness or death. Recalling and sharing holidays, vacations, and special events with family or school friends allows young people to see that they have made a difference in the lives of others and that they are part of a larger community, even though their time may not be of the quality or quantity they would have wished.

NURSING PROCESS

Assessment

In preparing to utilize self-reflection interventions with clients assess the following parameters:

- the ability of the client to read and write. If the client cannot read or write, the techniques can be simply modified to use audiotape recordings or a family member, friend, or member of the health care team can act as transcriber of the information.
- what goals are to be attained and the level of interest that the client expresses in reaching those goals
- the level of experience that the client has with each of the techniques to be used
- if the client understands that the purpose of the intervention is to enhance self-esteem, review and interpret recurrent themes, increase creativity, and integrate new information into the life process—and not in any way to invade the client's privacy

- the belief system of the client to ensure that the planned intervention is congruent with the client's reality and values
- any homework done during or since previous sessions

Nursing Diagnoses

Nursing diagnoses compatible with the techniques described in this chapter and that are related to the nine human response patterns of Unitary Person are as follows:

• Communicating:	Impaired verbal communication
• Relating:	Impaired social interaction Alteration in family process Social isolation
• Valuing:	Spiritual distress
• Choosing:	Impaired adjustment Ineffective family coping Ineffective individual coping
• Moving:	Diversional activity, deficit
• Perceiving:	Disturbance in self-concept Powerlessness
• Knowing:	Alteration in thought process
• Feeling:	Anxiety Grieving, anticipatory and dysfunctional

Client Outcomes

Table 17-1 guides the nurse in client outcomes, outcome criteria, and evaluation for the use of self-reflection as a nursing intervention.

Plan and Interventions

Experience with the techniques will give the nurse increasing expertise in knowing which of these self-reflection tools should be employed.

Before the Session

- Learn to trust and cultivate your intuition. Self-reflection is intuitive.
- Center yourself before the session. For example, each time you hesitate before entering a room, take a deep breath and let it out, feeling your relaxation. As you use this technique, notice how you enhance the quality of your client contact.
- Become personally familiar with the strategy you are presenting to your client.

Table 17-1 Client Outcomes: Self-Reflection

Outcomes	*Outcome Criteria*	*Evaluation*
1. Client will demonstrate increased effective individual and family coping skills.	1. Client will demonstrate effective individual and family coping skills as seen by: a. Increased quality and quantity of verbal communication with staff and family b. Decrease in frequency of disagreements and arguments c. Decrease in use of alcohol, drugs, or food to cope with stressors	1. Client demonstrated increased coping skills by increasing communication with staff and family and decreasing dependence on food, drugs, alcohol, and arguments.
2. Client will demonstrate feelings of self-worth generated by insights gained through diary and journal keeping.	2. Client will demonstrate feelings of self-worth generated by insights gained through diary and journal keeping as evidenced by: a. Verbalized feelings of self-worth b. Ability to point out successes and accomplishments with pride when questioned c. Increased assertive behaviors d. Increased participation in self-care and other activities	2. Client demonstrated increase in self-worth after working with diaries or journals. This was seen through an ability to point out successes, increased verbalization of self-pride, increased assertive behavior, and increased participation in self-care and other activities.
3. Client will verbalize feelings of continuity and belonging to a larger group as identified by life review.	3. Client will verbalize feelings of continuity and belonging to a larger group as evidenced by: a. Increased participation in group or one-to-one discussion of family and community ties b. Increased discussion of personal items, photos, family members, and their relationships c. Increased participation in community or family activities	3. Client verbalized feelings of belonging through discussion of personal items, family members, and a sense of community. Increased participation in group activities was observed.

Table 17-1 continued

4. Client will demonstrate an ability to move through a previously difficult situation, thought process, or memory by using clustering strategies.	4. Client will demonstrate an ability to move through a previously difficult situation, thought process, or memory as evidenced by: a. Increased verbalization of situation, thought process, or memory in appropriate ways b. Increased ability to sleep c. Appropriate expression of anger or sadness	4. Client demonstrated ability to deal with and move through previously stressful situation or memory as evidenced by increased positive verbalization, increase in healthful sleep pattern, and appropriate expressions of emotion after work with clustering strategy.

- Complete all necessary medical or nursing care so that the client will be able to work for the period of time necessary to complete the intervention.
- Provide an opportunity for physical and emotional comfort, such as encouraging the client to empty the bladder and adjust lighting and room temperature if necessary.
- Explain the purpose of the intervention in light of the client's perceived needs at the moment.
- Enlist the client's cooperation in determining goals for the session.
- Provide for privacy if the client wishes it.
- Have pencil, pen, crayons, markers, paper, and other supplies for writing and drawing on hand.
- Have a tape recorder and music tapes available.

Beginning the Session

- Describe to the client the intervention that you feel is appropriate and what the client may expect to achieve by utilizing the strategy.
- Provide the client with appropriate materials and instruction.
- Guide the client through a relaxation exercise as necessary to decrease anxiety and facilitate inner work.
- Discuss the completed homework from any previous session.
- Determine the needs of the client based on client input and any previous sessions.

During the Session

- Provide support for the client in terms of your physical presence and encouragement if you are using a verbal intervention or time alone if the client desires that to complete a written assignment.
- Reassess at intervals the client's understanding of both the strategy and the expected outcome to be obtained.
- Allow yourself to be used as a sounding board for questions and insights that arise from the process.
- Allow adequate time for the comfortable completion of the process or for the client to reach a point where the process can continue without your involvement until the next session. Some techniques, such as journal entries, are ongoing and the client need only be given materials, instruction, and time alone to work until a scheduled follow-up session. Most sessions require 20–60 minutes.

Closing the Session

- Bring gently the client's attention back to the room. Reorient, if necessary, to time and place.
- Discuss the work that has been accomplished if the client is comfortable doing so or provide privacy if needed for the client's work.

- Answer any questions that the client may have and assist in interpretation of the work if invited to do so.
- Encourage further work on an individual basis.
- Arrange for follow-up sessions.

Specific Interventions: Self-Reflection

Keeping Diaries and Journals (Basic to Advanced)

Diaries or journals may be single sheets of paper or more elaborate notebooks with a variety of categories and divisions, such as those used by participants in Ira Progoff's Journal Workshops (Advanced work). Exhibit 17-1 lists different categories into which Progoff suggests dividing a working journal. Keeping in mind that there is no right way (and therefore no wrong way) to keep a diary, the following general guidelines are suggested.

Writing in a book or notebook is preferable to using loose pieces of paper. The book can be selected for its appeal to the eye and touch, as well as for its ease of use. A beautifully bound blank book adds to the ritual and implied importance of the record keeping more so than a looseleaf notebook filled with school paper. If the client is confined to bed, perhaps even supine in a critical care unit, allowances must be made for ease of use. A simple steno pad is useful in these circumstances, because it is light-weight, small, easy to hold, and has a firm backing to support the hand.

Exhibit 17-1 Progoff Journal Categories

Period Log
Daily Log
Dialogue Dimension: Special Personal Section
Dialogue with Persons
Dialogue with Works
Dialogue with Society, Group Experiences
Dialogue with Events, Situations and Circumstances
Dialogue with the Body
Depth Dimension, Ways of Symbolic Contact
Dream Log, Description, Context, Associations
Dream Enlargements
Twilight Imagery Log
Imagery Extensions
Inner Wisdom Dialogue
Life/Time Dimension, Inner Perspectives
Life History Log, Recapitulations, and Rememberings
Stepping Stones
Intersections, Roads Taken and Not Taken
Now, The Open Moment

Source: Adapted from *At a Journal Workshop* by I. Progoff, pp. 301–320, with permission of Dialogue House, © 1975.

The writing instrument, like the diary itself, should combine utilitarian features with visual and sensual pleasures. How many of us have spent many happy moments in an office supply store picking out just the right pen or pencil for a particular project?

We must provide private time to quiet the mind and the spirit and allow inner material to surface. Privacy for the document must be guaranteed, if this is an issue for the writer. Most of us are able to find a secure location for our diaries. Privacy for the hospitalized client may be more difficult to find, but certainly not impossible. Many hospitalized clients wish to share their diaries with significant people in their lives and feel no need for privacy. Rather than creating their records alone, they may wish to dictate their thoughts to a loved one or even record them on audiotapes.

Diaries can help us determine our individual rhythms so that we can modify schedules, treatments, and activities to nurture these rhythms. A diary developed at the Institute of Living, a Hartford psychiatric hospital, uncovered patterns of recovery and drug reactions that never before had been noticed in hospital patients.[18] Diligent use of diaries, perhaps with computer-aided interpretation, may help us predict the appropriate timing of certain medications, surgical procedures, and other interventions.[19]

Structured diaries (Exhibits 17-2A and 17-2B), when used in a clinical setting, become a place to record symptom frequency and severity, the client's inner reactions to them, as well as the efficacy of various relief modalities. They become a treasure of patterns and possibilities.

The diary is an excellent place to explore the feelings surrounding illness, the fears associated with a perceived or real loss of independence or power, and, in the case of family members, the financial and physical responsibilities of caring for an ill or disabled relative. If one allows these concerns to flow onto a piece of paper and visualize them, some of the unknown fears and deeper emotions are more easily understood.

Writing Letters (Basic)

In addition to the love and support conveyed to and by clients through letters, writing letters may also be used as a cathartic process to express anger, disappointment, and other deep emotions. Old emotional wounds can be finally healed through the process of writing a letter that says on paper all the things that have been kept inside in some cases for decades. The letter is reread and kept for a period of time until the client feels the emotions have quieted. Then the client can do with the letter as he or she wishes. The client may choose to keep it, or it may be torn up, burned, buried, or otherwise disposed of in an appropriately ceremonial ritual.

Letters can help a client achieve a sense of peace within a difficult, unresolved situation. They may be addressed to objects, body parts, future offspring, or deceased friends or family members. The case histories at the end of this chapter contain marvelous examples of the power of letters.

Negotiating Contracts (Basic to Advanced)

When introducing the concept of making a contract to a client, ask the following questions[20]:

- What would you most like to change about your life right now?
- How can you begin the first step in that change?

Exhibit 17-2A Symptom Chart

This diary of a client with migraine headaches shows symptom severity rated on the 1 to 5 scale, hand temperatures before and after relaxation-imagery practice (an indication of the depth of relaxation achieved, see Chapter 11), medications taken, and some general comments on the day's activities.

Rate the degree to which you experience your symptom (pain, anxiety, etc.) at least four times during the day. Chart the times you listen to your tape or practice your relaxation exercises, and your hand temperature before and after practice.

Symptom severity range:
1 = absent or very mild
2 = present but can be ignored
3 = moderate, can't be ignored
4 = severe and interfering
5 = incapacitating

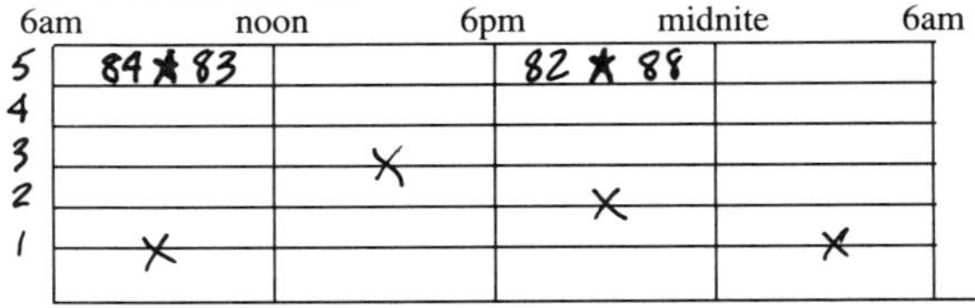

MONDAY: 5/18 Pretty good day 'til after lunch c̄ Frank, felt my shoulders tighten up while doing accounts good dinner out, better by bedtime - slept real well.

medications: Inderal 40 mg × 3, Aspirin 2 at 2 pm.

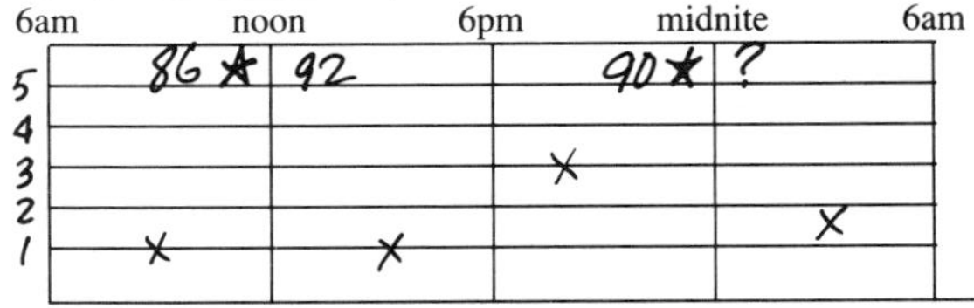

TUESDAY: 5/19 - Quiet day at work - rushed around after work, Picked up June's mom, took them both to party at Hanson's. Didn't practice 'til right before bed - fell asleep with tape - No headache -

medications:

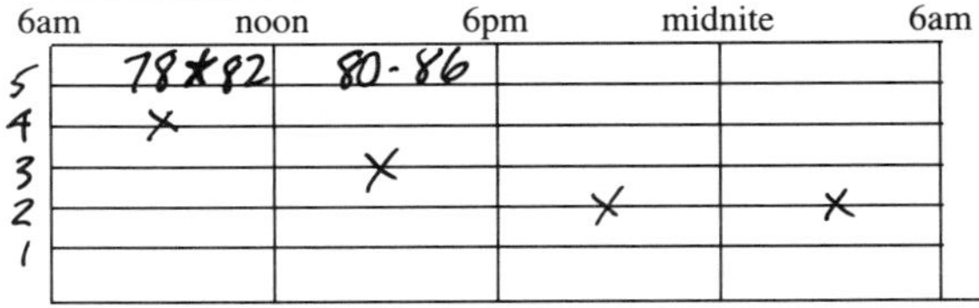

WEDNESDAY: 5/20 Woke up with headache & nausea - felt a little better after breakfast & Tape - saw two clients - practiced again after lunch & left work early - worked out & ran 1.5 miles - some headache in evening but not bad - woke up once but went right back to bed.

medications: MIDRIN 8 am + 1 pm

Exhibit 17-2A continued

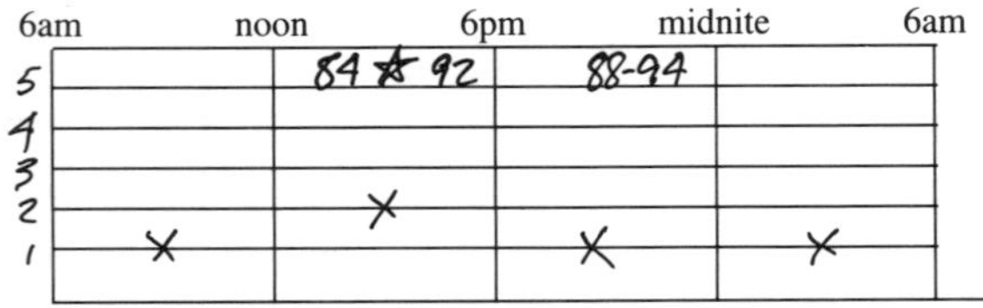

THURSDAY: 5/21 A good day! Shoulders tightened a bit in afternoon but generally felt fine—long conversation with Frank in evening—settled lots of "Stuff"! Slept well

medications: "

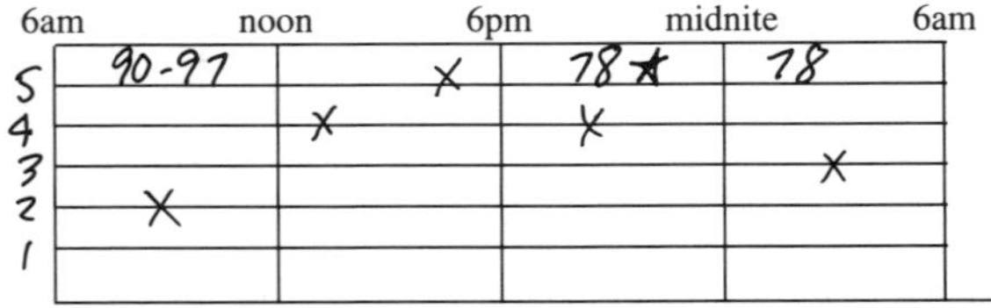

FRIDAY: 5/22 Felt OK in morning—big blow up at staff meeting—had to fire S.F.—big scene—head really pounding by dinner—went out with Frank but felt awful—Tape didn't help much—bed real late.

medications: "—Valium 5mg—4p.m.

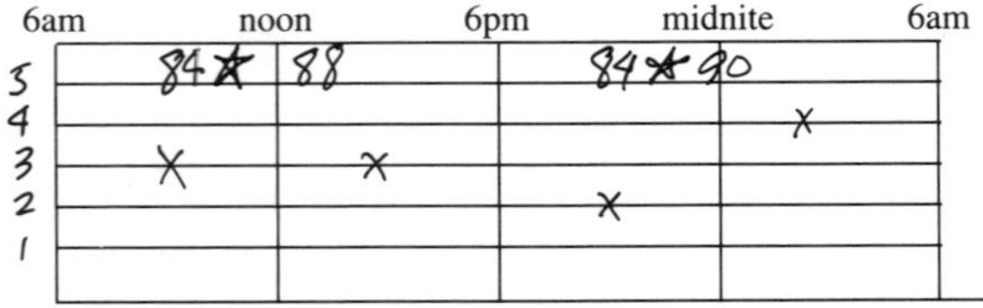

SATURDAY: 5/23 No headache, just felt "run over" Couldn't seem to accomplish much—finally ran in afternoon—Couldn't get to sleep—had to take Dalmane finally

medications: "Dalmane 15 mg 2am

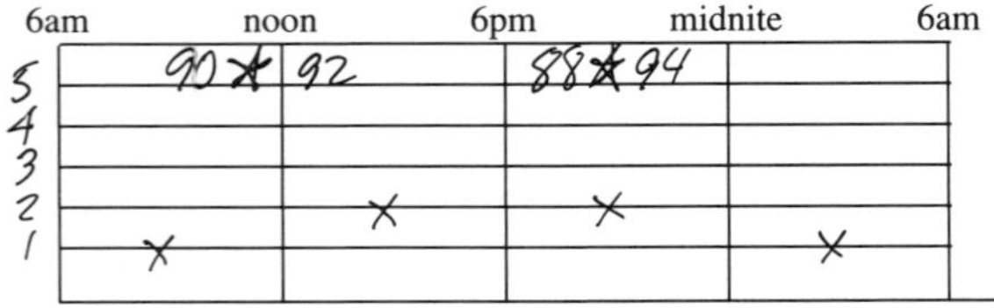

SUNDAY: 5/24 Better today—lunch with Fred and Susan. Tennis in the afternoon—felt a little uptight about work tomorrow but OK after relaxation—Hand Temp seems to be improving.

medications: "

Exhibit 17-2B Diary Sheet

This diary sheet shows the client's comments concerning her symptoms and interventions during the week. The shaded-in area on the human figures indicates areas of perceived muscle tension throughout the week.

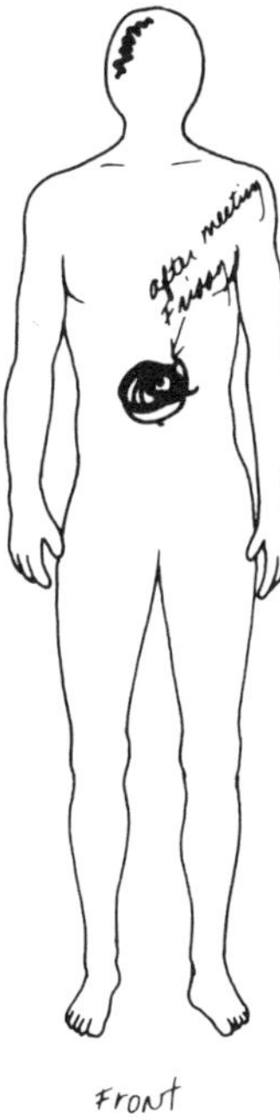

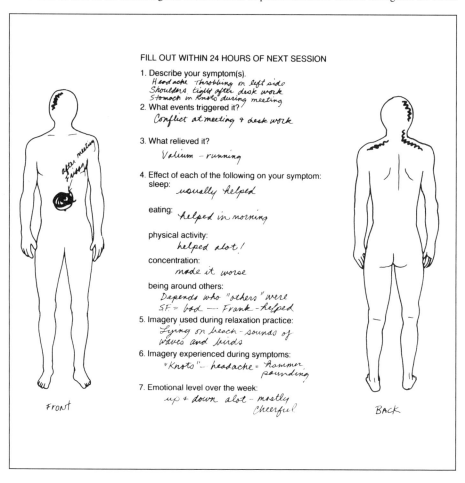

FILL OUT WITHIN 24 HOURS OF NEXT SESSION

1. Describe your symptom(s).
   Headache throbbing on left side
   Shoulders tight after desk work
   Stomach in knots during meeting
2. What events triggered it?
   Conflict at meeting & desk work
3. What relieved it?
   Valium – running
4. Effect of each of the following on your symptom:
   sleep: usually helped
   eating: helped in morning
   physical activity: helped alot!
   concentration: made it worse
   being around others: Depends who "others" were SF = bad — Frank – helped
5. Imagery used during relaxation practice:
   Lying on beach – sounds of waves and birds
6. Imagery experienced during symptoms:
   "Knots" – headache = hammer pounding
7. Emotional level over the week:
   up & down alot – mostly cheerful

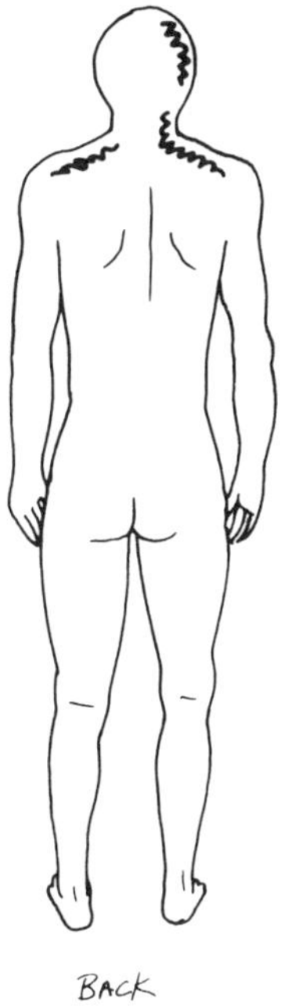

- On what date would you like to achieve that goal?
- How can you reward yourself for success?
- How will your life be different when you succeed?
- How can I help?

Contracts may be verbal, but are more likely to be taken seriously by all parties if they are written. If written, they should be signed by both the client and nurse. They should always contain these key elements:

- a specific, realistic, measurable goal or goals to be reached
- a time limit for completion, as well as specific times to evaluate progress
- statement of the responsibilities of both parties (the client and the nurse, client and spouse, etc.)
- a clear reward for accomplishing the stated goal

In our era of litigation, clients may find the word "contract" threatening or uncomfortable. If so, the contract may be referred to as an agreement or bargain. When helping a client draft a contract, the nurse must assume the role of facilitator, rather than originator. After presenting the concept of contracting and pointing out some of the reasons such an approach may be valid in the client's particular circumstances, your further involvement should be in the form of guidance and support. The greater the client input, the greater the client compliance with the terms of the contract.

The contracting process has five steps[21]:

1. *Problem identification and priority ranking:* mutual agreement on problem to be resolved
2. *Contract development:* a description of the responsibilities and actions of both the client and clinician
3. *Contract implementation:* a focus on the carrying out of the individual responsibilities
4. *Contract evaluation:* mutual evaluation of the outcome of the contract, including a renegotiation of the terms if necessary
5. *Contract termination:* target date for successful completion of the contract

Goal Setting. The following discussion of goal setting is useful with all clients, but becomes particularly important when helping clients determine the limits of a contract.

Goals, time frame, evaluation, and rewards should be primarily client-generated. Never presume you know a client well enough to decide the goals toward which that client is to strive. Goals should be specific, concrete, measurable, and offer a good chance of successful completion.

It is important to help clients institute beliefs that will allow them to dictate their own lives and their own experience. Setting goals facilitates this because it serves as a reminder that they have the power to create new experiences in their lives.

Follow these guidelines for helping clients set goals[22]:

- Examine the rewards or secondary gains that you get from lack of health awareness or from being sick. Fix a goal that will allow you to get that same reward in a way that takes the form of health, not sickness.
- Look at activities you have always wanted to do, but have not because of a lack of time, money, or whatever. Encouraging yourself to do these things can be a way to put more meaning in your life.
- Use the 2X-50 rule of goal setting. After stating the goal as it first comes to mind, double the amount of time allowed to accomplish it or reduce its difficulty by 50 percent. For example, *unreasonable goal:* "I will lose 10 pounds in the next

month.'' *Reasonable goals:* ''I will lose 5 pounds in the next month'' or ''I will lose 10 pounds in the next 2 months.''

Either of these last two goals is within reach and therefore more likely to be attained, give the client a sense of achievement, build self-esteem, and foster the enthusiasm to set further goals.

Rewards. Appropriate rewards for successful completion of a contract are often difficult for a client to determine. Many people feel uncomfortable rewarding themselves and fail to realize the importance of rewards in learning and maintaining new behavior patterns. Help the client keep in mind that rewards need not cost money or even be tangible in order to maintain enthusiasm for reaching the agreed-upon goal. See Exhibit 17-3 for examples of rewards.

Under some circumstances the nurse may reward the client for completion of a goal by providing reinforcers. Reinforcers may be candy, small toys, tokens to be used as trade, or special privileges. They are especially useful with children or others in residential settings who have difficulty determining rewards and taking responsibility for dispensing these rewards. Reinforcers, as do all rewards, must be congruent with the difficulty of the goal achieved and need not be time consuming or expensive.

Exhibit 17-4 shows a contract agreed upon by Mrs. Smith and her nurse. Mrs. Smith was having difficulty following a low-salt diet. After discussing the applications of contracts to cases similar to hers, she wrote up and signed the contract, stayed within its guidelines, and began to make significant changes in her eating behavior. This self-

Exhibit 17-3 Rewards

The following are responses from a group of health care workers to the question, ''How do you reward yourself for accomplishing a goal"?

1. Take a picnic to the country (or to a city park).
2. Buy a new record or tape.
3. Browse in a bookstore or hardware store.
4. Take a bubble bath and stay in 30 minutes longer than usual.
5. Work on a hobby or project.
6. Buy an item for my craft or hobby.
7. Spend time alone with a special friend.
8. Go to a movie or rent a videotape.
9. Take time alone just to sit and think.
10. Go to a free concert or play in the park.
11. Take a half-day off to go fishing.
12. Cook a special meal or go out for a special dinner.
13. Read in the bathtub.
14. Start a new project.
15. Walk on the beach.
16. Treat myself to a manicure or pedicure.
17. Make a phone call to an old friend.
18. Take a continuing education short course in something new.
19. Take a nap.

Exhibit 17-4 Contract

Starting today, August 18, I will not use a salt shaker at the table for 2 consecutive weeks. At the end of those 2 weeks, I will reward myself by taking my boys fishing for the afternoon. The following Monday I will telephone my nurse, and we will write a new contract based on my blood pressure readings and my goals for the month of September.

Signed: Angela Smith

Signed: Robert Long, RN

Source: Adapted from *Journal of Holistic Nursing*, Vol. 2, No. 1, pp. 21–23, with permission of American Holistic Nurses Association, © 1987.

reflection intervention helped her reach her goal, gain insight into her behavior, and become an active participant in her health care.

Beginning an Intuition Log (Basic)

Suggest to clients the value of beginning an intuition log in a small notebook that can be carried with them. Each time a flash of insight occurs or they hear a small, quiet, inner voice or sense a vague impression or feeling, it is to be recorded in the log. Encourage them to let the intuitions flow and record them without judging their correctness.

Keeping an intuition log and answering questions concerning the information gathered from intuitions can strengthen the intuitive skills.[23] These questions cover the content of the intuition, how it appeared, and what you were doing just before its appearance. This information is similar to dream interpretation logs and may be modified to fit both dreams and intuitions.

Over a period of weeks, clients will become more secure differentiating the form and feeling of successful intuitions from those more likely to be false. Tell clients that, as with any skill, accuracy and confidence increases with practice. With validation of increasing skill level, they will become comfortable acting on intuitive insights in many day-to-day decisions.

The following are excerpts from a nurse's intuition log.

> On the way to work I kept feeling that I had left the house without everything I needed for the day. When I got to the hospital I found I had left my stethoscope on the dresser. . . . Felt uneasy about leaving Mrs. R. alone with her son-in-law. When I returned to her room they were arguing and her frequency of PVCs had gone up from 2 per minute to over ten per minute. . . . Before leaving I just knew I had to say goodnight to Sam and tell him what a good job he had done during the code. I found him in the break room where he confessed he had been concerned and was really relieved to know he had done well.

Notice that all the entries concern nonverbal, right-hemispheric descriptions, using such words as "feel" and "knew." By listening to and acting on information from both sides of the brain, we move closer to a whole brain model of the nursing world. Many of our holistic nursing interventions have one foot planted firmly on intuitive ground. Far from abandoning traditional nursing skills, we are bringing them with us into a new era of balanced, whole nursing practice.

Learning from Dreams (Basic to Advanced)

The following techniques can be suggested to clients to help them use dreams as self-reflection interventions. The basic skill of recording one's dreams can move into advanced levels with the application of various interpretation skills.

Sleep and dream researchers, LaBerge and Gackenbach, have developed techniques to help dreamers become more involved and in control of their dream state. Some dreamers are actually aware that they are dreaming and are able to direct the "story-line" and outcomes of their dreams to some extent. These people are referred to as lucid dreamers. The techniques of lucid dreaming may be used to enhance self-confidence, promote personal growth and improve both physical and emotional health.[24] As an extension of guided imagery, it may be used to gather inner knowledge and creativity.

LaBerge's primary exercise to induce lucid dreaming is outlined in Exhibit 17-5.

To make use of the hypnopompic state of consciousness that occurs just as one is awakening, it is useful to record affirmations on a cassette tape that switches on at a predetermined time. Positive self-statements drift into the conscious mind as one awakens and affect the self-image throughout the day. See Chapter 16 for affirmations.

Dreams, combined with nonsleep imagery, are powerful sources of inner knowledge and interpretation of feelings and symptoms. A dream log, similar to the intuition log, can become a storehouse of information to be interpreted by the client alone or with the help of a nurse or therapist. Looking at a dream log with an eye for people, animals, locations, color, patterns, associated feeling, and repetitive themes will help the client begin to explore meanings and interpretations. Some dream images seem to speak for themselves, whereas others are more obscure in their meaning. Vaughan's questions

Exhibit 17-5 Lucid Dreaming Guidelines

- Ask yourself frequently during the day if you are dreaming, and look for evidence to prove to yourself that you are not. LaBerge suggests reading something, looking away, and then reading it again. If it reads the same way twice, you are probably not dreaming.
- Tell yourself that you want to recognize a nighttime dream the next time one occurs.
- As you prepare to go to sleep remind yourself that you want to recognize that you are dreaming when you begin to do so. This is the same technique as reminding yourself during the day to fill your car with gas on the way home.
- If you awaken during the night from a dream, imagine returning to it immediately. This may be enough to allow you to dream lucidly when you return to sleep.
- Practice this exercise as often as possible over several nights, and record your results in your log as soon as you awaken.

Source: Adapted from *Omni*, p. 1, with permission of OMNI Publications International, Ltd., © April 1987.

concerning dream content (Exhibit 17-6) may help with interpretation and clarification. See Chapter 10 for further imagery interpretation tools that may be applied to dreams.

Building Mind Maps and Clusters (Basic)

Clustering of thoughts and ideas, also referred to as "mind mapping" by some authors, is similar to free association.[25] It is an excellent tool to begin a flow of ideas as a means of seeing interconnections between people, problems, or solutions. Whenever you or a client become "stuck," try this intervention to see the multitude of possibilities and patterns offered by any situation.

In addition to the supplies listed in the "Before the Session" section, you will need large sheets of newsprint pads, construction paper, or even typing paper, depending on whether you are working with bedridden or ambulatory clients. Some clients even do clustering on small scraps of paper, but the visual impact and creativity flowing from large pieces of paper are to be sought.

After allowing yourself or your client a few moments for inner quieting and centering, a central word or theme statement concerning the problem or situation to be dealt with is written in the middle of a large piece of paper and circled. This theme word may be a name, a symptom, a short statement of the problem, a desired outcome, a perceived block, or an image, symbol, or metaphor. This and several other chapters of this book began as a single key word.

As associated words and ideas arise, they are written around the central word, circled, and connected to the center and/or each other with appropriate lines. Figure 17-1 shows an example of how this cluster grows into a meaningful web of ideas to form this chapter.

This activity should proceed like a brainstorming session in that nothing should be censored and no idea or connection should be too tenuous to be ignored. In as little as a

Exhibit 17-6 Dream Interpretation

- What is an appropriate title for this particular dream? Is there an obvious message to this dream? Is there a particular message that might have some relevance to your life at present?
- What is the predominant feeling tone of this dream?
- What are the principal qualities of the different characters in the dream? Are you aware of these qualities in yourself?
- Can you view the dream from the point of view of one of the other characters in the dream?
- Is this dream a recurring dream? Is the theme familiar, or does it seem entirely new?
- Does this dream seem to be a "big dream" or does it seem to be an ordinary dream?
- If you were to make an affirmation for yourself from this dream, what would it be?
- Is there any particular action you would like to undertake as a result of what you have learned from this dream?
- Would you like to continue this dream in your imagination?
- Would you like to give this dream a different ending?
- If you could redream this dream, how would you change it?

Source: Reprinted from *The Inward Arc* by Frances Vaughan, pp. 175–176, with permission of Shambhala Publications, Inc., © 1986.

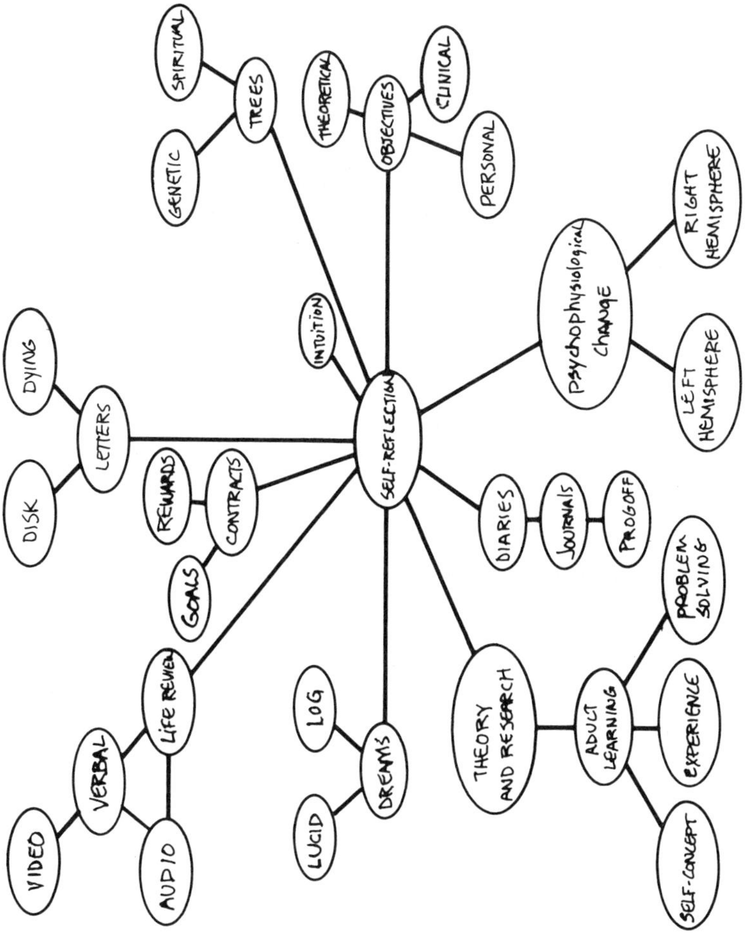

Figure 17-1 Example of the Process of Clustering

few minutes, your web-like grouping of key words will begin to point to relationships and possibilities of which you were probably unaware.

This shift from a nebulous, indeterminate form to a focus on pattern and relationships is called the *trial-web shift* and is a state that occurs during any creative act.[26] From seemingly disconnected random words and thoughts there suddenly emerges a direction, a clarity of purpose that may lead a person out of the dark and into a solution.

As your clustering project begins to feel complete, you or your client may wish to take another few moments to center and enjoy the visual and felt pleasure of what has been created. The cluster may be discussed as soon as it is complete or kept for further refinement and insight over a period of several days or weeks. This process frequently opens a period of insight and creativity that can last for the entire length of a project, therapeutic intervention, hospitalization, or relationship.

Reminiscing and Life Review (Basic to Advanced)

The life review process is basic when in the form of simple recounting of past events to a friend, family member, or interested health care provider. It can progress into more complex levels of transpersonal focusing and inward reflection if the client wishes to explore those levels. Support and skill in dealing with the advanced strategies come with training received at workshops or seminars and with clinical experience. Begin with the basic strategies and as your skills and interest develop, move into the more advanced interventions.

Life review may be simply verbal, coming from the client in the small time periods while being bathed or receiving other nursing care. Journal keeping and letter writing may also be used for life review purposes, and some clients and families may prefer the more complete and personal record of audio or video recording of reminiscence sessions.

Encourage family members to bring in old photographs to be discussed and identified or to make a scrapbook of treasures. Asking open-ended questions about personal items or photos in the client's room will often stimulate discussion and elicit information that will help you provide more personal and meaningful care.

The life review process may involve one session or many, which vary in length depending on the client and what needs to be explored. The intervention cannot be done if one is rushed, for the process is one of unfolding and opening.

To facilitate the life review process, do the following:

- Encourage self-expression by the client.
- Involve family members and friends.
- Keep the information and process confidential.
- Begin the process when the client has sufficient physical strength and a mood of openness.
- Listen with focused attention.
- Use touch when appropriate.
- Allow the client periods of silence and a time to retreat if needed.

Be aware that this is an active imagery process using the creativity of both client and nurse.

Group therapy situations with a creative guide can also open doors to the past. Discussions of the "old days," first jobs, wars, public figures, personal and national losses, and triumphs will lead to many insights for both clients and guides. Having clients bring items from their past, such as old quilts, newspaper clippings, photos, and letters, will stimulate lively discussions.[27] Be alert for members of a group who need to be silent with their own thoughts and be prepared to come to them individually to help them explore their memories when they are ready.

Conscious Dying. Spurred on by the work of Cecily Saunders, Elizabeth Kubler-Ross, Stephen Levine, and Richard Boerstler (see Suggested Readings), we have begun to be more open about dying and more aware of how it can truly be a transformation—a time of remembering, of growth, and of peaceful completion of this life.

When clients are in the end stages of this life, the process of life review begins as any other. The needs of the client and family are assessed, outcomes determined, and the intervention begun with frequent evaluations. The nurse helps the client review the important memories of the past and rehearse events coming in the future. This helps ease the potential feelings of psychologic isolation common to the dying, helps deal with unresolved conflicts, maintain self-esteem, gain insight into past and present relationships, and emphasize positive aspects of the client's life.

Encourage the client to review decisions over which he or she still has some control. Such decisions may concern medications, treatments, daily routines, special requests about a funeral, will, and whom the client wishes to receive certain personal belongings. The client may also be helped to deal with unresolved dilemmas, such as belief in an afterlife, higher guiding powers, or connections with others.

When death is an inevitable outcome of the immediate situation, clients may need to take time to prepare themselves and their family members. Unfortunately, many have not dealt with the emotional or physical details of the process and will require assistance to do so. As Stephen Levine says:

> In a way, it seems strange that we are so unprepared for death, considering how many opportunities we have to open to what is unexpected or even disagreeable. Each time we don't feel well, each time we have the flu or a kidney stone, or a pain and stiffness in the back, we have the opportunity to see that sooner or later some pain or illness is going to arise that won't diminish but will increase until it displaces us from the body. We can use each situation as an extraordinary opportunity to practice the death chant, to practice Gandhi's closeness with God. We are reminded again and again of the process we are. Continually opportunities arise to practice letting go of this solidness, to tune to the ongoing process, to sense the spaciousness in which it's all unfolding.[28]

Numerous relaxation imagery exercises are appropriate means of helping the client practice "letting go of this solidness." The ability to let go of pain, both physical and emotional, eases the client through difficult procedures and conflicts with friends and family and into a sense of calm and self-direction. See Chapter 11 for exercises to help clients experience death with peace and dignity.

As death approaches, self-reflection may take on more immediate forms, such as talking or simply sitting and maintaining physical touch with a loved one or nurse. The barriers that prevented communication earlier may lift as the burden of the ego is laid aside and clients find it easier to say the things to family and friends that were not forthcoming earlier.

Clients may need to complete certain projects before they allow themselves to let go of life. They may wish to contact those with whom they have had misunderstandings in order to straighten things out and feel that they are leaving their relationships with a sense of closure and peace. Facilitating this need by arranging nursing care in blocks and allowing the client to spend time alone with particular friends and family members—while also helping to set limits on the demands of others, according to the client's wishes—is a vital advocacy role of the nurse as the end of life approaches.

Evaluation

The nurse must evaluate with the client whether the outcomes established before the session were met (Table 17-1). The interventions described in this chapter, for the most part, take place over fairly long periods of time, such as weeks or months. For this reason they must be periodically reviewed and re-evaluated even though they are not yet felt to be completed. Continued support and feedback are necessary.

Case Studies

Case Study No. 1

Setting:	Client's home; use of letters
Client:	59-year-old Aldie Hine, diagnosed with terminal lung cancer, 15 months before his death
Nursing Diagnoses:	1. Anticipatory grieving 2. Spiritual distress 3. Powerlessness 4. Social Isolation: all related to the diagnosis of lung cancer

Virginia Hine, Aldie's wife, has given us a beautiful and powerful example of the healing power of letters in her book, *Last Letter to the Pebble People,* written a few months after the death of her husband Aldie. Through letters, personal contact, and telephone calls, a spiritual network was built to help carry Aldie and his family through his final days.

The opening letter, sent to the "biologic family, nonkin family, close friends, and a few concerned professional colleagues," reads:

> We propose to organize ourselves to tap the healing energy-force by coming together each day at 5:00 P.M. for 10 or 15 minutes by ourselves or with anyone who is moved to come here at this time. In silence we will concentrate our love and thoughts on these ideas and hopes. . . . We ask anyone, anywhere, who wants to join us in thought to do the same thing, perhaps at the same time of day if this is fitting. We will be sitting near a little fountain lined with stone which we built together during the last 2 months. We recognize the power of symbolic acts and objects. We have each put a pebble in the lower

> pool to remind us daily of our commitment to a power beyond ourselves. We ask that anyone who wants to join us in our faith in life send us a pebble or small stone from some place you have loved. Each day at the joining time, Aldie will put into the pool any pebbles that have come, and the name of its sender will be in our hearts with gratitude. Each pebble will be to us a symbol of the love and concern people have expressed for us, and we know already how strengthening this has been.[29]

Life review can also be an important aid in the process of letting go peacefully into death. As Aldie Hine approached the last few days of his life, he lay in his bed and reminisced with his wife and family. "He experienced a very moving sense of 'laying aside the burden of the ego' as he put it. 'I might have come to this without illness . . . but the prospect of death spurs the sense of letting go. The process of dying speeds up the transformation'"[30]

Aldie Hine died at home, 15 months after his initial diagnosis of lung cancer, but he did so surrounded in body, mind, and spirit by a far-flung web of love and support; in a multitude of ways he died the "good death."

Case Study No. 2

Setting:	Client's home
Client:	46-year-old male with ruptured L5-S1 disk; at bedrest for 4 weeks before surgery
Nursing Diagnoses:	1. Activity intolerance (severe) 2. Alteration in comfort (severe pain) 3. Impaired mobility (inability to move about the environment; secondary to severe pain): related to acute pain of L5-S1 ruptured disk

The following is an extraordinary example of a letter written by a client to his disease process. It is full of insight and represents an attempt to come to terms with the fact of illness—to enter it fully, exploring the meaning it contains and trying to find a personal path through the labyrinth of adversity.

To My Ruptured Disk

> I am writing this because, although we've communicated rather intimately in the past month, it may help me to nail things down in words. You know, words, my addiction. Can't help it. Don't want to. They're part of me. Like you.
>
> A month ago I took to bed, where I've been since. Before that there was a lot of pain for several weeks. I pushed through it, sometimes with the help of pain pills and a lot of denial. You know, trying to "work through" the problem, hoping (believing?) it would eventually resolve. Not so.
>
> In the past month a wonderful collection of friends have come to my aid, some from traditional medical-surgical circles and some from the holistic-alternative (HA) arena. You know how it is. Both sides, really, are so suspicious

of the other. Disk, I've had 17 treatments of one sort or another in the past 4 weeks: massage, acupuncture, shiatzu, reflexology, psychic healing, cranio-sacral manipulation, various nutritional therapies, and prayer. Yes, lots of prayer, more than I will ever know about. I think I like that the best, prayer. Cuts right to the heart of the matter, you know. Straight to the Power Source, no funny paraphernalia, theories, or intermediary complexities. Yet in spite of it all, here I lie, flat on my back, pillows under my knees, with My Friend Pain burning its presence at the moment down the left leg into the ankle.

One of the many surprises you have up your sleeve, disk, is the way you affect the interactions of people. You function like a love magnet, pulling toward you the care and caring of many people. You have evoked yet greater love from my wife toward me in this process, which I had previously considered to be rather maximal already. Illness does that. Remarkable!

Some friends have suggested imagery to unleash the power of thought in an aggressive manner against the offending site—a tumor, e.g., or, in your case, a ruptured disk. Then in some way the offending piece of the body is disposed of—dissolved, dispatched from the body, sent packing in some way or other. Well, here's the problem.

I cannot regard you as an object. (It may seem as if I do, talking to you this way, but this is just a device for self-conversation.) I am you, and you are I. How can I inflict self-injury, self-mutilation on you, through masculine, aggressive, and destructive images? It would be like shooting myself in the foot. Something's wrong for me with that approach, although I have seen it work for others. And the same thing goes for the pain. Project it outside the body, they say. Get **rid** of it! But all these approaches violate something I deeply feel, which is, first, that you and the pain are **not** objects that can be treated in this way and, secondly, that I am intrinsically and indissolubly connected with you. Treating you as an object asks me to violate one of the most deeply held convictions I have: that the world is not made of external sets of objects, whether existing outside in the world or inside my body. These approaches are off base, at least for me.

And so I lie here hurting, and think about the pain—knowing that while I am thinking about the pain I am really thinking about **me.** The Buddhist masters always bring one back to the question: "Who is it that is suffering?" That's the lesson, a lesson about the self. Getting rid of the pain, treating the pain as if it were an object, is not the primary goal. Even at its height—when it is searing, burning, from buttock to foot, I still know the pain is myself, and that there is a larger Self of which the "hurting self" is a part. The larger Self does not hurt; it is pain-free. That's what I know, disk, that's what I understand.

This pain and this illness, disk, is a great training ground for understanding more about the self. There is the tendency to allow one's entire awareness and sense of person to begin to revolve around the fact of hurting and the fact of being sick. The illness and pain try to dominate everything in sight, extending beyond oneself, even, to involve others. Pain and illness are a dictator, a conqueror, trying to sweep all before them. The test, then, is how to meet their challenge. It can only be done by giving a proper answer to the Zen master's question, "Who is it that is suffering? Who is it that is sick?" The right answer wins the day; the wrong one allows the pain and sickness to completely control one's entire being.

And you, disk? You are like the pain: part of me. No, not a "part" in the usual sense. Again, the interconnectedness. Still, dear disk, in 4 days I've commissioned a neurosurgeon to cut you out. He'll do it, then send you as a surgical specimen to the pathologist. I know **you** know the surgery is not what it seems, however, and that you are not misled by such procedures. The fact is, surgery or not surgery, there is no separating you or me. Even after you are cut out of me, the connection remains. No getting away from each other, even if we tried. It's a **nonlocal** world, disk, and you know it. Spatial separation is not primary. Can't be: the world doesn't work that way. When people bemoan the loss of body parts they're wailing for nothing, for the contact remains at some deep level. And it's the deep levels that mean the most.

One of my HA friends said, "The solution is not to remove the problem." He does not understand that removal, in principle, is impossible. And so you and I are going to engage in a paradoxical procedure: In the process of removal, there is no removal. In the act of excision, there is no excision. Sounds like Zen double-talk, yes?

Surgery, then, is not what it seems. There is no violation of the body that is possible, once the nonlocal nature of the world is felt, once it is realized that spatial separation is impossible at the deepest levels of nature. "When the electron vibrates, the universe shakes," Eddington put it. Connection holds, even across galactic distances, dear disk. So we'll be together, you and I, even after the operation. My HA friend can stop worrying: no violation of the body is possible, except in the minds of those who do not sense the inseparability of all things.

What will happen after surgery? Will it be a "success?" Will I be free of pain and gradually regain function? Yes, it is extraordinarily likely, but who knows for sure? In any case, "success" and freedom from pain are only one part of the double movement, of concern only to the lesser self. In the other domain where the Self lives there can be no success as there is no failure. There, operations don't come out right or wrong, good or bad. So the "outcome" of the surgery, while important at one level, is of no ultimate importance. Now, don't get me wrong. I want the pain eradicated, and I've hired the most skillful surgeon I can find, and I've tried to cover all the bases to insure "success." There are two levels to this, and it is indeed a **double** movement. No sense in denying it.

But beyond the desire to "get well" is the sure certainty that wellness is already there, in place, having never left the scene in the first place. I say this because I believe one cannot say that the universe is "right" or "wrong." It simply is. Therefore I place no ultimate value on the eventual outcome of all this. One cannot improve on perfection.

So, disk, I just wanted to get these things out on the table. Clear the air, you know. Hope you enjoy surgery. Should be fascinating, eh? Nonlocally!

The client was asked why he had engaged in this form of self-exploration, writing down his thoughts in the way he did. He replied:

> I have an attitude of reverence toward my body. It's the ''carrier'' of my consciousness. I have a respect for it because of this special relationship. I feel a special need to address it before I commit it to the surgeon. This ruptured disk—this part of me that is literally in the wrong place and pressing on a nerve and causing me a lot of pain—is as valuable a part of me as my brain, my heart, my lungs. I want to have a conversation with it, to ''make peace'' with it, if you will, before I allow the surgeon to cut it out of me. As explained in my letter, it still will be a part of me, because I don't think things can ever be separate in an ultimate sense, but there's still some things I need to say to it before the moment of surgery.
>
> You see, it's a matter of respect. The American Indians used to address the plants and animals before they killed them for food. This is the same idea. It isn't some sentimental ritual. It's a feeling of connectedness with all things, including my body parts, that I feel I must respond to.
>
> After my conversation with my disk, I felt peaceful. Like I had finished something that needed to be done. I felt at one with my body, that I was holding nothing back. I was ready to go forward without any reservation whatsoever. No fear. And with the sure knowledge that I had been completely honest with my body and my innermost self in dealing with this enormous problem.

He was asked what does all this have to do with getting well?

> A lot. Think what happens when people get ready to have surgery, or any other type of medical treatment. A lot of emotions are stirred up. Almost everybody experiences apprehension and fear. With some people the fear is just tremendous. All these feelings don't stay in the mind. It's well known that they enter the body through various pathways. They affect the heart, the immune system, the inflammatory response—probably all the major organ systems are affected in some degree. If these fears and apprehensions aren't dealt with, they interfere with healing. Another way to look at it is the positive approach: If you want to get well faster and more completely, deal with all your ''stuff'' beforehand! It's all those concealed emotions, all the denial that people carry into surgery and other kinds of treatments, that can boomerang. So it's really a very practical thing for me to write a memorandum to my disk before having surgery.

SUMMARY

We have seen how a variety of tools and interventions can provide us access to inner awareness and healing. By using these ourselves and offering them to our clients we can all reach for higher levels of wellness and understanding of the life process. Each of the interventions covered can be successfully woven into the fabric of our nursing practice and experience for our mutual enrichment.

DIRECTIONS FOR FUTURE RESEARCH

1. Develop and test evaluation tools to measure reliably the psychophysiologic effects of self-reflection methods.
2. Develop interpretation guidelines for unconscious material arising from dreams and clustering techniques.
3. Determine changes in behavior, perceived quality of life, and social interaction during and after reminiscence therapy.
4. Measure the effectiveness of various rewards and reinforcers in client contracts.
5. Evaluate if life review process and conscious dying techniques work to decrease client and family anxiety and fear around death.

NURSE HEALER REFLECTIONS

After reading this chapter the nurse healer will be able to answer or begin the process of answering the following questions:

- What inner knowledge, as well as factual records, can I create by keeping a *journal*?
- How can I facilitate new health behaviors in my clients by using *diaries* and *contracts*?
- What do I experience about my imagery and creativity when I use *clustering* techniques?
- How can I ease the emotional pain of death for my clients with the *life review process*?
- What can I learn from becoming an active participant in my *dreams*?

NOTES

1. Piero Ferrucci, *What We May Be* (Los Angeles: Jeremy P. Tarcher, Inc., 1982), p. 143.
2. Donald A. Bille, "Patient/Family Teaching in Critical Care," in *Critical Care Nursing: Body-Mind-Spirit,* ed. Cornelia Vanderstaay Kenner, Cathie E. Guzzetta, and Barbara Montgomery Dossey (Boston: Little, Brown and Co., 1985), p. 116.
3. Ira Progoff, *At a Journal Workshop* (New York: Dialogue House Library, 1975), p. 9.
4. Frances E. Vaughan, *Awakening Intuition* (Garden City, NY: Anchor Books, 1979), p. 9.
5. Ibid., p. 51.

6. Patricia Gerrity, "Perception in Nursing: The Value of Intuition," *Holistic Nursing Practice* 1, no. 3 (May 1987): 70.
7. Tristine Rainer, *The New Diary* (Los Angeles: Jeremy P. Tarcher Inc., 1978), p. 17.
8. Ibid., p. 9.
9. Ira Progoff, *At a Journal Workshop* (New York: Dialogue House, 1975), p. 10.
10. Leslie Kolkmeier, "Contracting in an Outpatient Setting," *Journal of Holistic Nursing* 2, no. 1: 21–23.
11. Carl Jung, *Man and His Symbols* (Garden City, NY: Doubleday, 1964), p. 50.
12. Frances Vaughan, *Awakening Intuition,* p. 119.
13. Ernest Hartmann, "Dream", in *World Book Encyclopedia,* (Chicago: Field Enterprises Educational Corp., 1975), p. 276.
14. Jeanne Achterberg, *Imagery in Healing* (Boston: New Science Library, 1985), p. 54.
15. Frances Vaughan, *Awakening Intuition,* p. 144.
16. Diane B. Hamilton, "Reminiscence Therapy," in *Nursing Intervention: Treatments for Nursing Diagnoses,* ed. Gloria Bulechek and Joanne McCloskey (Philadelphia: W.B. Saunders, 1985), pp. 139–151.
17. A. McMahon, and P. Rudick, "Reminiscing," *Archives of General Psychiatry* 10, no. 3 (1961): 292–298.
18. Gay Gaer Luce, "Body Time", in *Ways of Health,* ed. David Sobel (San Diego: Harcourt, Brace, Jovanovich, 1979), p. 405.
19. Leland Kaiser, "The Next Medical Frontier: Computer and Robotic-Enhanced Health Care," *Group Practice Journal* 35 (November/December 1986): 5–11.
20. Leslie Kolkmeier, "Contracting in an Outpatient Setting", pp. 21–23.
21. Gloria M. Bulechek and Joanne Comi McCloskey, *Nursing Interventions* (Philadelphia: W.B. Saunders Co., 1985), p. 94.
22. Cathie E. Guzzetta and Barbara Montgomery Dossey, *Cardiovascular Nursing: Bodymind Tapestry* (St. Louis, MO: The C.V. Mosby Company, 1984), p. 47.
23. Philip Goldberg, *The Intuitive Edge* (Los Angeles: Jeremy P. Tarcher, Inc., 1983), pp. 209–210.
24. Steven LaBerge, "Power Trips: Controlling Your Dreams," *OMNI,* April 1987, p. 1.
25. Joanne McDonald, *Mind Mapping, Caring in a Technological Age*. Proceedings of the 11th Annual National Teaching Institute of the AACN, 1984, p. 237.
26. Gabrielle Lusser Rico, *Writing the Natural Way* (Los Angeles: Jeremy P. Tarcher, Inc., 1983), p. 90.
27. Gloria Bulechek and Joanne McCloskey, *Nursing Interventions,* p. 145.
28. Stephen Levine, *Who Dies?* (Garden City, NY: Anchor Press, Doubleday, 1982), p. 32.
29. Virginia Hine, *Last Letter to the Pebble People* (Mars Hill, NC: St. Alden's in the Weeds, 1977), p. 28.
30. Ibid., p. 74.

SUGGESTED READINGS

Boestler, Richard. *Letting Go*. Watertown, MA: Associates in Thantology, 1982.

Gendlin, Eugene. *Focusing*. Boston: Bantam Books, 1978.

Hanh, Thich. *The Miracle of Mindfulness*. Boston: Beacon Press, 1976.

Trumpa, Chogyam. *Shambhala: The Sacred Path of the Warrior*. Boston: Shambhala Publications, 1983.

Welwood, John. *Awakening the Heart*. Boston: Shambhala Publications, 1983.

appendix **A**

NANDA Diagnosis Qualifiers

Cathie E. Guzzetta

Exhibit A-1 outlines the definitions for diagnostic qualifiers that were approved by the North American Nursing Diagnosis Association. These diagnostic qualifiers provide a common terminology for understanding the nursing diagnoses found in Taxonomy I (refer to Chapter 6) and for developing new and revising old diagnoses.

Exhibit A-1 NANDA Diagnosis Qualifiers

Category 1	
Actual:	Existing at the present moment; existing in reality
Potential:	Can, but has not yet, come into being; possible
Category 2	
Ineffective:	Not producing the desired effect; not capable of performing satisfactorily
Decreased:	Smaller; lessened; diminished; lesser in size, amount, or degree
Increased:	Greater in size, amount or degree; larger, enlarged
Impaired:	Made worse, weakened; damaged, reduced; deteriorated
Depleted:	Emptied wholly or partially; exhausted of
Deficient:	Inadequate in amount, quality, or degree; defective; not sufficient; incomplete
Excessive:	Characterized by an amount or quantity that is greater than necessary, desirable, or usable
Dysfunctional:	Abnormal; impaired or incompletely functioning
Disturbed:	Agitated; interrupted, interfered with
Acute:	Severe but of short duration
Chronic:	Lasting a long time; recurring; habitual; constant
Intermittent:	Stopping and starting again at intervals; periodic; cyclic

Source: The North American Nursing Diagnosis Association, St. Louis, Mo., 1986.

appendix B

Unitary Person Assessment Tool Prototype*

Cathie E. Guzzetta, RN, PhD, FAAN
Associate Professor and Chair
Cardiovascular Nursing
The Catholic University of America
Washington, D.C.

Shelia D. Bunton, RN, MSN
Major, Army Nurse Corps
Tripler Army Medical Center
Tripler Army Medical Center, Hawaii

Linda A. Prinkey, RN, MSN, CCRN
Staff Nurse
Open Heart Recovery Room
St Joseph's Hospital
Towson, MD

Anita P. Sherer, RN, MSN, CCRN
Cardiopulmonary Rehabilitation Nurse Specialist
Alexandria Hospital
Alexandria, VA

Patricia C. Seifert, RN, CNOR, MSN
Assistant Nursing Coordinator
Cardiac Surgery
The Fairfax Hospital
Falls Church, VA

The Unitary Person Assessment Tool prototype is a nursing data base that was developed from the North American Nursing Diagnosis Association's Unitary Person Framework and Taxonomy I. (To understand this assessment tool it is essential that the reader refer back to the Unitary Person Framework and Taxonomy I sections in Chapter 6.)

Within the Unitary Person Framework, a *nursing diagnosis is defined as a judgment about the health of the unitary person based on the data collected from the nine human response patterns*. The Unitary Person Assessment Tool prototype was developed to incorporate the signs and symptoms necessary for nurses to formulate such judgments based on the data collected from the nine human response patterns. (Refer to Chapter 6 which discusses the nine human response patterns.) In developing the Unitary Person Assessment Tool prototype it was necessary to operationalize the concepts of unitary person to create a data base that was practical and realistic in measuring human response patterns. The challenge then was to develop a data base that would translate theory into bedside practice. Because our clinical area of expertise was in cardiovascular critical care nursing, we developed the data base prototype to assess the problems of the cardiovascular critically ill patient. The objectives of the project were to develop a Unitary Person Assessment Tool prototype which would:

---

*Cathie E. Guzzetta, Shelia D. Bunton, Linda A. Prinkey, Anita P. Sherer, and Patricia C. Seifert, *Clinical Assessment Tools for Use with Nursing Diagnoses* (St. Louis: Mosby Year Book, 1989): pp. 15–22.

- be developed from the Unitary Person Framework
- be organized according to the classification schema of Taxonomy I
- focus on cardiovascular critically ill patients
- include the standards of cardiovascular nursing[1] and the process standards of critical care nursing[2]
- be tested and refined in clinical practice

Exhibit B-1 reveals the outcome of the Unitary Person Assessment Tool prototype which has been refined and revised after testing in clinical practice. All nine human response patterns have been included. Specific signs and symptoms pertinent to each category and to most nursing diagnoses have been incorporated. Relevant nursing diagnoses associated with the data have been placed in the right-hand column of the assessment tool. When assessing signs and symptoms that may affirm the existence of a particular diagnosis, you can circle the diagnosis in the right-hand column. The circled diagnosis does not confirm the existence of a particular problem, but should alert you to a possible problem or alteration. After the assessment has been completed, you can visually scan the possible problems in the right-hand column, synthesize the data to determine whether other clusters of signs and symptoms also support the existence of the problem, and then formulate a judgment as to whether the actual diagnosis is present.

The diagnoses in the right-hand column may be repeated in more than one place. They may also be repeated in other subcategory alterations as appropriate. The nursing diagnoses in the right-hand column are intended as a guide to focus thinking and direct more detailed attention to the collection of data relative to a possible problem. This column is not meant to be static or absolute. You should not feel limited by the diagnoses in this column because other diagnoses that are not listed may exist related to a pattern of concern.

In developing this data base we found the need to rearrange the order of the nine major human response patterns to allow pertinent historical and interview data to emerge before specific physiologic data were collected. The exchanging category, which reflects complex physiologic data, was rearranged to provide a logical head-to-toe assessment. Data were organized to prevent repetition of assessment parameters. The vascular and cardiac categories (under alteration in circulation) were combined because from a clinical viewpoint it was not logical to separate these areas. Other lower level categories were added because they were highly relevant to the cardiovascular patient population being assessed (e.g., risk factor profile). Some lower level categories were deleted because they generally were not relevant problems for cardiovascular patients (e.g., potential for violence).

The Unitary Person Assessment Tool can be used as a prototype for assessing various kinds of patients. Thus it is possible to use this prototype to assess labor and delivery patients or spinal cord injured patients in a rehabilitation setting by combining, deleting, adding, rearranging, and changing the appropriate assessment parameters to meet the needs and requirements of a particular patient population or setting. If you are working in a cardiac rehabilitation setting, for example, you may wish to delete the detailed hemodynamic monitoring parameters while adding specific questions to assess cardiovascular prevention, stress management, and teaching knowledge. In contrast, if you work primarily with a gerontologic population, you may wish to delete many of the hemo-

Exhibit B-1 Unitary Person Assessment Tool: A Prototype*

Name: ______ Age: ______ Sex: ______
Address: ______ Telephone: ______
Significant other: ______ Telephone: ______
Date of admission: ______ Medical diagnosis: ______
Allergies: ______ Dyes: ______

	Nursing Diagnosis (Potential or Altered)
Communicating—A pattern involving sending messages	
Read, write, understand English (circle) ______	Communication
Other language ______	Verbal
Intubated ______ Speech impaired ______	[Nonverbal]
Alternate form of communication ______	
Valuing—A pattern involving the assessment of relative worth	
Religious preference ______	Spiritual state
Important religious practices ______	
Cultural orientation ______	
Cultural practices ______	
Relating—A pattern involving establishing bonds	
[Alterations in Role]	
Marital status ______	[Role performance]
Age and health of significant other ______	Parenting
______	Sexuality patterns
Number of children ______ Ages ______	
Responsibilities in home ______	
Financial support ______	Family processes
Occupation ______	
Job satisfaction/concerns ______	
Physical/mental energy expenditures ______	
Sexual relationships (satisfactory/unsatisfactory) ______	
Physical difficulties related to sex ______	
______	
[Alterations in Socialization]	
Quality of relationships with others ______	Impaired social interaction
Patient's description ______	
Significant other's description ______	
Staff observations ______	
Verbalizes feelings of being alone ______	Social isolation
Attributed to ______	
Knowing—A pattern involving the meaning associated with information	
Previous hospitalization/surgeries ______	Knowledge deficit
______	
Educational level ______	
History of the following diseases:	
Heart ______	
Lung ______	
Liver ______ Kidney ______	
Cerebrovascular ______ Rheumatic fever ______	
Thyroid ______	
Diabetes ______ Medication ______	
Current health problems ______	
______	

continues

Exhibit B-1 continued

	Nursing Diagnosis (Potential or Altered)
Current medications ______	Knowledge deficit
______	
Risk factors — Present — Knowledge of	
1. Hypertension ______ ______	
2. Hyperlipidemia ______ ______	
3. Smoking ______ ______	
4. Obesity ______ ______	
5. Diabetes ______ ______	
6. Sedentary living ______ ______	
7. Stress ______ ______	
8. Alcohol use ______ ______	
9. Oral contraceptives ______ ______	
10. Family history ______	
Knowledge of planned test/surgery ______	
Misconceptions ______	
Readiness to learn ______	[Learning]
Learning impeded by ______	Thought processes
Feeling—A pattern involving the subjective awareness of information	
Alterations in comfort	
Pain/discomfort	
Onset ______ Duration ______	Pain
Location ______ Quality ______ Radiation ______	Chronic
Associated factors ______	[Acute]
Aggravating factors ______	[Discomfort]
Alleviating factors ______	Chronic
	Acute
Alterations in emotional integrity	
Recent stressful life events ______	Anxiety
Verbalizes feelings of fear or anxiety ______	Fear
Source ______	
Physical manifestations ______	
Moving—A pattern involving activity	
[Alterations in activity]	
History of physical disability ______	Impaired physical mobility
Limitations in daily activities ______	Activity intolerance
Exercise habits ______	
[Alterations in rest]	
Hours slept/night ______ Difficulties ______	Sleep pattern disturbance
Sleep aids (pillows, medications, food) ______	
[Alterations in recreation]	
Leisure activities ______	Deficit in diversional activity
Social activities ______	
[Alterations in activities of daily living]	
Home maintenance management ______	Impaired home maintenance management
Size and arrangement of home (stairs, bathroom) ______	

Exhibit B-1 continued

	Nursing Diagnosis (Potential or Altered)
Housekeeping responsibilities ______	Impaired home maintenance
Shopping responsibilities ______	management
Health maintenance	
Health insurance ______	Health maintenance
Regular physical check-ups ______	
Alterations in self-care	Self-care
Ability to perform ADL: Independent ____ Dependent ____	Feeding
Specify deficits ______	Bathing
Discharge planning needs ______	Dressing
	Toileting
Perceiving—A pattern involving the reception of information	
Alterations in self-concept	
Patient's description of himself/herself ______	Body image
Effects of illness/surgery on self-concept ______	Self-esteem
______	Personal identity
[Alterations in meaningfulness]	[Meaningfulness]
Verbalizes hopelessness ______	Hopelessness
Verbalizes powerlessness ______	Powerlessness
Sensory/perceptual alterations	
Vision impaired ____ Glasses ______	Visual
Visual examination ______	
Auditory impaired ____ Hearing aid ______	Auditory
Auditory examination ______	
Kinesthetics impaired ____ Romberg ______	Kinesthetic
Gustatory impaired ______	Gustatory
Tactile impaired ____ Examination ______	Tactile
Olfactory impaired ____ Examination ______	Olfactory
Reflexes: Biceps R __ L __ Triceps R __ L __	Reflexes
Brachio-radialis R __ L __ Knee R __ L __	
Ankle R __ L __ Plantar R __ L __	
Exchanging—A pattern involving mutual giving and receiving	
Alterations in nutrition	
Teeth, gums, lesions ______	Oral mucous membrane
Dentures ______	
Ideal body weight ______	More than body requirements
Height ______ Weight ______	
Eating patterns	
Number of meals per day ______	
Special diet ______	Less than body requirements
Where eaten ______	
Food preferences/intolerances ______	
Food allergies ______	
Caffeine intake (coffee, tea, soft drinks) ______	
Appetite changes ______	
Presence of nausea/vomiting ______	
Current therapy	
NPO ____ NG suction ______	
Tube feeding ______	
TPN ______	

continues

Exhibit B-1 continued

	Nursing Diagnosis (Potential or Altered)
Laboratory results	
NA ____ K ____ Cl ____ Glucose ____________	
Cholesterol ______ Triglycerides ______ Fasting ______	
[Alterations in physical regulation]	
[Immune]	
Lymph nodes enlarged ___ Location ______________	Infection
WBC count _________ Differential ______________	Hypothermia
Alteration in body temperature	Hyperthermia
Temperature _________ Route ________________	Ineffective thermoregulation
[Alterations in physical integrity]	
Skin integrity _______ Rashes _______ Lesions _______	Impaired skin integrity
Petechiae ___________ Surgical incision ___________	Impaired tissue integrity
Bruising ____________ Abrasions ______________	
[Alterations in circulation]	
Cerebral (circle appropriate response)	Cerebral tissue perfusion
Pupils / Eye opening	
L 2 3 4 5 6 mm / None (1)	
R 2 3 4 5 6 mm / To pain (2)	
Reaction: Brisk _____ / To speech (3)	Fluid volume
Sluggish ________ / Spontaneous (4)	Deficit
Nonreactive _______	Excess
Best verbal / Best motor	
Intubated (0) / Flaccid (1)	
Mute (1) / Extensor response (2)	Cardiac output
Incomprehensible sound (2) / Flexor response (3)	
Inappropriate words (3) / Semipurposeful (4)	
Confused conversation (4) / Localized to pain (5)	
Oriented (5) / Obeys commands (6)	
Glasgow coma scale total ____________	
Neurological changes/ symptoms ______________________________	
[Cardiac]	
Apical rate and rhythm ____________	Cardiopulmonary tissue perfusion
PMI ____________	
Heart sounds/ murmurs ______________________________	
Dysrhythmias ______________________________	
Pacemaker __________	Fluid volume
BP: Sitting R ___ L ___ Lying R ___ L ___ Standing R ___ L ___	Deficit
	Excess
A-Line reading ______________________	
Cardiac index __________ Cardiac output __________	Cardiac output
CVP _________ PAP _________ PCWP _________	
IV fluids ______________________	
IV cardiac medications ______________________	
______________________________	
Serum enzymes ______________________	

Exhibit B-1 continued

	Nursing Diagnosis (Potential or Altered)
Peripheral	Peripheral tissue perfusion
Pulses: A = absent B = bruits D = Doppler	
+3 = bounding +2 = palpable +1 = faintly palpable	
Carotid R __ L __ Popliteal R __ L __	
Brachial R __ L __ Posterior tibial R __ L __	
Radial R __ L __ Dorsalis pedis R __ L __	Fluid volume
Femoral R __ L __	Deficit
Jugular venous distention R __ L __	Excess
Skin temperature ______ Color ______	
Edema ______ Capillary refill ______	Cardiac output
Clubbing ______ Claudication ______	
Gastrointestinal	
Liver: Enlarged ______ Ascites ______	GI tissue perfusion
Renal	
Urine output: 24 hour ______ Average hourly ______	Renal tissue perfusion
BUN ______ Creatinine ______ Specific gravity ______	
Urine studies ______	Fluid volume
	Deficit
	Excess
	Cardiac output
[Alterations in oxygenation]	
Rate ______ Rhythm ______ Depth ______	Ineffective airway clearance
Labored/unlabored (circle) Chest expansion ______	
Use of accessory muscles ______	Ineffective breathing patterns
Orthopnea ______	
Breath sounds ______	Ineffective gas exchange
Complaints of dyspnea ______ Precipitated by ______	
Cough: Productive/nonproductive ______	
Sputum: Color ______ Amount ______ Consistency ______	
LOC ______ Splinting ______	
Arterial blood gases ______	
Oxygen percent and device ______	
Ventilator ______	
Alterations in elimination	
Bowel	Bowel patterns
Abdominal physical examination ______	Constipation
Usual bowel habits ______	Diarrhea
Alterations from normal ______	Incontinence
Urinary	
Bladder distention ______	Urinary patterns
Color ______ Catheter ______	Incontinence
Usual urinary pattern ______	Retention
Alteration from normal ______	
Choosing—A pattern involving the selection of alternatives	
Alterations in coping	
Patient's usual problem solving methods ______	Ineffective individual coping
Family's usual problem solving methods ______	Ineffective family coping
Patient's method of dealing with stress ______	

continues

Exhibit B-1 continued

	Nursing Diagnosis (Potential or Altered)
Family's method of dealing with stress ______	
Patient's affect ______	
Physical manifestations ______	
[Alterations in participation]	
Compliance with past/current health care regimen ______	Noncompliance
Willingness to comply with future health care regimen ______	

ADL = activities of daily living; A-line = arterial line; BP = blood pressure; BUN = blood urea nitrogen; CVP = central venous pressure; GI = gastrointestinal; IV = intravenous; LOC = level of consciousness; NG = nasogastric; NPO = nothing by mouth; PAP = pulmonary artery pressure; PCWP = pulmonary capillary wedge pressure; PMI = point of maximal impulse; TPN = total parenteral nutrition

dynamic monitoring variables while adding variables that are pertinent to the elderly population (e.g., impact of recent losses, ability to ambulate and transfer, independence in self-care activities, history of falls, accidents, injuries, etc.). Moreover, the Unitary Person Assessment Tool prototype can also be modified as a short screening tool to rapidly evaluate patients. This work has already been accomplished in a forthcoming book in which the Unitary Person Assessment Tool prototype has been adapted to many specific patient populations and settings.[3]

The benefits from using the Unitary Person Assessment Tool prototype are multiple. Because the data measure human response patterns, the data collected are pertinent to nursing diagnoses and are collected from a holistic and nursing point of view. The tool permits evaluation of specific signs and symptoms to assist the nurse in validating the existence of a particular nursing diagnosis. We have found that when the tool is used in practice, the data are so rich that nursing diagnoses appear to "fall out" after the assessment. Continued use of this tool in various practice settings will be beneficial in easing problems with nursing diagnoses and in refining the Unitary Person Framework. We invite any correspondence related to the use or further refinement of this work.**

**Direct correspondence to Anita P. Sherer, RN, MSN, CCRN, 6327 Teakwood Court, Burke, VA 22015.

NOTES

1. American Nurses' Association Division of Medical-Surgical Nursing Practice and American Heart Association Council on Cardiovascular Nursing, *Standards of Cardiovascular Nursing Practice*, (Kansas City: American Nurses' Association, 1981), p. 1ff.
2. American Association of Critical-Care Nurses, *Standards for Nursing Care of the Critically Ill*, (Reston, Va.: Reston Publishing Co., 1981), p. 1ff.
3. Cathie E. Guzzetta, Shelia D. Bunton, Linda A. Prinkey, Anita P. Sherer, and Patricia C. Seifert, *Clinical Assessment Tools for Use with Nursing Diagnoses* (St. Louis: Mosby Year Book, 1989): pp. 15–22.

appendix **C**

Holistic Nursing Assessment Tool

Pamela Potter Hughes, RN, BSN, MA

Name ______________________ Date of Birth ____________ Sex ______
Address ______________________________ Telephone ____________
Significant Other ______________________ Telephone ____________
Date __________ Education ____________ Employment ____________
Medical Diagnosis ____
Reason for Seeking Holistic Nursing Care ____________________________

Height ______ Weight ______ B/P ______ T ______ P ______ R ______

	Nursing Diagnosis *(Potential/Altered)*
COMMUNICATING—A pattern involving sending messages	
Verbal:	[Communication, altered]
Nonverbal:	Verbal Nonverbal
VALUING—A pattern involving the assigning of relative worth	[Spiritual State, altered] Spiritual Distress
RELATING—A pattern involving establishing bonds	
Role (marital status, children, parents):	Role Performance, altered Parenting, altered Parental Role Conflict [Work] Sexual Dysfunction
Occupation:	Family Processes, altered
Sexual Relationships:	Sexuality Patterns, altered
Socialization:	[Socialization, altered] Social Interaction, impaired Social Isolation

Name: ____________________ Date: ______________

Nursing Diagnosis
(Potential/Altered)

KNOWING—A pattern involving the meaning associated with information

Orientation: Thought Processes, altered
[Orientation]
[Confusion]

Memory: [Memory]

Previous Illnesses/Hospitalizations/Surgeries:

Identified Health Problems (Present/History):

Current Medications (Medication Allergies):

Risk Factors (Smoking, Family History, etc.):

Perception/Knowledge of Health/Illness: Knowledge Deficit (Specify)

Expectations of Holistic Health Intervention:

Readiness To Learn (Ready, Willing, Able): [Learning]

FEELING—A pattern involving the subjective awareness of information

Comfort: [Comfort, altered]
Pain, chronic
Pain, acute
[Discomfort, chronic]
[Discomfort, acute]

Emotional Integrity States: [Grieving]
Anticipatory
Dysfunctional
Anxiety
Fear
[Anger]
[Guilt]
[Shame]
[Sadness]
Post-Trauma Response

Name: ____________________ Date: ______________

	Nursing Diagnosis *(Potential/Altered)*
MOVING—A pattern involving activity	
Activity (Physical Mobility Limitations):	[Activity, altered] Activity Intolerance Impaired Physical Mobility
Rest:	Fatigue Sleep Pattern Disturbance [Hypersomnia] [Insomnia] [Nightmares]
Recreation:	Diversional Activity Deficit
Environmental Maintenance:	Impaired Home Maintenance Management [Safety Hazards]
Health Maintenance:	Health Maintenance, altered
Self-Care:	Bathing/Hygiene Deficit Dressing/Grooming Deficit Feeding Deficit Toileting Deficit
PERCEIVING—A pattern involving the reception of information	
Sensory Perception:	[Sensory Perception, altered] Visual Auditory Kinesthetic Gustatory Tactile Olfactory Unilateral Neglect
Self-Concept:	[Self-Concept, altered] Body Image Disturbance Personal Identity Disturbance

Name: ____________________ Date: ______________

Nursing Diagnosis
(Potential/Altered)

Self-Esteem
Disturbance
—Chronic Low
—Situational

Meaningfulness:

[Meaningfulness, altered]
Hopelessness
Powerlessness

EXCHANGING—A pattern involving mutual giving and receiving

Nutrition:

[Nutrition, altered]
[Nutritional Deficit]

< or > Body
Requirements

Oral Mucus Membranes,
impaired

Elimination:

[Bowel Elimination,
altered]
Bowel Incontinence
Constipation: colonic
Constipation: perceived
Diarrhea

GI Tissue Perfusion

Renal/Urinary:

[Urinary Elimination,
altered]
Incontinence (specify)
Retention
[Enuresis]

Renal Tissue Perfusion

Physical/Tissue Integrity:

[Tissue Integrity,
impaired]
Impaired Skin Integrity
[Injury: risk]
Aspiration
Disuse Syndrome
Poisoning
Suffocation
Trauma

Name: ____________________ Date: ______________

	Nursing Diagnosis *(Potential/Altered)*
Physical Regulation:	
Immune:	[Physical Regulation, altered] Infection: risk Altered Protection Thermoregulation, ineffective —Hypothermia —Hyperthermia
Circulation:	Cardiac Output, decreased [Tissue Perfusion, altered] Cardiopulmonary Cerebral Peripheral [Fluid Volume, altered] Deficit Deficit: risk Excess
Oxygenation:	[Respiration, altered] Airway Clearance, ineffective Breathing Pattern, ineffective Gas Exchange, impaired
Hormonal/Metabolic Patterns:	[Menstrual Patterns] [Premenstrual Syndrome]

CHOOSING—A pattern involving the selection of alternatives

Coping:	Individual Coping, ineffective Adjustment, impaired
Judgment/Decisions:	Conflict: decisional Coping: defensive Denial: impaired
Participation:	Noncompliance
Family Coping:	[Family Coping, ineffective] Compromised Disabled

ADDITIONAL COMMENTS:

Therapeutic/Healing Touch

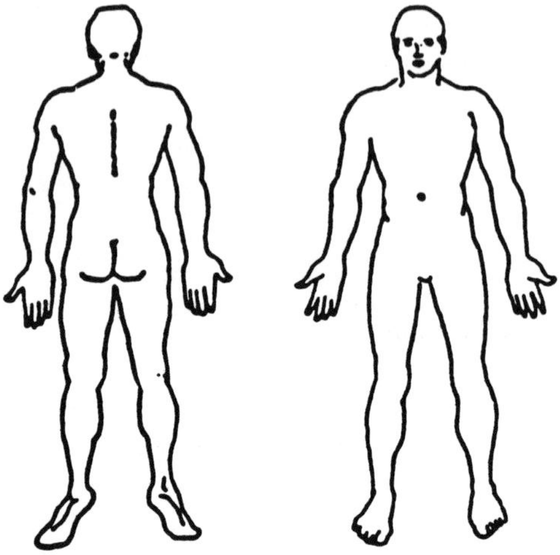

Goals [Health-Seeking Behaviors]

1. ______________________
2. ______________________
3. ______________________
4. ______________________
5. ______________________

Prioritized Nursing Diagnosis/Problem List

1. ______________________
2. ______________________
3. ______________________
4. ______________________
5. ______________________

Signature ______________________ **Date** ______________

Holistic Nursing Care Plan

Name: ____________________
Date: ______________

Client Goals:
1. ________________________________
2. ________________________________
3. ________________________________
4. ________________________________

Nursing Diagnosis and Related Factors	*Client Outcomes/ Outcome Criteria*	*Therapeutic Intervention*	*Evaluation*

Client Signature ____________________

Holistic Nursing Assessment Tool: Developed by Pamela Potter Hughes, RN, BSN, MA

Source: Adapted from Cathie E. Guzzetta, Shelia D. Bunton, Linda A. Prinkey, Anita P. Sherer, and Patricia C. Seifert, *Clinical Assessment Tools for Use with Nursing Diagnoses* (St. Louis: C.V. Mosby), 1989.

Index

A

Absolute, 30
Abstract imagery, 224
Accelerated learning, 271
Acting, 135
Active attention, 15
Active goal-directed states, 35
Active listening, 28, 45, 46
Acupressure, 332-334, 339, 345
Acute care settings, 72, 335
Adult education principles, 359-360
Aerobic exercise, 160, 162
Affirmations, 18-20
After-images, 224
Aldosterone, 89
Alfalfa, 174
Aloneness, 306
Altered states of consciousness (ASC), 24, 33, 35, 215, 363
Ambience, 182
American Heart Association, 117, 175
American Holistic Nurses' Association, 69, 117-121
American Nurses' Association, 66, 107, 117
Anchoring, 243-244
Angiotensin, 93, 185
Animism, 59
Anniversary phenomenon, 50
Applicability of knowledge, 360
Aquinas, Thomas, 63
Asclepions, 60-61, 333
Assessment
  definition, 103
  development of tools, 103-104
  environmental control, 187-188
  imagery, 233-234
  intuitive thinking, 105-107
  motivational factors, 140
  music therapy, 275-276
  nutrition, exercise, and movement, 170-171
  play and laughter, 296
  receptivity, 105
  relationships, 312
  relaxation, 205-206
  self-reflection, 364-365
  touch, 341
  worksite wellness needs, 142
Associations, 247
Atomism, 58, 64
Attitudes, 134, 139
Audio cassette libraries, 278-279
Authenticity, 31-32, 130, 310
Autogenic training, 196, 199, 212

Autonomic nervous system, 84-86, 88, 91, 228
Awareness, 31, 205
Ayurvedic healing, 61-62

B

Basic vulnerability, 45
Behavior modification, 141
Being-in-the-world, 25
Beliefs, 46, 134, 139, 203-204
Beta endorphins, 93
Bidirectional information, 91, 93
Biobehavioral therapies, 88, 91. *See also specific therapies*
Biodance, 4, 13
Biofeedback, 81, 196, 200-201, 203, 215
Biomedical model, 104
Bodymind connection, 25, 34, 41, 78, 80, 81, 129
  definition, 13
  environmental factors, 186
  imagery and, 228
  merging with music intervention, 281
  nutrition, exercise: and movement factors, 164
  play and laughter and, 293
  relationships and, 309
  relaxation and, 201
  self-reflection, 360
  touch and, 337-338, 340
  See also Psychophysiology
Body-mind-spirit, 5, 25, 60, 63, 64, 68, 131
Body scanning, 196, 205
Body therapy, 332
Bone healing script, 255-256
Boundaries, 14, 308
Brain
  centers, 83-84
  hemispheric functions, 33-34, 87, 227, 228, 231-232, 268, 361
  mind modulation and, 84, 86, 89, 91, 93
Breathing, 209, 212, 219, 301
Burn graft script, 257-258

C

Calcium, 162, 174
Cancer, 162, 186
Cardiac conditioning, 168, 171
Cardiorespiratory endurance, 170
Cardiovascular changes, 316-317
Cardiovascular disease, 162
Caring process, 25-26
Caring touch, 332
Cartesian dualism, 63, 150
Cartoon collections, 300
Cassette tapes, 271, 278-279, 300
Centeredness, 40, 45
Centering, 44-45, 175, 332, 340
Chakras, 62, 270
Change, 47, 132, 308
Ch'i, 61, 334
Chiron myth, 43
Choice potential, 17, 20
Cholesterol-lowering diet, 174
Choosing, 135, 245
Christian healing, 62-64, 363
Circle of human potential
  affirmations, 18-20
  choice, 17
  emotions, 15-16
  mental, 14-15
  physical, 14
  relationships, 16-17
  spirit, 16
Classical music, 271, 273
Client outcomes, 117
  definition, 115
  environmental control, 188
  imagery, 234
  music therapy, 276
  nutrition, exercise, and movement, 172
  play and laughter, 297
  relationships, 312
  relaxation, 206
  self-reflection, 365
  touch, 342
Clock time, 267
Closed family system, 308-309
Clustering, 358, 378, 380
Cognitive strengthening, 141

Cohesiveness in relationships, 17
Color, 270
Communications
  anchorig, 243-244
  eye positions, 243
  neuropeptide system, 91-93
  process, 45
  relationships and, 309
Compassionate guide, 203
Competition, 294, 299
Concrete imagery, 224
Conflict, 45, 134
Conscious dying, 381-382
Consciousness, 70, 71, 80, 84, 94, 129
Consciousness raising, 68, 141
Contracts, 358, 362-363, 370, 373-376
Control, 203
Co-participants, 26
Coping, 141, 229, 293-294, 359
Counseling, 306, 309
Creative movement, 170, 175-176
Creativity, 270
Crises, 306
Cues, 106, 141, 205, 209
Cymatics, 264

D

Daily practice, 44
Dance, 170
Dance of life, 13, 16, 43
Daydreams, 225, 363
Denial, 310
Descartes, Rene, 63-64, 149
Diaries, 358, 359, 362, 369-370
Dietary fiber, 174
Digestion, 166
Discipline, 131
Disease, 80, 228-229
Disturbance, 267
Divine sleep of the saints, 363
Door to the inner mind intervention, 215-216
Dorsal horn, 93
Drawing
  cartoons, 300
  case studies, 251
  family and group, 246-247
  guidelines, 244-245
  mandalas, 247-250
  symbolism, colors, and association, 247
  symptom/disease, 245-246
Dreams, 225, 358, 363, 377-378
Dunbar, Flanders, 65-66
Dunn, Halpert, 66
Dying, 381-382

E

Ecominnea, 182
Effleurage, 351
Eidetic imagery, 225
Eidetic psychotherapy, 227
Embedded commands, 232
Emotions, 93, 269, 270, 315
Emotions potential, 15-16, 19
Empty chair intervention, 323-324, 327-328
Enactive mode, 227
Enchanted world, 63
Endocrine system, 86-89, 91
Endorphins, 88, 293
End-result imagery, 224, 228
Endurance, 160
Energy meridian, 332, 334, 339
Energy transduction, 80-81
Enkephalins, 88
Enmeshment, 308
Entropy, 308
Environment
  attitudes toward, 186-187
  bodymind connections, 186
  food irradiation, 185-188
  definitions, 182
  hazards, 182-183
  meat and poultry supplementation, 186
  noise pollution, 183, 185, 190
  nurse healer objectives, 181-182
  nurse healer reflections, 193-194
  nursing process and, 187-190, 192-193
  passive smoking hazard, 188
  research directions, 193
Environmental control committees, 190

Environmental Protection Agency (EPA), 182
Ergonomics, 182
Estebany, Oskar, 335
Ethics
  American Nurses' Association, 66
  holistic, 71
Etiology, 108
Evaluation
  definition, 116
  environmental control, 192-193
  imagery, 250-251
  music therapy, 282-283
  nutrition, exercise, and movement, 177
  play and laughter, 300-301
  relationships, 325
  relaxation, 216
  self-reflection, 382
  touch, 352
  wellness programs, 142
Events, 267
Exercise
  benefits of, 168-169
  definitions, 160-161
  guidelines, 168
  health factors, 162-163
  interventions, 175
  nurse healer objectives, 159-160
  nurse healer reflections, 178
  nursing process, 170-173, 177
  purpose, 166, 168
  research directions, 178
Existential identity, 29
Expanding awareness, 213
Expanding the senses, 280-281
Experience, 359
Experiential time, 267
Experimental listening, 274
Eye positions, 243

F

Facilitators, 44
Family systems, 306-309
Family therapy interventions, 246, 322-323
Fantasy, 225
Far Eastern healing, 61, 333, 363
Fear of failure, 47
Feedback, 13, 80, 307, 308
Fehmi, Lester, 201
Felt sense, 317, 319, 320
Fish oils, 174
Fitness, 160, 163, 166-167, 175
Flexibility, 160, 170
Focusing inward, 31, 317, 319
Food irradiation, 185-186
Foot-in-the-door strategy, 141
Foot reflexology, 332, 339-340, 345
Forgiveness, 306
Frequencies, 264, 265
Froebel, Friedrich Wilhelm August, 291
Frozen images, 227
Future pacing, 244

G

Game playing, 299-300. *See also* Play and laughter
Garlic, 174
Gastrointestinal system, 88, 93
General adaptation syndrome (GAS), 78
General imagery, 224
Genes, 89
Golden Moment, 212
Great Chain of Being, 29
Greeks
  healing, 60-61, 263, 363
  play theory, 291
Green, Alyce, 200
Green, Elmer, 200
Group drawing, 246-247
Growth, 48-49
Guided imagery, 215, 338
  definition, 225
  disease treatment, 228-229
  scripts, 238-243, 255-258
Guided Imagery and Music (GIM), 271, 272
Guides, 40, 42-43, 203, 283, 364
Gut feeling, 93, 105

H

Hallucinations, 225
Hardiness, 128, 132-134
Harmonic environment, 182
HDL (high-density lipoprotein), 160
Healee, 25
Healer, 25, 41-42
Healing, 14, 39
  ancient history, 58-63, 333
  definition, 4
  future of, 69-73
  holistic health care, 64-69
  human science basis, 25-26
  modern sense, 41
  nurse healer objectives, 57-58
  nurse healer reflections, 74
  post-Scientific Revolution history, 63-69
  research directions, 74
  spirituality basis, 26, 28
Healing awareness, 4, 14, 17, 31-32
Healing sites, 72-73
Healing the whole person, 13
Health, 80, 109, 129, 151
Health Belief Model (HBM), 139
Health-illness continuum, 151
Health-oriented nursing diagnoses, 109, 114-115
Heart rate, 175
Heisenberg's Uncertainty Principle, 148, 153
Hemispheric functions, 33-34, 87, 227, 228, 231-232, 268, 361
High-calcium diet, 174
Higher potentials, 35
Higher Self. *See* Transpersonal self
High-level wellness, 66
Hippocratic Oath, 61
Holism, 4, 5
Holistic ethics, 71
Holistic health, 57
Holistic nursing models, 104
Holistic nursing standards, 117-121
Homeodynamic mechanisms, 308
Hormones, 86-88, 91, 93
Hospice, 72
Hospital music, 273-274
Human caring process, 26
Human motivational model, 136-141
Human potentials
  actualizing, 3
  circle of, 13-20
  definitions, 4
  maximization of, 5, 14
  nurse healer objectives, 3-4
  nurse healer reflections, 21
  relaxation interventions, 214
  research directions, 20-21
  self-assessment, 5-13
  whole person, 5
Human science, 25-26
Humor, 290, 293-295, 299, 300
Hypnagogic imagery, 225
Hypnagogic sleep, 363
Hypnopompic imagery, 225
Hypnopompic state, 377
Hypnosis, 83, 94, 196, 199-200, 215-216
Hypometabolic state, 34, 214, 268
Hypothalamus, 88, 89, 91. *See also* Limbic-hypothalamic system

I

Illness, 151, 228-229, 309
Imagery, 31, 94
  assessment, 233-234
  case studies, 251-258
  client outcomes, 234
  definitions, 224-225
  disease treatment, 229-230
  drawing, 244-251
  eliciting of, 227-228
  empowering the spoken word, 231-233
  evaluation, 250
  function of, 223
  interpretation of, 230-231
  interventions, 238-250
  learning and, 226-227
  music and, 270, 271
  nurse healer objectives, 223-224
  nurse healer reflections, 259
  nursing diagnosis, 234
  nursing process, 233-238, 250-251

physiology and, 84, 225-226
plan and intervention, 234-238
relaxation and, 219
research directions, 259
script use guidelines, 238
scripts, specific, 238-242
storytelling and, 322
touch therapies and, 345
wellness and, 228
Imagination imagery, 225
Immune system, 89-91
Implementation, 116
Incubation sleep, 363
Indian healing, 61-62, 333
Individuation, 73, 308
Induced imagery, 224
Informational substrate, 93
Information flow, 80, 94, 105
Information theory, 78, 80
Information transduction, 80-81, 84, 86, 89
Inner awareness interventions, 215
Inner guide script, 242-243
Institute for Music and Imagery, 271-272
Insulin, 93
Intention, 40, 44, 47, 333
Interconnectivity, 308
Interpersonal awareness, 68
Interpersonal growth, 48, 49
Interspersal technique, 232-233
Intersubjectivity, 26
Interventions
criteria, 115-116
environmental control, 190
exercise, 175
imagery, 234-250
movement, 175-176
music therapy, 276
nutrition, 174
play and laughter, 297-300
relationships, 314-325
relaxation, 208-216
self-reflection, 365, 368-382
touch, 342-352
Intimacy, 306
Intimacy awareness, 317
Intuition, 33, 40, 105-107, 317, 337, 361
Intuition logs, 376-377
Inward arc, 30
Inward journey, 5, 28, 30, 39
Isolation, 17, 306-307
Iso-principle, 274
"I" statements, 317

J

Joke collections, 300
Journals, 358, 359, 362, 369-370, 380

K

Katha Upanishad, 32
Knowing, 105, 361

L

Laughter. *See* Play and laughter
LDH (low-density lipoprotein), 160
Learning, 47, 226-227, 271
Lecithin, 174
Left hemispheric function, 33-34, 227, 228, 231-232, 268, 361
Letters, 358, 359, 362, 370, 380, 382-386
Lexical mode, 227
Life mission, 131-132
Life potentials, 40, 47
Life review, 358, 363-364, 380-383
Light and shadow, 43-44
Limbic-hypothalamic system, 78, 82, 83, 86-87, 89, 93
Limbic system, 93, 269
Linkages, 232
Listening, 28, 45-46, 274, 282, 322
Loneliness, 306
Love, 40, 42, 44, 306
Lucid dreaming, 377
Lymphocytes, 89, 91

M

Macrominerals, 166
Mandalas, 247-250
Mantras, 196, 199

Massage, 333, 338-339, 345
Maximal heart rate, 160
Meaning, 49-51, 227
Meat supplementation, 186
Medical paradigms, 68
Medications, 204-205
Meditation, 24, 40, 196, 198-199, 214
Meditative music, 271, 273
Memory, 84, 226-227, 267, 364
Memory imagery, 225
Mental Aikido, 203
Mental potential, 14-15, 19
Metaphors, 232
Mindfulness, 202
Mind-gene process, 89
Mind mapping, 378, 380
Mind modulation, 14
  autonomic nervous system, 84-86
  definition, 78
  endocrine system, 86-89
  immune system, 89-94
  neuropeptide system, 91-94
  relaxation effects, 201
  See also Psychophysiology
Minerals, 160, 166
Miso, 165
Mission, 131-132
Monocytes, 93
Mood, 93
Mother Theresa, 72
Motivation, 128, 134, 136-141
Motivational gap, 137, 139
Movement
  definitions, 160-161
  forms of, 163-164
  interventions, 175-176
  nurse healer objectives, 159-160
  nurse healer reflections, 178
  nursing process factors, 170-173, 177
  research directions, 178
  use of programs, 169-170
Multiple Risk Factor Intervention Trial (MRFIT), 68-69
Muscle strength, 170
Music therapy
  bodymind connections, 269-270
  case studies, 283-285
  clinical settings, 272
  definitions, 264-266
  function of, 263-264
  goal, 267
  history, 263
  imagery, emotions, and senses, 270
  individual preference factors, 274
  interventions, 278-282
  movement and, 176
  nurse healer objectives, 264
  nurse healer reflections, 285-286
  nursing process, 275-278, 282-283
  psychophysiologic responses, 268-269
  relaxation and, 338
  research directions, 285
  scripts, 280-282
  selection of music, 272-276
  sound principles, 265-266
  state of consciousness and, 267
  storytelling and, 322
  uses and outcomes, 270-272
Music bath, 280
Music Rx tapes, 273

N

NANDA Diagnosis Qualifer, 384
Natural systems theory, 78-80
Negentrophy, 108
Networks
  bodymind, 80
  nurse-client, 46
  social, 16-17, 309
Neuroanatomic model, 84
Neurolinguistic programming (NLP), 243
Neuromuscular retraining, 215
Neuropeptides, 78, 91, 93-94
Neurosecretion, 86-87
Neurotransmitters, 78, 84, 91
New Age music, 273
New Games, 299-300
New World view, 64-65
Nightingale, Florence, 65
Nociception, 226
Nodal points, 93
No exit syndrome, 50

Noise pollution, 183, 185, 190
Nontraditional foods, 165-166
Nontraditional music, 273, 281
North American Nursing Diagnosis Association (NANDA), 107-109
Novel stimuli, 81
Nowness, 45
Nurse-client relationship, 105, 106, 121
Nurse healer
  centering, 44-45
  characteristics, 42
  definitions, 4, 40-41
  future role, 73
  guiding role, 42-43
  healing role, 41-42
  listening skills, 45-46
  meaning factors, 49-51
  nurse healer objectives, 39-40
  nurse healer reflections, 52
  polarity factors, 43-44
  purpose, 48-49
  research directions, 52
  working with others, 46-47
  woundedness factors, 43
Nursing diagnosis, 104
  definition, 102, 107
  environmental control, 188
  imagery, 234
  music therapy, 276
  nutrition, exercise, and movement, 171-172
  play and laughter, 296-297
  process, 107-108
  relationships, 312
  relaxation, 206
  self-reflection, 365
  standardization of terms, 107
  Taxonomy I, 109-114
  touch, 341-342
  Unitary Person Framework, 108-109
  Unitary Tool Assessment Protype, 391
  wellness diagnoses, 109, 114-115
Nursing models, 103, 104
Nursing orders, 115
Nursing process
  assessment, 103-107, 140, 142, 170-171, 187-188, 205-206, 233-234, 275-276, 296, 312, 341, 364-365
  case studies, 176-177, 190-191, 216-219, 251-258, 283-285, 301-302, 382-386
  client outcomes, 115, 117, 172, 188, 206, 234, 276, 297, 312, 342, 365
  definitions, 102
  environmental control, 187-190, 192-193
  evaluation, 116-117, 142, 177, 192-193, 216, 250-251, 282-283, 300-301, 325, 352, 382
  framework, 102-103
  imagery, 233-238, 250-251
  implementation, 116
  music therapy, 275-278, 282-283
  nurse healer objectives, 101-102
  nurse healer reflections, 124
  nursing diagnoses, 107-109, 114, 171-172, 188, 206, 234, 276, 296-297, 312, 341-343, 365
  nutrition, exercise, and movement, 170-173, 177
  plan, 115-116, 173, 190, 208-211, 234-238, 276, 296-299, 314-315, 342-344, 365, 368-369
  play and laughter, 296-300
  relationships, 312-315, 325
  relaxation, 205-211, 216
  research directions, 124
  self-reflection, 364-382
  standards of care and, 117-123
  touch, 341-344, 352
  See also Interventions
Nurturance, 14
Nutrition
  case study, 176-177
  definitions, 160
  dietary goals, 161, 164, 166
  digestive process, 166
  disease and, 161-162
  food irradiation, 185-186
  interventions, 175
  meat and poultry supplementation, 186
  nontraditional foods, 165-166
  nurse healer objectives, 159-160
  nurse healer reflections, 178
  nursing process, 170-173, 177

research directions, 178
vitamins and minerals, 166

O

Obstacle removal, 325
Occupational Safety and Health Administration (OSHA), 183
Omnidirectional information, 80, 105
Open family system, 308
Open Focus, 196, 201, 213
Opiates, 93
Optimalearning, 271
Optimal states of consciousness (OSC), 24, 34, 35
Orientation of staff, 121
Oscillation, 264
Osteoporosis, 162
Outcomes. *See* Client outcomes
Outward arc, 30

P

Pain, 196-197, 200, 201
Pain control scripts, 239
Pantanjali-derived psychophysiologic principle, 32
Paradigm
definition, 58, 102
fitness, 163
medical, 68, 70
nursing, 103
research, 150
wellness, 66-69
Paranormal events, 84
Parasympathetic nervous system, 84, 86
Passive non-goal directed states, 35
Passive smoking, 186
Passive volition, 203
Perceptions, 14, 15, 17, 31, 46, 267, 309. *See also* Intuition
Perennial philosophy, 24, 29
Permanent dance, 132
Personal growth, 48, 49
Personal space, 182
Person-centered caring standards, 121-123
Phenomenal field, 25, 26
Physical activity. *See* Exercise; Movement
Physical potential, 14, 18
Physiologic measurents, 152
Physiology. *See* Psychophysiology
Pineal gland, 226
Pituitary, 86, 87
Placebo, 78
Placebo effect, 78, 81-82, 336
Place of conflict, 45
Plans
definition, 115
environmental control, 190
imagery, 234-238
music therapy, 276
nutrition, exercise, and movement, 173
play and laughter, 296-299
relationships, 314-315
relaxation, 208-211
self-reflection, 365, 368-369
touch, 342-344
Play and laughter
adults and, 294-295
cartoon collections, 300
coping role, 293-294
definitions, 40, 290-291
game playing, 299-300
history of theory, 291-293
interventions, 299-300
language and, 293
nurse healer objectives, 290
nurse healer reflections, 302-303
nursing process, 296-300
player's role, 295-296
research directions, 302
silly behavior cultivation, 299
winning and, 294
work setting, 295
Polarities, 40, 43-44
Popular music, 273
Positive attitudes, 131
Poultry supplementation, 186
Prayer, 214-215
Preparatory play, 291
Preparatory sensory information, 229-230

Presence in the moment, 31, 44, 47
Pressure manipulation, 339-340
Pressure pulse wave, 265
Prizing, 135
Problem-Etiology-Signs/Symptoms (P-E-S) format, 107-108
Problem solving, 132, 226-227, 360
Procedural touch, 333
Process, 4, 15
Process imagery, 224
Progressive Muscle Relaxation (PMR), 197, 199, 211-212
Projection, 310, 323-324
Protective shield/space script, 240-241
Pseudo-listening, 45-46
Psychic wholeness, 63
Psychologic measurements, 152
Psychoneuroimmunology (PNI), 89
Psychophysiologic, 4
Psychophysiologic self-regulation (PPSR), 24, 33-35
Psychophysiology
  autonomic nervous system, 84-86, 91
  brain centers, 83-84
  definitions, 78-79
  endocrine system, 86-89, 91
  genes, 89
  human potential and, 13, 14
  imagery and, 225-229
  immune system, 89-91
  music therapy and, 265-266, 268-269
  neuropeptide system, 91-94
  nurse healer objectives, 77-78
  nurse healer reflections, 95
  Pantanjali-derived principle, 32
  placebo effect, 81-82
  play and laughter and, 293
  relationships and, 309
  relaxation and, 34, 201
  research directions, 95
  self-reflection and, 360-361
  state-dependent learning, 79, 82-83, 226-227
  theories of, 79-81
  trends, 94-95
Psychosynthesis, 227-228
Psychotherapeutic materialism, 47
Psychotherapy, 226, 227, 309, 324
Purpose, 48-49

Q

QR for Kids program, 213
Qualitative research, 148-153
Quality of care. *See* Standards of care
Quantitative research, 148-152
Quiet heart intervention, 214
Quieting response, 212

R

Radical aliveness, 5
Rationalization, 310
Reaction formation, 310
Real listening, 45
Receptive role playing, 325
Receptivity, 105, 106
Receptors, 79, 88, 88-91, 93
Red ball of pain script, 239
Reductionism, 58, 64, 148, 149, 334
Reflexology, 339-340, 345
Reframing, 47, 79, 91, 227, 232, 271, 361
Regression, 310
Relationship potential, 16-17, 19-20
Relationships, 45
  bodymind connections, 309
  case studies, 326-328
  counseling and psychotherapy, 309-310
  defenses in, 310
  definitions, 41, 306
  family, 306-307
  functions, 305
  interventions, 315-325
  nurse healer objectives, 305-306
  nurse healer reflections, 328-329
  nursing process, 312-315, 325
  research directions, 328
  types, 307-309
Relaxation
  benefits, 198
  bodymind connection, 201

case studies, 216-219
caveats, 203-205
commonalities, 202-203
definitions, 41, 196-197
function of, 197-198
interventions, 211-216
music therapy and, 267, 270, 271, 274
nurse healer objectives, 196
nurse healer reflections, 220
nursing process, 205-211, 216
research directions, 220
storytelling and, 322
tapes, 205
techniques, 198-201
touch therapy and, 340
Relaxation Response (RR), 24, 34, 197, 201, 214
Reminiscence therapy, 358, 363-364, 380-382
Renewal centers, 72-73
Repatterning, 271
Repression, 310
Research
definition clarification, 151
definitions, 148
evaluation of holistic interventions, 151-153
future directions, 153-154
holistic research methods, 149
methodological problems, 149-151
objectivity factors, 153
nurse healer objectives, 147, 148
nurse healer reflections, 154
research needs, 153-154
scientific investigation, 153
variable identification, holistic, 151
wellness model, 148
Research needs
environmental control, 193
healing, 74
human potentials, 20-21
imagery, 259
music therapy, 285
nurse healer, 52
nursing process, 124
nutrition, exercise, and movement, 178
play and laughter, 302
psychophysiology, 95
relationships, 328
relaxation, 220
research, 153-154
self-reflection, 387
touch, 353
transpersonal self, 35-36
wellness, 143
Resistance, 18
Resolution, 41, 44, 46
Resonance, 264, 265
Resonant, 265
Resources, 306
Resting heart rate, 160
Return to balance, 212
Reverberating feedback loop, 307
Rewards, 141
Right hemispheric function, 33-34, 87, 227, 228, 231-232, 268, 361
Risk taking, 132
Rock music, 272

S

Schiller, Johann, 64
Schumann's Resonance, 266
Scientific method, 149-151
Scripts, imagery, 238-242
Scripts, relaxation, 211-215
Self, 25, 30
Self-assessments, 5-14
Self-care, 34-35, 41
Self-change principles, 46-47
Self-concept, 359
Self-confidence, 106
Self-dialogue, 15, 242
Self-discovery, 5, 228
Self-experience, 46
Self-healing, 14
Self-help groups, 141
Self-help tapes, 271
Self-hypnosis, 197, 200, 216
Self-image, 14, 47, 128, 131
Self-reflection
adult education principles, 359-360
bodymind connection, 360
case studies, 382-386
definitions, 358

interventions, 369-382
methods, 360-364
nurse healer objectives, 358
nurse healer reflections, 387
nursing process, 364-369, 382
research directions, 387
Self-reflective experiential exercises, 322, 324-325
Self-regulation, 34-35, 151-153, 197
Self-responsibility, 41, 66-68, 70, 128, 131
Self-talk, 18, 215, 294
Self-validation, 306
Selye, Hans, 65
Senate Select Committee on Nutrition, 161, 164
Senses, 225-226, 243, 270, 280-282
Shamanic cultures, 58
Shamans, 58-60, 263, 333
Shiatzu, 333, 334, 339, 345
Signs/symptoms, 108
Silliness, 299, 300
Skillful listening, 282
Skillpower, 132
Skin hunger, 336
Smoking, 174, 186
Smuts, Jan, 65
Social support, 140, 141
Societal changes, 70-71
Sodium-potassium pump, 89
Somatic response, 227
Sonic, 265
Sound, 265-266, 269-270
Specialization, 73
Special/safe place script, 238-239
Spirit, 29
Spirit potential, 16, 19
Spirituality, 24, 26, 28
Spontaneity, 300, 306
Spontaneous imagery, 224, 236
Sprouted seeds, 166
Standards of care
definition, 102
holistic nursing, 117-121
person-centered caring, 121-123
subspecialties, 117
State-bound information, 226
State-dependent learning, 79, 82-83, 228-227
States of consciousness
altered, 24, 33, 35, 215, 363
hemispheric function, 33-34
optimal, 24, 34, 35
music therapy and, 267
psychophysiologic self-regulation, 34
skills for change of, 35
usual, 33
Stem phrase completion, 322-323, 326-327
Storytelling, 321-322
Strength, 161, 170
Strength diagnoses, 114-115
Stress, 14, 65, 89, 183, 197, 272, 309, 315-316
Stress management, 130
Stressors, 183, 306
Stretching, 176
Subacute care settings, 72
Subjective motivational state, 137
Subliminal suggestions, 271
Suggestology, 271
Super Learning, 271
Surrounding space, 176
Symbolism, 247
Sympathetic nervous system, 84, 86, 215
Sympathetic resonance, 265, 266
Symptom/disease drawing, 245-246
Synergy, 133
Synesthesia, 232, 270

T

Tacit dimension, 105
Tai Chi, 163, 164, 170
T'ai Chi t'u, 137
Tape libraries, 278-279
Tape recorders, 279
Tapes, 271, 278-279, 300
Target heart rate, 161, 175
Taxonomy I, 102, 109-114
Teaching competence, 47
Telematics, 58, 71
Tension awareness, 211-212
Therapeutic double bind, 232

Therapeutic message, 333, 338-339, 345, 350
Therapeutic touch (TT), 333, 336-337, 340-341, 345-348
Time, 202, 204, 267
Tissue repair, 93
Tobacco products, 186
Tofu, 165
Toning and groaning, 281
Touch
  bodymind connection, 337-338, 340
  case studies, 348-352
  concepts of, 334-335
  cultural variations, 334
  definitions, 332-333
  function of, 331
  history, 333-334
  interventions, 344-348
  nurse healer objectives, 331-332
  nurse healer reflections, 353
  nursing process, 341-344, 352
  nursing studies, 335-337
  research directions, 353
  types, 338-341
Toxic substances, 182
Trace elements, 166
Transactional psychologic therapy (TP), 315-317
Transcend, 24, 29
Transcendence, 16, 29
Transduction, 80-81, 84, 86, 89
Transpersonal, 41, 48, 197
Transpersonal growth, 48, 49
Transpersonal human care, 25-26
Transpersonal self
  definitions, 24
  Great Chain of Being, 29
  healing, 26, 28
  healing awareness, 31-32
  inward arc, 30-32
  nurse healer objectives, 23-24
  nurse healer reflections, 36
  psychophysiologic principle, 32-33
  perennial philosophy, 29
  research directions, 35-36
  states of consciousness, 33-35
Transpersonal view, 4, 16
Trial-web shift, 380
Truism, 231-232
Trypsin, 335

U

Unifying concepts, 16
Unitary Person Assessment Tool Prototype, 391
Unitary Person Framework, 102, 108-109. *See also* Nursing diagnoses
Use of self, 44
Usual states of consciousness (USC), 24, 33

V

Value indicators, 135
Values clarification, 128, 130, 134-136, 141
Viability, 308
Videotapes, 300
Virtual Time, 267
Visualization. *See* Imagery
Visual-motor behavioral rehearsal (VMBR), 34-35
Vitamins, 160, 166
Volition, passive, 203
Vomeronasal system, 226
Vulnerability, 45

W

Warmup exercises, 175-176
Weber, Max, 64
Weber, René, xi-xiii, 25
Wellness
  assumptions about, 130
  changing and risk taking, 132
  definitions, 128
  framework, 129-130
  hardiness, 132-134
  health care change and, 128-129
  human motivational model, 136-141
  life mission, 131-132
  modeling, 130-131
  nurse healer objectives, 127-128

nurse healer reflections, 143
research directions, 143
values clarification and, 134-136
worksite programs, 141-142
work spirit, 133-134
Wellness diagnoses, 109, 114
Wellness paradigm, 66-69
White light of healing energy script, 240
Wholeness, 5, 13-14
Whole person wheel, 13
Willpower, 132
Winning, 294
Working with others, 46-47
Worksite wellness programs, 141-142
Work spirit, 133-134
Worry and fear script, 241-242
World view, 64
Wounded healer, 41, 43

Y

Yin and yang, 61
Yoga, 32, 62, 183, 216
Yogurt, 165-166

Z

Zone therapy, 339